# Using WordPerfect®
## 3rd Edition

Deborah Beacham
Walton Beacham

Revised for Version 4.2
by Ron Person

Que™ Corporation
Carmel, Indiana

Using WordPerfect®, 3rd Edition.

Library of Congress Catalog No.: 87-050315
ISBN 0-88022-295-6

91   90   89   88          12   11   10

Interpretation of the printing code: the rightmost number of the first series of numbers is the year of the book's printing; the rightmost number of the second series of numbers is the number of the book's printing. For example, a printing code of 88-1 shows that the first printing of the book occurred in 1988.

*Using WordPerfect*, 3rd Edition, is based on WordPerfect Version 4.2. References are made, where appropriate, to WordPerfect Version 4.1. Text and figures assume WordPerfect 4.2 as the standard.

# ■ About the Authors

Deborah and Walton Beacham are the coauthors of another microcomputer software book, *Using DisplayWrite*, published by Que Corporation. Formerly a Computer Systems analyst with the U.S. Postal Service, Deborah is currently a Systems Consultant for a Washington, D.C., computer firm.

Walton studied corporate management with an engineering focus at Georgia Tech. He became a staff writer for *Business Week* magazine and a contributor to *Nation* magazine. He also has written eight books and edited fifty others. Formerly president of Corporate Communication Associates, he is currently vice president of a major reference book publishing company. His duties include marketing and sales, as well as product content and development.

■

*Cursor Movement p 42*

*Acquisitions Editor*

Pegg Kennedy

*Editors*

Kathleen A. Johanningsmeier
Rebecca Whitney
Gail S. Burlakoff

*Product Director*

Patricia Q. Stonesifer

*Editorial Assistant*

Ann K. Taylor

*Technical Editors*

Karen Rose
Dean Ellis

*Production*

Dan Armstrong
Kelly Currie
Jennifer Matthews

# Table of Contents

# 6  Using the Block Function To Rearrange Your Text ............... 119

■ SECTION TWO

# Polishing Your Documents

■ SECTION THREE

# Creating Special Documents

## 13  Using Special Characters and Document References

■ SECTION FOUR

# Streamlining with WordPerfect

## 14 Using Macros To Streamline Editing and Printing ... 311

## 15 Combining Documents with Merge ... 341

# 16 Using Sort and Select

# Acknowledgments

For Edna and Jack

# Trademark Acknowledgments

Que Corporation has made every effort to supply trademark information about company names, products, and services mentioned in this book. Trademarks indicated below were derived from various sources. Que Corporation cannot attest to the accuracy of this information.

1-2-3 and Lotus are registered trademarks of Lotus Development Corporation.

COMPAQ is a registered trademark of COMPAQ Computer Corporation.

dBASE III and Ashton-Tate are registered trademarks of Ashton-Tate Company.

IBM, IBM PC, IBM PC AT, and Quietwriter are registered trademarks and IBM Personal System/2 and IBM PC XT are trademarks of International Business Machines Corporation.

LaserWriter and LaserWriter Plus are registered trademarks of Apple Computer, Inc.

Microsoft is a registered trademark of Microsoft Corporation.

MultiMate Advantage is a trademark of Multimate International, an Ashton-Tate company.

MultiMate is a registered trademark of Multimate International, an Ashton-Tate company.

SuperCalc is a registered trademark of Computer Associates International, Inc.

WordPerfect is a registered trademark of WordPerfect Corporation.

WordPerfect Library is a trademark of WordPerfect Corporation.

WordStar and MicroPro are registered trademarks of MicroPro International Corporation.

Screen reproductions in this book were created by means of the Inset program from Inset Systems Inc., Danbury, Connecticut.

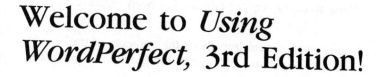

# Welcome to *Using WordPerfect*, 3rd Edition!

**A**t the beginning of each chapter you'll find a preview because most of us appreciate knowing what we can expect to find before we actually begin reading. If you begin each chapter with the preview, you'll be able to make early decisions about which sections will be particularly helpful. If you are new to WordPerfect®, you'll probably read each section carefully—if you've used WordPerfect before, you may decide to skip from one section to another.

Each chapter preview includes a synopsis of the functions and features presented in the chapter as well as hints that will make WordPerfect easy to use.

In this preview (which really previews the entire book's structure) you'll find:

- A "Using This Book" section that will help you move through each chapter quickly and successfully by providing information about the structure of the chapters

- A short discussion called "What, Exactly, Is WordPerfect?" that suggests what WordPerfect can do for you

- A section called "The Table of Contents at a Glance" that is helpful if you are looking for a particular section of the book, and want to find it quickly. Although the "at a Glance" section does tell you a little about each chapter, it does not include all of the

1

subheadings you'll find in the formal Table of Contents. The "Table
of Contents at a Glance" is an efficient way to introduce yourself
to what's covered in this book

Now that you have a better idea of what lies ahead, read on and learn
how WordPerfect will permit you to carry out your daily tasks with
greater efficiency and effectiveness.

# Using This Book

Each chapter in *Using WordPerfect,* 3rd Edition, has been organized in
this way:

- Each chapter begins with conversation about the contents of the
  chapter, including hints about special features and functions—and, ways
  to use WordPerfect more effectively

- Chapters 2 through 6 include a *Quick Start* section that permits those
  of you who are new to WordPerfect to practice the keystroke
  procedures presented in the chapter. The *Quick Start* practices offer
  you an opportunity to reinforce the concepts presented in the body of
  each chapter by applying them in a "real life" example. Some of you
  may elect to do the *Quick Start* section before reading the main part of
  the chapter. That's great! Each *Quick Start* contains enough information
  to "walk you through" the WordPerfect features and functions discussed
  in that chapter. *Quick Start* practices include most of the information
  presented in the chapter—but the information is presented in a
  "nutshell"

- All WordPerfect concepts, features, functions, and procedures are
  written and presented to support the "real life" application of
  WordPerfect. Examples are designed to illustrate how WordPerfect is
  used (everyday!) in business, industrial, professional, and educational
  environments

Bruce Bastian, Chairman of the Board of WordPerfect Corporation, relates
that his inspiration for the WordPerfect word-processing program came in
response to the human need for an uncomplicated word-processing
program that would eliminate the feeling of frustration that too often
accompanies so-called "user-friendly" word-processing packages.

*This book supports Mr. Bastian's premise that learning word processing
shouldn't be complicated and frustrating.*

# New to WordPerfect?

If you are new to WordPerfect, *Using WordPerfect,* 3rd Edition, provides complete explanations of all of the command keys and menus that you must use to cause WordPerfect to carry out its functions.

After WordPerfect becomes a bit more familiar to you, you'll find that those command key and menu explanations have allowed you to decrease the time you've spent learning WordPerfect.

If you've spent time using WordPerfect but sometimes have trouble when you print, merge, sort, or execute macros, this book provides practical suggestions for both avoiding difficulty and for solving problems—if problems occur.

A frequent WordPerfect-user will find the chapters on special applications for macros, sorting, and merging useful.

# What, Exactly, Is WordPerfect?

WordPerfect is a word-processing program that, since its release in 1982, has continued to attract a large and enthusiastic audience. The claim that WordPerfect combines ease-of-use with power and flexibility to arrive at a word-processing package that supports new users, intermediate users, and WordPerfect power-users, is validated by its number-one rating in word-processing software sales.

WordPerfect's strengths are enhanced by the speed with which it manages mailing lists, files, memos, and billings. WordPerfect's Math function for columns of calculations permits you to incorporate data tables into typical financial reports easily. Because the Sort and Merge features are fast and easy to manipulate, WordPerfect is an excellent tool for assembling, comparing, and organizing information.

WordPerfect also provides access to ASCII files created by other software programs such as Lotus® 1-2-3® and dBASE® II and III. This capability allows you to interchange data management, spreadsheet and other word-processing data files.

In addition to all the essential elements users look for in a good word-processing system, WordPerfect offers:

- The capability to sort and select lines, paragraphs, and merge-records from within WordPerfect with a few simple keystrokes

- Macro chaining, which allows you to string a series of keystrokes together—one causing the other to execute

- File protection, which prevents an unauthorized user from reading your files

- An on-line Help feature that, with the press of a key, permits you to read a screenful of information about any WordPerfect feature. You do not have to leave your document to use the Help feature

- A thesaurus that displays a list of synonyms and antonyms on your screen. From the list of synonyms and antonyms, you may select the word that most clearly and vividly expresses your ideas

- Windows that divide your editing screen so that you may work on two separate documents at the same time

- The capability to use the cursor to draw charts and graphs and enclose text in boxes

# The Table of Contents at a Glance

*Chapter 1.* Chapter 1 details (step-by-step) how to install WordPerfect, how to use disks, and how to select your printer. At the end of the chapter, you'll be ready to go with WordPerfect!

*Chapter 2.* "Using WordPerfect To Create a Document" includes information about your keyboard, and the cursor. The chapter uses a short *Quick Start* exercise to introduce you to WordPerfect's wordwrap feature, cursor movement, and the Enter key.

*Chapter 3.* In a practical and procedural way, Chapter 3 explains how to make basic editing changes in your document. Deleting unwanted text, moving text, inserting text, changing letters to uppercase or lowercase, and erasing lines of text are five of the editing procedures discussed.

*Chapter 4.* Saving, retrieving, and printing your document are explored in Chapter 4. You will learn also how to name your document files, and how to use the Exit key to save your document and exit to begin another task.

*Chapter 5.* This chapter permits you to practice (if you choose to work through the *Quick Start* exercise) enhancing the look of your text by underlining words and phrases, turning regular lettering into bold lettering, and centering selected text between the margins. You will learn also how to delete the hidden function codes that are inserted when you press a function key.

*Chapter 6.* Chapter 6 completes the learning-how-to-use-WordPerfect section of the book. The last of the fundamental WordPerfect concepts is presented in Part 5 of the *Quick Start* practice—marking blocks of text to be moved, centered, deleted, and saved. The chapter talks about using windows and the Switch function to work on two documents in one operation.

*Chapter 7*. Proofreading your document is the focus for this chapter. Proofreading includes searching for and replacing words or phrases that are either incorrect or inappropriate. Proofreading also covers how to use WordPerfect's dictionary to look up correct spellings and meanings, and how to use the thesaurus to find the most suitable words to convey your ideas.

*Chapter 8*. This chapter describes how to organize, and add visual interest to your document's text by changing standard margins, setting tabs, indenting lines of text, adding or deleting the space between lines of text, and hyphenating words and phrases.

*Chapter 9*. You also can make changes in the format of your document's page by creating pages of different length, changing the size of the paper on which your document is printed, changing the size of the top margin, and changing the size of the bottom margin. Chapter 9 presents these, and other, page formatting options.

*Chapter 10*. Using the full potential of your printer's options is examined in this chapter. Among other things, you'll learn how WordPerfect allows you to: print less than a full page of text, print what is displayed on your screen, print on odd-sized paper, and format multi-paged documents. The section called "Troubleshooting Your Printer" is an important section you must be certain to read.

*Chapter 11*. The remaining topics (beginning with Chapter 10) move into the more specialized features of WordPerfect. If you are responsible for editing a newsletter or if you are required to organize the material you write into columns of text, you'll find chapter 11 helpful. How to create newspaper-style and parallel columns of text is discussed, and an example of each is offered to illustrate how you might apply each feature in your work.

*Chapter 12*. If you must create columns of figures for financial reports, you'll need to spend time with Chapter 12. This chapter addresses setting the tabs necessary for creating math columns, entering numbers and operators, calculating a subtotal and a grand total, creating a formula, and printing your report.

*Chapter 13*. Special formatting features such as aligning numbers with tab align, specialized characters (subscripts, superscripts, and formulas), line drawing, and outlines are described and illustrated for users who create documents that require more specialized formatting capabilities.

*Chapter 14.* Macros are automatic keystroke procedures that *you* create to streamline your editing and printing efforts. Most people skip this chapter because they believe creating and using macros is a difficult process. Chapter 14 will convince you that creating macros is not difficult at all. Included in the chapter are the "Eleven Frequently Used Macros" including memo formatting, saving, creating windows, executing Switch, and printing.

*Chapter 15.* Merging documents will save you time and effort when you have repetitive tasks such as completing form letters, standard forms and contracts, or mailing lists to perform. The chapter explains how to create both the primary and secondary files, how to create a data file, how to use merge with the Mail option, how to create mailing labels, and how to compile reports with merge.

*Chapter 16.* Using the sort and select feature covers selecting the type of sort you intend to execute, setting the keys to be used in sorting, selecting the records to be sorted, and performing sorts. An example that encourages you to practice the sort-and-select procedure utilizing a number of variables is included in Chapter 16.

*Chapter 17.* The last chapter, "Managing Your System," explains how to customize WordPerfect using the Set-up menu. The chapter also discusses both converting WordPerfect text to ASCII characters and converting WordPerfect text to Lotus 1-2-3 text. You will want to read the section "Protecting Your Files From Unauthorized Users," as well.

The *Appendix* presents a list of WordPerfect codes that can be viewed from the Reveal Codes screen. This appendix also includes a reproduction of the function-key template used on the enhanced keyboard for the IBM® PC, XT™, and AT, and the keyboard for the IBM PS/2™ computers.

And, if you haven't already noticed, there is a color-coded, desktop, tear-out card at the back of your book. Take a moment to look it over. You'll find the *Keyboard Command Map* and the illustrated *Function Keys Chart* invaluable as you learn WordPerfect.

You can use WordPerfect on a number of popular computers. Remember that template names, and the number and position of function keys, differ from keyboard to keyboard. This book assumes that you are using an IBM PC keyboard. If you are using a different keyboard, you may have to make allowances for the differences between the IBM PC keyboard and the one you are using. WordPerfect requires 256K and runs on DOS version 2.0 as well as later versions of DOS.

*Using WordPerfect*, 3rd Edition, will help you with the features and functions of both WordPerfect version 4.1 and WordPerfect version 4.2. Text and figures assume WordPerfect version 4.2 as the standard. The differences between the two versions are noted wherever appropriate. Although the two versions are very similar, some macros may not work because of a change in menu choices. Refer to Chapter 14 for more information about macros.

By now you should have a clearer picture of how this book will help you integrate WordPerfect's features and functions in your daily work. Whether you are an author working at home, a research assistant in a legal office, a student completing your dissertation, a secretary in a medical office, or a manager in an insurance office—whatever your word-processing needs—you are ready to apply WordPerfect to your own special tasks.

# Learning WordPerfect Basics

To: Communications Department Staff
From: John Roberts
Re: Computer Equipment and Software

Well, you asked and asked and we finally got approval! I'm pleased to announce that tomorrow morning we'll accept delivery of six microcomputers and six printers. They'll be installed over the lunch hour.

After much deliberation we've selected *WordPerfect Version 4.2* software—it will fulfill both immediate and future word-processing needs.

This week's priority, then, is learning the basics of WordPerfect. By this time next week you should:

- Have WordPerfect installed and running
- Be able to create and edit a WordPerfect document
- Provide samples of the kinds of improvements we can make in the customer report layout

We'll discuss your WordPerfect accomplishments at our regular meeting.

J. Roberts

# CHAPTER 1

# Getting Started

If WordPerfect has already been installed on the system you are using, you'll probably just skim this chapter and go on to Chapter 2. If WordPerfect has not been installed on your system, you'll find this chapter a tremendous help. Because this section is written in easy-to-understand format, you can follow the installation procedure step-by-step; and before you know it, you'll be up and running in WordPerfect.

As you'll discover, there are six basic steps you must complete:

- A process called "booting your system"

- Formatting the disks you'll use to make working copies of WordPerfect master disks

- Then, copying the WordPerfect master disks

- Actually starting WordPerfect

- Selecting your printer so it can communicate with WordPerfect

- And, exiting WordPerfect

You'll find tips and hints sprinkled throughout this chapter that will permit you to install WordPerfect without a troublesome moment.

# Installing WordPerfect

You must complete six steps to install WordPerfect on your system. They are:

1. Booting your system

2. Formatting your working disks

3. Copying the WordPerfect master disks

4. Starting WordPerfect

5. Selecting your printer

6. Exiting WordPerfect

Each of the six steps is described in the sections that follow. If you are using a dual floppy disk system, you must carry out *all* six steps. You will find the procedures you must follow listed in the sections titled "If You Are Using a Dual Floppy Disk System . . . ."

If you are using a hard disk system, you must carry out only *five* of the six steps listed. You will find instructions for booting your system, copying the master disks, starting WordPerfect, selecting your printer, and exiting WordPerfect in the sections called "If You Are Using a Hard Disk System . . . ."

# Booting Your System

*Booting* is a word that is used to describe the process of starting up your computer. On a dual floppy disk system, booting involves inserting the DOS disk into Drive A, turning on the computer, and typing in the date and time.

On a hard disk system, booting usually involves simply turning the computer on.

### Booting Your System If You Are Using a Dual Floppy Disk System . . .

1. Insert the DOS disk in Drive A

2. Turn the computer on

3. Type the **date** (for example, 5/17/87)

4. Press Enter

**5.** Type the **time** (for example, 14:15)

**6.** Press Enter

This prompt will appear on your screen:

    A>

### *Booting Your System If You Are Using a Hard Disk System . . .*

**1.** Turn the computer on

**2.** Type the **date** and **time** if your system does not enter them for you automatically

This prompt will appear on your screen:

    C>

# Using Floppy Disks

If you are using WordPerfect on an IBM PC, XT, AT, or compatible, the complete set of program disks comes on *six* 5 1/4-inch floppy disks. For IBM Personal System/2 computers, the WordPerfect program is contained on *three* 3 1/2-inch microfloppy disks. A fourth "demo" disk provides new users with an overview of WordPerfect, the WordPerfect Library, and MathPlan.

Both types of disks can be compared to the traditional filing cabinet found in most office settings. Just as you store paper files in a cabinet, you store files created with WordPerfect on disks.

Although disks are tougher than they might appear—especially the 3 1/2-inch microfloppy disks—they require care as you handle them:

- Magnetic fields damage disks. Keep disks away from magnetic paper clip holders, paperclips from these holders, message magnets, scissors, or the ends of fluorescent lights

- Disks are susceptible to extreme changes in temperature—don't store them near a heat source or leave them in your car in subzero weather or in the heat of summer

- The recording surface can be damaged if you spill liquids on it (this is especially true for 5 1/4-inch floppy disks)

- X-rays damage disks—it's generally a good idea to hand-carry disks around the security gates in airports or factory guard houses

- The 5 1/4-inch floppy disk's recording surface can be damaged if you write on the disk label with a ball point pen—use a felt-tip pen or create the label before affixing it to the disk jacket

## Formatting Your Working Disks

If you are using a hard disk system, you don't need to format disks for working copies. Skip this step and go to "Copying WordPerfect's Master Disks."

Formatting means preparing your disks for use. If you plan to run WordPerfect on an IBM PC, XT, AT, or compatible, you will need to format six blank disks so that you can copy the program information stored on the six WordPerfect *master disks* to what will become your newly formatted *working disks*. If you plan to run WordPerfect on an IBM PS/2 computer, you will need to format three blank disks, which will subsequently become your working disks. You cannot store information on an unformatted disk.

## Formatting Disks If You Are Using a Dual Floppy System . . .

1. If your computer uses 5 1/4-inch disks, write these labels on six blank disks:

   *WordPerfect-Working*

   *Speller-Working*

   *Thesaurus-Working*

   *Printer 1-Working*

   *Printer 2-Working*

   *Learning-Working*

   If you have an IBM PS/2 computer, write these labels on three blank 3 1/2-inch floppy disks:

   *WordPerfect/Learn-Working*

   *Speller/Thesaurus-Working*

   *Printer 1/Printer 2-Working*

With the DOS disk in Drive A:

2. Type **format b:/s** and press Enter

**3.** Insert the blank disk labeled

*WordPerfect-Working* (5 1/4-inch disk)

or

*WordPerfect/Learn-Working* (3 1/2-inch disk)

in Drive B

**4.** Press Enter when prompted.

After the disk light goes out this message will appear on your screen:

Format another (Y/N)?

**5.** Type **N** and press Enter.

When you type N, you are telling your computer that you do not want to format another disk with the **/s** format option.

Now, go on to format your five (or two) remaining working disks:

**6.** Type **format b:** and press Enter.

**7.** Remove the

*WordPerfect-Working* (5 1/4-inch disk)

or

*WordPerfect/Learn-Working* (3 1/2-inch disk)

disk from Drive B.

**8.** Insert the blank disk labeled

*Speller-Working* (5 1/4-inch disk)

or

*Speller/Thesaurus-Working* (3 1/2-inch disk)

in Drive B.

**9.** Press Enter when prompted

This message will appear on your screen:

Format another (Y/N)?

**10.** Type **Y** and press Enter

**11.** Remove your

*Speller-Working* (5 1/4-inch disk)

or

*Speller/Thesaurus-Working* ( 3 1/2-inch disk )

from Drive B.

12. Insert the blank disk labeled *Thesaurus-Working* ( 5 1/4-inch disk) in Drive B

13. Press Enter

14. Repeat steps 10 through 13 for the remaining three blank 5 1/4-inch disks. For IBM PS/2 computers, you will only need to format one additional blank disk.

When you have formatted all of your working disks and this message appears on your screen:

```
Format another (Y/N)?
```

15. Type **N** and press Enter.

If you are using 5 1/4-inch disks, put write-protect tabs over the square notch on the side of each WordPerfect *master* disk. For 3 1/2-inch microfloppy disks, take a pencil and move the write-protect tab down to the "open" position.

WordPerfect will not run if you "write protect" your working disks.

You may wish to format another disk now to be used later as a disk to hold the documents you create with WordPerfect. If you like, name the disk *Documents*. As you create more and more documents, you'll label your document disks more precisely but, for now, *Documents* will do.

# Copying WordPerfect Master Disks

One of the most important "rules" of system management is to *make working copies of all program master disks.* The second most important rule is to *file those master program disks in a safe and physically separate location.*

If you follow this guideline, you have all but eliminated the possibility of damaging the master program disk. If your working copy becomes damaged, it is a simple matter to make another copy from the master. If, on the other hand, your master disks become damaged, you are essentially "shut down" until you purchase another copy of the software.

## Copying WordPerfect Master Disks If You Are Using a Dual Floppy Disk System

1. Insert the master disk labeled

   *WordPerfect* (5 1/4-inch disk)

   or

   *WordPerfect/Learn* (3 1/2-inch disk)

   in Drive **A**

2. Insert the working disk labeled

   *WordPerfect-Working* (5 1/4-inch disk)

   or

   *WordPerfect/Learn-Working* (3 1/2-inch disk)

   in Drive **B**

3. Type **copy a:*.* b:**

4. Press Enter

Your system has finished copying the WordPerfect program to your working disk when this message appears on your screen:

   (number)`files copied`

5. Repeat Steps 1 through 4, substituting the correct master disks and the correct working disks until all the master disks have been copied.

## Preparing To Copy the WordPerfect Master Disks If You Are Using a Hard Disk System . . .

Because of the differences between the floppy disk system and the hard disk system, you will not copy the master disks to working disks—rather, you will create a subdirectory (see fig. 1.1) in which you will store the programs housed on the master disks.

1. Type **md\wp**

The letters "md" mean "make directory." The letters "wp" identify the directory for "WordPerfect."

2. Press Enter.

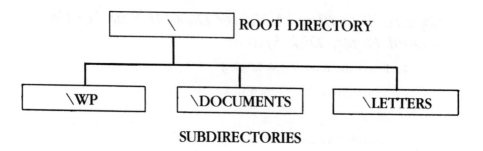

*Fig. 1.1. Directory structure.*

Now, move to your *wp* subdirectory to copy the master disks:

> **3.** Type **cd\wp**

The letters "cd" mean "change directories."

> **4.** Press Enter

You are now ready to copy the WordPerfect program files to your hard disk.

**Note:** To continue installation, choose either of the following two sections, depending on what type of computer you are using:

- an IBM PC, XT, AT, or compatible—which uses 5 1/4-inch floppy disks

  or

- an IBM PS/2 computer—which uses 3 1/2-inch microfloppy disks

## *Copying the Master Disks To Your Hard Disk (IBM PC, XT, AT, or Compatibles)*

> **1.** Insert the *WordPerfect* master disk in Drive A
>
> **2.** Type **copy a:*.***
>
> **3.** Press Enter

Your system will then copy the WordPerfect program to the *C:\wp* directory (although the directory and the WordPerfect program are both named *wp*, the computer is able to tell them apart). This message will appear on your screen:

> (number)files copied

4. Insert the *Speller* master disk in Drive A

5. Type **copy a:*.\***

6. Press Enter

The speller program will be copied from Drive A to your *wp* directory.

7. Insert the *Thesaurus* master disk in Drive A

8. Type **copy a:*.\***

9. Press Enter

The thesaurus program will be copied from Drive A to your *wp* directory.

10. Remove the *Thesaurus* master disk from Drive A

11. Insert the *Learning* master disk in Drive A

12. Type **copy a:wphelp.fil**

13. Press Enter

14. Type **copy a:wphelp2.fil**

15. Press Enter

Only the help program will be copied from Drive A to your *wp* directory.

If you want to complete the tutorial on the *Learning* master disk, check the *WordPerfect Installation and Appendices* booklet that comes with your WordPerfect documentation.

## *Copying the Master Disks To Your Hard Disk (IBM PS/2 Computers)*

For WordPerfect on IBM PS/2 computers, you must selectively copy the main program files from the *WordPerfect/Learn* master disk to your hard disk.

1. Place the *WordPerfect/Learn* master disk in Drive A

2. Type **copy a:wp.exe**

3. Press Enter

The main program file (WP.EXE) is copied to your *wp* directory.

This message will appear on your screen:

```
(number)files copied
```

4. With the *WordPerfect/Learn* master disk still in drive A, type
**copy a:*.fil**

5. Press Enter

The files WPRINTER.FIL, WPFONT.FIL, WPHELP.FIL, and WPHELP2.FIL are copied to your *wp* directory.

6. Remove the *WordPerfect/Learn* master disk from Drive A

7. Insert the *Speller/Thesaurus* master disk in Drive A

8. Type **copy a:*.***

9. Press Enter

The speller and thesaurus programs will be copied from Drive A to your *wp* directory.

10. Remove the *Speller/Thesaurus* master disk from Drive A

Unless you want to complete the WordPerfect tutorial, installation of WordPerfect on your hard disk is now complete.

If you want to complete the tutorial on the *WordPerfect/Learn* master disk, check the *WordPerfect Installation and Appendices* booklet that comes with your WordPerfect documentation. This booklet provides the steps for creating a separate *learn* directory where you would copy the learning files.

**Important note:** If you follow the documentation's recommendation— create a *learn* directory and copy all the files on the *WordPerfect/Learn* master disk to this directory—you will need to *delete* the files WPHELP.FIL, WPHELP2.FIL, WP.EXE, WPRINTER.FIL, and WPFONT.FIL from this directory because (if you followed the preceding steps) these files were copied to your *wp* directory.

To delete WPHELP.FIL, WPHELP2.FIL, WP.EXE, WPRINTER.FIL, and WPFONT.FIL from your *learn* directory, follow these steps:

1. Type **cd\learn** to move to the *learn* directory

2. Press Enter

3. Type **erase a:*.fil**

4. Press Enter

5. Type **erase a:wp.exe**

6. Press Enter

The *learn* directory now contains only those files that are appropriate.

# Starting WordPerfect

The next step in installing WordPerfect is to start WordPerfect.

## *Starting WordPerfect If You Are Using a Dual Floppy Disk System . . .*

1. Insert your

   *WordPerfect-Working* disk (5 1/4-inch disk)

   or

   *WordPerfect/Learn-Working* disk (3 1/2-inch disk)

   in Drive A

2. Type **b:**

3. Press Enter

You are now in Drive B.

4. Type **a:wp**

5. Press Enter

You have started WordPerfect. The screen illustrated in figure 1.2 is displayed on your monitor and will continue to display at start-up until you've installed your printer. Press any key to display a WordPerfect clean screen.

## *Starting WordPerfect If You Are Using a Hard Disk System . . .*

With the DOS prompt C> on your screen:

1. Type **cd\wp**

2. Press Enter

You are now in your WordPerfect directory.

3. Type **wp**

4. Press Enter

You have started WordPerfect. When you become more familiar with how you'll use WordPerfect, turn to Chapter 17 for a discussion about managing your system.

```
                        Welcome to WordPerfect


        Before you begin, place the template      You start with a clear screen.  As
        over the function keys.  The template     you type and edit a document, the
        is color-coded.                           status line shows your position in
                                                  the document.
        Color     Press
        Red       Ctrl key + function key         When you are ready to print, press
        Green     Shift key + function key        the Print key.  When you are ready
        Blue      Alt key + function key          to save a document, press the Exit
        Black     Function key alone              key.

        The Help key, which is labeled on         If something unexpected happens, try
        your template, gives you a brief          pressing the Cancel or Backspace
        summary of WordPerfect's features.        key.

              After you Select Printers, you will not see this message.

           We hope you enjoy using WordPerfect -- press any key to begin.
```

Fig. 1.2. Screen displayed after starting WordPerfect prior to selecting a printer.

# Restarting Your System from an Incorrect Shutdown

Always exit WordPerfect the correct way—use the Exit (F7) key.

If someone accidentally turns off the power while WordPerfect is on the screen, you will lose the document that last appeared on the screen. If you saved a copy of your document to disk, that copy *is* retrievable.

When you restart WordPerfect after a power failure, this message will appear at the bottom of your screen:

> Are other copies of WordPerfect currently running? Y/N

If the computer lost power while WordPerfect was running:

  1. Type **N**

If you are working on a network, check to see if anyone else is running WordPerfect. If no one is running WordPerfect:

  1. Type **N**

If you are working on a network, and others *are* running WordPerfect:

  1. Type **Y**

WordPerfect will respond to the Y by asking you to name a directory where it can store temporary working files. Make sure that the directory you name is different than the directories being used by other network WordPerfect users.

# Selecting Your Printer

As you perform the following steps you will be telling WordPerfect what kind of printer it will be sending documents to. WordPerfect and your printer must be "linked" properly; otherwise they won't "talk" to one another and you won't be able to print the documents you have created on the screen.

## *Selecting Printers*

1. Insert the

   *Printer 1* master disk (5 1/4-inch disk)

   or

   *Printer 1/Printer 2* master disk (3 1/2-inch disk)

   in Drive A on a hard disk system or Drive B on a floppy disk system

2. Start WordPerfect

3. Press the Print key (Shift-F7)

4. Type 4 Printer Control

The Printer Control screen in figure 1.3 is displayed.

```
Printer Control                      C - Cancel Print Job(s)
                                     D - Display All Print Jobs
1 - Select Print Options             G - "Go" (Resume Printing)
2 - Display Printers and Fonts       P - Print a Document
3 - Select Printers                  R - Rush Print Job
                                     S - Stop Printing
Selection: 0

Current Job

Job Number: n/a                      Page Number:  n/a
Job Status: n/a                      Current Copy: n/a
Message:    The print queue is empty

Job List

Job  Document            Destination          Forms and Print Options



Additional jobs not shown: 0
```

*Fig. 1.3. Printer Control screen.*

5. Type 3 to Select Printers

The Printer Definition screen in figure 1.4 is displayed.

6. Press the right-arrow key until Printer 1 displays in the lower left corner

WordPerfect can assign printer model definitions to each of six different printers. You are about to assign a printer model definition to what WordPerfect thinks is the first of six possible printers.

If your Printer Definition screen, shown in figure 1.4, includes the names of the printers connected to your computer, SKIP to Step 9. If your printer's definition does not show on the screen the appropriate definition must be retrieved from one of the *Printer* disks.

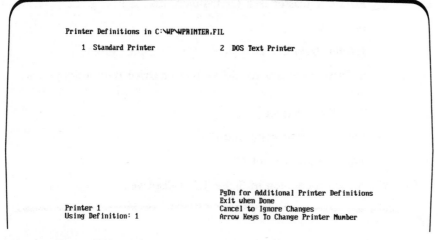

```
Printer Definitions in C:\WP\WPRINTER.FIL

    1  Standard Printer            2  DOS Text Printer

















                                   PgDn for Additional Printer Definitions
                                   Exit when Done
        Printer 1                  Cancel to Ignore Changes
        Using Definition: 1        Arrow Keys To Change Printer Number
```

*Fig. 1.4. Printer Definition screen.*

If there are no printers on the screen or your printer is not on the screen, view the complete list of printers:

7. Press PgDn for additional printer definitions

8. Follow the screen directions and type the letter of the drive containing the *Printer* disk

You can view the complete list by pressing PgDn to move forward from screen to screen; to move to the previously displayed page in the list, press PgUp.

> If your printer is not listed on any of the pages on the *Printer 1* (5 1/4-inch) disk:
>
> 1. Press F7
>
> The system has returned you to the Printer Control menu.
>
> 2. Remove your *Printer1-Working* disk
>
> 3. Insert your *Printer2-Working* disk
>
> 4. Type 3
>
> 5. Press PgDn and enter the letter of the drive containing *Printer 2* disk
>
> Continue to move through the screens as you did on the first disk.

**9.** Type your **printer model number**

**10.** Press Enter

After you type the printer model number WordPerfect will display additional menus from which you must specify the port (the plug on your computer) to which the printer is connected.

Generally, dot-matrix printers (parallel printers) and letter-quality printers (serial printers) are connected to *LPT1* ports (type **0**); often letter-quality printers are connected to *COM1* ports (type **4**) as well.

If you are using a serial printer, you will be asked to supply the printer's *baud rate*, *parity*, *stop bits*, and *character length*. Check your printer manual for the correct settings.

**11.** Type the **number of the port** your printer is using

**12.** Type **1** if you are using continuous paper with your printer

Or

**12.** Type **2** if you are using hand fed paper with your printer

Or

**12.** Type **3** if you are using sheet fed paper with your printer

After selecting the type of paper, you will be returned to the Printer Definitions screen.

**13.** Return to Step 6 if your computer uses more than one printer

Make sure the *Printer* number is different for each additional printer definition you select.

**14.** Press Exit (F7) to leave the Select Printers menu

Pressing Cancel (F1) will signal WordPerfect to ignore the printer selections you've made.

**15.** Press Enter to return to your WordPerfect typing screen

## *Initializing the Apple LaserWriter*

If you're printing with the Apple LaserWriter® or LaserWriter® Plus, you will need to prepare the LaserWriter by sending a file to the printer from your computer.

The file that you'll send is one of two files WordPerfect uses when printing in near-typeset quality on the LaserWriter. These two files, LASERWRT.PS and INITLWRT.PS should have been automatically copied to your \wp directory when you installed the LaserWriter definition.

To prepare the LaserWriter:

**1.** Turn your printer on

Wait for the test page. Once the test page is ejected and the printing light stops blinking, you'll copy the INITLWRT.PS file to the LaserWriter with the DOS *copy command*:

**2.** Type **copy c:\wp\initlwrt.ps com1:**

The copy command copies the file from the \wp directory on a hard disk. INITLWRT.PS and LASERWRT.PS must reside in the same directory as WP.EXE

If your computer is set up differently, use the *dir* command to find the location of the file.

**3.** Press Enter

Make sure the COM port in the copy command matches the COM port you specified when installing the LaserWriter definition. End the copy statement with COM2 if you connect your LaserWriter to the second serial port.

You can copy the INITLWRT.PS file to the printer while WordPerfect is running. Temporarily go to DOS without quitting WordPerfect:

**1.** Press the Shell key (Ctrl-F1)

**2.** Type **1**

Once you see the DOS prompt:

**3.** Type **copy c:\wp\initlwrt.ps com1:**

After the copy is complete, return to your document:

    4. Type **exit**

    5. Press Enter

## *What If Your Printer Won't Print?*

There are a number of reasons why your printer may not work. Some are very simple and others are very complex. The following list may help you. Start with the first checkpoint on the list and hopefully you'll find the answer before you get to the last checkpoint:

1. Check to be sure that the power is on by first checking the printer control panel lights, then check the plugs and outlet.

2. Be certain that the *On Line* light is on. The light indicates that the printer is connected electronically to the computer. Press the On Line button until the light comes on.

3. Check that cables are secure. Does the printer print with other programs?

4. If your printer is a serial printer (letter quality printers are usually serial) then verify the baud rate, parity, and COM port to which your printer is attached. The baud rate and parity are in your printer manual. Other information will be available from your dealer or a consultant.

5. Reselect the printer from the master disk labeled *Printer 1*. If your model is not shown, check on the *Printer 2* disk. Remember that if you are using WordPerfect on an IBM PS/2 computer, *all* the printers are listed on one disk: the *Printer 1/Printer 2* master disk. If neither *Printer* disk contains a definition of your printer, then choose a similar model from the same manufacturer. If a similar model from the same manufacturer is not available, then choose STANDARD PRINTER, one of the printer definitions immediately available without using the *Printer* disks.

6. If your printer prints, but does not print correctly, then call WordPerfect Corp. at the toll-free support line in Orem, Utah for further suggestions.

WordPerfect Corp. continually updates and adds to the printer definitions on the *Printer* disks. If your printer is new, call WordPerfect and ask if a new printer definition is available.

# Quitting WordPerfect

It is important that you exit WordPerfect correctly. Exiting WordPerfect incorrectly causes the document displayed on your screen to be "lost," and an error message appears the next time you start WordPerfect.

When you are ready to stop work with WordPerfect:

  **1.** Press the Exit key (F7)

This message will appear at the bottom of your screen:

    Save Document? (Y/N)

This question provides you with one last opportunity to save your document before exiting. Be careful! If your document has not been saved to disk, you cannot retrieve it later on.

  **2.** Type **Y** if you want to save the file

  **3.** Type the **file name**

  **4.** Press Enter

    Or

  **1.** Type **N** if you do not want to save the file

This message will appear on your screen:

    Exit WP? (Y/N)

  **1.** Type **Y** to exit WordPerfect and return to DOS

    Or

  **1.** Type **N** to clear the screen and return to WordPerfect

    Or

  **1.** Press the Cancel key (F1) to stay in WordPerfect but leave the screen as it is

To recap, you have booted your system, formatted disks, copied the WordPerfect master disks, started WordPerfect, selected your printer, and exited WordPerfect. Many users consider these tasks to be the most difficult part of learning any new software program!

Chapter 2 will show you how to use your system to create a basic WordPerfect document so that you can begin creating letters, memos, agendas, reports, and manuscripts.

# Creating a Document

In this chapter you'll begin creating WordPerfect documents by entering text, using Status Line information, and moving the cursor. Some of the features and functions discussed in this chapter are:

- Moving rapidly to any point in your document

- Using the Status Line to check cursor location

- Giving commands with function key combinations

- Canceling menus and restoring deleted text

- Accessing Help

If you're a first-time WordPerfect user—or a WordPerfect user simply itching to get into the program—try your hand by beginning with the *Quick Start* section in this chapter. Then, after you've tried the *Quick Start* fundamentals, go back and read the rest of the chapter for the details.

*Quick Start* Part 1 will guide you through starting WordPerfect, entering text, moving through text, inserting blank lines, and quitting WordPerfect. Remember, although *Quick Starts* do present the basic concepts, *Quick Starts* do not pursue every concept in detail—the main part of the chapter does.

31

# The Status Line

As illustrated in figure 2.1, the *Status Line* appears at the lower right of your screen. That line of information is called the Status Line because the information that appears describes the *cursor's* status. The cursor is the small blinking line that marks the spot (on your screen) where the next character you type will appear.

The first item on the Status Line appears in the lower left corner of your screen—the current document name (which includes the full path name). From time to time, the document name will be temporarily replaced by WordPerfect messages and prompts. Chapter 17 describes how you may change your system default so that the document name will not display.

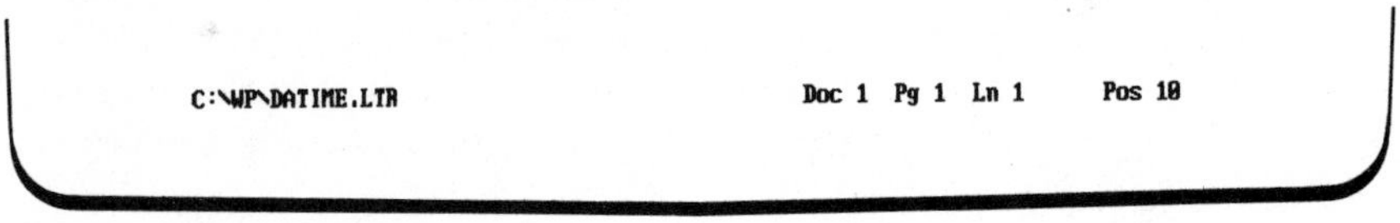

```
     C:\WP\DATIME.LTR                    Doc 1  Pg 1  Ln 1      Pos 10
```

*Fig. 2.1. The Status Line screen.*

The second item in the Status Line (*Doc*) indicates which of two available documents is currently displayed on your screen (WordPerfect is able to hold two documents in memory simultaneously). The Status Line identifies the documents as either *Doc 1* or *Doc 2*. The name of the current document is displayed in the lower left corner of the screen.

The number of the page on which the cursor currently rests is displayed next in the Status Line following the *Pg* indicator.

The number following the Status Line indicator *Ln* indicates on which line of your document's page the cursor currently rests.

The last item (*Pos*) in the Status Line indicates in which column on your document's page the cursor currently rests. The position indicator will be helpful as you become more familiar with WordPerfect. The position indicator will appear in uppercase letters (*POS*) if the Caps Lock key is activated for typing in uppercase letters. When the position indicator blinks, the Num Lock key is activated to allow you to use the numeric keypad keys to type numbers rather than using numeric keypad keys to move the cursor. When you create bold lettering, the position indicator number changes from regular type to bold type. And, when you underline text the position indicator number is underlined.

As you move the cursor, the numbers in the Status Line change to reflect the new column, line, and page cursor position.

In the lower left section of your screen, you'll find the name of the current file as well as the messages and prompts generated by your system as you work. Status Line information appears only on your screen; it doesn't appear in your printed document. (WordPerfect 4.1 screens do not display the name of the file.)

# Using Your Keyboard

The WordPerfect keyboard is divided into three basic sections. Figure 2.2 illustrates the keyboard for the IBM PC and compatibles; figure 2.3 illustrates the keyboard for IBM PS/2 computers. One major difference between the two keyboard layouts is that the PS/2 keyboard houses the function keys in a horizontal row above the number keys at the top of the keyboard. WordPerfect uses function keys 1-10 on both keyboards, and each function key is capable of carrying out four distinct tasks depending on whether the key is used by itself or in conjunction with another key.

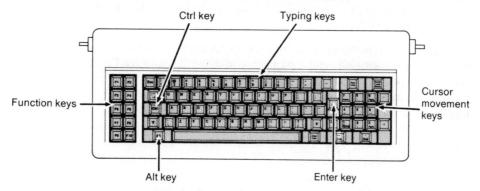

*Fig. 2.2. Keyboard configuration for WordPerfect.*

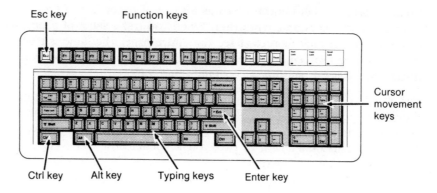

*Fig. 2.3. Keyboard for IBM PS/2.*

The keys at the far right of the keyboard are capable of carrying out several tasks. Notice that four of the keys contain arrows. You will use those keys to move the cursor as you create and edit WordPerfect documents. When the Num Lock key is activated, those cursor arrow keys become numeric keys with which you may carry out math functions. The keyboard for the IBM PS/2, like that shown in figure 2.3, provides you with a *duplicate* set of cursor arrow keys that can be used to move the cursor even if the Num Lock key is activated.

The Home, PgUp, End, and PgDn keys that surround the cursor arrow keys allow you to move the cursor more quickly (than the cursor arrow keys) within your document. The IBM PS/2 keyboard comes with duplicate keys for Home, Page Up, Page Down, and End to allow you to use these keys if the Num Lock key is activated. Note also that the PS/2 keyboard provides duplicate Insert and Delete keys (these will be discussed later).

The keys that lie between these two sections respond much as regular typing keys—with a few special exceptions. The *Alt* and *Ctrl* keys are used with other keys to provide capabilities that an individual key would not have if used by itself.

The *Enter* (or Return) key can be used as a carriage return, and to insert blank lines in your text. The IBM PS/2 comes with duplicate Enter keys. WordPerfect does have an automatic return feature called *wordwrap*. As a matter of course, when the cursor reaches the right margin at the end of the line you are currently typing, your system automatically moves the cursor to the left margin of the next line so that you may continue uninterrupted typing. Practice using wordwrap in the *Quick Start* section at the end of this chapter.

## Comparing Your Computer to a Typewriter

Think of WordPerfect's *clean screen* as a sheet of paper and of the keyboard as the keys on a typewriter. When you roll a sheet of paper into a typewriter's carriage, you can't see the entire page. The same is true of your computer's screen: you see only a limited number of lines of your document's page at one time—generally about 24.

Just about everything else is similar to working on a typewriter. With a little practice, you'll be able to set headings, margins, and page number positions as quickly with your computer as you can now on a typewriter. After you create a document or two, you'll wonder how you ever composed text on a typewriter!

Unlike a conventional typewriter, WordPerfect sets margins for letters automatically. You must change the margin settings if you want them to appear at other than the 10 and 74 *default* settings. Standard WordPerfect system settings are called default settings. Each time you start WordPerfect, the system defaults are automatically set. The left margin is automatically set at 10, and the right margin at 74. Tabs are positioned every 5 spaces across the line, and text is automatically single-spaced and printed without page numbers.

## More About Function Keys

As you create WordPerfect documents, you will routinely use the function keys to give your computer instructions called *commands*. These commands are illustrated on the template for the IBM PC, XT, AT, and compatibles (see figure 2.4) and on the tear-out card in the back of this book. If you are using the IBM Enhanced Keyboard for the PC, XT, or AT, the command template is shown in the appendix. This template can be used on the PS/2 keyboard as well. Commands are color-coded for easy use:

- Black indicates that the function key is used alone

- Green indicates that you must hold the Shift key down and press the appropriate function key

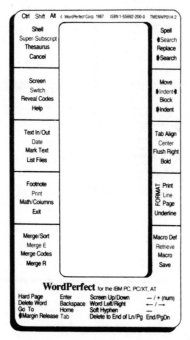

*Fig. 2.4. WordPerfect's keyboard function key template.*

- Blue indicates that you must hold the Alt key down and press the appropriate function key

- Red indicates that you must hold the Ctrl key down and press the appropriate function key

Function keys work in several ways:

- Some function keys are used to turn a feature on and off. For instance, you will learn that to create bold type you must first press the function key F6, type the text to be bolded, and press F6 to end the bold feature

- Some function keys ask you to make choices from a menu. As an example, pressing Ctrl-F7 causes your system to display the Footnote menu

- And, some function keys start a feature that is ended by pressing the Enter key. An example is the centering feature which you begin by pressing Shift-F6 and you end (after typing the text to be centered) by pressing the Enter key

You may display the function key template (illustrated in fig. 2.5) on your screen by pressing the Help key (F3) twice.

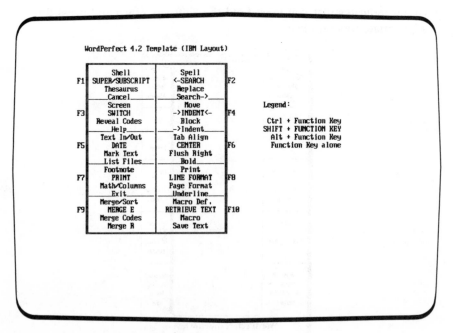

*Fig. 2.5. On-line function key template.*

Your WordPerfect documentation includes a color-coded and alphabetized list of features and the keystrokes associated with those features. Figure 2.6 presents fifteen frequently used WordPerfect features and their commands, and the card in the back of this book provides a desktop reminder of key locations and function commands.

| Feature | Keystroke |
| --- | --- |
| Block | Alt-F4 |
| Cancel | F1 |
| Exit | F7 |
| Help | F3 |
| Indent | F4 |
| Line Format, Margins | Shift-F8, 3 Margins |
| Line Format, Tabs | Shift-F8, 1 2 Tabs |
| List Files | F5 |
| Move | Ctrl-F4 |
| Print (current doc) | Shift-F7, 1 Full Text |
| Reveal Codes | Alt-F3 |
| Save | F10 |
| Search | F2 |
| Spell | Ctrl-F2 |
| Switch (between docs) | Shift-F3 |

*Fig. 2.6. Fifteen of the most frequently used WordPerfect features and their commands.*

## The Cancel/Undelete Key

The function key that can really provide peace of mind is the *Cancel key* (F1). You might call it an "oops" key.

Press the Cancel key (F1) when you accidentally get into the wrong menu and want to back out without making a choice. The Cancel key acts also as an *undelete key* with which you can restore text you have mistakenly deleted.

Whenever you see a menu on the screen that you would like to leave without making a choice, press Cancel (F1) to back up through previous menus until you reach the typing screen.

Remember, this works in only *two* situations: with menus and with a command called the Block function. Pressing the Cancel key won't undo commands such as Bold, Underline, or Center. (The Bold, Underline, or

Center function keys are removed with the Reveal Codes key covered later in Chapter 6.)

The Cancel key also restores any of the last three text items you deleted. In this case, an "item" means those characters (numbers, letters, punctuation) deleted before moving the cursor. If you are on the typing screen (and not in a menu) when you press Cancel (F1), the last item deleted will temporarily display at the cursor's current location (see fig. 2.7). It doesn't matter whether the last item deleted was a single letter or multiple pages of text.

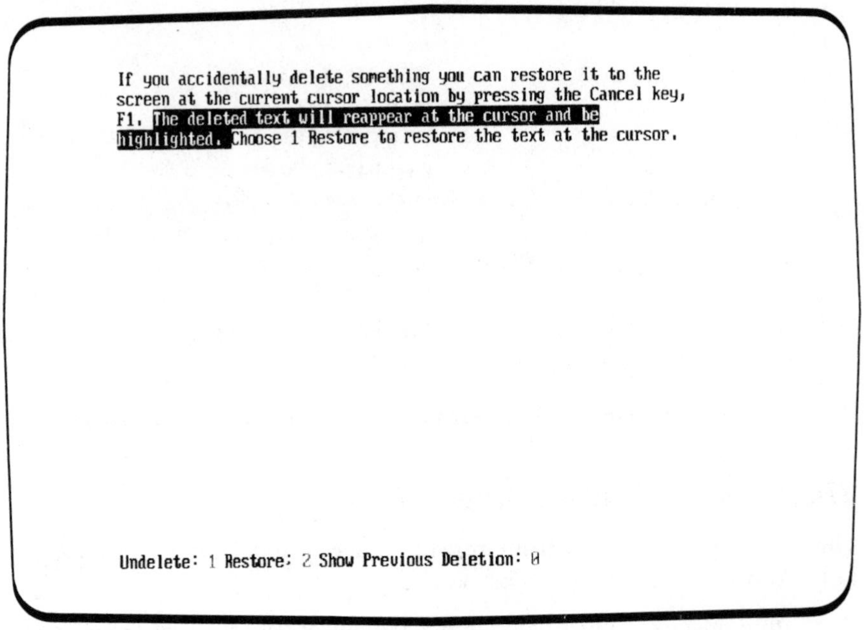

```
     If you accidentally delete something you can restore it to the
     screen at the current cursor location by pressing the Cancel key,
     F1. The deleted text will reappear at the cursor and be
     highlighted. Choose 1 Restore to restore the text at the cursor.












     Undelete: 1 Restore; 2 Show Previous Deletion: 0
```

Fig. 2.7. Using Cancel (F1) from the typing screen.

To restore one of the last three items you deleted (you'll learn how to delete in Chapter 3):

1. Move the cursor to the location where the deleted item should reappear

You do not have to place the cursor at the deletion's original location.

2. Press Cancel (F1)

The deleted item will show on screen as highlighted text. If you want to return to typing without restoring:

**3.** Press Cancel a second time

Or

**3.** Press **1** to restore the deleted text

Or

**3.** Press **2** to view another of the three deleted items

As you can imagine, the Cancel key can give you confidence. It lets you back out of menus, and restores text you may have deleted by mistake.

# Using the Cursor

After you load WordPerfect, you will notice that the cursor appears at the top left corner of the screen. The cursor marks the location where the first character you type will appear and, as you will discover later in these chapters, the cursor also marks the location in your text where codes (such as those used to create new margin settings) will be entered.

## Cursor Movement Keys

If you try to move the cursor on a clean screen with the cursor arrow keys, nothing will happen. WordPerfect won't permit the cursor to move where nothing exists—imagine your cursor hitting an invisible shield covering the screen. The cursor will only move over typed text or over blank characters (spaces) created with the space bar.

You can move the cursor by: typing text, pressing the space bar, pressing the Tab key, or pressing the Enter key (which will move the cursor down the screen along the left margin). After you've entered text, you can use the arrow keys to move the cursor.

Pressing the space bar moves the cursor forward, but it also inserts blank characters. In WordPerfect 4.2 the cursor will attempt to maintain its column position as you move up or down through a document. The cursor in WordPerfect 4.1 moves to the left edge of the screen, when it meets a blank line, and stays there during further vertical motion.

You can use any of these procedures to move the cursor back to the top left corner of the screen:

• Press the left-arrow key until the cursor rests at the left margin. Press the up-arrow key until the cursor reaches the top of the screen

- Press the Home key and then press the up-arrow key. You can also move to the bottom of any screen you have filled by pressing the Home key and then pressing the down-arrow key

- Press the minus key or the plus key on the *numeric keypad* to move the cursor to either the top or the bottom of the screen, respectively

- Press the Home and any arrow key to move quickly to the edge of the screen indicated by the direction of the arrow

- Press Ctrl-arrow to move the cursor a word at a time

# Scrolling

*Scrolling* is a word used to describe the act of moving the cursor through the pages of your document—line by line. You can scroll forward or backward through the document. Although you can alter the number of lines on a page, WordPerfect documents generally contain 54 lines per page. In a document several pages long, scrolling line by line is a time-consuming task. WordPerfect allows you to scroll quickly through your document using the options described in the following section.

## *Using PgDn, PgUp, and Go To*

Use the PgDn or PgUp keys to move the cursor a page at a time. When you press one of these keys, this prompt appears on the Status Line:

    Repositioning

Use the Go To function to move to any page in the document by following this procedure:

1. Check the page number on the Status Line

2. Press Go To (Ctrl-Home)

3. Type the **number of the page** you want to move to

4. Press Enter

The screen display will change, and the cursor will rest at the top of the specified page. Remember that PgDn, PgUp, and Go To work only if there are other pages to "go to" in the document.

The Go To key can be used with other keys. For instance if you want to move the cursor to the next character, press the Go To key, then type the character you want to move the cursor to.

22222222222222

## Moving the Cursor a Specific Number of Lines or Characters

You can move the cursor any number of lines by using the Esc (Escape) key. This prompt appears on the screen when you press Esc:

n=8

8 is the system default. You can change the default by replacing it with the number of lines you want to move and then pressing the appropriate arrow key (up or down).

The cursor will move in the direction indicated by the arrow key and exactly the number of lines you entered when prompted. Pressing the arrow key clears the Esc function.

Table 2.1 summarizes the cursor commands.

**Table 2.1**
**Summary of Cursor Movement Keys**

| Horizontal Movement | Keys |
| --- | --- |
| Character left or right | Left- or right-arrow key |
| Word right | Ctrl-right arrow |
| Word left | Ctrl-left arrow |
| Right edge of screen | Home-right arrow |
| Left edge of screen | Home-left arrow |
| Right end of line | Home-Home-right arrow, or End |
| Far left of line | Home-Home-left arrow |
| Far left of line (preceding all hidden command codes) | Home-Home-Home-left arrow |
| To space following specific character (nonnumeric) | Ctrl-Home-[character] |
| Move text right to next tab | Tab (normal, insert mode), or Indent |
| Jump cursor to next tab | Tab (typeover mode 4.2 only) |
| Move left and enter blank space | Backspace (typeover mode) |

| Vertical Movement | Keys |
| --- | --- |
| Line up and down | Up- and down-arrow keys |
| Top of screen | Home-up arrow or minus key (–) on numeric keypad |
| Bottom of screen | Home-down arrow or plus key (+) on numeric keypad |
| Top of current page | Ctrl-Home-up arrow |
| End of current page | Ctrl-Home-down arrow |
| Top of previous page | PgUp |
| Top of next page | PgDn |
| Beginning of document | Home-Home-up arrow |
| Beginning of document (preceding all hidden command codes) | Home-Home-Home-up arrow |
| End of document | Home-Home-down arrow |
| Go To page # | Ctrl-Home-[#]-Enter |
| # lines up | Esc-[#]-up arrow |
| # lines down | Esc-[#]-down arrow |

## Using On-Line Help

WordPerfect has an on-line Help feature that can be accessed as you work. Help permits you to research any of the function keys, as well as the Esc key, Del key, Ins key, Backspace key, Tab key, Home key, and the cursor arrow keys. Simply press the Help key, F3, and the Help menu appears (see fig. 2.8).

Then press the key or letter of the command about which you want to know more. For example, if you press the Print key (Shift-F7), the Print Help menu is displayed (see fig. 2.9). From within the Print Help screen you can learn more about Printer Control by pressing 1. After you have reviewed the Help information, return to your file either by pressing Enter or by pressing the space bar.

Note that if you are using a dual floppy disk system, you must insert your *Learning-Working* (5 1/4-inch) disk or *WordPerfect/Learn* (3 1/2-inch microfloppy) disk in drive B in order to access the Help feature. To make the on-line Help feature available without swapping disks, copy both *wphelp.fil* and *wphelp2.fil* from the *Learning* (5 1/4-inch) disk or from the *WordPerfect/Learn* (3 1/2-inch microfloppy) disk to your document storage disk.

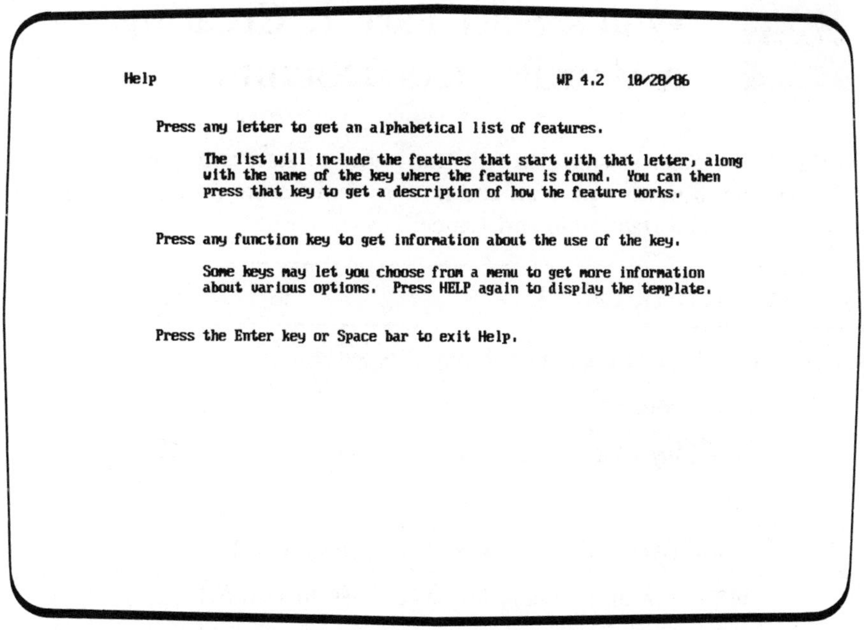

```
Help                                    WP 4.2    18/28/86

     Press any letter to get an alphabetical list of features.

          The list will include the features that start with that letter, along
          with the name of the key where the feature is found.  You can then
          press that key to get a description of how the feature works.

     Press any function key to get information about the use of the key.

          Some keys may let you choose from a menu to get more information
          about various options.  Press HELP again to display the template.

     Press the Enter key or Space bar to exit Help.
```

Fig. 2.8. On-line Help menu screen.

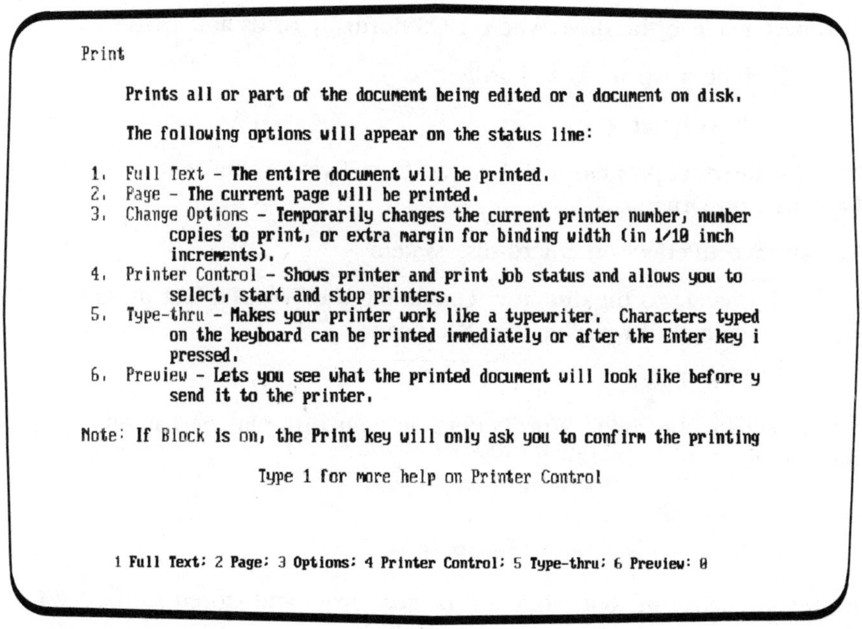

```
Print

     Prints all or part of the document being edited or a document on disk.

     The following options will appear on the status line:

1.  Full Text - The entire document will be printed.
2.  Page - The current page will be printed.
3.  Change Options - Temporarily changes the current printer number, number
          copies to print, or extra margin for binding width (in 1/10 inch
          increments).
4.  Printer Control - Shows printer and print job status and allows you to
          select, start and stop printers.
5.  Type-thru - Makes your printer work like a typewriter.  Characters typed
          on the keyboard can be printed immediately or after the Enter key i
          pressed.
6.  Preview - Lets you see what the printed document will look like before y
          send it to the printer.

Note: If Block is on, the Print key will only ask you to confirm the printing

               Type 1 for more help on Printer Control


   1 Full Text; 2 Page; 3 Options; 4 Printer Control; 5 Type-thru; 6 Preview: 0
```

Fig. 2.9. Print Help menu.

# Quick Start Part 1: Creating a WordPerfect Document

In this *Quick Start* session you will learn how to start and exit WordPerfect, how to type text, and how to move around on-screen. You'll also use the important Help and Cancel keys.

## Starting WordPerfect

To start WordPerfect on a dual floppy disk system:

1. Insert your

   *WordPerfect-Working* (5 1/4-inch disk)

   or

   *WordPerfect/Learn-Working* (3 1/2-inch disk)

   in Drive A and a blank formatted disk in Drive B

2. After the DOS prompt A> type **b:**

3. Press Enter

You have made B the drive where DOS normally reads and writes.

4. Type **a:wp** to start WordPerfect

5. Press Enter

The WordPerfect program will be read from Drive A, but your work will be stored on Drive B.

To start WordPerfect on a hard disk system:

1. Change to the directory containing the WordPerfect program by typing **cd\wp** after the DOS prompt C>

2. Press Enter

The directory containing WordPerfect on your disk may be named differently.

3. Type **wp**

4. Press Enter to start WordPerfect

Until you change it, your work will be read from and stored to the \WP directory.

## Checking Your Screen

If the printer is installed, a blank typing screen will appear. If text appears, the printer has not been installed. You must press the space bar to continue.

As you work through *Quick Start* watch the Status Line at the bottom of the screen. The *Pg*, *Ln*, and *Pos* indicators show the page, line, and column position of the cursor. Notice that when WordPerfect starts the cursor is on page 1, line 1, and column position 10.

*Quick Start* assumes the original WordPerfect default margins of 10 and 74. If your margins are different, the screen appearance and location of your cursor may differ from this example.

## Typing Text

You will type a paragraph and quickly recognize the first major difference between a typewriter and a word processor.

1. Type the following paragraph without pressing the Enter (carriage return) key. Type it as one continuous stream, stopping only at the last period. As you type, watch the words wrap to the next line when they pass the right margin. (Don't worry about typing mistakes, you'll correct them later.) Now, type:

**One of the great advantages of word processors is that you can type continuously until you reach the end of a paragraph. Only then should you press the Enter (carriage return) key. As you type, any words that pass the right margin automatically wrap to the next line.**

2. Now, press the Enter key once to end the paragraph and move to a new line

3. Press the Enter key a second time to insert a blank line

4. Type the second paragraph, again watching the cursor position reflected on the Status Line

5. Press the Enter key after the last period in the paragraph

**Should you change margin widths, or insert and delete text, the sentences will automatically wrap themselves to the next line when they pass the right margin. If you end lines by pressing Enter, the computer assumes you are marking the end of a**

**paragraph. When you modify margins or insert and delete text the
lines ending with an Enter key will not wrap to the next line.
They will break abruptly.**

Your screen should look like the screen illustrated in figure 2.10.

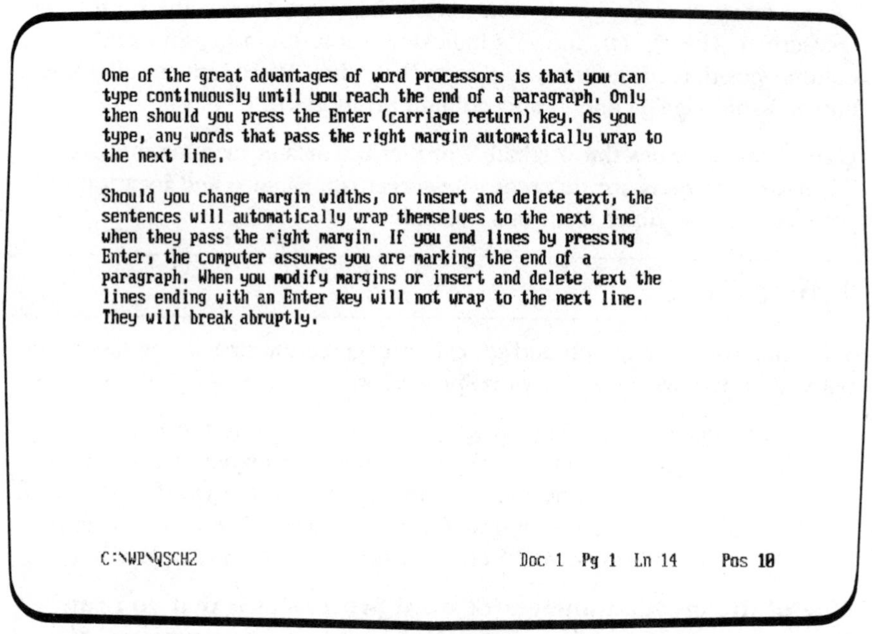

```
One of the great advantages of word processors is that you can
type continuously until you reach the end of a paragraph. Only
then should you press the Enter (carriage return) key. As you
type, any words that pass the right margin automatically wrap to
the next line.

Should you change margin widths, or insert and delete text, the
sentences will automatically wrap themselves to the next line
when they pass the right margin. If you end lines by pressing
Enter, the computer assumes you are marking the end of a
paragraph. When you modify margins or insert and delete text the
lines ending with an Enter key will not wrap to the next line.
They will break abruptly.



C:\WP\QSCH2                          Doc 1  Pg 1  Ln 14      Pos 10
```

*Fig. 2.10. Screen display for Quick Start Part 1: Typing Text.*

## Moving the Cursor

The cursor moves only where there is text or there are blank characters.
The four arrow keys move the cursor in the direction in which the arrow
is pointing. (If the Pos indicator on the Status Line is flashing, press the
Num Lock key to switch the numeric pad so the arrow keys will work.)

   1. Press the up-arrow key until the cursor rests on the first
      character of the first line

If necessary, press the left-arrow key to move the cursor to the first
character on the first line

   2. Press and release the right-arrow key three times to move right
      three characters

3. Hold down the right-arrow key to move the cursor continuously to the right

Holding the cursor down repeats the keystroke. Watch the cursor wrap to the next line when it passes the right margin.

4. Move the cursor to the blank line between paragraphs

5. Press the right arrow

Instead of moving right, the cursor moves down. There was no character to the right, so the cursor moved to the next character below.

6. Move the cursor to a full line of text, then press and release the Home key, next press the right arrow

Pressing Home, releasing, and then pressing an arrow moves the cursor to the last character position on-screen in the arrow's direction.

7. Press Home, release, then press the up arrow to move to the top of the screen

## Inserting Blank Lines

You can insert blank lines and divide paragraphs into new paragraphs with the Enter key.

1. Move to the blank line between paragraphs

2. Press the Enter key to insert a blank line

You can see the second paragraph move down as hard carriage returns are inserted. A hard carriage return is an invisible code that is inserted in your document each time you press the Enter key. Later (Chapter 17), you'll discover that WordPerfect permits you to make a change in the hard return default which causes WordPerfect to insert a visible screen symbol each time you enter a hard return.

3. Continue pressing the Enter key until you see the Pg and Ln indicators in the Status Line reflect that you are on a new page

You will see also that the break between pages appears as a line.

4. Move the cursor to the *I* in the word *If* in the paragraph that now appears on the second page

5. Press Enter

This procedure ends the preceding sentence and starts a new paragraph at the *I*

**6.** Press Enter again to insert a new blank line between the two paragraphs on page two

Your screen should now look like figure 2.11.

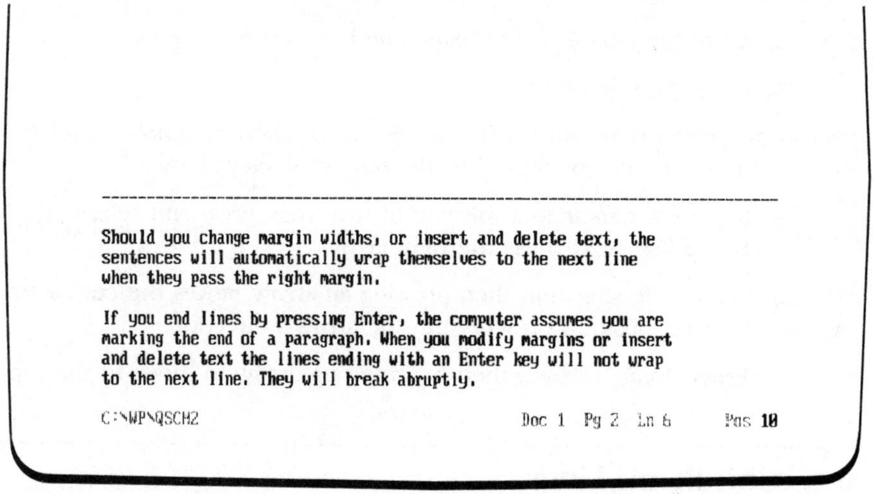

```
------------------------------------------------------------------



    Should you change margin widths, or insert and delete text, the
    sentences will automatically wrap themselves to the next line
    when they pass the right margin.

    If you end lines by pressing Enter, the computer assumes you are
    marking the end of a paragraph. When you modify margins or insert
    and delete text the lines ending with an Enter key will not wrap
    to the next line. They will break abruptly.

    C:\WP\QSCH2                              Doc 1  Pg 2  Ln 6      Pos 10
```

*Fig. 2.11. Screen display after dividing paragraph two.*

## Moving between Pages

Now you have two pages in which you can use page movement commands.

**1.** Press the PgUp key to move to the top of the preceding page

**2.** Hold down the Ctrl key and at the same time, tap the Home key to start the Go To command

**3.** Type **2**, the page number you want to go to

**4.** Press Enter

**5.** Press Home-Home-up arrow key to go to the very top of the document

**6.** Press Home-Home-down arrow key to go to the very bottom of the document

## Removing Blank Lines

You can remove the blank lines you've inserted and rejoin the paragraphs with the Backspace key. (On your keyboard, the Backspace key is generally located along the top row of typing keys and is identified by a left arrow.)

1. Move the cursor to the first character in the third paragraph

2. Press the Backspace key

You have deleted one of the hard carriage returns left by pressing the Enter key. The third paragraph moves up.

3. Press the Backspace key again and the third paragraph will rejoin the end of the second paragraph

4. Move to the first character in the second paragraph

5. Press the Backspace key to delete hard carriage returns that create the blank lines

The paragraph will move up.

6. Continue pressing the Backspace key until the second paragraph passes through the page break and moves to its original position after the first paragraph

Because of the paragraph's position on the screen it will be difficult to determine when you have reached the end of the first paragraph until the second paragraph actually joins Paragraph one. Insert blank lines between the two paragraphs by pressing Enter, twice.

## Using the Function Keys

Two of the purposes of the function keys are to cause a feature or function to activate (such as the centering feature), or to cause a menu to be displayed (which offers you additional word-processing choices). To display the Margin menu:

1. Press the Line Format key (Shift-F8)

2. Type 3 to choose Margins

Do not change the margin settings. This exercise is only to see the menu. Leave the menu on-screen for the next step.

## Using Cancel (F1)

To get out of the Margin menu—or any menu from which you don't want to make a choice:

    **1.** Press F1 (the Cancel key)

If you press the Cancel key when you are not in a menu, WordPerfect will ask if you want to restore one of the last three items deleted. In this *Quick Start* you have been deleting carriage returns so you won't see very much restored.

## Using Help (F3)

The Help command is a resource that you can use to review infrequently used commands.

    **1.** Press Help (F3) and read the screen

    **2.** Type **M** to access Help for margins

The screen advises you to press Shift-F8 for margin help. Shift-F8 is also the function key combination for margins.

    **3.** Press the Line Format key (Shift-F8)

    **4.** Type **3** to access information about margins

    **5.** Press the space bar to return to the typing screen

To see a keyboard template of the function key commands:

    **6.** Press Help (F3) twice

    **7.** Press the space bar to return to the typing screen

## Exiting WordPerfect

When you are finished exploring how to type and move on the WordPerfect screen you can exit with the following steps. *Do not exit WordPerfect by turning off the computer.*

    **1.** Press the Exit key (F7)

This prompt will appear on your screen:

    Save Document? (Y/N)

    **2.** Type **N**

Since this is practice, you don't need to save it.

This prompt will appear on your screen:

> Exit WP? (Y/N)

3. Type **Y** if you want to exit WordPerfect

   Or

3. Type **N** if you want to clear the screen and continue typing

Chapter 2 described how to enter text using wordwrap, how to insert blank lines, and how to use the cursor to move through your documents. You have learned most of what you'll need to know about using function keys with WordPerfect, and after another chapter or two, you'll be ready to produce complete documents with WordPerfect.

Some of the important points to remember about typing and moving within your documents are:

- [ ] The cursor moves over text or blank characters
- [ ] Type paragraphs continuously, ending them with the Enter key
- [ ] Use Backspace to rejoin paragraphs and lines
- [ ] Move to the edge of a line with Home-arrow key
- [ ] Move to the beginning or end of the document with Home-Home-up/down arrow
- [ ] Move to any page with the GoTo key (Ctrl-Home)

The function keys are important because you'll use them to execute or select special commands or features. When using function keys remember:

- [ ] Function keys display a menu or cause immediate action
- [ ] Execute function key combinations, such as Shift-F8, by holding down the first key as you quickly press the function key
- [ ] Back out of menus by pressing Cancel (F1)
- [ ] Help is only one keystroke away, the F3 key

*Use* the Help and Cancel keys! Exploring WordPerfect commands with Help and Cancel will help you learn the many ways that WordPerfect commands and functions can be used to make your work easier.

Even the cursor movement keys can be used in combination. You'll find some of the key combinations in table 2.1 to be very handy when used with other functions. For example, Ctrl-right/left arrow moves the cursor a word at a time in either direction, and Ctrl-Backspace deletes the current word. A handy combination when editing!

With what you know already you're ready to start editing.

# Editing Your Document

In the last chapter you learned how to enter text, how to move the cursor, and how to use the Enter key. You didn't, however, learn how to correct the mistakes made while typing.

Don't be concerned; in this chapter you'll learn how easy it is to make corrections. In fact, you'll find that writing and editing with WordPerfect is a new and far more efficient way of composing and writing.

No longer will the ghost of your fourth grade teacher hover over your shoulder searching for every misspelled word and misplaced comma. With WordPerfect you can type as thoughts come to you and worry about catching misspellings, errors in grammar, and incorrect punctuation later.

Once your thoughts are on the screen you can go back to cut the superfluous and dress up the important—correcting and polishing with the insert and delete commands. You won't have to write right the first time! You can get your ideas right, and correct the words later.

WordPerfect permits you to delete unwanted text and insert additional text in several ways. Each approach works best in a specific situation. After you've scanned the information at the beginning of the chapter, take a few minutes and try the *Quick Start*—experiment with the different methods.

If you find you want to learn more about a particular method, you can read about it in the section of the chapter that describes the insert or the delete procedure in greater detail. Remember that *Quick Start* Part 2 doesn't cover every topic discussed in the chapter.

This chapter demonstrates how to:

- Delete characters to the left of the cursor with Backspace

- Delete characters above the cursor with the Del key

- Delete one word at a time with Ctrl-Backspace

- Delete any amount of text with the flexible and powerful Block delete command

The chapter also demonstrates two procedures for adding text to an existing document:

- Inserting so that the existing text moves to make room for new text

- Typing over text so that the original text is replaced with new text

Finally you'll learn how to clear your old work from the screen to start afresh. You'll also be reminded that you can restore what you've previously deleted.

# Deleting

One of the greatest frustrations for anyone who creates letters, memos, reports, brochures, newsletters—literally any kind of written communication—is to review what you have written only to discover that the document contains incorrect or inappropriate text.

It used to be that deleting text (even as little text as two or three words) required completely retyping the document—making a change on one page necessitated changes to all of the others. With WordPerfect, you can delete as much, or as little, text as you like and your system adjusts the remaining text automatically.

## Using the Delete and Backspace Keys
## To Delete Characters

Use the Del key to delete characters that lie directly above the cursor. Use the Backspace key to delete characters that lie to the left of the cursor. Because both keys perform similar functions, you can use whichever one is convenient to the current cursor location.

To delete with the Del key:

1. Use the arrow keys to place the cursor under the character to be deleted (see fig. 3.1)

2. Press Del

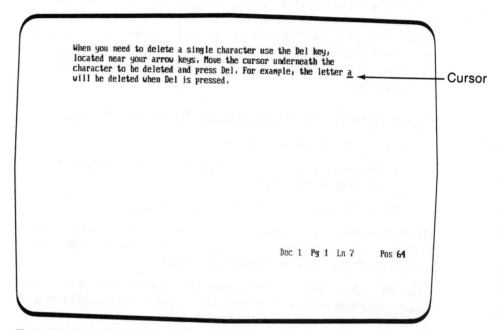

Fig. 3.1. Using the Delete key to delete a character.

Hold down the Del key to delete multiple characters. The text to the right of the deleted characters will move to fill in the gap.

When you need to delete characters starting from the end of a word or sentence it's often easiest to use the Backspace key.

To use the Backspace move the cursor so that it is one character to the right of the character you wish to delete. *The character that lies above the cursor will not be deleted.*

When you press the Backspace key, the character to the left of the cursor is erased. Any text to the right moves one character position to the left.

Hold the Backspace key down to delete multiple characters to the left. (On some keyboards the Backspace key is not labeled. It appears as a lone left-arrow key at the upper right of the keyboard.)

The 4.2 version of WordPerfect responds differently (than the 4.1 version) when backspacing in the Typeover mode. The Typeover mode enables you to type new characters over existing text, replacing the original character just the way a typewriter would. Backspace in Typeover mode in WordPerfect 4.1 deletes the character to the left of the cursor and brings the text together to fill the gap. WordPerfect 4.2 replaces the character to the left with a blank character, leaving the previous text in the original column positions.

## Using the Ctrl-Backspace Keys To Delete Words

If you need to delete an entire word:

1. Place the cursor anywhere in the word or in the blank space to the right of the word

2. Hold down Ctrl while you press the Backspace key

The Ctrl-Backspace key combination deletes the word above the cursor or it deletes the word to the left of the cursor if the cursor is positioned under a blank space directly following the word.

Frequently, editing involves deleting unnecessary words and phrases from within paragraphs. One of the easiest ways to cut words and phrases is to move from word to word with the Ctrl-arrow keys and selectively delete whole words with Ctrl-Backspace. You can become very fast with this method since your left little finger never moves from the Ctrl key. Your right hand jumps between cursor key and Backspace key.

## Deleting Carriage Returns To Delete Lines

As you discovered in the *Quick Start* in Chapter 2, blank lines are inserted into your text when you press the Enter key. Each time you insert a blank line, a hidden carriage return code is inserted in the text as well. Should you want to remove one of these blank lines:

1. Move the cursor to the left margin at the beginning of the blank line

2. Press Del

The hidden carriage return code is deleted and the lines of text move up.

In some cases a blank line may contain a return code and blank character entered with the space bar. You may have to press Del more than one time to delete the blank characters before you reach the hidden return code on the same line.

## Using Delete to EOL To Erase Lines of Text

Place the cursor where you want to begin erasing text. If you press the Ctrl-End key (called the Delete to EOL command), WordPerfect erases everything from the cursor position through the end of the line.

To erase several lines at a time, use the Esc key as a *repeater*.

1. Count the number of lines you want to erase following the cursor

2. Press Esc

This message appears in the Status Line:

    n=8

3. Type the number of lines you want to erase

4. Press Delete to EOL (Ctrl-End)

WordPerfect erases the number of lines you have specified.

## Using Delete to EOP To Erase a Page of Text

You can erase text that lies between the cursor's current position and the end of the current page with almost the same keystroke as Deleting to EOL. In this case, after positioning your cursor, press Ctrl-PgDn (Delete to EOP). The text that appears between the cursor and the bottom of that page will be deleted after you respond Y to the prompt:

    Delete Remainder of Page? (Y/N)N

## Using the Block Delete Command To Erase Blocks of Text

One of the most powerful and flexible commands in WordPerfect is the Block command. Although Chapter 6 is devoted to using the Block command, we will take a look at how the Block command can be used to delete any amount of text—from one character to many pages. The word "block" is used in word processing to describe a body of text that can consist of as little text as several characters or as much text as an entire document.

To use Block delete:

1. Move the cursor to the first character in the block you want to delete

2. Press the Block key (Alt-F4)

This message will appear (flashing) in the lower left corner of the screen:

Block on

When the message is displayed, any cursor movements will highlight text.

The highlighted text is known as the Block. The character at which you started will always be an "anchored" corner of the block. You can highlight more text by moving the "free corner" of the block with the cursor arrow, PgDn, PgUp, and Go To (Ctrl-Home) keys.

For example, if you want to delete multiple pages you can turn on the Block on one page, use Go To to move to another page, and all of the text on the pages in between will be highlighted.

3. After moving the cursor to highlight the text, check the screen to be certain that only text to be deleted is highlighted

4. Press the Del key to delete the highlighted text

This message will appear on your screen:

Delete Block? (Y/N)

5. Type **Y** to delete the block of text

You can get out of the Block command at any time by pressing Cancel (F1).

# Restoring Deleted Text

Because WordPerfect "remembers" the last three portions of text deleted, text removed with any of the deletion commands can be restored to the document.

To restore text:

1. Place the cursor where you want the deleted text to be restored

2. Press Cancel (F1)

WordPerfect displays the most recently deleted text in a highlighted rectangle, as shown in figure 3.2.

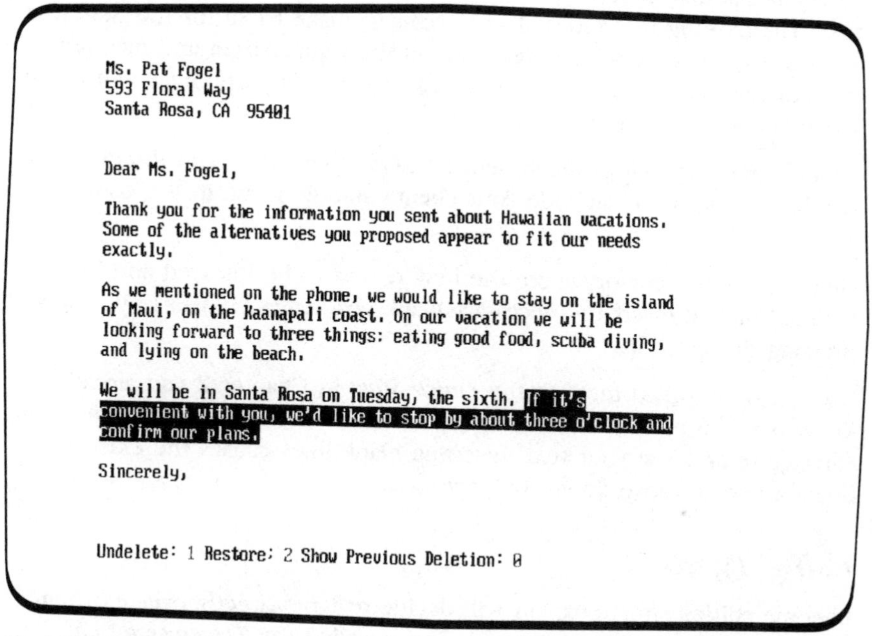

```
    Ms. Pat Fogel
    593 Floral Way
    Santa Rosa, CA  95401


    Dear Ms. Fogel,

    Thank you for the information you sent about Hawaiian vacations.
    Some of the alternatives you proposed appear to fit our needs
    exactly.

    As we mentioned on the phone, we would like to stay on the island
    of Maui, on the Kaanapali coast. On our vacation we will be
    looking forward to three things: eating good food, scuba diving,
    and lying on the beach.

    We will be in Santa Rosa on Tuesday, the sixth. If it's
    convenient with you, we'd like to stop by about three o'clock and
    confirm our plans.

    Sincerely,



    Undelete: 1 Restore; 2 Show Previous Deletion: 0
```

*Fig. 3.2. Deleted text.*

**3.** Type **1** to restore the text

Typing 2 from the menu displays the second most recent deletion. Typing 1 while that text is displayed restores it to the document.

# Adding Text to Your Document

Just as deleting text is a part of the editing process so is inserting text. As you review your documents, you'll find that some of what you have written needs enhancement. The following sections describe how easy it is to make what you have written better by inserting additional text; or by refining the existing text by typing over it with new text.

## Using Insert

WordPerfect normally operates in what is known as an *Insert mode*. Insert mode means that as you type, the new characters are inserted into existing text. The existing text moves to the right to make room for the new text. As you type, sentences may push beyond the right margin and may not immediately wrap to the next line. Don't worry. The sentences will adjust when you move to the next line.

As an example, you'd probably select Insert mode when you discover that you have forgotten to include your client's middle name in the contract you're writing.

Simply place the cursor where the new text is to be inserted and begin typing. You can insert the necessary blank characters (spaces) by simply pressing the space bar.

Note: If you worked through the *Quick Start* in Chapter 2 you already know that you press the Enter key to insert blank lines (and accompanying carriage returns) in your text. Inserting blank lines causes the existing lines of text to move down the page.

## Using Typeover

In some editing situations you will decide to type directly over existing text so that new text replaces old. This is called the *Typeover mode*.

You'd probably select Typeover mode if you've mistakenly typed your client's middle name as "Jane" and it should be "Dane."

To switch to Typeover mode:

1. Place the cursor where you want the new text to begin

2. Press the Ins key to turn the Insert mode off

This prompt appears at the lower left of the screen:

    Typeover

3. Type your text

As you type, the new text *replaces* the existing text.

To turn off Typeover, press the Ins key again. The prompt disappears, indicating that the function is off.

The Typeover function replaces text that has been marked for bold or underline, *only* if the cursor lies between the bold/underline code and the first character. If the cursor precedes the code, the text marked for bold/

underline is moved forward, not replaced. Chapter 5 discusses formatting codes at length.

# Changing Letters to Uppercase or Lowercase

If, as you are reviewing your document, you decide that it would be more effective to type an especially important series of sentences in uppercase letters, you can change from lowercase lettering to uppercase lettering quickly by following this procedure:

Mark the sentences you wish to change to uppercase lettering as a block:

1. Place the cursor at the beginning of the text to be changed to uppercase

2. Press Block (Alt-F4)

This message appears in the prompt section of the screen:

    Block on

3. Move the cursor to the end of the text

The block will be highlighted.

4. Press Switch (Shift-F3)

5. Type 1 for uppercase lettering

You'd type 2 to select lowercase lettering.

After the highlighted text changes to the appropriate case, the Switch menu disappears. The prompt, Block on, remains on the screen; it can be turned off by pressing Block (Alt-F4) or by pressing Cancel (F1).

# Rewriting the Screen

There may be times (as you insert text) that existing lines of text seem to "fall off" the right edge of the screen. To restore "lost" lines, press the down-arrow key.

Pressing the down-arrow key forces WordPerfect to *rewrite the screen*, bringing all the text into view. You can press Rewrite (Ctrl-F3) then Enter to bring the "lost" lines into view as well.

# Clearing a Document To Start Anew

WordPerfect is slightly different from other word processors in a way that makes WordPerfect more powerful than other word processors—but, that slight difference can even confuse experienced word-processing operators.

That difference is, in WordPerfect you must *clear the current document* from the screen before you start work on a new document or retrieve a new document from disk.

If you do not clear the current document before starting a new document, or before retrieving a document from disk, the old and the new documents will merge with one another. They will link together as one document. As you might imagine, it can cause a lot of confusion when you print or edit. Finding unwanted and unrelated text at the end of your previous work or at the beginning of your new work can be an unhappy surprise!

To clear the current document before starting a new document or before retrieving a document from disk:

> **1.** Press Exit (F7)

This prompt appears on your screen:

> Save Document? (Y/N)

> **2.** Type **Y**

> **3.** Type the **file name** to save the current document to disk

There are rules for creating file names; you'll find out about those rules in the next chapter.

> Or

> **2.** Type **N** if you don't need to save the work or if it has already been saved

The next prompt that will appear on your screen is:

> Exit WP? (Y/N)

> **3.** Type **N** to erase the screen and return to typing

If you type Y it means, *"Yes, I want to exit WordPerfect."*

If you are confused by any of the terms or procedures presented in this section, don't worry; you will learn more about naming and saving your documents in Chapter 4.

# Quick Start Part 2: Editing Your Document

In this *Quick Start* you will use two of WordPerfect's most useful functions, insert and delete. With the insert and delete methods presented here you will be able to change words and correct spelling so that the first copy you print will be the only copy you print.

## Getting Ready for Quick Start

Start WordPerfect using the steps described in Chapter 2's *Quick Start*.

1. Type this letter *including* the mistakes. The mistakes will give you something to edit

Remember, press the Enter key only at the end of paragraphs or at the end of partial lines like the address.

Ms. Pat Fogel
593 Floral Way
Santa Rosa, CA 95401

Dear Ms. Fogel;

Thank you for the information you sent about Hawaian vacatoisn. Some of the alternatives you proposed appear to be fine and dandy.

As we mentioned on the phone, we would like to stay on the island of Maui. On our vacation we will be looking forward to three things, eat, dive, and relax.

We will be in Santa Rosa on Tuesday, the fifth. If it's convenient with you, we'd like to stop by about three o'clock and confirm our plans.

Sincerely,,,,,,

Your typed copy should look like the screen shown in figure 3.3. (If your WordPerfect margins are different from the defaults 10 and 74, the location of words on the line may be slightly different from this example.)

```
        Ms. Pat Fogel
        593 Floral Way
        Santa Rosa, CA  95401

        Dear Ms. Fogel;

        Thank you for the information you sent about Hawaian vacatoisn.
        Some of the alternatives you proposed appear to be fine and
        dandy.

        As we mentioned on the phone, we would like to stay on the island
        of Maui. On our vacation we will be looking forward to three
        things, eat, dive, and relax.

        We will be in Santa Rosa on Tuesday, the fifth. If it's
        convenient with you, we'd like to stop by about three o'clock and
        confirm our plans.

        Sincerely,,,,,,


    C:\WP\QS2                                Doc 1  Pg 1  Ln 1      Pos 18
```

*Fig. 3.3. Practice letter screen display.*

## Using Backspace To Delete a Character

There are two ways to delete single characters: the Delete key which is labeled Del, and the Backspace key which is usually located by itself on the keyboard and labeled with a left pointing arrow. To delete a character using the Backspace key:

1. Place the cursor after the semicolon following Fogel in the salutation

2. Press the Backspace key. You have deleted the semicolon and moved the cursor left

3. Now, type a **comma** (,)

## Inserting a Single Character

It's easy to insert a single character (or an entire phrase). Just move the cursor to the location where you want to begin inserting text, and start typing.

**1.** Move the cursor beneath the last *a* in the word *Hawaian*

The cursor is in the position where you want to insert the missing letter *i*

**2.** Type the letter **i**

Notice that when you type *i* the letter appears at the cursor location and existing text moves right to make room.

## Deleting Multiple Characters

In WordPerfect it's easy to make corrections by typing in the new text, then pressing the Del key to remove the old text. You can use this method to correct the mistyped word *vacatoisn*

**1.** Move the cursor underneath the *o* in the word *vacatoisn*

**2.** Type in the correct letters **ions**

Notice how the existing text shifts to the right.

**3.** Press the Del key once to delete the *o*

**4.** Press and briefly hold the Del key down to delete *isn*

The Del key and Backspace repeat when held down.

## Moving the Cursor One Word at a Time

As you edit it's frequently more convenient to move the cursor from word to word than from letter to letter.

**1.** Place the cursor on any word in the first line of your letter and press the Ctrl-right arrow key combination

Watch the cursor skip an entire word to the right.

To press Ctrl-right arrow, hold down the Ctrl key, then quickly press the right arrow. (If you see a number appear instead of the cursor moving, you have accidentally pressed Shift-arrow.)

**2.** Hold down the Ctrl-right arrow combination and continue to jump words

3. Stop so the cursor rests on the first letter (*b*) in the phrase *be fine and dandy*.

## Deleting Entire Words

Two handy editing key combinations are the Ctrl-arrow combination which moves the cursor a word at a time and the Ctrl-Backspace combination which deletes an entire word.

1. Press Ctrl-Backspace to delete the word *be*

Remember to hold the Ctrl key down as you press Backspace.

2. Press and hold Ctrl-Backspace to word-delete the phrase *fine and dandy*.

3. Type **fit our needs exactly.**

## Inserting a Long Phrase

WordPerfect permits you to insert long phrases as well as single letters.

1. Move the cursor under the period (.) following the word *Maui*

2. Press the space bar once and type the phrase **on the Kaanapali coast**

Watch the screen as the text is inserted.

## Deleting to the End of the Line

Sometimes it's convenient to delete from the cursor's current position to the end of the same line.

1. Place the cursor under the comma preceding the phrase *eat, dive, and relax*.

2. Press Ctrl-End to delete from the cursor to the end of the line

Notice that the cursor stays in place for you to type in a correction.

3. Type : **eating good food, scuba diving, and lying on the beach.**

## Using Typeover

The insert feature of WordPerfect makes adding new text easy. In some instances, such as forms and tables, you may want to type over the top of existing text just as a typewriter does.

1. Move the cursor to the first *f* in *fifth*

2. Press the Insert key

Notice that the word *Typeover* appears in the lower left corner of your screen.

3. Type **six**

You will type over *fif* to create the new word *sixth*

4. Press the Insert key a second time to turn Typeover mode off

Notice that the Typeover prompt disappears from the screen.

## Using the Repeat Key

You can repeat many WordPerfect functions with the Escape key. In this example you will delete five commas with three keystrokes.

1. Move the cursor to the first comma (,) following *Sincerely*

2. Press the Esc key

The prompt n=8 will display in the lower left corner.

3. Type **5**

You have told your system that you want to repeat your next keystroke five times.

4. Press the Del key

The Esc key repeats the Del key five times, deleting the extra commas. Use the repeat ability of Esc to insert lines, delete spaces, and draw underlines. It's a time-saver.

## Deleting a Block of Text

One of the most powerful and flexible ways of deleting a block of text of any size is with the Block command. With the Block command you simply highlight all of the text you want deleted, then press the Del key.

1. Move to the word *If* in the last sentence

2. Press Block (Alt-F4) to turn on the Block command

The prompt `Block on` appears in the lower left corner of your screen.

3. Press the right-arrow key until the cursor appears under the *y* in the word *you*

Notice how the text that the cursor passes over is highlighted.

When the cursor appears under the *y*:

4. Press the down arrow to highlight one entire row at a time

Everything that is highlighted can now be deleted.

5. Press the Del key

This prompt appears on your screen:

`Delete Block? (Y/N)`

6. Type **Y** to delete the highlighted text

## Restoring Deleted Text

If you delete something and then decide you liked it as it first appeared, don't despair. For example, you can restore the sentence that you've just deleted with the Block delete command.

If you want the letter to make sense, leave the cursor after the word *sixth* in the final sentence. However, you could move the cursor anywhere in the letter and restore the deletion.

1. Move the cursor to the location where the text to be restored will appear

2. Press Cancel (F1)

The last deleted item, the Block delete in this case, appears in highlight on the screen.

Figure 3.4 illustrates how the text about to be restored displays in highlight.

```
        Ms. Pat Fogel
        593 Floral Way
        Santa Rosa, CA  95401

        Dear Ms. Fogel,

        Thank you for the information you sent about Hawaiian vacations.
        Some of the alternatives you proposed appear to fit our needs
        exactly.

        As we mentioned on the phone, we would like to stay on the island
        of Maui, on the Kaanapali coast. On our vacation we will be
        looking forward to three things: eating good food, scuba diving,
        and lying on the beach.

        We will be in Santa Rosa on Tuesday, the sixth. If it's
        convenient with you, we'd like to stop by about three o'clock and
        confirm our plans.

        Sincerely,



        Undelete: 1 Restore; 2 Show Previous Deletion: 0
```

*Fig. 3.4. Highlighted text to be restored.*

**4.** Type **1** to Restore the deleted text

Type 2 if you want to see the previous deleted item. Press Cancel to return to typing without making a choice.

Because the Block command is the most powerful and flexible command in WordPerfect, Chapter 6 is devoted to a thorough discussion of Block command applications.

## Clearing the Current Document from Memory

*This is an important command.* You must clear the current document from the screen before you retrieve another document from disk or before you start a new document. If you do not clear the current document, the new document and the old document will merge into one.

To clear the current document from memory:

**1.** Press Exit (F7)

This prompt appears on your screen:

> Save Document? (Y/N)

    **2.** Type **Y** to save the document

    **3.** Type the **name of the document**

You'll learn all about naming documents in Chapter 4. For now, however, type in a name that contains less than eight letters.

    **4.** Press Enter

This prompt appears on your screen:

> Exit WP? (Y/N)

    **5.** Type **N** because you do not want to exit WordPerfect, you only want to clear the screen

You also could type Y to exit WordPerfect and return to DOS, or you could press Cancel (F1) to cancel the command to erase the current document.

## Exiting WordPerfect

Now that you have cleared the screen, you may want to go on to try the *Quick Start* in Chapter 4. If you'd prefer not to go on, here's how to exit WordPerfect:

    **1.** Press Exit (F7)

This prompt appears on your screen:

> Save Document? (Y/N)

    **2.** Type **N**

This prompt appears on your screen:

> Exit WP? (Y/N)

    **3.** Type **Y** to exit WordPerfect and return to DOS

This chapter explored the two fundamental capabilities designed into all word-processing software, inserting and deleting text. The insert and delete features alone make a word processor more valuable and timesaving than a typewriter. In the chapters to come, you will discover many more WordPerfect features that will help you use your time more effectively and efficiently.

Remember that there are many ways to delete text. You'll be most satisfied if you learn all the ways and use each in the appropriate situation:

☐ Delete unwanted characters to the left of the cursor with the Backspace key

☐ Delete unwanted characters above the cursor with the Del key

☐ Delete a word at a time with Ctrl-Backspace

☐ Delete any amount of text with the flexible and powerful Block delete command

You can easily add impact to your words by inserting new text, adding new ideas, replacing ineffective words, and supplying added detail. To insert new text or type over existing text:

☐ Move the cursor to the location where you want to insert text and begin typing

☐ Replace existing text by pressing the Insert key, then typing new text over old

While you're "trying on" different words and phrases you may delete words you wish you'd saved. With WordPerfect you can restore them. To "undelete" text:

☐ Restore one of the last three deletions by moving to the location where the text is to appear and pressing Cancel (F1). Then, follow the menu instructions

Finally, you must clear your completed work before starting new work:

☐ Clear the screen by pressing Exit (F7), before you retrieve a document from disk, or before you begin a new document

You've taken more than a few steps since beginning this book—now you can create and edit basic WordPerfect documents! The next chapter will show you how to save your documents, how to retrieve them from disk, and how to print them.

# Saving, Retrieving, and Printing Your Document

Now you can type and edit basic WordPerfect documents! But, if you're going to use WordPerfect as more than a typewriter, you're going to need to know how to save your work to disk, how to retrieve the documents you've saved, and of course, how to print your documents. *Saving, retrieving,* and *printing* are the next three important functions that will be introduced.

In this chapter you'll discover how WordPerfect uses function keys to display menus. If you want to learn WordPerfect *well*—and, if you want to learn *how* to learn more on your own, then:

- *Don't* press the keystrokes described in the rest of this book *until* you compare those keystrokes to their function name on the WordPerfect template

- *Don't* choose any item from a screen menu *until* you read all the choices in the menu

If you follow these two rules you'll remember *where keys are located,* and you'll remember *menu features that will enhance the way you use WordPerfect* later on.

Some of the more important procedures you'll explore in this chapter are:

- How to save your documents to disk

- How to save parts of a document to disk

- How to clear the screen before retrieving a new document

- How to create a "boilerplate" to save yourself the work of typing frequently used paragraphs and pages

- How to print the current document, or documents in the queue, from disk

- How to continue working on a document while another document is printing

As you've probably discovered by now, one of the nicest things about *Using WordPerfect*, 3rd Edition, is that the book permits you to decide how to learn about WordPerfect.

If you're already familiar with WordPerfect, you can elect to simply scan the detail sections of the chapter—reading about only those features that aren't familiar to you.

If you're new to WordPerfect, you can choose to start with this chapter's *Quick Start*; in this case, a guided tour of the save, retrieve, and print features. Then, after you've tried the *Quick Start*, go back and read about the features you've used.

Some of you may feel more comfortable first reading the chapter and then trying the *Quick Start*—the choice is yours!

# Saving Your Work

The caution *save your work frequently* cannot be overemphasized. Horror stories from people who have labored over their documents for hours—only to lose all of their work because of a power failure, or a thunder storm, or (worse yet!) someone else's carelessness—have sent the warning far and wide.

---

■ **Caution**

---

**Save your work frequently**

---

If you are working on a long document—save your work every fifteen minutes. Saving is easy! You must remember that what you see on the screen is nothing but a *temporary* display. Only documents that have been saved to disk enjoy a measure of security. As soon as the power goes off in your computer, whatever is on the screen disappears forever—unless you have saved it to disk.

## Naming Your Document File

The Save Key (F10) can be used at any time while you are working on a document. After you press the Save key, this prompt appears on the screen:

```
Document to be Saved:__
```

You'll respond by typing the name you want to assign to the document. You can type the name in uppercase or lowercase letters.

For example, LEtters, LETTERS, letters, and lEttErs are identical file names as far as your computer is concerned. Just as people have first and last names, file names have two parts. The first name can contain from one to eight characters; the last name can contain from zero to three characters. The last name is referred to as the *file name extension*. If both a first and last name are used, separate them with a period (.):

*Example*: LETTERS.JLS

Avoid using punctuation marks except for the period between the first name and the extension, and don't include blank spaces between characters. If you press the space bar, the Enter key, or an arrow key, WordPerfect assumes that you have finished typing the file name.

For instance, if you try to save your document under the file name L. ;addRESSES WordPerfect names the file L

If you want to include a blank character in a file name, use the hyphen or underscore key instead (LET-RS.JLS or LET_RS.JLS). A few other symbols are allowed in names, but most are not. It's easiest to use just the hyphen or underscore.

Select file names that are descriptive. The file name should quickly identify the document for you. One file-naming strategy that works well is to reserve the three-letter file name extension as a descriptor that defines the category in which the file belongs.

In the example above, LETTERS.JLS could be the name you'd assign to a letter that goes to your client, John L. Smith.

And, you can keep track of the number of times that a document is revised by reserving the seventh and eight characters in the first name for the version number as in the example that follows.

The ninth revision of a budget forecast could be saved logically as
BDGFRC09.RPT. While this file name might look long and cumbersome at
first glance, it translates nicely to: *Budget Forecast Version 09.Report*. The
file name extension identifies that budget forecast document as a report.

## Using the List Files Screen

File name space restrictions don't offer you very much latitude in
describing a file's contents, but you can actually find out quite a bit about
a document before retrieving it from disk.

The List Files screen (see fig. 4.1) displays both the date and time the file
was saved as well as the size of the file (there are about 2000 bytes per
full page of typing). Using the *Look* option from the List Files screen
permits you to take a peek at a file without retrieving it.

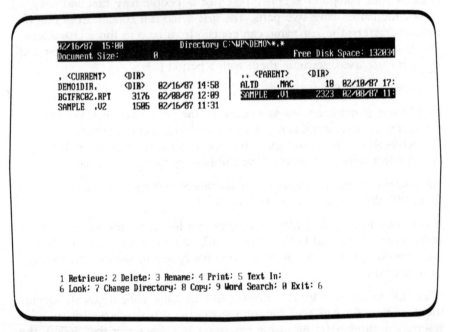

```
02/16/87  15:00               Directory C:\WP\DEMO\*.*
Document Size:       0                             Free Disk Space: 132034

   . <CURRENT>   <DIR>              .. <PARENT>   <DIR>
   DEMO1DIR.    <DIR>   02/16/87 14:58    ALTD    .MAC      10  02/10/87 17:
   BGTFRC02.RPT  3176   02/08/87 12:09    SAMPLE  .V1     2323  02/08/87 11:
   SAMPLE  .V2   1505   02/16/87 11:31








   1 Retrieve: 2 Delete: 3 Rename: 4 Print: 5 Text In:
   6 Look: 7 Change Directory: 8 Copy: 9 Word Search: 0 Exit: 6
```

*Fig. 4.1. List Files screen.*

In just a few moments you can create a summary of each of your
documents. The summary can be created and edited from anywhere in
your document text. A document summary includes such information as:
the file name, the date it was created, the author's name, and short
comments that may help you to later identify the document.

Figure 4.2 illustrates the Document Summary screen.

1. Press Text In/Out (Ctrl-F5) to display the Text In/Out menu

2. Select **A** Create/Edit Summary option

WordPerfect automatically enters the file name and the creation date.

3. Type the **author's name**

4. Type any **comments** describing the document

5. Press F7 to exit the comment section of the screen

6. Press Enter to exit the Document Summary screen

And, the cursor appears in the text at the point where you left off.

To display the document summary just press Ctrl-F5, D and respond to the prompt by typing Y. To display the comments section, type Y. To cancel the summary display, repeat these steps but type N to the document summary prompt.

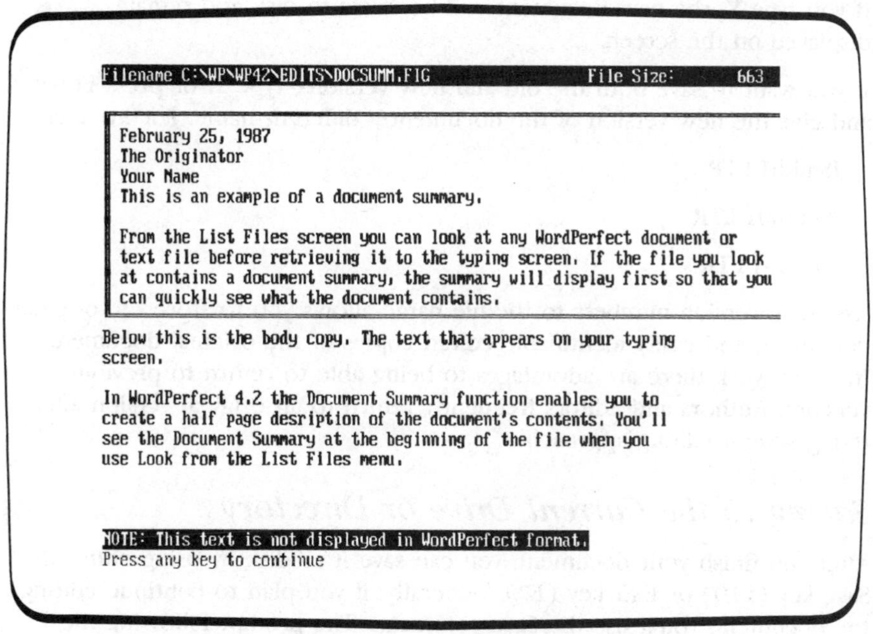

```
Filename C:\WP\WP42\EDITS\DOCSUMM.FIG          File Size:      663

  February 25, 1987
  The Originator
  Your Name
  This is an example of a document summary.

  From the List Files screen you can look at any WordPerfect document or
  text file before retrieving it to the typing screen. If the file you look
  at contains a document summary, the summary will display first so that you
  can quickly see what the document contains.

Below this is the body copy. The text that appears on your typing
screen.

In WordPerfect 4.2 the Document Summary function enables you to
create a half page desription of the document's contents. You'll
see the Document Summary at the beginning of the file when you
use Look from the List Files menu.


NOTE: This text is not displayed in WordPerfect format.
Press any key to continue
```

*Fig. 4.2. Document Summary screen.*

## Using the File-Naming Procedure

Assume that you have created a letter that will be mailed to your client, John L. Smith. You can save your document under any of these file names:

JSmith.LTR    JonSmith    LETTER.JLS

>  **1.** Press F10, the Save key

This prompt appears on your screen:

>  `Document to be Saved:`

>  **2.** Type **JSmith.LTR** (or whatever name you have selected)

>  **3.** Press Enter

From this point on, whenever you save that document, WordPerfect prompts:

>  `Document to be Saved: C:\WP\JSMITH.LTR`

If you make changes to your document and want those changes saved so they replace the existing file on disk, press Enter without changing the file name. This prompt will appear on your screen:

>  `Replace B:JSMITH.LTR (Y/N)N`

If you type Y, the new document will be saved to disk and remain displayed on the screen.

If you want to save both the old and new versions, type N or press Enter and give the new version of the document a different name. For instance:

>  JSmith1.LTR

>  JSmith01.LTR

>  JSmith-1.LTR

Assigning version numbers to the file name allows you to store the original document, and easily identifiable edited copies of the original document. In some work there are advantages to being able to return to previous versions. Authors and editors frequently return to an original version after trying several editing approaches.

## *Saving to the Current Drive or Directory*

After you finish your document, you can save it to disk by using either the Save key (F10) or Exit key (F7). Generally, if you plan to continue editing the document, you'll use the Save command. The prompt following the Exit command asks whether you want to save the text. This prompt is intended more as a safeguard against carelessness than as a means of filing.

If you started the WordPerfect program on your floppy disk system by typing:

>  **1.** A>B:

>  **2.** B>A:WP

your documents will be saved to Drive B disk when you type a file name.

If you want to save a document to Drive A type:

**A:JSmith01.LTR** (substitute your file name)

Because Drive A is usually reserved for program and system data, it is not recommended that you save document files on the A disk drive. WordPerfect takes up most of the space on Drive A.

If you are using WordPerfect on a hard disk; program, system, and document files generally reside on Drive C.

When you press the Save key (F10), the save prompt will tell you on which disk and in which directory the document will be stored, for example:

```
Document to be Saved: C:\WP\JSMITH01.LTR
```

The document file named JSmith01.LTR will be saved on Drive C, in the \WP directory.

If you want to save the file to another disk, type: the letter of the disk drive that you want the document saved to, a backslash, the name of the directory, another backslash, and the file name. Press Enter.

## Creating Backup Files

In WordPerfect 4.2 you can use the arrow and Del keys to delete and edit a *path* and file name without completely retyping it.

If you are using a hard disk system, it is important to create a *backup* by saving to another drive or to another disk. On a hard disk system, most of your work is done on Drive C. It is an excellent idea to save a final copy of important work to a floppy disk in Drive A. Store the backup disks in a physically separate location. Then, should your office be destroyed by fire, or your computer fail (or be stolen), you will have backup copies of important work.

WordPerfect will back up your files automatically with either the timed backup option, or the original backup option (which saves the original copy of your file). The original backup option works like WordStar® *.BAK* files. The options are explained fully in Chapter 17, *Managing Your System*, in the section called "Setting Backup Options."

## Saving Specific Parts of Your Document

In the last chapter you used the Block command to delete a block of text. Because the Block command is very flexible, it can be used also to save any block of continuous text to its own separate file. The Block command can be used with many WordPerfect functions—be sure to read Chapter 6 for more information about how you can use the Block function.

Saving blocks of text can be very useful if there are parts of a document that you'd like to save (in individual files) and use later on. The *Quick Start*, in this chapter, illustrates how you can save specific paragraphs to disk, retrieve them, then insert them into another document.

To save the block of text:

   **1.** Move the cursor to the first character in the block of text you want saved

   **2.** Press Block (Alt-F4)

This message appears on your screen:

     Block on

   **3.** Move the cursor to the last character of the text you want to save

As you move the cursor, the text that will be saved is highlighted.

   **4.** Press Save (F10)

This prompt replaces the *Block on* prompt on your screen:

     Block Name:

   **5.** Type the **file name** (as you normally would when saving a document)

   **6.** Press Enter

The disk drive light will flash momentarily as the highlighted text is saved as a separate document.

If a file already exists with the name you have selected, WordPerfect will prompt you to either Cancel the command or Replace the existing file.

## Saving to a Subdirectory

If you're using a hard disk system, and if you've created subdirectories (such as WPLETTER and WPMEMOS), you'll probably want to save your documents to a designated subdirectory.

To save your document to a specific subdirectory:

   **1.** Press Save (F10)

   **2.** Type the **letter of the disk drive**

   **3.** Type :\

4. Type the **name of the directory**

5. Type \

6. Type the **name of the subdirectory**

   *Example:* **c:\wp\wpletter**

7. Type the **name of the file**

   *Example:* **C:\WP\WPLETTER\JSMITH.LTR**

8. Press Enter

## Using the Exit Key To Save and Exit

When you press Exit (F7) to save a document, this prompt appears on your screen:

```
Save document? (Y/N) Y
```

If you press Y, you'll see the prompts that create a document file name as you saw when you used the Save key.

You move through the same steps, with one exception—instead of remaining in the document after the Save operation, a prompt will ask:

```
Exit WP? (Y/N) N
```

If you press N or any other key (except Y or Cancel), a blank screen will appear, and you can start a new document.

If you press Cancel (F1) the document remains on the screen, and you may continue to work on it.

If you press Y, the screen clears, and WordPerfect returns to the operating system. A>, B>, or C> will appear in the lower left corner of the screen.

At that point, you can:

1. Turn the computer off

   Or

1. Replace the WordPerfect disk with another program disk

   Or

1. Reload WordPerfect by typing **WP** after the DOS prompts A> or C>

   Or

1. Reload WordPerfect by typing **A:WP** after the DOS prompt B>

# Retrieving a Document

When you want to work on a file saved to disk, you have two options for retrieving your document. If you don't know the exact file name, you can use the List Files key (F5) to check the name in the directory before retrieving the document (see fig. 4.3). If you know the exact file name, you can use Retrieve (Shift-F10).

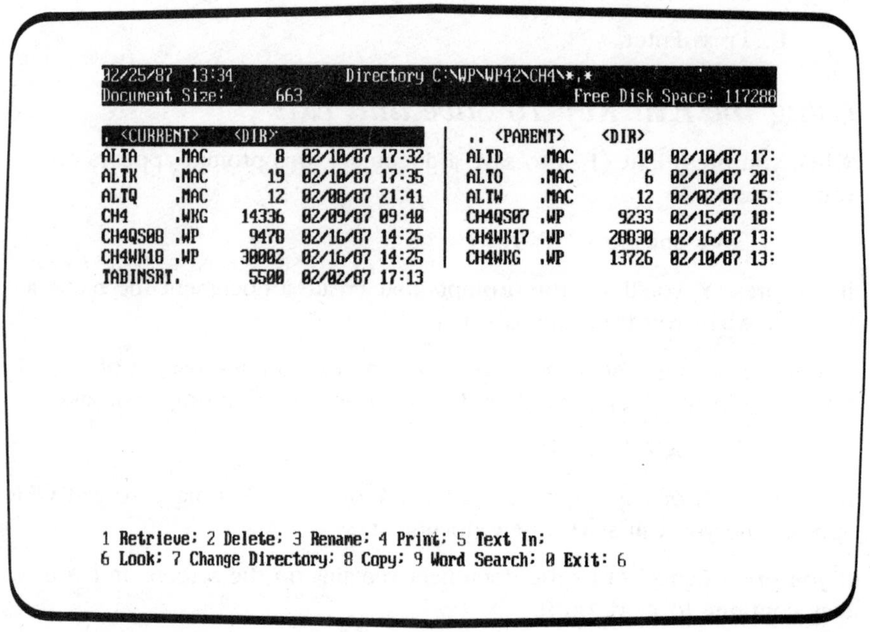

```
02/25/87  13:34          Directory C:\WP\WP42\CH4\*.*
Document Size:      663                    Free Disk Space: 117288

.  <CURRENT>    <DIR>            ..  <PARENT>    <DIR>
ALTA    .MAC       8  02/10/87 17:32    ALTD    .MAC      10  02/10/87 17:
ALTK    .MAC      19  02/10/87 17:35    ALTO    .MAC       6  02/10/87 20:
ALTQ    .MAC      12  02/08/87 21:41    ALTW    .MAC      12  02/02/87 15:
CH4     .WKG   14336  02/09/87 09:40    CH4QS87 .WP     9233  02/15/87 18:
CH4QS88 .WP     9470  02/16/87 14:25    CH4WK17 .WP    20830  02/16/87 13:
CH4WK18 .WP    30002  02/16/87 14:25    CH4WKG  .WP    13726  02/10/87 13:
TABINSRT.        5500  02/02/87 17:13




1 Retrieve; 2 Delete; 3 Rename; 4 Print; 5 Text In;
6 Look; 7 Change Directory; 8 Copy; 9 Word Search; 0 Exit: 6
```

*Fig. 4.3. List Files screen.*

## ▩ Beware

Beware! If you retrieve a document from disk while a second document is displayed on your screen, the document displayed on your screen and the document you have retrieved from disk will combine to form a third document.

If you work through the Quick Start you will see how combining documents can be beneficial. If, however, you are not aware that the mix is occurring, the results can be very confusing. To prevent documents from merging, use the Exit key (F7) to clear the old document before retrieving the new document.

## Retrieving When You Know the File Name

If you are certain that you know the name of the file, the easiest way to retrieve a stored document is to use the Retrieve command (Shift-F10).

Before you give the command, check to see that you have a blank typing screen. Remember, if you don't clear your screen before you retrieve a file, WordPerfect will combine the file on the screen with the file you are retrieving.

When you press Retrieve, this prompt will appear on the screen:

Document to be Retrieved:

Type the file name if the file is in your current directory. If the file is in another directory or on another disk, type the entire path and file name.

*Example:* **C:\WP\MEMOS\RAISES.V2**

Press Enter, and the file will be *loaded* so that you can begin editing. The loaded file becomes the working document, which does not affect the document stored on the disk. The file stored on the disk remains there—untouched. The document that you see (and edit) on your screen is a copy of the original.

## Retrieving from a List of File Names

If you're not certain that you know the correct name of the file, check the file directory by pressing List Files (F5).

Depending on the drive currently set as the storage drive, you'll see one of the following designations in the lower left corner of the screen:

Dir B:\*.*

Dir C:\WP\*.*

Press Enter to see a list of all the documents on the named drive. To see the files on a drive other than the one designated:

1. Press Cancel (F1)

2. Press List Files (F5)

3. Type the **drive letter**

4. Type a **colon** (:)

5. Type the **path name** (such as \WP\MEMOS)

6. Press Enter

When you find the file name in the directory:

7. Highlight the file name using the arrow keys (see fig. 4.4)

8. Type **1** (Retrieve)

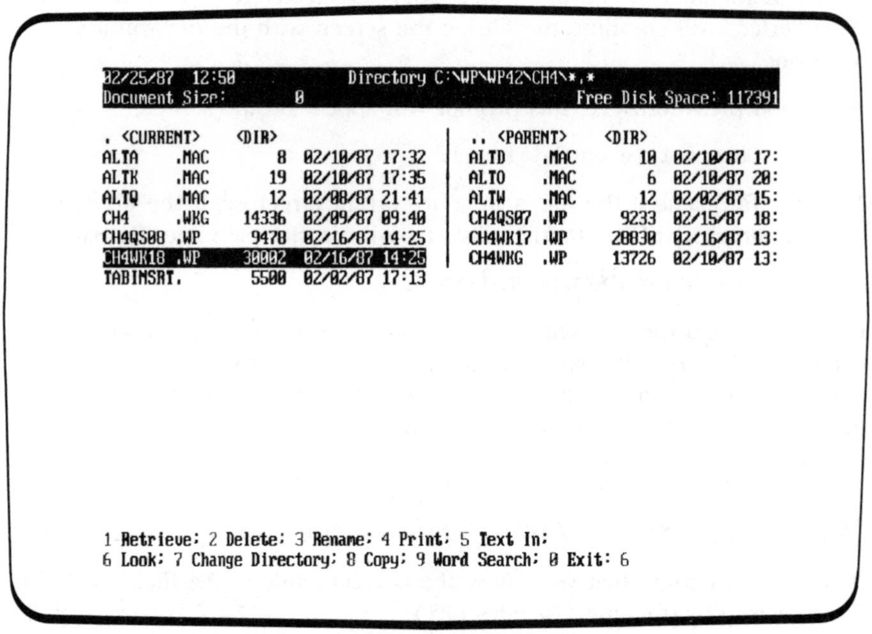

```
02/25/87  12:58          Directory C:\WP\WP42\CH4\*.*
Document Size:         0                    Free Disk Space: 117391

. <CURRENT>    <DIR>              .. <PARENT>    <DIR>
ALTA    .MAC        8  02/10/87 17:32    ALTD    .MAC       10  02/10/87 17:
ALTK    .MAC       19  02/10/87 17:35    ALTO    .MAC        6  02/10/87 20:
ALTQ    .MAC       12  02/08/87 21:41    ALTW    .MAC       12  02/02/87 15:
CH4     .WKG    14336  02/09/87 09:40    CH4QS07 .WP      9233  02/15/87 18:
CH4QS08 .WP      9478  02/16/87 14:25    CH4WK17 .WP     20030  02/16/87 13:
CH4WK18 .WP     30002  02/16/87 14:25    CH4WKG  .WP     13726  02/10/87 13:
TABINSRT.         5500  02/02/87 17:13




1 Retrieve; 2 Delete; 3 Rename; 4 Print; 5 Text In;
6 Look; 7 Change Directory; 8 Copy; 9 Word Search; 0 Exit: 6
```

*Fig. 4.4. Highlighted file name on List Files screen.*

The file you've selected will appear on the screen.

If the document you want to retrieve is stored on another disk or resides in another subdirectory, select option 7 Change Directory from the List Files menu.

The subdirectory name that you type automatically becomes the new default. Until you change the default again, documents are saved in this subdirectory. List Files (F5) automatically displays the files on this disk or in the subdirectory.

## ■ Caution

Caution: Never try to retrieve WordPerfect system files. They are coded files. Trying to look at them while WordPerfect is running can cause serious damage to the program disk.

To return to a blank screen from the directory display, press Cancel (F1) or press the space bar.

Remember, before retrieving a file, clear the screen. Otherwise, WordPerfect will combine the document retrieved with the document currently displayed on-screen.

## *Retrieving Files into Working Documents*

WordPerfect capabilities have been lauded by legal professionals because the program saves substantial time and manpower when it is used to prepare legal documents containing common phrases and paragraphs. If you are responsible for preparing contracts, proposals, bids, wills, and other legal documents, there is a good chance that you will use WordPerfect. One of the examples in this *Quick Start* demonstrates how frequently used paragraphs can be saved to disk and merged into an existing document.

Standard legal paragraphs or phrases that exist in one document, and are needed in other documents, can be saved as a separate file using the Block save command. The Block save process is described earlier in this chapter. Once the paragraph or phrase is saved to disk, it can be retrieved and inserted anywhere in the document on your screen.

Inserting a document from disk into the document on-screen is very easy:

1. Move the cursor to the location within the document displayed on the screen where you want the document stored on the disk to be inserted

2. Retrieve the document on disk using either List Files (F5) or Retrieve (Shift-F10)

The document from the disk will be inserted in the document displayed on the screen, moving existing text down to make room for the newly added text.

Unless the document being retrieved has its own margin and tab settings it will adhere to the margin and tab settings established for the document on-screen. (Chapter 8 describes how to set margins and tabs.)

# Printing Your Document

With WordPerfect what you see on the screen is what you get in print! It's comforting to know that your text will be formatted on paper exactly as it appears on the screen.

The following sections describe the fundamentals of printing. For more information, reference Print Format, displayed by pressing Ctrl-F8 (see fig. 4.5). With Print (Shift-F7), (see fig. 4.6) you can choose 3 Print Options and 4 Printer Control options to control details of printing such as binding width, printer selection, and the number of printed copies.

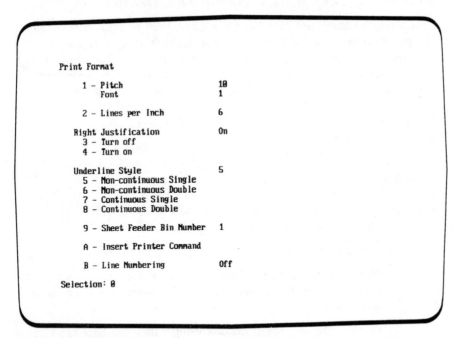

```
Print Format

        1 - Pitch               10
            Font                1

        2 - Lines per Inch      6

    Right Justification         On
        3 - Turn off
        4 - Turn on

    Underline Style             5
        5 - Non-continuous Single
        6 - Non-continuous Double
        7 - Continuous Single
        8 - Continuous Double

        9 - Sheet Feeder Bin Number    1

        A - Insert Printer Command

        B - Line Numbering      Off

    Selection: 0
```

Fig. 4.5. Print Format screen.

WordPerfect offers an advantage, not always available with other word processors. While your documents are printing, you can continue to work on the screen. And, you can establish a document queue (a waiting line for documents) so you don't have to stop work to start the next print job.

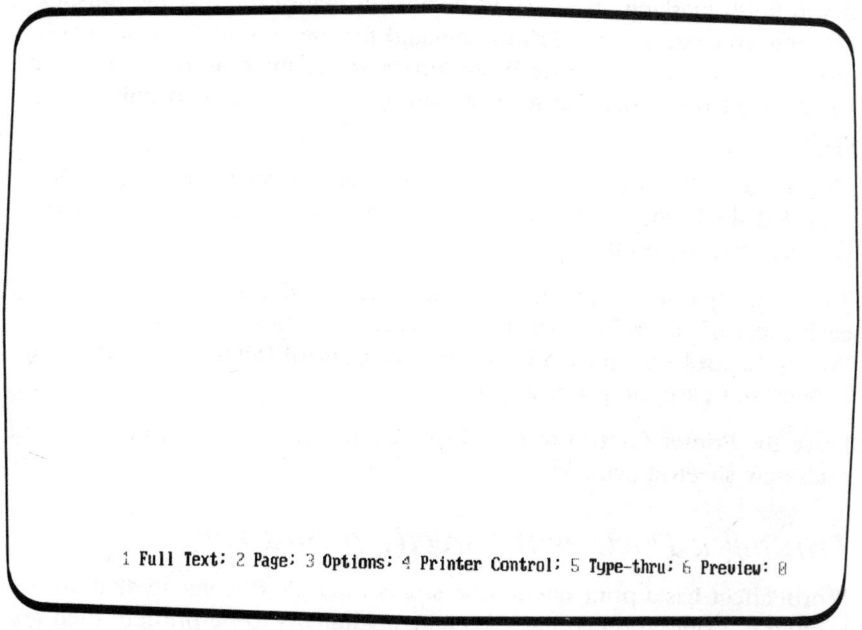

1 Full Text; 2 Page; 3 Options; 4 Printer Control; 5 Type-thru; 6 Preview: 0

*Fig. 4.6. Print (F7) screen.*

## Previewing Your Printing in WordPerfect 4.2

What you see on your screen is your document's *body copy*. The screen display does not include headers, footers, and footnotes. If you are using WordPerfect 4.2 you can preview on-screen exactly what will print on paper by pressing the Print key (Shift-F7), then choosing 6 Preview.

You will be prompted for previewing the full document or the current page. (Previewing a large document can take some time.) You may not be able to preview a large document on a dual floppy disk system if there is insufficient storage space on the Drive B disk. Press Cancel (F1) to stop the preview.

## Printing the Document Displayed on Your Screen

If the document to be printed appears on the screen, press Print (Shift-F7) and select item 1 Full Text.

After you've given the Print command, the document can be cleared from the screen. While one document prints, you can start a new document or retrieve a file from disk.

If you finish working on a second document before the first file finishes printing, you can give the Print command for the second file just as you did for the first one. Because WordPerfect stores multiple print jobs, you can go right on working instead of waiting for the printer to finish each job.

The printer will not start printing automatically, if you're printing with hand fed single sheets of paper, or if you specified "single sheet" when you installed the printer.

The printer pauses before printing each page to give you time to insert each sheet of paper. To start the first sheet, you must go back to the Printer Control screen by pressing Printer Control (Shift-F7,4) and typing G once you have the paper aligned.

Leave the Printer Control screen displayed and type G after you've aligned each new sheet of paper.

## Printing a Document Directly from Disk

WordPerfect has a print queue that stores multiple documents that are waiting to print. You can line up many documents to be printed, then go back to your typing. WordPerfect will print from the queue as you type.

You can print a file stored in Drive B or Drive C without retrieving it. And, there are several ways to do it.

1. Press Print (Shift-F7)

2. Type 4 for Printer Control

The menu in figure 4.7 appears. Notice that you are able to check documents in the queue.

3. Type **P** (Print a Document)

4. Type the **name of the document**

If the file you want to print resides in a directory other than the current directory type the drive name preceding the file name as in this example:

**B:JSmith01**

Because WordPerfect prompts for the beginning and ending page numbers, you can select specific pages from your document.

Another way to print from the disk is to use the List Files (F5) function. When you press Enter, you see a list of the files on the disk, as shown in figure 4.8. Move the cursor to highlight the desired file and select 4 to print it.

*Fig. 4.7. Printer Control menu.*

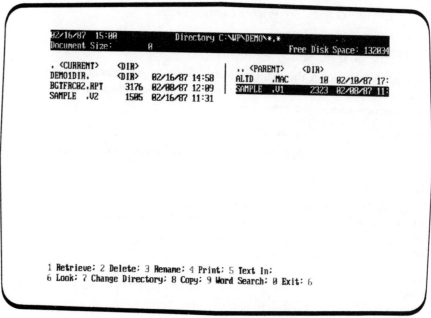

*Fig. 4.8. Highlighted file for print.*

## *Stopping the Printer Momentarily*

Because you will experience (as we all do) the exasperation caused by a jammed printer or a printer that runs out of paper halfway through a print job, you need to know how to stop and resume printing!

To stop the printer:

1. Press the Print key (Shift-F7)

2. Type 4 to choose Printer Control

On the upper right quadrant of the Printer Control screen is the alphabetical menu that controls the printer.

3. Type S for Stop Printing

The printer will stop and a message will appear at mid-screen telling you to advance the paper to the next page.

If your printer has a large *print buffer* (temporary character storage in the printer), it may continue to print up to a full three pages after you have typed S. Most printers have less than one page of buffer and will stop soon after you press S.

When you have repositioned the paper and are ready to restart from the top of the last page:

4. Type G from the Printer Control menu

## *Canceling a Print Job*

To completely cancel the printing instructions so you can start over, or when you want to remove a document from the list of documents in the print queue—cancel the print job.

To cancel any (or all) print jobs:

1. Press Print (Shift-F7) to move to the Printer Control menu

2. Type 4 Printer Control

In the alphabetical menu at the top right corner of the Printer Control screen you will see the command C - Cancel Print Job(s).

3. Type C

A prompt will appear at mid-screen asking you which print job to cancel.

4. Type an **asterisk** (*)

5. Press Enter

All print jobs that are printing and those in the queue waiting to be printed will be canceled.

WordPerfect assigns a job number to each document printing. If you have several print jobs in the queue, make a note of the job numbers. WordPerfect keeps a running tab of job numbers. If you enter the number for a specific job, only that job is canceled, all others continue printing.

# Quick Start Part 3: Saving and Printing Your Document

The *Quick Starts* in Chapters 2 and 3 have shown you how to create, enter, and edit a simple document. This *Quick Start* will guide you through saving and printing your document.

In a demonstration of just one of the ways WordPerfect can increase your efficiency you'll discover the timesaving benefits of *Block Save* by saving a part of a document as a separate file and retrieving it into another document. This process of piecing together existing document parts is known as *boilerplating*—it can save you a great deal of time and work as you create documents that share the same phrases and paragraphs.

## Typing Your Practice Document

Before you can practice saving, retrieving, and printing your documents, you must have some text to work with. Type the three paragraphs that follow. Make sure you enter three paragraphs because you will save each paragraph to disk separately. Type the title *Paragraph* and its associated number at the top of each paragraph. You will use the titles for reference later. Begin typing:

**Paragraph 1**
**Every person who has worked with computers for very long has a favorite story about how critical work was lost when a file was destroyed. Of course, the reason the story is told is that there was no backup copy.**

**Paragraph 2**
**There are three simple precautions you can use to prevent losing work. If you don't take these precautions, somehow, somewhere, at the worst possible time, Murphy's law will reach out and destroy your work.**

**Paragraph 3**
**1. Save your work to disk every fifteen minutes in case of equipment or power failure. Occasionally, use a new version number in the file name so you have copies of both new and old work.**

**2.   Make a copy of your work onto a disk other than the hard disk or disk you work with. Physical damage could destroy your single working copy.**

**3.   If your work is very important, take a third copy to a physically separate location. Fire, theft, or sabotage can destroy originals and backup copies in the same building.**

## Saving Your Work

To save your documents in the current disk or directory:

**1.** Press Save (F10)

This prompt will appear on your screen:

    `Document to be Saved:`

If you have saved the document before, the previous disk designation, path name, and file name will follow the prompt. In WordPerfect 4.2 you can edit the path and file name.

**2.** Type the file name **SAMPLE.V1**

Leave no spaces in the name and use only one period. The V1 in the name extension stands for *version 1*. You don't have to use a version number but it can help organize your work.

**3.** Press Enter

If you are using a dual floppy disk system, the light on Drive B will signal as the document is stored. If you are using a hard disk system the hard disk light will flicker for just a moment. These lights come on when you are reading from or writing to the disks. In WordPerfect 4.2 you will see the path and file name appear in the lower left corner of the screen.

## Editing a File Name in WordPerfect 4.2

WordPerfect 4.2 permits you to edit the path and file name displayed after the `Document to be Saved:` prompt appears. WordPerfect 4.1 users must retype the entire name if a change is necessary. If you saved the file named SAMPLE.V1 and you use WordPerfect 4.2, follow these steps to practice editing a file name whether you use a hard disk or a floppy disk system:

**1.** Press Save (F10)

**2.** Press the right-arrow key until it rests under the number 1

**3.** Press Del to delete the 1

**4.** Type **2**

**5.** Press Enter to save the file with the new name SAMPLE.V2

If a file with the same name had already existed you would have been asked to cancel the command or replace the existing file.

## Clearing the Screen

WordPerfect expects you to clear the screen before retrieving a new document. If you do not clear the screen, the document currently displayed on your screen and the retrieved document will combine to form one. As you will see later in this *Quick Start*, merging documents can be handy, but for now:

**1.** Press Exit (F7)

This prompt appears on your screen:

     Save Document? (Y/N)

**2.** Type **N** since you have already saved the document

In response to the prompt Exit WP? (Y/N)

**3.** Type **N**

You will not exit WordPerfect, but you will clear the screen.

## Retrieving a File from Disk

If you are not certain of the name under which the document is stored, you can review file names, file sizes, and the date on which files were stored to disk, with List Files.

From the List Files menu (such as the one shown in fig. 4.9) you can retrieve the file, look at the file's contents, delete the file from disk, and perform other file management functions.

These steps will retrieve the document you saved under the name *SAMPLE.V1*:

**1.** Press the List Files key (F5)

The bottom left of the screen will show the disk and directory.

**2.** Press Enter to accept the current path name

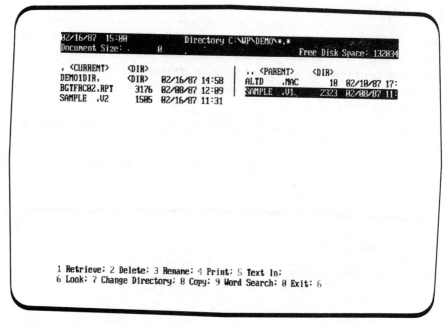

Fig. 4.9. List Files screen.

Figure 4.9 shows the List Files menu at the bottom of the screen and files similar to those that may display on your screen.

Select files or directories by moving the highlight to a name and then choosing a number from the menu.

3. Press the right-arrow key to highlight a name in the right column

4. Press the down-arrow or PgDn key to move down your screen

5. Press the PgUp key until you are at the top of the list

6. Type **S**

Then, pause. The cursor moves to the first file that starts with *S*. Since you intend to retrieve *SAMPLE.V1* this method can save many keystrokes.

7. Press the space bar or arrow key to redisplay the List Files menu

8. Move to highlight *SAMPLE.V1*

9. Type **1** to select Retrieve

Your screen will return and the *SAMPLE.V1* document will appear.

## Printing Your Document

Because video displays are heavy to carry and very difficult to fold or slide into a back pocket, computer manufacturers make printers to produce paper copies of your work. If you have gone through the printer installation process described in Chapter 1 then you can print your document, *SAMPLE.V1*.

Make sure that your printer is on and that the top of the paper is aligned with the top edge of the strike plate.

1. Press the Print key (Shift-F7), 4, to display the Printer Control menu shown in figure 4.10

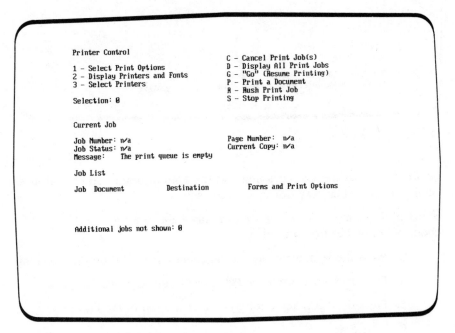

```
Printer Control
                              C - Cancel Print Job(s)
  1 - Select Print Options    D - Display All Print Jobs
  2 - Display Printers and Fonts   G - "Go" (Resume Printing)
  3 - Select Printers         P - Print a Document
                              R - Rush Print Job
  Selection: 0               S - Stop Printing


  Current Job

  Job Number: n/a             Page Number: n/a
  Job Status: n/a             Current Copy: n/a
  Message:    The print queue is empty

  Job List

  Job  Document         Destination        Forms and Print Options



  Additional jobs not shown: 0
```

*Fig. 4.10. Printer Control menu.*

2. Type **1** from the Print menu for Full Text

This selection will print the entire document that is on the screen. If you have a printer that is installed for Single Sheet Feed, then the printer has not started printing. You will have to continue with these steps after you have rolled a sheet into the printer.

**3.** Press Print (Shift-F7) again

**4.** Type 4 Printer Control

A message at mid-screen in the Printer Control menu will tell you when to type G. WordPerfect pauses the printer to let you insert a sheet of paper, then waits for you to type G to let it know when to print.

**5.** Type **G** to tell the computer to Go

Notice that the Printer Control menu on the upper left corner of the screen contains commands other than G. They include: S to Stop, C to Cancel, and so forth.

## Saving Sections of Your Document with Block Save

The Block command enables you to save any amount of continuous text as a document, separate from the original. That is, you can designate a section of continuous text from your document and save that section to disk under its own name. With the *SAMPLE.V1* document on the screen you can practice saving each of the three paragraphs under a separate file name.

This section of *Quick Start* will show you how to retrieve your practice paragraphs—in the order in which you want them to appear in your new document.

**1.** Move the cursor to the *P* in the title *Paragraph 1*

**2.** Press the Block key (Alt-F4)

Notice the flashing prompt Block on that appears in the lower left corner of the screen.

**3.** Press the down-arrow key to highlight an entire line at a time

**4.** Press the right- or left-arrow key until all of the text in *Paragraph 1* is highlighted

Figure 4.11 illustrates how your screen should look.

**5.** Press Save (F10)

This prompt appears at the lower left corner of your screen:

Block Name:

**6.** Type **PARAGRAF.1**

**7.** Press Enter

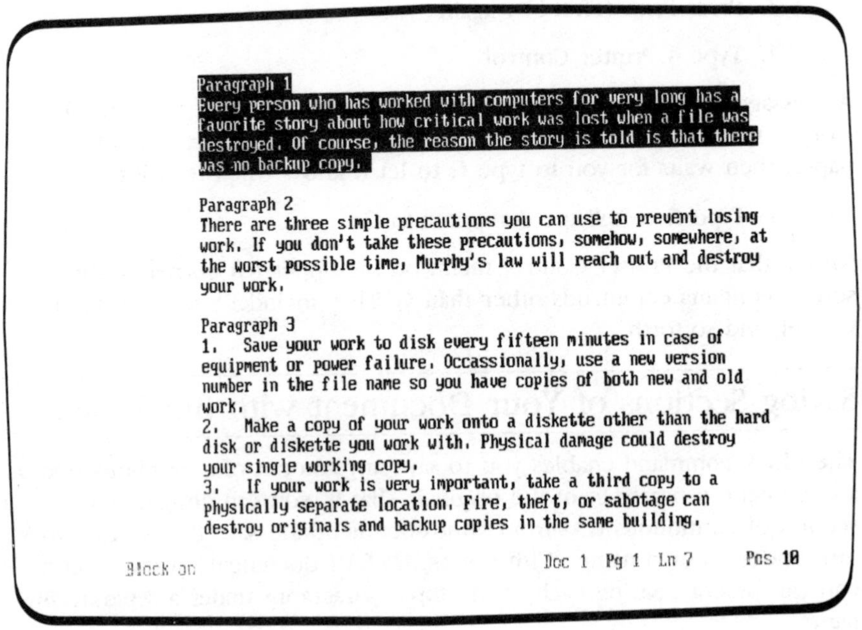

Paragraph 1
Every person who has worked with computers for very long has a favorite story about how critical work was lost when a file was destroyed. Of course, the reason the story is told is that there was no backup copy.

Paragraph 2
There are three simple precautions you can use to prevent losing work. If you don't take these precautions, somehow, somewhere, at the worst possible time, Murphy's law will reach out and destroy your work.

Paragraph 3
1. Save your work to disk every fifteen minutes in case of equipment or power failure. Occassionally, use a new version number in the file name so you have copies of both new and old work.
2. Make a copy of your work onto a diskette other than the hard disk or diskette you work with. Physical damage could destroy your single working copy.
3. If your work is very important, take a third copy to a physically separate location. Fire, theft, or sabotage can destroy originals and backup copies in the same building.

Block on Doc 1 Pg 1 Ln 7 Pos 10

*Fig. 4.11. Saving a highlighted block of text.*

The disk light will flicker as the paragraph is saved.

**8.** Press Cancel (F1)

The Block command is canceled.

**9.** Complete Steps 1 through 7 for *Paragraph 2* and *Paragraph 3*

Save each paragraph with the file names *PARAGRAF.2* and *PARAGRAF.3* respectively.

## Retrieving Document Text Anywhere in Your Document

Because you have saved the three paragraphs under separate file names, you can retrieve them to a blank screen or to an existing document. You can retrieve and insert them in any order you wish.

**1.** Move the cursor to the *P* in *Paragraph 2*

The file you'll retrieve from disk will insert itself at the cursor's location and move the existing text down.

**2.** Press the Retrieve key (Shift-F10)

You can use this key to retrieve files if you are certain that you know the names of those files.

**3.** Type the file name **PARAGRAF.3**

**4.** Press Enter

The disk light will flicker as the file is read and *Paragraph 3* will suddenly appear between *Paragraph 1* and *Paragraph 2.*

**5.** Move to a new location in the document on-screen

You can even retrieve a file into the middle of existing text.

**6.** Complete Steps 2 through 5 so that you retrieve *PARAGRAF.1* or *PARAGRAF.2* to a new location

From this point forward you'll begin to notice that, with WordPerfect, there are many ways to carry out the same function. Take fifteen minutes before the work day starts (for a few weeks) and experiment with the WordPerfect commands you haven't used. Your fifteen-minute investment will pay off in new approaches to WordPerfect that will save you time—and ultimately make your work easier.

In this chapter you've discovered that there are several ways to save text with WordPerfect. For example, you can:

- ☐ Save a document with the Save key, F10

- ☐ Save a document with the Exit key, F7

- ☐ Save part of a document with the Block save method

Retrieving a file is another example of the flexibility of WordPerfect. If you clear the previous document from the screen before retrieving then you can:

- ☐ Retrieve with the List Files key (F5) when you can't remember the name of the file

- ☐ Retrieve with the Retrieve key (Shift-F10) when you do know the exact file name

To merge the disk file into the document on the screen:

- ☐ Move the cursor to the insert point and retrieve with List Files (F5) when you can't remember the name of the file

- ☐ Move the cursor to the insert point and retrieve with Retrieve (Shift-F10) when you do remember the file name

You can print a document either from within the document currently displayed on the screen, or from a list of documents saved to disk. All the Print commands originate from the Print key (Shift-F7). Don't confuse the Print key with the Print Format key (Ctrl-F8). The Print Format key controls features such as pitch and justification. Remember, WordPerfect permits you to work on your documents while other documents are printing.

Now you're ready to move on to Chapter 5 where you'll discover how to add *visual impact* to your documents using enhancements such as centering, bold print, and underlining. Chapter 5 will introduce you to the Reveal Codes function—a powerful feature used to uncover (and delete) hidden codes. These elusive codes are inserted from WordPerfect menus to control such features as underlining, margin settings, and page formatting.

# Adding Impact to Your Words with the Bold, Underline, Centering, and Reveal Code Features

**A**t first glance Chapter 5 appears to explain only how to add visual interest to your documents using the bold, underline, and text centering features. Then, the chapter turns right around and explains how to *remove* the codes that instruct WordPerfect to create bold, underlined, and centered text.

Such a simplistic view of Chapter 5 is not altogether appropriate, however. Because what you will be exploring in Chapter 5 is not just how to enhance the look of your text; but, how to insert and remove very powerful hidden codes in your work. WordPerfect uses these system codes in far-ranging applications—to bold text, to change margins, to reset tabs, to set print pitch, to change type fonts, and so on. In fact, almost every *format change* (a change in the way your printed document will look) or text enhancement is effected using embedded codes.

As you move through this chapter, you'll learn that you can embed hidden codes in your document in two ways. Some codes, such as the codes for text centering, margin settings, and tab settings, are inserted by pressing a single function key. All of the text that follows the embedded code is affected.

Other codes, such as the codes that create bold and underlined text, are inserted at the beginning of a block of text and, again at the end of the block of text. Only the text that lies between the embedded codes is affected. To create bold text, for example, the Bold key is pressed to "turn on" the bold feature, the text is typed, then the Bold key is pressed again to "turn off" the bold feature. Only the text that lies between the "on" code and the "off" code is bold text.

WordPerfect codes are easy to understand. The codes embedded to create bold text are: [B] to turn on the bold feature and [b] to turn off the bold feature. These codes are inserted automatically when you press the bold function key. Preview the codes by looking over the Codes Table in the Appendix.

# Enhancing Text

You can add visual impact to your text in a number of WordPerfect-ways. Call attention to a particularly important word (or words) by printing the text in bold face or cause your reader to take action by underlining a phrase or focus your audience's attention by centering the lines of a quotation within your report.

All of these text enhancements are performed by pressing a single function key, and typing the text. And, as you already know, for some text enhancements you will need to press the function key a second time to turn the enhancement feature off.

Some enhancements, such as *italic text*, are a function of your printer. The italic text feature, for instance, is selected as a Font from the Print Format key (Ctrl-F8). On some printers you may need to insert a special Printer Control code to access fonts.

The Print Format menu also enables you to select the style of underlining to be printed, although not all underlining styles may be available for your printers. You will find more about printer-related text enhancements in Chapter 11.

## *Centering Text*

Most people who use WordPerfect use the centering feature to create titles and headings for their reports, lists, personnel rosters, and transparencies (for overhead projectors). If you want to center lines of text that already exist in a document, refer to the Block command in Chapter 6.

The center command is very easy to use but can cause a strange display when used incorrectly. If you press the Center key (Shift-F6) in a line that already contains text, you may cause some of the text to disappear. Use the Reveal Codes key, described later in this chapter, to remove the hidden centering code that was inserted when you pressed Center (Shift-F6).

## Centering Text between Margins

Centering text horizontally between margins is easy. If you have not yet entered the text you want to center:

**1.** Move the cursor to the left margin of the line you want to center

**2.** Press Center (Shift-F6)

The cursor centers between the two margins. As you type, the text adjusts left and right to stay centered. When you have finished typing the text you want centered:

**3.** Press Enter

The line is ended and you have turned off the centering function.

If you need to center text that has already been typed, use the Block command, described in Chapter 6.

## Centering Text around a Character Position

If you need to center text around a character position, make sure there are no codes, characters, or spaces on the line, then press the space bar to move the cursor to the character position you want as the center. Press the Center key, Shift-F6, and begin to type. The text will center around the character position where you pressed Center.

In WordPerfect 4.2 you can use centered tab settings to center multiple headings on a line (Chapter 8 describes the procedure).

## Typing Bold Text

Bold text appears brighter (or a different color) on your screen; it appears darker and stronger than regular type when printed on paper. Bold text is an excellent way to emphasize important headings or specific items in your work.

The Bold feature needs to be turned on before you type the text and turned off after the last character to be bold is typed. As you reach the point in your document where you want bold text to appear:

**1.** Press Bold (F6)

**2.** Type the text to appear bold

The text you type after pressing the Bold key will appear brighter (or a different color) on screen. The Pos indicator in the Status Line will also reflect the brightness or color change. Should the bold text not appear brighter on a monochrome screen, adjust both contrast and intensity settings for the display.

When you have typed the text that will appear bold:

    **3.** Press Bold (F6)

If you forget to press F6 the second time, everything you type will be bold. Refer to Chapter 6 to bold existing text.

## Creating Underlined Text

Creating underlined text is just as easy as creating bold text. When you reach the point in your document that you want text to appear underlined:

    **1.** Press Underline (F8)

Pressing F8 turns on the underlining feature.

    **2.** Type the text you want to appear underlined

The underline feature remains on until you turn it off. When you have finished typing the text to be underlined:

    **3.** Press Underline (F8)

Both the text you have selected to be underlined and the Pos number in the Status Line will appear underlined (or colored, or highlighted) on your screen. If the underlined text looks the same as plain text on your screen, refer to the Set-up Menu section of Chapter 17.

Although WordPerfect permits you to select different types of underlining styles through the Print Format key (Ctrl-F8), some printers will not work with all underlining styles. Check your printer manual and Chapter 11 for more information about printer capabilities.

## Typing within Bold or Underlined Text

This section describes two subtle aspects of the bold and underline features. First, any time you insert text into a highlighted block of text that is marked for Bold or Underline, the inserted text is also highlighted. For example, consider this bold text:

    **As you may have read in the January issue**

If you insert the words *and February* and add the letter *s* to the word *issue* in this phrase, they will appear bold as well:

**As you may have read in the January and February issues**

You also can extend the bold (or underline) range by moving the cursor into the existing range (see fig. 5.1).

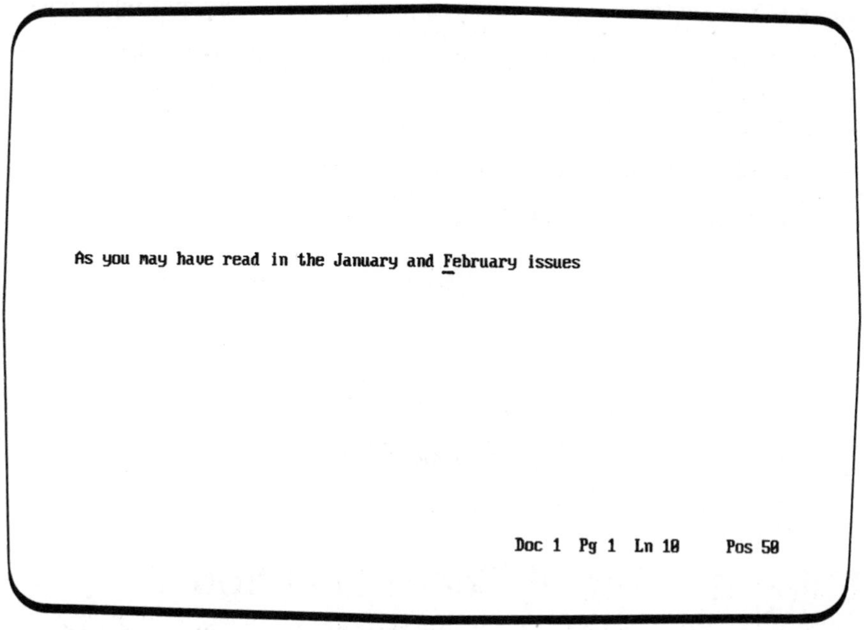

As you may have read in the January and February issues

Doc 1  Pg 1  Ln 10      Pos 50

*Fig. 5.1. Moving the cursor into existing bold range.*

Now, move the cursor one space at a time beyond the last text character in the range.

Watch the column position number in the Status Line for a change in display when you use your cursor to move left or right from within a bold or underlined range.

When the cursor reaches the embedded codes (the code that turns bold or underlining on and off), the numeric value of the character position number will not change as you move the cursor to the right or left. When the column position number is displayed in bold, then you know that your cursor is within the bold range, and any text that is inserted will also appear as bold text.

The same thing happens when you're working with underlined ranges; the character position number will appear with an underline (or in a different shade or color if you have a graphics card or color monitor) while the cursor is within the underlined range.

### Using More Than One Enhancement

You can use both underline and bold at the same time by turning on both features. You can even type a centered phrase that is bold and underlined.

To begin *multiple enhancements*, press the function keys associated with the enhancement and press the function keys a second time when you reach the end of the text you want to enhance.

For example, to create a centered bold and underlined phrase:

1. Press Center (Shift-F6)

2. Press Bold (F6)

3. Press Underline (F8)

4. Type the phrase

5. Press F6 to turn the Bold enhancement off

6. Press F8 to turn the Underline enhancement off

7. Press Enter to end the line and center the phrase

# Using the Reveal Codes Function

One of the most important functions in WordPerfect is its Reveal Codes function. The codes, which you embed in your documents to effect format changes and text enhancements, can be removed using the Reveal Codes feature.

As you already know, when you press the function key that signals WordPerfect to center text, or to underline text, or to change the margins in your document, you are actually instructing WordPerfect to insert hidden codes into the text. The codes are hidden so they won't clutter the typing screen.

Those hidden codes tell WordPerfect (and your printer) how each character should look, and how the document's text should be formatted when it is printed. Nearly all of the WordPerfect text enhancement and formatting functions cause a hidden code to be embedded in your documents.

As mentioned earlier, codes are straightforward, and easy to recognize and remember. For example, when you press the Bold key (F6) the code [B] is inserted to turn on the bold feature. Any text you type after the [B] code will appear on-screen as bright or a different color. When printed, that same text will be emphasized. Pressing F6 a second time inserts the code [b] to turn off bold. WordPerfect understands that the text that lies between the [B] and [b] codes is to be printed in bold type.

## Displaying Hidden Codes

WordPerfect permits you to view embedded codes on your screen so that you can remove those codes you no longer need or want. When you remove codes (such as bold or underline codes), your document text reacts as though the code were never inserted.

To see the hidden codes and delete them, use the Reveal Codes key. When you press Reveal Codes (Alt-F3) the screen splits into two sections.

The upper half, shown in figure 5.2, displays the normal typing screen which contains the current cursor position.

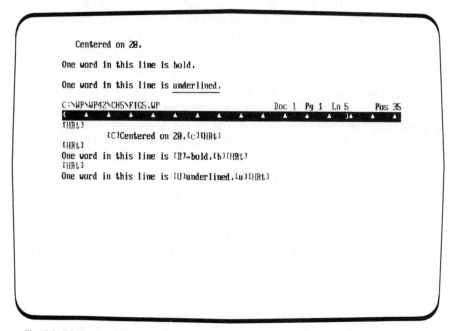

*Fig. 5.2. Displaying hidden codes.*

The lower half of the screen displays the same text that appears on the top half of the screen, but the hidden codes are displayed. The bar between screens displays the tab and margin settings for the line on which the cursor currently rests.

Although the codes are terse, they are easy to understand as you become more familiar with WordPerfect functions. If you see a code that you don't immediately recognize, check the Codes list in the Appendix. Some hidden codes such as tab settings include numbers that indicate the column position of the tabs.

## Deleting Hidden Codes

Hidden codes can be deleted in two ways:

- While the Reveal Codes screen is displayed

- While the normal typing screen is displayed

The easiest method of deleting codes is while the Reveal Codes screen is displayed. The typing screen method is described also because you will encounter this method as you work.

## Deleting Codes Using the Reveal Codes Screen

On the lower portion of the Reveal Codes screen, shown in figure 5.3, you can see the hidden codes and the affected text. Because you can *see* the codes and their *exact positions* in the text, the codes are easy to delete. Notice, as you delete codes from the lower portion of the Reveal Codes screen, that the effect on your document is displayed on the upper screen.

There may be times when text will look strange to you because two functions, such as center and indent, are used on the same line of text. "Competing" codes, accidentally entered on the same line, may cause text to disappear. In these cases, the Reveal Codes screen can show you the hidden text and codes on the line. You can then delete the code you do not want to make the typed line appear correct.

To delete a code on the Reveal Codes screen or to edit a typing screen that looks strange, follow these steps:

1. Move the cursor to the location in your document where the format changes, the enhanced text begins, or the strange-looking text starts

2. Press Reveal Codes (Alt-F3)

3. Move the Reveal Codes cursor so that it is directly to the right of the hidden code you want removed

The Reveal Codes cursor appears as a bright flashing cursor in WordPerfect 4.2 and appears as a flashing circumflex [^] in WordPerfect 4.1.

The normal cursor in the upper screen mimics the position of the cursor in the Reveal Codes screen.

4. Press the Backspace key to delete the hidden code

To return to the normal typing screen:

5. Press the Cancel key

Or

5. Press the space bar

Or

5. Press the Enter key

Note: You can stay in the Reveal Codes screen and delete multiple codes or characters. But, you can only *delete* while on the Reveal Codes screen. *You cannot insert text or codes.* Move through your text with the arrow keys, PgUp, and PgDn. When you press any typing key you will be returned to the normal typing screen.

## Deleting Codes from the Typing Screen

Although you cannot see the hidden codes from the typing screen, the Backspace and Del will remove a hidden code embedded in your document.

As you know, there is a hidden [B] at the beginning of bold text and a hidden [b] at the end of bold text. If you move the cursor two or three characters beyond the end of the bold text and backspace slowly, you will eventually backspace against the [b]. When the backspace is about to remove the embedded bold code, this message will flash in the lower left corner of the screen:

Delete [Bold]? (Y/N)

If you type Y, the [b] code will be deleted. Typing N or pressing a cursor key will leave the code intact. Deleting either end of the [B] [b] combination will cause the enhanced text to revert to normal text.

When you delete text with the Del key you may also delete embedded codes. The same prompt will appear in the lower left corner of your screen.

## ■ Beware

Beware! If you delete the text that lies between enclosing codes, be certain to delete the codes as well. If you delete the text only, you leave behind two hidden codes that enclose no text. Should the cursor ever fall between these codes, your text may magically appear bold or underlined.

If something like this happens, or if you prefer to delete codes that you can see, use the Reveal Codes.

# Quick Start Part 4:
# Enhancing Your Text

Don't let the fact that *Quick Start* Part 4 looks short and quick detract from its importance! You'll try your hand at typing bold, underlined, and centered text—but, removing hidden codes is the more global lesson you'll take away from this exercise.

You'll then be able to apply the process used to remove hidden text-enhancement codes to other codes that control text appearance and document format.

This *Quick Start* demonstrates how to enhance text as you type. Chapter 6 will show you how to change existing text.

Figure 5.3 shows the lines you'll be creating as they will be displayed on your screen. Each line is centered, bold, or underlined as the text indicates. After you've created these lines, you'll reveal and delete the hidden codes for center, bold, and underline, causing the text to return to normal.

```
                          This line is centered.

        Centered on 28.

    One word in this line is bold.

    One word in this line is underlined.















    C:\WP\WP42\CH5\FIG5.WP              Doc 1  Pg 1  Ln 8      Pos 18
```

*Fig. 5.3. Practice lines for Quick Start Part 4.*

## Centering a Line between Margins

To center each line between the right and left margins as you type:

Make sure the cursor is against the left margin.

1. Press Center (Shift-F6)

The cursor will move to the midpoint between margins.

2. Type **This line is centered.**

3. Press Enter

Pressing Enter at the end of the centered line ends the centering command and returns typing to normal. If you want to center a number of lines of text (a quotation, perhaps), turn to Chapter 6 for an explanation of the procedure.

4. Press Enter to move the cursor down for the next example

## Centering a Line around a Character Position

If you want to center text around a character position on a blank line, here's how:

Make sure the cursor is on a blank line.

1. Using the space bar, move the cursor to character position 20

These steps will center your text around character position 20:

2. Press the Center key (Shift-F6)

The cursor will not move.

3. Type **Centered on 20.**

Notice how the text shifts to center around column 20.

4. Press Enter to end centering and return to normal typing on the next line

5. Press Enter to move the cursor down for the next example

## Creating Bold Text

WordPerfect's Bold feature must be turned on before you type the text that is to appear in bold, and turned off at the end of the text that you wish to appear in bold. To create bold text:

1. Type **One word in this line is**

2. Press the Bold key (F6) once to turn on the Bold function

Notice that the Pos number at the lower right corner of your screen indicates, by its changed appearance, that Bold is on.

3. Type **bold.**

Notice that the word *bold* in the sentence—*One word in this line is* ***bold.***—appears either in bold type, or in color on your screen. When it is printed, the word *bold* will be printed in bold type.

4. Press the Bold key (F6) a second time to turn the Bold function off

The Pos number returns to normal.

5. Press Enter to end the sentence

6. Press Enter to insert a blank line before the next example

## Creating Underlined Text

The Underline feature must be turned on before typing the text to be underlined, and turned off after typing the text to be underlined. To underline text:

1. Type **One word in this line is**

2. Press Underline (F8) to turn on underlining

Notice that the Pos number at the lower right corner of your screen indicates, by its changed appearance, that Underline is on.

3. Type **underlined.**

The word *underlined* in the sentence—*One word in this line is* <u>*underlined.*</u>—appears underlined, highlighted, or colored on your screen. When it is printed the word *underlined* will be printed as underlined text.

4. Press F8 (Underline) to turn the underlining function off

The Pos number returns to normal type.

5. Press Enter to end the sentence

Your screen should look like the screen illustrated in figure 5.3.

## Typing Text within the Bold and Underline Range

To insert text within a bold or underline area follow these steps:

1. Move the cursor to the location within the bold or underlined text where you want to insert additional text

As you move the cursor over one end of the bold or underlined area, the Pos number changes to reflect that you have move the cursor into a bold or underline range.

2. Type the text to be inserted

The inserted text will appear bold or underlined.

## Revealing the Hidden Codes in Text

You can both view and delete the hidden codes that cause WordPerfect to enhance text and change your document's format, with the Reveal Codes key. The Reveal Codes key will display a split screen; the top portion displays the normal text screen, and the bottom portion displays text and the hidden codes.

Practice removing the bold, underline, and center codes using these steps:

1. Move the cursor to the *b* in the word *bold* on the line containing bold text

2. Press Reveal Codes (Alt-F3)

The Reveal Codes screen shown in figure 5.2 will appear. The bottom half of the Reveal Codes screen shows the normal text plus the hidden codes [B] and [b].

If you are using WordPerfect 4.1 the cursor appears as a flashing circumflex [^] on the Reveal Codes screen.

3. Use any cursor movement key to move the cursor to the first character position to the right of the first bold code [B]

The Reveal Codes cursor may already rest at that position because of the cursor move in Step 1.

4. Press the Backspace key to remove the [B] code from the Reveal Code screen

The text on the upper screen is no longer bold. Removing the [B] at the beginning of bold text or the [b] at the end of bold text removes the bold feature.

    **5.** Use the cursor movement keys and Backspace key to move through the Reveal Codes screen deleting the hidden underline codes [U] [u], and the center codes [C] [c]

Notice the results on the upper portion of the screen. When you delete the center code on a line centered around a character position (20), the line remains indented 20 spaces. To return the text to the left margin:

    **6.** Delete the spaces

    **7.** Press the Cancel key to return to the typing screen

    Or

    **7.** Press the space bar to return to the typing screen

    Or

    **7.** Press Enter to return to the typing screen

In one or two quick keystrokes, you can add visual impact to your printed words by embedding a hidden code in your document's text. WordPerfect uses hidden codes to change document formats, enhance characters, and control the printer.

WordPerfect uses two types of embedded codes: those codes that are entered when you press a single function key (margin settings), and those that are turned on when you press a function key, and turned off when you press the same function key a second time (underline and bold, for instance). Hidden formatting codes such as margin and tab settings codes are mentioned in this chapter only as a concept. Formatting is described fully in Chapter 8.

If you've changed your mind about using one of the document enhancement features, you can easily delete the hidden codes. You can use the Del or Backspace keys, on the typing screen, to locate and delete an unwanted hidden code; or you can display and delete the codes with the Reveal Codes function.

Because the Reveal Codes screen permits you to view the hidden codes, the Reveal Codes screen may be the only way you'll be able to isolate and decipher a problem with overlapping tabs, indents, or centering.

Although this chapter has described how you can enhance text *while* you are typing your document, there will be times that you will want to add impact to your words *after* you have typed your document. Chapter 6 will help you do just that—enhance your existing text using the Block function.

# Using the Block Function
# To Rearrange Your Text

Chapter 6 marks the end of the first section of *Using WordPerfect*, 3rd Edition. At the conclusion of this chapter you will be able to use all of those basic—and very powerful—WordPerfect features and functions that permit you to create, edit, and print most of the kinds of documents used in business, industry, education, and the military.

As you complete the last *Quick Start*, take time to reflect on the word-processing skills you've acquired in this short time. You should feel excited about moving on to the second section of this book, knowing that (with each subsequent chapter) you will be adding to your base of WordPerfect knowledge at a dramatic rate.

Chapter 6 introduces three topics:

- Using the Block command to isolate blocks of text within your document; and then applying WordPerfect features to those blocks of text in several ways

- Using the Move commands to create written communication that is clear, concise, and complete

- Working with two WordPerfect documents at one time

By now, you may be feeling comfortable enough with WordPerfect that you'd like to try the *Quick Start* before reading the chapter. You'll find this *Quick Start* particularly interesting, because you'll cut pieces from one part of the document and paste them in another part of the document.

You'll even open a second WordPerfect document and move text between two documents.

Remember, even if you are successful in performing all of the *Quick Start* procedures, you've not learned all there is to learn about the topics. The body of the chapter contains information that is not included in the *Quick Start*. Reading the chapter after you've done the *Quick Start* is a good way to both reinforce and add to your learning.

Some of the procedures you'll explore in this chapter are:

- Blocking text so that a WordPerfect feature (such as underline or print) affects only the blocked text

- Moving sentences, paragraphs, or pages with the Move function

- Moving as many as three segments of text, at one time, with Delete, and Cancel (Restore)

- Loading and working with two documents

- Splitting the screen to view two documents at once

- Moving text between two documents displayed on the screen

# Using the Flexible and Powerful Block Function

The most powerful and flexible command in WordPerfect, the Block command, is used with other WordPerfect functions to isolate specific segments of text so that only the "blocked" segment of text is affected by the selected WordPerfect function.

Some of the things you can do with the Block command are:

- Underline or make bold a block of existing text

- Move a block of text of any size

- Delete a block of text of any size

- Print a portion of a document

- Save a portion of a document

You can use many WordPerfect features with the Block function. Table 6.1 lists WordPerfect features that are compatible with the Block function.

**Table 6.1**

*WordPerfect Features Compatible with the Block Function*

| | | |
|---|---|---|
| Bold | Delete | Mark Text |
| Replace | Sort | Move |
| Spell | Superscript | Subscript |
| Center | Print | Flush Right |
| Save | Underline | Upper/Lower Case |

If you do not see a specific feature listed in table 6.1, then you must assume that the feature is not used with the Block function. For example, to change margin settings in a portion of your document, the Line Format key is used, not the Block function. Although the Block function is flexible, it is not so flexible that it can be used with all WordPerfect features.

## Marking Text as a Block

WordPerfect must be told exactly which segment (block) of text is to be changed or affected. Use the Block function to highlight the text (block) you wish to change or manipulate in some way.

To mark a block of text:

1. Check table 6.1 to make sure that what you want to do will work with the Block function

2. Move the cursor to the first character that will begin the block of text you want affected

3. Press Block (Alt-F4)

This message flashes in the lower left corner of your screen:

    Block on

Using the cursor arrow keys, PgDn, PgUp, or Go To (Ctrl-Home):

4. Move the cursor to the right of the last character in the block of text

As you move the cursor, WordPerfect will highlight all of the text that will be affected by the function you select in the next step.

    **5.** Press the key that is used to identify the function that will affect the block you have highlighted

If the function key you select will not work with the Block function, WordPerfect will signal you with a beep. To back out of the command, press Cancel (F1).

Some commands such as a block print or block delete require confirmation.

    **6.** If a Yes/No (Y/N) type of prompt appears at the lower left of the screen, answer it by typing Y for yes and N for no

The function selected in Step 5 will execute, affecting only the highlighted block of text. If the block highlighting remains after the function is complete:

    **7.** Select another function from table 6.1

        Or

    **7.** Press Cancel (F1) to remove the highlighting

As you are blocking text (highlighting it), don't limit yourself to using the left- and right-arrow keys. You can use all the normal cursor movement keys. For example, to highlight an entire line, press the down arrow, to highlight from the cursor to the bottom of the current screen press Home-down arrow, and to highlight multiple pages use the Go To (Ctrl-Home) command.

## Turning Off the Block Function

In most cases, the Block function is turned off when the task is completed. If you need to turn off Block after turning it on:

    **1.** Press Cancel (F1)

        Or

    **1.** Press Block (Alt-F4) a second time

The Block on prompt will disappear from the screen.

## Changing an Existing Block of Text to Bold or Underlined Text

In Chapter 5 you created underlined and bold text as you typed the text for the first time. If the text you wish to bold or underline already exists, use the Block command to tell WordPerfect which text should be enhanced.

1. Repeat Steps 1 through 4 (in the section "Marking Text as a Block") to mark your block of text

2. Press Bold (F6) to bold the block of text

Or

3. Press Underline (F8) to underline the block of text

The Block function turns off automatically when finished.

*A Timesaving Tip*: Because bold and underline are normally used to enhance a few words within a phrase, you can save time by turning on the Block, then using the Ctrl-right arrow to highlight one word at a time. When all the needed words are highlighted, press the Bold or Underline key.

On monochrome screens with graphics adaptors (such as Compaq), the underline is most frequently displayed as highlighted text. Since the block is also highlighted, there may be no change in text appearance when you press the Underline key to underline a block of text. You'll know that the command worked because, after the function has executed, the text remains highlighted while the flashing Block on prompt disappears.

## Centering a Block of Existing Text

It's as easy to center a block of existing text as it is to make it bold or underlined.

Mark the block of text you want to center, and press Center (Shift-F6). The block of text will center between the left and right margins.

The Block center function does have one limitation you need to be aware of. If the block of text contains full-lines in paragraph form, there isn't much blank space left between the margins for centering. The fact that the text is centered may not be readily apparent.

And, there is a caveat that applies to the Block center function as well—if there is any chance that you'll need to return the block to left justified text, save a copy before centering.

Centering changes each line so that it no longer word wraps or left justifies. This happens because WordPerfect's centering function places a Hard Return (just as though you pressed Enter) at the end of each centered line. If you need to change the centered block of text back to the standard text format, use the Reveal Codes function to delete the Hard Return codes, [HRt]. To refresh your memory, return to Chapter 5 for information about using Reveal Codes.

## Deleting Blocks of Text

Block delete is the most efficient way to delete more than one or two characters. In a few keystrokes, you can delete an unwanted sentence or three full pages of text.

1. Block the text you want deleted

2. Press Del

To make sure that you didn't accidentally press the wrong key, WordPerfect displays this prompt:

    Delete Block? (Y/N)

3. Type **Y** to delete the block of text and turn the Block function off

    Or

3. Type **N** and you are returned to the highlighted block

Remember, you can recover the last three deleted items in WordPerfect by pressing the Cancel key (F1).

Later in this chapter you will discover how to use the Block delete function and the Cancel function to move as many as three different blocks of text to new locations (at the same time!).

## Saving Blocks of Text

WordPerfect's Block save function can help you become more efficient (and effective) when you're working with documents that contain repetitive text. An example of repetitive text might be a standard clause in a lease or a standard paragraph that appears several times in a contract for the purchase of a home.

If your documents contain frequently used phrases, paragraphs, or specifications—you need to use Block save. If you tried the Quick Start in Chapter 4, you first saved a block of text, and then retrieved the "saved text" into another document. This process is an efficient and an effective way to eliminate the need for retyping phrases and paragraphs that you frequently use within the same document or in several documents.

To use the Block save function, you must first save the blocked (highlighted) portion of any document into a file (to which you have assigned a name). Each of these separate files can then be retrieved into another document, in the order in which you want them to appear.

Block save enables you to build a library of standardized pieces that can be reconstructed to form a larger document. And, you can perform the Block save as easily as you perform any other Block function:

1. Use the Block function to highlight everything you want saved in one file

2. Press Save (F10)

This prompt appears on your screen:

Block name:

3. Type the **file name**

Select a file name that clearly identifies the phrase, paragraph, or pages you are saving. You can include a drive letter and path name before the file name.

4. Press Enter to save the block

The block will stay highlighted.

5. Press Cancel (F1) to return to normal typing

## Printing Blocks of Text

When you want to print only a portion of a document, use Block print in this way:

1. Block the text you want printed

2. Press Print (Shift-F7)

This prompt will appear on your screen:

Print Block? (Y/N)

3. Type **Y** to print

If you want to Block print several pages use the Go To to move quickly to the end of the Block.

1. Place the cursor on the first character of the block

2. Press Block (Alt-F4)

3. Press Go To (Ctrl-Home)

4. Type the **number of the page** you want to Go To

5. Press Enter

Once the pages are highlighted, you can make adjustments in the amount of text to be blocked (highlighted) with the arrow keys.

The block will print with page breaks and formats exactly as they appear on-screen.

If you are starting the Block print in the middle of a page, the end-of-the-page code (page break) may be reached before all of the text you wish to print can be printed. To print all of the text you have designated as a part of your block, press Ctrl-Enter (which embeds a code called a Hard Page break) directly before the block. Delete that same Hard Page break code using Backspace after you have printed the block of text.

If the words *page break* sound unfamiliar, don't worry; in Chapter 9, you'll learn more about how WordPerfect uses page breaks.

# Moving Text

It was pointed out, in an earlier chapter, that the Insert and Delete functions are two very important advantages of word processing. There is another, equally dramatic and important, word-processing capability that you must know about—moving text. Being able to move text whenever and wherever you like (whether that text is a sentence or a paragraph) permits you to organize and refine your written thoughts quickly and easily—as many times as you like!

There are three ways to move text in WordPerfect. The most flexible method is the Block move. The Block move functions are:

| Function | Keys | Feature/Advantage |
|---|---|---|
| Move | Ctrl-F4 | Move exactly one sentence, paragraph, or page |
| Block, Move | Alt-F4, Ctrl-F4 | Move a single text segment of any size. Move columns or rectangles |
| Block, Delete, Restore | Alt-F4, Ctrl-F4, F1 | Delete then restore to a new location up to three text segments of any size |

## Moving Text Using the Move Command

If you are moving or copying *exactly* one sentence, or one paragraph, or one page:

1. Place the cursor within the sentence, paragraph, or page you want to move

2. Press Move (Ctrl-F4)

The menu shown at the bottom of figure 6.1 is displayed.

Pressing 1, 2, or 3 highlights the sentence, paragraph, or page that contains the cursor.

After you select the text to be moved you are asked to choose whether you want to *copy* or *cut* your selection. In WordPerfect 4.2 you have the additional option of *deleting* your selection.

3. Type **1** Cut if you want to remove the original text so it can be moved

   Or

3. Type **2** Copy to leave the original in place and move a duplicate

   Or

3. Type **3** Delete if you want to delete your selection

After choosing Cut, Copy, or Delete the menu will disappear. Of course, if you choose Cut or Delete, so will the text!

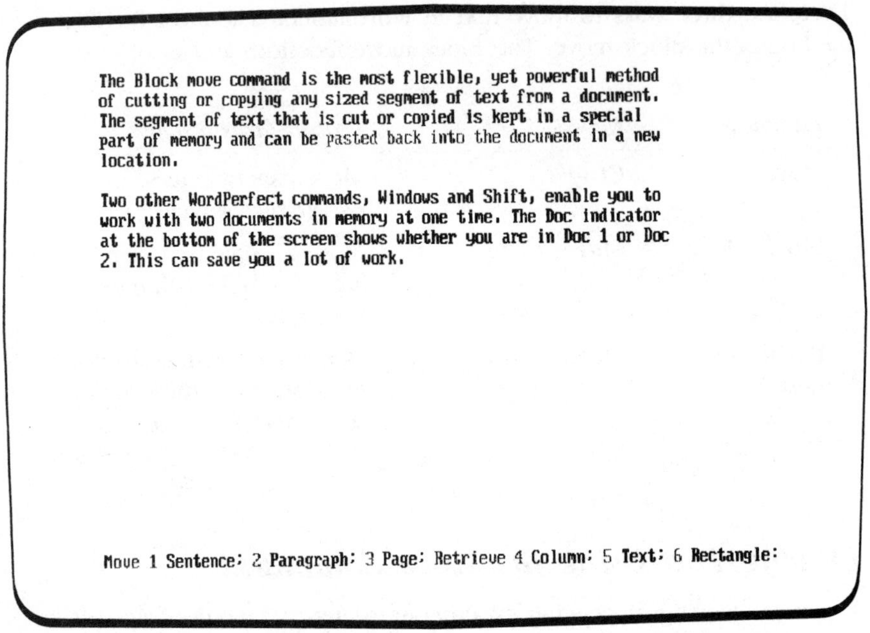

```
     The Block move command is the most flexible, yet powerful method
     of cutting or copying any sized segment of text from a document.
     The segment of text that is cut or copied is kept in a special
     part of memory and can be pasted back into the document in a new
     location.

     Two other WordPerfect commands, Windows and Shift, enable you to
     work with two documents in memory at one time. The Doc indicator
     at the bottom of the screen shows whether you are in Doc 1 or Doc
     2. This can save you a lot of work.




     Move 1 Sentence; 2 Paragraph; 3 Page; Retrieve 4 Column; 5 Text; 6 Rectangle:
```

*Fig. 6.1. Move menu when Block is off.*

The text that you highlighted resides in your computer's temporary memory, waiting to be *pasted* into the document.

> **4.** Move the cursor to the location within your document where you want the text to appear
>
> **5.** Press Move (Ctrl-F4)

Notice that the Move menu has two sides. The three options on the left select what will be *moved* and the three choices on the right select what will be *retrieved*. Because you want to retrieve the text you cut or copied:

> **6.** Type **5** Text

## Moving Blocks of Text

As you become more involved in editing your WordPerfect documents, you'll notice that you rarely move exactly one sentence, one paragraph, or one page. More often you'll decide to move parts of sentences and paragraphs. For these types of moves you'll select the Block move option.

You'll use the Block move option to move columns and rectangles of text. If you type financial data, the column move function will save you time and the frustration of moving financial data figure by figure.

## Marking the Block of Text

To review what you learned earlier in this chapter: To Block text, move the cursor to the first character in the block of text you want to move. Press the Block key, Alt-F4. The prompt, Block on, will flash in the lower left corner of the screen. Move the cursor to the end of the text to be moved. All the text to be moved will be highlighted.

## Cutting or Copying the Block of Text

After blocking the text to be moved, press Move (Ctrl-F4). The Move menu illustrated in figure 6.2 is different than the Move menu displayed when the Block is not on.

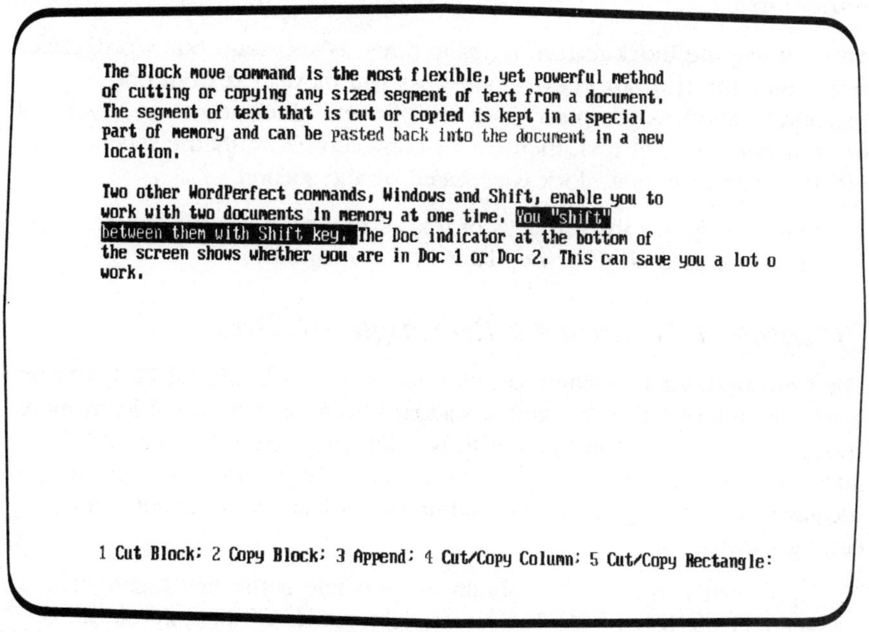

```
    The Block move command is the most flexible, yet powerful method
    of cutting or copying any sized segment of text from a document.
    The segment of text that is cut or copied is kept in a special
    part of memory and can be pasted back into the document in a new
    location.

    Two other WordPerfect commands, Windows and Shift, enable you to
    work with two documents in memory at one time. You "shift"
    between them with Shift key. The Doc indicator at the bottom of
    the screen shows whether you are in Doc 1 or Doc 2. This can save you a lot o
    work.










    1 Cut Block; 2 Copy Block; 3 Append; 4 Cut/Copy Column; 5 Cut/Copy Rectangle:
```

*Fig. 6.2. Move menu when Block is on.*

If you choose 1 Cut Block the highlighted block of text will disappear from the screen and will be stored in temporary memory so it can be pasted elsewhere in the document.

Selecting 2 Copy Block causes WordPerfect to create an image of the highlighted text in memory that can be pasted into your document later. The original text remains on the screen.

If you select 1 or 2, the highlighting disappears.

## Pasting Text

If you have chosen cut or copy, move to the location in your document where the first character of the moved text is to appear. Press the Move key (Ctrl-F4) to move the block of text back into the document.

The Move menu that appears this time will look like the one illustrated in figure 6.1. Choices on the right side of the menu are used to retrieve or move text into your document. Since you cut or copied text, type 5 to retrieve text.

You can use the Block feature as many times as you want but WordPerfect stores only the text last cut or copied. As you move text from one location to another, you must work on only one block at a time. If you cut or copy one block of text, then cut or copy another, only the second block remains; the first block is replaced by the second.

To move as many as three blocks of text at one time use the Delete and Restore move method described later in this chapter.

## Blocking a Column or Rectangle of Text

The procedure for blocking a column of text or a rectangular body of text is slightly different than marking a standard body of text. You'll learn more about tabular columns in Chapter 8; but, let this section serve as an introduction to the Block function as it applies to moving columns and rectangles of text—refer to this section as you learn more about using columns text.

The upper left corner of the column or rectangle is the first highlighted character in the text block. The lower right corner of the column or rectangle will be the last highlighted character. The lines of text that lie between these corners will contain highlighting that extends past the column or rectangle corners to the edge of the margins, but it's only the corners you mark that count.

## Cutting or Copying a Tabular Column or Rectangle

Once you have marked the corners of the column or rectangle for the beginning and the end of the block, press Move (Ctrl-F4). WordPerfect permits you to select from five Block move types.

Choice 4 enables you to cut or copy tabbed and indented columns of text (numeric columns or lists, for instance). Choice 5 permits you to cut a rectangle of text from a body of copy.

Choose 4 or 5 and another menu will appear to ask if you want to: 1 Cut, 2 Copy, or 3 Delete.

Type 1 or 2 if you want to move the highlighted column or rectangle. (The delete choice is available in WordPerfect 4.2 only.)

If you cut a column from a tabular space, the other columns will move to the next tab setting to the left. If you cut a rectangle, the text on either side of the cut moves to fill the hole.

## Pasting Tabular Columns or Rectangles

After you have cut or copied a column or rectangle of text, you can paste it into your document by moving to the appropriate tab setting at the new location. Press Move (Ctrl-F4) and type 4 to retrieve the column, or type 6 to retrieve the rectangle.

If you're pasting a column, the tabs will adjust to the tab settings that exist at the location in the document where you are inserting the column. Existing columns that are aligned on tabs will move over to accommodate the newly inserted column.

If you cut or copy a column, but (by mistake) signal WordPerfect to retrieve text or a rectangle, you will get unreliable results.

## Using the Delete Key To Move Text

So far, you have been introduced to only those methods that allow you to move one block of text at a time.

Using the Delete key to move text permits you to store as many as three blocks of text in temporary memory at one time. And, you can selectively paste them into your document wherever you want.

First, delete the blocks of text you want to move using the Block delete method described earlier in this chapter. When you delete a fourth block, the first will be lost from memory. Only the last three deletions can be restored.

Once you have deleted the text, move the cursor to the location in your document where you want one of the deleted blocks of text pasted.

Press the Cancel key (F1). At the cursor you will see a highlighted copy of the text most recently deleted. A short menu will appear at the bottom left of the screen.

Type 1 to restore the highlighted text as it appears on-screen. Type 2 to display one of the other deleted blocks of text.

If the highlighted text is not the text you wish to paste into the current location, press 2 until the correct text is displayed. When you have found the text you want restored, type 1. You can restore text to the document as many times as you wish, but only the last three deleted items are remembered.

# Windows and Multiple Documents

WordPerfect's reputation is built around a number of its very powerful word-processing features. One of WordPerfect's most powerful features permits you to create and edit two documents at the same time. You can view the documents separately or split the screen into *windows* to view both documents at once.

If you have trouble visualizing the split-screen concept, think of your WordPerfect screen as a desk upon which two documents are lying one above the other. One important advantage to the WordPerfect split screen is that you can cut and paste text from one document to the other using just a few keystrokes.

## *Switching between Documents*

To see the document that is not currently displayed:

    **1.** Press Switch (Shift-F3)

As you press Switch, look at the Doc number on the Status Line. The indicator will change from Doc 1 to Doc 2. Each press of Switch moves you from one document to the other.

Don't be surprised when Doc 2 first appears. Since Doc 2 doesn't contain a typed document yet it will be blank. The typing in Doc 1 is still in the computer, it's just not displayed.

## Opening a Window

To split the screen so you can see the other document:

    **1.** Press Screen (Ctrl-F3)

Notice that Screen and Switch share F3. From the Screen menu:

    **2.** Type **1** (Window) to open a window into a second document

WordPerfect prompts you to enter the number of lines for the document displayed. The default setting (24 lines—the size of a full screen of text) appears in the prompt.

    **3.** Type **11** to split the screen in half

You can specify any number of lines.

    **4.** Press Enter and the top window will open

When you open the window it may display as a blank window if the second document doesn't contain text.

The *Tab Ruler* divides the screen. Each window has its own Status Line as illustrated in figure 6.3. Each triangle on the Tab Ruler represents a tab setting. The left or right brackets ([]) display the positions of the left or right margins. Left or right braces ({}) display when a tab and margin share the same space.

Press Switch (Shift-F3) to move the cursor between the documents, just as you did when each document used the full screen. As the cursor switches, the triangles point to the window that contains the cursor.

## Closing a Window

The procedure for closing a window is to increase the number of lines in the current window so that the document fills the screen. Suppose, for example, that Document 1 has 14 lines and Document 2 uses the remaining 10 lines on the screen. To expand Document 1 to fill the entire screen:

    **1.** Press Switch (Shift-F3) to move the cursor into the window you want to enlarge

    **2.** Press Screen (Ctrl-F3)

    **3.** Type **1** Window

    **4.** Type **24** or a greater number

    **5.** Press Enter

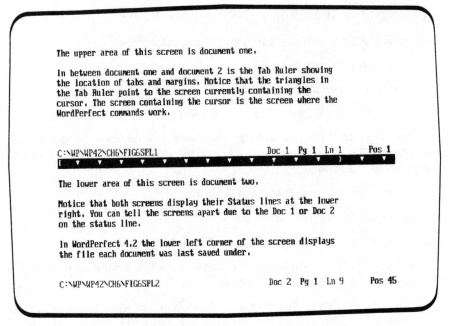

The upper area of this screen is document one.

In between document one and document 2 is the Tab Ruler showing
the location of tabs and margins. Notice that the triangles in
the Tab Ruler point to the screen currently containing the
cursor. The screen containing the cursor is the screen where the
WordPerfect commands work.

C:\WP\WP42\CH6\FIG6SPL1                        Doc 1  Pg 1  Ln 1        Pos 1

The lower area of this screen is document two.

Notice that both screens display their Status lines at the lower
right. You can tell the screens apart due to the Doc 1 or Doc 2
on the status line.

In WordPerfect 4.2 the lower left corner of the screen displays
the file each document was last saved under.

C:\WP\WP42\CH6\FIG6SPL2                        Doc 2  Pg 1  Ln 9        Pos 45

*Fig. 6.3. Opening a window.*

This procedure increases the number of lines displayed from Document 1
from 14 to 24. Document 1 now fills the screen.

You must exit both documents displayed in the windows before
WordPerfect will let you exit the program. Press Exit (F7) and respond to
the prompts. When you exit one document you'll be transferred to the
other document if it contains text.

## Adding a Tab Ruler without Windows

As you work with columns of text, you may want to see where the tabs
are set. You can display the Tab Ruler, used to divide windows, without
displaying the two windows by decreasing the number of lines in the
visible window so that the Tab Ruler creeps into view at the bottom.

1. Press Screen (Ctrl-F3)

2. Type 1 Window

This prompt will appear on your screen:

#Lines in this Window:

3. Type 23

4. Press Enter

## Moving Text Blocks between Documents

All of WordPerfect's features can be used in a window. You can use the text, column, and rectangle moves described earlier in this chapter to move text and columns between documents. Just cut or copy the text, columns, or rectangles from one document, press Switch, and paste into the second document.

# Quick Start Part 5:
# Using Block Functions

*Quick Start* Part 5 teaches two of the most powerful WordPerfect techniques—using the Block function with other WordPerfect features, and moving blocks of text.

You can move blocks of text using several methods. To begin, become familiar with the Block move demonstrated in this *Quick Start*; then try other methods to fit more specific text move needs. The Block move is by far the most flexible.

Before you can work through *Quick Start* 5 you will need some text to work with. Enter this text on a clear screen:

**The Block move command is the most flexible, yet powerful method of cutting or copying any sized segment of text from a document. The segment of text that is cut or copied is kept in a special part of memory and can be pasted back into the document in a new location.**

**Two other WordPerfect commands, Windows and Shift, enable you to work with two documents in memory at one time. You "shift" between them with Shift key. The Doc indicator at the bottom of the screen shows whether you are in Doc 1 or Doc 2. You can even use the Block Move commands to cut a block of text from one document and paste it into another. This can save you a lot of work.**

## Enhancing Existing Text

In Chapter 5 you created bold and underlined text. In this exercise you will bold part of the first paragraph, even though it has already been typed.

1. Move the cursor to the *p* in the word *pasted* on the next to the last line of the first paragraph

2. Press Block (Alt-F4) to turn the Block command on

This flashing message appears on your screen:

    Block on

> **3.** Press the right arrow so the cursor moves across and highlights
> the words *pasted back into the document*

The highlighted text is the text you want bold. Figure 6.4 illustrates how
the blocked area appears.

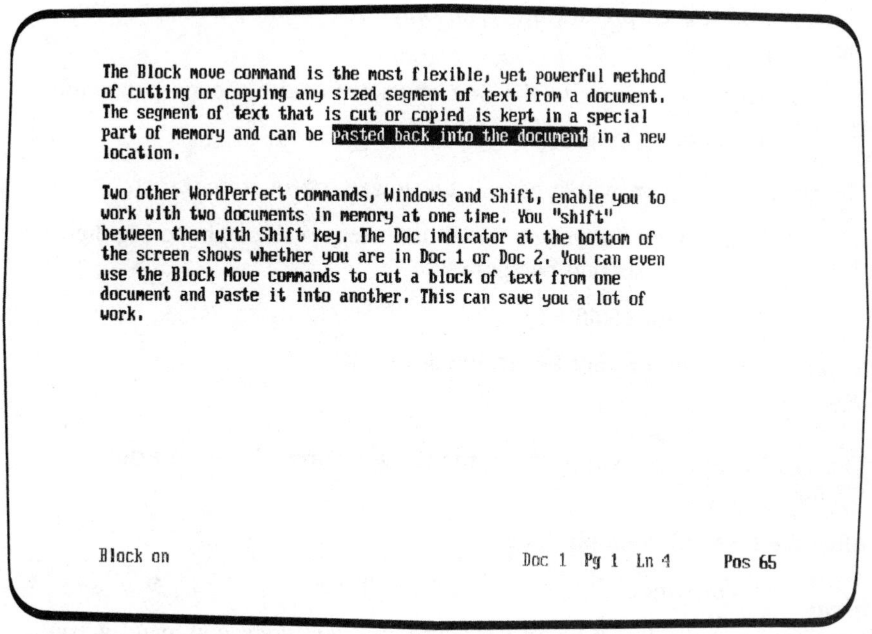

```
The Block move command is the most flexible, yet powerful method
of cutting or copying any sized segment of text from a document.
The segment of text that is cut or copied is kept in a special
part of memory and can be [pasted back into the document] in a new
location.

Two other WordPerfect commands, Windows and Shift, enable you to
work with two documents in memory at one time. You "shift"
between them with Shift key. The Doc indicator at the bottom of
the screen shows whether you are in Doc 1 or Doc 2. You can even
use the Block Move commands to cut a block of text from one
document and paste it into another. This can save you a lot of
work.




Block on                                   Doc 1  Pg 1  Ln 4      Pos 65
```

*Fig. 6.4. Blocked text for bold.*

> **4.** Press Bold (F6)

The text that was highlighted will now display as bold by changing color
or appearing brighter. You can use this same technique of Blocking and
pressing a function key to underline or center text.

The Block command turned itself off automatically after the Bold function.

## Printing Blocks of Text

Whether you want to "show off" the perfect paragraph or hand out six pages of a fifty-page report, you'll want to print only a part of your document. Use the Block print command.

As you probably guessed, you'll use the same procedure for Block print as you use for all of the other Block commands.

Block the text, then press Print. Print only the second paragraph with these steps:

> **1.** Move the cursor to the first character of the second paragraph
>
> **2.** Press Block (Alt-F4)

The flashing Block on will appear at the lower left of your screen.

> **3.** First, move the cursor down and then to the right to highlight the entire second paragraph
>
> **4.** Press Print (Shift-F7)

In response to the prompt Print Block? (Y/N)

> **5.** Type **Y**

The highlighted text will print on the printer currently set in Print Options.

After the text has been printed:

> **6.** Press Cancel (F1) to turn off the Block

You can leave the Block on and execute another Block command if you wish.

## Deleting a Block of Text

The Del key works fine for single characters, Ctrl-Backspace works well on words, Ctrl-End deletes the line, but when you really need a flexible way to delete text, use Block delete.

> **1.** Move the cursor to the *Y* in the phrase *You can even* . . . in the second paragraph
>
> **2.** Press Block (Alt-F4)

This prompt appears in the lower left of your screen:

    Block on

**3.** Press the right-arrow key to highlight the entire sentence

*You can even use the Block Move commands to cut a block of text from one document and paste it into another.*

    **4.** Press the Del key

Figure 6.5 illustrates how your screen should look.

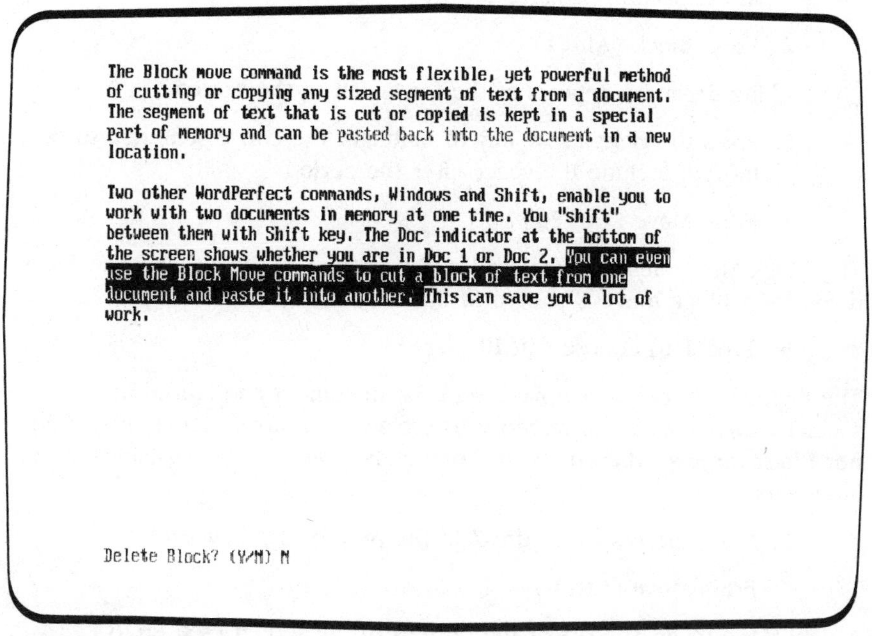

```
The Block move command is the most flexible, yet powerful method
of cutting or copying any sized segment of text from a document.
The segment of text that is cut or copied is kept in a special
part of memory and can be pasted back into the document in a new
location.

Two other WordPerfect commands, Windows and Shift, enable you to
work with two documents in memory at one time. You "shift"
between them with Shift key. The Doc indicator at the bottom of
the screen shows whether you are in Doc 1 or Doc 2. You can even
use the Block Move commands to cut a block of text from one
document and paste it into another. This can save you a lot of
work.
```

```
Delete Block? (Y/N) N
```

*Fig. 6.5. Blocked text for delete.*

This prompt appears on your screen:

    Delete Block? (Y/N)

**5.** Type **Y**

All the highlighted text will be deleted. Don't forget you can restore the last three deletions with the Cancel key.

## Moving a Block of Text in the Same Document

You no longer have to use scissors and tape to reorganize your writing—use WordPerfect's Block move. The Block move function permits you to type your words as you think of them, then go back and reorganize and refine.

In this exercise you will move the second sentence in paragraph two so that it follows the sentence that is currently third.

1. Move the cursor to the *Y* in the phrase *You "shift" between . . .* in the second paragraph

2. Press Block (Alt-F4)

The flashing Block on appears at the lower left of the screen.

3. Press the right-arrow key to highlight the entire sentence to be moved. Include the space after the period

4. Press Move (Ctrl-F4)

The Block Move menu is displayed at the bottom of the screen. The Move menu for a Block move is shown in figure 6.2.

5. Type 1 to choose Cut Block

The highlighted text is removed from the document and stored in a special *scrapbook* area of memory. There are two Move menus. If you do not Block the text, then the Cut Block choice will not be available on the Move menu.

6. Move the cursor to the *T* in the phrase *This can save . . .*

7. Press Move (Ctrl-F4)

A new Move menu appears at the bottom of the screen (see fig. 6.1).

8. Type 5 to choose Text from the right side of the menu

Notice in figure 6.1 that the Retrieve commands are on the right side of this menu. If you choose the wrong retrieve command you may get very strange results!

## Switching between Two Documents

When you are working on similar documents, it's convenient to have both documents readily available. In WordPerfect you can store two documents in memory and switch back and forth between them. You can use all WordPerfect commands in either document.

To type in Document 2:

1. Look at the Doc number on your current screen. It should say Doc 1. You are in document number one

2. Press Switch (Shift-F3) to switch to Doc 2

Don't panic when the screen goes blank. Doc 1 is still in memory, it's just hidden. The screen is blank because Document 2 doesn't contain any typing yet. Notice the Doc 2 on the Status Line at the bottom right.

3. Type **This is document 2.** on the first line

4. Press Switch (Shift-F3) to switch back to Doc 1

See, your work is still there!

## Moving Blocks of Text between Documents

One of the greatest advantages of working on two documents at once is being able to cut blocks of text from one document and paste them into the other.

You should currently be in Doc 1. If you are not, press Switch (Shift-F3).

You can use techniques from the previous exercises to copy the first paragraph from Doc 1 and paste it into Doc 2. To try this procedure:

1. Move the cursor to the first character of the first paragraph in Doc 1

2. Press Block (Alt-F4)

3. Press the arrow keys to highlight the entire first paragraph

4. Press Move (Ctrl-F4)

5. Type **2** to select Copy Block

The paragraph remains on the screen of Doc 1 and a duplicate image of the paragraph is stored in temporary memory.

6.  Press Switch (Shift-F3) to switch to Doc 2

7.  Move the cursor to the end of the sentence

8.  Press Move (Ctrl-F4) to display the Move menu

9.  Type 5 Text to retrieve the paragraph you cut from Doc 1

## Exiting Multiple Documents

Exit multiple documents the same way you exit a single document, by pressing Exit (F7), and responding to the prompts. When you exit one document you will automatically be transferred to the other document if it contains text.

The three concepts you learned in this chapter take you giant steps beyond conventional writing methods. Before long, you'll use the Block function whenever you need to enhance a section of existing text.

Before leaving the chapter, make sure you have read over the table that shows what functions work with Block. When you want to use a Block command follow these steps:

1.  Move to the beginning of the text

2.  Press Block (Alt-F4)

3.  Highlight the block using cursor movement keys

4.  Press the function key for the command to affect the block of text

If the Block highlight does not disappear, then press Cancel (F1).

Once you understand how to Block text it's only a short step to moving blocks of text.

1.  Block the text you want to move

2.  Press Move (Ctrl-F4) and type 1 Cut or 2 Copy

3.  Move to the point in your document where the text is to be inserted

4.  Press Move (Ctrl-F4) and select 5 Text from the Retrieve side of the menu

When you want to work with two documents you only need to remember two keys:

- ☐ Switch (Shift-F3)
- ☐ Screen (Ctrl-F3)

You can do any WordPerfect function in either document.

This is the final *Quick Start* chapter. The *Quick Starts* have presented all of the procedures you'll need to create, edit, save, and print simple documents using standard WordPerfect margin and tab settings.

Don't feel uncomfortable if you must refer to the chapter or look through the *Quick Starts* to remember a function or keystroke combination. Because it's natural to forget those keystrokes that you don't use frequently, it's important to practice using WordPerfect features and functions every day. If you take the few minutes to look up a technique, you'll remember it next time.

If you are an occasional WordPerfect user, you can get by admirably with what has been covered so far. Don't forget to use the Index to look up special functions or topics.

If the word processor is a major tool in your profession, then don't stop here! Although you can get by with what you've learned so far, you'll forgo the professional results and time-savings available with other WordPerfect features.

Don't feel that you have to read every chapter in the rest of the book. Skim the table of contents, scan headings, and check the Index to see what features and techniques sound like they can help you. Then, when you find that you need them, give 'em a try.

# ■ SECTION II

# Refining Your Documents

To:        Communications Department Staff
From:   John Roberts
Re:         Feedback on New Computer System

Without exception, everyone is moving "full speed ahead" in WordPerfect! I know, because I have received more interoffice correspondence in the last week than in the previous quarter! While your efforts are commendable, don't totally abandon our "old style" communications—talking!

On a serious note though, I have noticed areas where we need improvement. Because these "challenges" are easily met with WordPerfect's features, I am convinced that by next week's report we will have met these goals:

- **Eliminate misspellings**—with the Spell-check feature there is no reason we should settle for less than completely accurate spelling! Check the Dictionary feature as well

- **Eliminate overused words and trite phrases**—please use your on-line Thesaurus, folks. There must be more descriptive words than "interact" and "overview." No more "bottom line," either!

- **Create more effective document formats**—relying on the same margin, page length, indent, and tab settings for every letter, memo, and report just doesn't make it! Your page layout must carry your message in the most efficient and effective way—use WordPerfect's formatting options to respond to *your audience's* communication needs too

J. Roberts

# Refining Your Document

Chapter 7 will help you put the stamp of excellence on your work. If you look upon the functions presented here as your personal quality-assurance measures, and use the techniques explored, you'll polish your documents so they are accurate and complete—void of the small editing flaws that annoy and distract your readers.

In Chapter 7 you'll discover how to search for specific words or phrases and replace them with alternate text, how to check your spelling for accuracy, how to look up alternate words (synonyms), how to mark text for notes and questions, and how to insert hidden comments that will not appear in the printed document.

There are four sections in the chapter. In the *Search and Replace* section you will learn that:

- Search and Replace will find characters, words, phrases, or functions

- Search can be used to find specific topics in your document

- Search can also be used to locate notes or questions you've previously marked in your document

- Extended Search searches headers, footers, footnotes, and endnotes

The *Document Comments* section describes how WordPerfect 4.2 permits you to insert "pop up" comments that can be viewed on the screen but do not print in your final document. The comments capability is useful if your work is reviewed by others—your boss or an editor, for instance.

The *Spelling* checker is a real bonus for both good and bad spellers. Before you make the final printed copy of your work, run the Spell checker to find and fix:

- Misspelled words

- Transposed letters and typographical errors

- Easily duplicated words such as the the or to to

When you find yourself using the same word over and over, or you need a word that is clearer and more dramatic than the word you have used, the *Thesaurus* will:

- List words with similar meanings (synonyms)

- List words with opposite meanings (antonyms), in WordPerfect 4.2 only

So, as a part of your regular create and edit cycle, use the functions presented in Chapter 7 to proof and polish your work—before printing the final copy of your document. You'll be pleased with the results.

# Searching for Words, Phrases, and Function Codes

WordPerfect makes it possible for you to easily locate specific characters, words, phrases, or functions that are a part of your document. If, in the process of creating your document, you have referred to your client as *Dane Smith* and your client's name is really *Jane Smith*, WordPerfect permits you to identify the location of each occurrence of *Dane*, and make the appropriate correction.

To search from the current cursor position forward, through the text, to the end of the document:

    **1.** Press →Search (F2)

This prompt will appear at the lower left of your screen:

    Srch:

    **2.** Type the characters or functions you want to search for

    *Example:* **Dane**

It's very common when learning the Search functions to press the Enter key after typing in the characters or functions you are searching for. If you do press the Enter key, the code [HRt] is entered as one of the characters being searched for.

   **3.** Press →Search again

WordPerfect begins searching, and stops when the characters or functions are found. WordPerfect will stop the first time it encounters the word *Dane*. To search for the next occurrence:

   **4.** Press →Search twice

You can search backward from the current cursor position to the beginning of the document:

   **1.** Press ←Search (Shift-F2)

This prompt will appear on your screen:

   Srch:Dane

   **2.** Type the characters and functions you want to locate. Your typing will replace any previous search characters

   **3.** Press Shift-F2 to activate the search

   Or

   **3.** Press F2 to activate the search

To repeat the same ←Search:

   **4.** Press Shift-F2, then F2

You won't have to reenter the characters, phrases, or functions you are looking for.

The Forward and Reverse Search commands *locate* text or functions in your document—they *do not replace* text or functions. To replace the located text automatically, use the Replace function.

## Defining Characters and Functions

To make the best use of the Search feature you must understand how to define the characters and functions you want to find.

WordPerfect differentiates between upper- and lowercase letters as it searches. To signal WordPerfect to search without differentiating between upper- or lowercase letters, type the Search characters in lowercase. If you type an uppercase letter, WordPerfect will look for only uppercase matches on that letter.

For example, if you ask WordPerfect to locate all occurrences of the word *search*, the cursor will stop on *search*, *Search*, and *SEARCH*. But if you ask WordPerfect to search for all occurrences of the word *Search*, the cursor will stop only on the word *Search* as it appears in your document.

You must be careful how you type in the characters or function keys you are searching for. For example, typing *the* will find the word *the* as well as *anaesthesia*. In such an instance, to locate only the word *the*, place a space before the word and a space after the word.

   *Example*: _the_

You can even find the word *final* at the end of a paragraph by entering the search phrase *final.[HRt]*

The code [HRt] is entered by pressing the Enter key. The Search function will only find occurrences of *final* that are followed by a period and the hard return (Enter key).

If you need to find a hidden code (such as pitch or tab settings) that is embedded in the document, go through the normal search procedure; but when the Srch: prompt appears, press the function keys that represent the hidden code. When the cursor moves to the code use the Reveal Codes key (Alt-F3) to reveal the code.

## Using Extended Search

To use the extended search feature (to extend search to headers, footers, footnotes, and endnotes), press Home before pressing →Search (F2), ←Search (Shift-F2), or Replace (Alt-F2).

## Marking Notes and Questions

Drafting an original work seems to move more smoothly when you work without interruption. Don't stop to research a name or number you have forgotten. If you interrupt your writing you may lose an idea, and you'll surely lose momentum. Rather than halting your progress, mark questions or comments with coded symbols. Once your rough draft is complete, you can use the Search function to quickly find the marks and add the needed text. Some marks that work well are:

| | |
|---|---|
| *** | to mark a comment or clarification |
| ### | to mark a number that must be inserted or verified |
| ??? | to mark text data that must be inserted or verified |

# Using Replace in Form Letters

WordPerfect's Replace features can be used to automatically find and replace specific text. For example, you might create and save a standard letter directed to Jones Associates. When you need to send the same letter to a different company (Ajax, Inc.), use the Replace command to locate and change the name to Ajax, Inc. throughout the letter.

If you use the same contract or document frequently, you may want to create a reusable document that contains imaginary names. You can later replace the imaginary names with the real names. For example, assume you frequently use the same contract proposal. Create your document using the "place keeper" *client* wherever the client's name should appear in the proposal.

The asterisks surrounding the word *client* will ensure that the Replace command will not work on the word client should it appear in the text or within a larger word. Save this document for reuse.

When you need a proposal, just replace *client* with the client's real name. To do this:

1. Move the cursor to the beginning of the document by pressing Home, Home, up arrow

2. Press the Replace key (Alt-F2)

This prompt will appear on your screen:

> w/Confirm?(Y/N)

3. Type **Y** if you want to visually check each location before a replacement occurs

Or

3. Type **N** if you want all occurrences of *client* replaced without first viewing them

Since *client* is a rare combination of letters it's probably safe to type N.

When this prompt appears:

> →Srch:

4. Type **\*client\***

5. Press Search (F2)

This prompt appears on your screen:

> Replace with:

The prompt is asking you what you will use to replace *client*.

**6.** Type **your client's name**

Once you have typed the real name:

**7.** Press →Search (F2)

The cursor will move through the document, stopping at each occurrence of *client* automatically replacing it with your client's name, or WordPerfect will ask you to: Confirm? (Y/N)N. When all of the occurrences of *client* have been replaced, the cursor will stop. At that point you can save, print, or edit the document as you would any document.

## Using Replace To Replace Commands

A very powerful use of the Replace function is finding hidden codes and either marking them or removing them. Using Replace to replace commands can be a great time-saver for jobs such as:

- Removing tabs selectively

- Removing margin settings

- Removing all hard page breaks

- Removing hard returns at the end of ASCII text lines

In WordPerfect you cannot search for commands with specific settings. For example, you cannot search for [Margin Set:1,65]. You can, however, find all occurrences of the command [Margin Set]. The other limitation you must be aware of as you replace commands is you cannot use a hidden code to replace another hidden code.

A technique you might find useful is searching for and selectively deleting hidden codes. For example, assume you want to remove a number of margins throughout your document:

**1.** Move the cursor to a location in your document that precedes the margin settings

**2.** Press the Replace key (Alt-F2)

This prompt appears on your screen:

w/Confirm? (Y/N)

**3.** Type **Y**

You'll have the opportunity to say yes or no to any replacement.

This prompt appears on your screen:

→Srch:

**4.** Press the function key and select the menu item of the hidden command you're replacing

In this example, press Line Format (Shift-F8) then choose 3 Margin. Notice that you won't be able to enter the specific margin settings you are looking for, but the prompt will indicate that WordPerfect is searching for a margin setting.

→Srch:[Margin Set]

**5.** Press the →Search key (F2) to continue

This prompt appears on your screen:

Replace with:

You cannot replace [Margin Set] with another code, but you can replace it with a *character string* (group of characters) or with nothing.

Since this example removes the margin settings, replace the [Margin Set] codes with nothing. Pressing the →Search key (F2) after the Replace with: prompt enters nothing.

From this point on the cursor will move to each margin setting and ask if you want it replaced. If you press Y then the margin code will be replaced with nothing. Type N to leave a margin code intact.

In some instances you will want to replace hidden codes with easily identified characters so you can return to make editing changes. In this case, enter the characters you've selected after the Replace with: prompt.

Using the Replace command can save time if you need to transfer a WordPerfect document to a word processor for which there is no document converter. To prepare your document for transfer, scroll through the document and replace hidden codes with appropriate characters. For example, replace [Tab] with the characters *Tab*.

Replace all the major hidden codes with characters and then save your WordPerfect document as an ASCII text file using the Text In/Out key

(Ctrl-F5). Nearly all word processors can read an ASCII text file. The user on the receiving word processor can replace your *Tab* characters with the appropriate command for the receiving word processor.

The Replace command also can save you considerable time if you receive an ASCII text file from someone else. ASCII files from word processors, databases, or spreadsheets have a hard return [HRt] (Enter key) at the end of each line. The codes prevent sentences from word wrapping when you add or delete text. To remove unwanted hard returns follow these steps:

    **1.** Replace all double [HRt][HRt] with **

Now, paragraph ends are marked with **

    **2.** Replace all single [HRt] with **nothing** (as described in the [Tab] example)

Lines will word wrap. If you find that words at the beginning and the end of lines merge, replace [HRt] with a space.

    **3.** Replace all ** with **[HRt][HRt]**

And, the end of paragraph marks are inserted in the document.

If the ASCII document has naturally occurring asterisks in the text you may need to select a different place holder.

# Adding Nonprinting Document Comments

One of the handiest features offered by WordPerfect 4.2 is the feature that permits you to add hidden comments to your writing—comments that don't appear in the printed document. The feature is a great aid when it's important to add notes to yourself while editing your own work, when analyzing work done by another, or when questioning an author whose work you are editing. The comments you insert are displayed on the screen inside a double-lined box like the one illustrated in figure 7.1.

To add a nonprinting comment:

    **1.** Move the cursor to the location on your screen where you want the first line of the comment to appear

    **2.** Press the Text In/Out key (Ctrl-F5)

    **3.** Select **B** Create Comment when the menu appears

```
The comments you type will appear on screen inside the double-
lined box. They will not print. If a comment box is used in the
middle of a sentence, you can move to the adjacent part of the
sentence with the right or left cursor arrow.

Delete Comments by going to Reveal Codes, Alt-F3, and using Del
or Backspace to remove the [Smry/Cmnt:] code.

╔═══════════════════════════════════════════════════════════════╗
║ This is an example of a Document Comment that can be entered in ║
║ WordPerfect 4.2 documents. Within this double-lined box you or your editor ║
║ can type comments that will help you improve or explain your work. You can ║
║ choose whether Document Comments display on the typing screen. The ║
║ Document Comment will not print. ║
╚═══════════════════════════════════════════════════════════════╝

(d)Editing Document Comments
When you need to edit a document comment, move the cursor
directly after where the comment appears on the screen, then
press the Text/In Out key, Ctrl-F5. When the menu appears select
C Edit Comment. Use normal WordPerfect editing procedures to edit
the comment. Press Exit, F7, when you are finished editing. Press
Cancel, F1, to disregard edits you have made.

C:\WP\WP42\CH7\CH7WK12.WP                    Doc 1  Pg 5  Ln 17    Pos 1
```

*Fig. 7.1. Nonprinting document comments.*

A double-lined box will appear at the top of the screen. You can type as many as 1,024 characters in the box.

4. Type your **comments**

5. Press the Exit key (F7)

If you use a comment box in the middle of a sentence, you can move to the words that lie adjacent to the box with the right or left cursor arrow.

## Editing Document Comments

To edit a document comment:

1. Move the cursor to the space that follows the last character in the comment

2. Press the Text/In Out key (Ctrl-F5)

3. Select **C** Edit Comment when the menu appears

4. Edit the comment using normal WordPerfect editing procedures

**5.** Press Exit (F7)

Or

**5.** Press Cancel (F1) to disregard edits you have made

## Hiding Document Comments

During routine typing you may not want document comment boxes cluttering your screen. During the editing and analysis phases of document creation however, comments *are* important; display them.

Switch between displaying and hiding comment boxes:

**1.** Press Ctrl-F5 to display the Text In/Out menu

**2.** Select **D** Display Summary and Comments

This prompt appears on your screen:

    Display Summary?(Y/N)

**3.** Type **Y** to display the comment box

Or

**3.** Type **N** to hide the comment box

Even when document comments are hidden, you can see them from the View option on the List Files menu. On the Reveal Codes screen you can see the first 100 characters after the [Smry/Cmnt:].

Delete comments by pressing the Reveal Codes key (Alt-F3) and using Del or Backspace to remove the [Smry/Cmnt:] code.

# Checking for Misspellings and Typographical Errors

WordPerfect's Speller is fast and easy to use. You can use the Speller to check a single word, to check a page of text, or to check your entire document for misspelling.

Because the Speller uses a phonetic matching system, it can identify the correct spelling of a word when, although you have misspelled the word, that misspelled word sounds like the correct spelling. An example is the misspelled word *peeple*. Although the word is misspelled, WordPerfect will identify the correct spelling *people*.

You can add words to the Speller dictionary and create specialized dictionaries that contain words commonly used in your profession. Often,

WordPerfect users create specialized dictionaries to house the technical jargon that is an accepted part of most technical and scientific environments. The Speller can even check for double words—the repetition of the same word in succession, such as to to.

**Note:** If you are using WordPerfect for the IBM PS/2, the Speller *and* the Thesaurus files are combined on one 3 1/2-inch master disk labeled *Speller/Thesaurus*. PS/2 users should keep this combination in mind when encountering subsequent references to the *Speller* disk.

## Spell Files

You will find three files on your *Speller* master disk. WordPerfect's dictionary is in the file named LEX.WP. This file contains a main word list and a common word list. The Speller first checks for words in the common word list (a list of frequently used words).

If the word isn't found there, the Speller checks the main word list. The words that you add to the dictionary during the spell-check process are stored in the file named {WP}LEX.SUP, the supplemental word list. The LEX.WP and {WP}LEX.SUP files are the files WordPerfect uses to check your documents.

WordPerfect also supplies a file named SPELL.EXE. By typing SPELL from the DOS prompt you can add to or remove words from the dictionary. With SPELL you can also create files of words for separate dictionaries.

WordPerfect 4.2 has a few corrections to the LEX.WP dictionary file. If you have added many words to the WordPerfect 4.1 dictionary you may want to continue using the WordPerfect 4.1 dictionary with WordPerfect 4.2. Be careful when copying files from the WordPerfect 4.2 master disks so that you only copy SPELL.EXE onto your working disk. If you want to keep your previous dictionary, do not copy the new LEX.WP on top of the older LEX.WP. Any supplementary dictionaries you have created in WordPerfect 4.1 will continue to work with WordPerfect 4.2.

Because the Speller dictionary requires a large amount of disk storage it must remain on its own 360K disk.

## Starting the Speller on a Dual Floppy Disk System

Before checking the spelling in a document, be sure that you have saved the document on the disk in Drive B. Once the document is saved remove the disk (from Drive B). Insert your copy of the Speller disk in Drive B. Do not remove the WordPerfect Program disk from Drive A. The WordPerfect disk must reside in Drive A while the Speller is being used in Drive B.

When you are finished checking spelling, put your working disk back in
Drive B. If you forget to put the working disk in Drive B you will save
your documents onto the Spelling disk. (That's not a problem, but it is
inconvenient and a waste of time.)

## Starting the Speller on a Hard Disk System

If your WordPerfect program is loaded on the hard disk, the Spell files are
immediately available. You won't have to switch disks. For the Spell
function to work correctly the spelling files must be in the same
subdirectory as WP.EXE. Refer to Chapter 17 for more information.

## Checking a Word, a Page, or an Entire Document

To run the Speller, press Spell (Ctrl-F2).

The Spell menu appears at the bottom of the screen as shown in figure
7.2. You can choose from six menu options: Word, Page, Document,
Change Dictionary, Look Up, and Count. Each of the options is described
in the text that follows. If you press any key other than the menu choices
(after the Spell menu appears) you'll exit the Speller and return to your
text file.

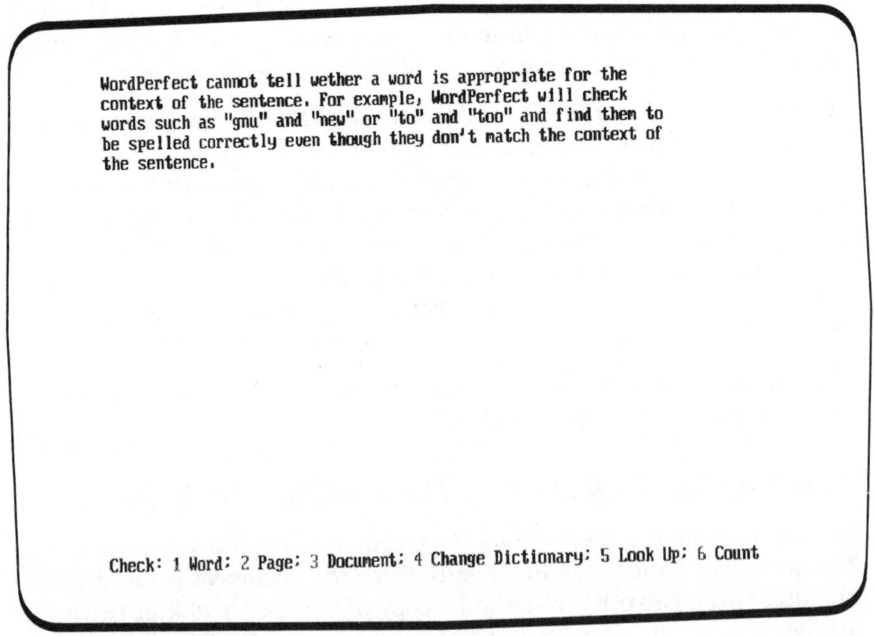

```
        WordPerfect cannot tell wether a word is appropriate for the
        context of the sentence. For example, WordPerfect will check
        words such as "gnu" and "new" or "to" and "too" and find them to
        be spelled correctly even though they don't match the context of
        the sentence.
```

```
        Check: 1 Word; 2 Page; 3 Document; 4 Change Dictionary; 5 Look Up; 6 Count
```

*Fig. 7.2. The Spell menu.*

To check the spelling of one word only, or to check just one word at a time: place the cursor anywhere in the word you want to check, press the Spell key (Ctrl-F2), and choose 1 Word.

If the word that lies above the cursor is misspelled (or cannot be matched in the dictionary), the Speller pauses, highlights or *tags* the word, and offers a choice of correct words. If the Speller finds the word that lies above the cursor in the dictionary, it is assumed to be correct, and the cursor jumps to the next word in your document. Figure 7.3 illustrates how a list of words is displayed when the incorrectly spelled *wether* appears in text being checked.

When you select option 2 Page or 3 Document on the first Spell menu, the program checks every word, on the page or in the document, against the dictionary. Headers, footers, and footnotes also are checked as part of the text. Chapter 9 discusses headers, footers, and footnotes.

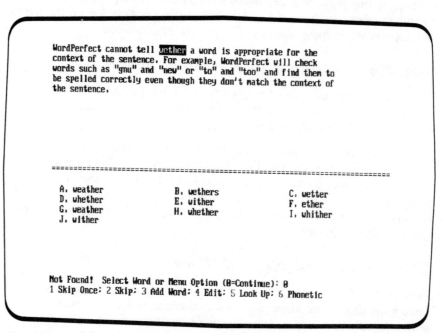

Fig. 7.3. A list of alternate spellings for the incorrect "wether."

To replace the highlighted word with a word from the dictionary list, type the letter preceding the dictionary's word. If you do not find a suitable replacement among the words listed, you can choose from the menu options listed at the bottom of the screen. This Spell menu offers the following options: Skip Once, Skip, Add Word, Edit, Look Up, and Phonetic.

## Skip Once/Skip: Skipping a Highlighted Word

If you seldom use the highlighted word and it is spelled correctly, you can skip it once by typing 1, Skip Once. To skip the word through the rest of the document, type 2, Skip. Although the Speller contains many commonly used proper names and acronyms, most of the words unrecognized by the Speller will be proper names or terminology specific to a particular subject.

The WordPerfect Speller stops the first time that WordPerfect encounters *character strings* that begin with a number. A character string is simply a series of characters that appear together; the word *character* is considered a string. At this point, you can instruct the Speller to skip words that contain numbers, such as 2nd or 5th, by selecting option 3 from the menu that appears when these numbered words are encountered.

## Add Word: Adding a Word to the Dictionary

If you use a highlighted word frequently and want WordPerfect to recognize it in the future, add the word to the dictionary. Make sure the word is spelled correctly, and type 3, Add Word.

WordPerfect takes a moment to add the word to the dictionary, and automatically resumes the spelling check. As soon as you add a word to the dictionary, WordPerfect begins recognizing that word. Any unit or group of characters, such as a company name, client's name, mathematical formula, or hyphenated family name, can be treated as a word and can be added to the dictionary.

## Edit: Editing a Highlighted Word

Sometimes a word is misspelled, but the dictionary does not suggest the correct spelling. If you know the correct spelling, you can correct the word manually by typing 4, Edit. A prompt instructs you to make the correction using normal editing keys and then press Enter. When WordPerfect is in Edit mode, you can use the keyboard as you usually do. After you press the Enter key, the spelling check continues.

## Look Up: Looking Up a Word

Look Up is option 5 on both the initial Spell menu and the menu displayed during the spelling check. You use this option to look up a word and check its spelling (if it's in the dictionary). Look Up can be used to locate the correct spelling of the highlighted word or any word for that matter! Look Up is great if a crossword puzzle has you stumped.

When you select Look Up, WordPerfect displays the prompt Word Pattern: at the bottom of the screen. You can type as much of the word as you know to be correct and use *wild cards* to fill in the unknown characters.

For example, if you can't spell hippopotamus, but you know it starts with *hip* and ends with an *s*, you can type *hip\*s* and press Enter.

You will see a list of all words that have hip as the first three letters and end with an s. There could be any number of different letters in between, because the asterisk (*) is a wild card symbol that represents any number of characters. Use a question mark (?) instead of an asterisk as a wild card for exactly one character.

You can mix wild cards in your pattern. For example the Look Up pattern of *p?rf\*t* will return *parfait* and *perfect*. The pattern *p\*rf\*t* returns *pluperfect* because the two *'s can match any group of one or more characters. The only restriction on words returned is that they start with *p*, end with *t*, and have *rf* somewhere in between.

## Phonetic Checking

The last option for handling a misspelling is a phonetic lookup for the highlighted word. Menu item 6 Phonetic checks the dictionary for words that sound like the word at the cursor position. Although WordPerfect automatically makes some phonetic suggestions, this choice forces the Speller to repeat its search for words with similar phonetic spelling.

## Double Words

The Speller causes the cursor to stop on a word that occurs two times in succession. Figure 7.4 illustrates the *double word* feature of WordPerfect's Speller.

When a double word is found, the program displays the Double Word menu shown at the bottom of figure 7.4. This menu enables you to skip over the first occurrence of *you*, delete the second occurrence automatically, edit the text, or turn off the double-word checking feature.

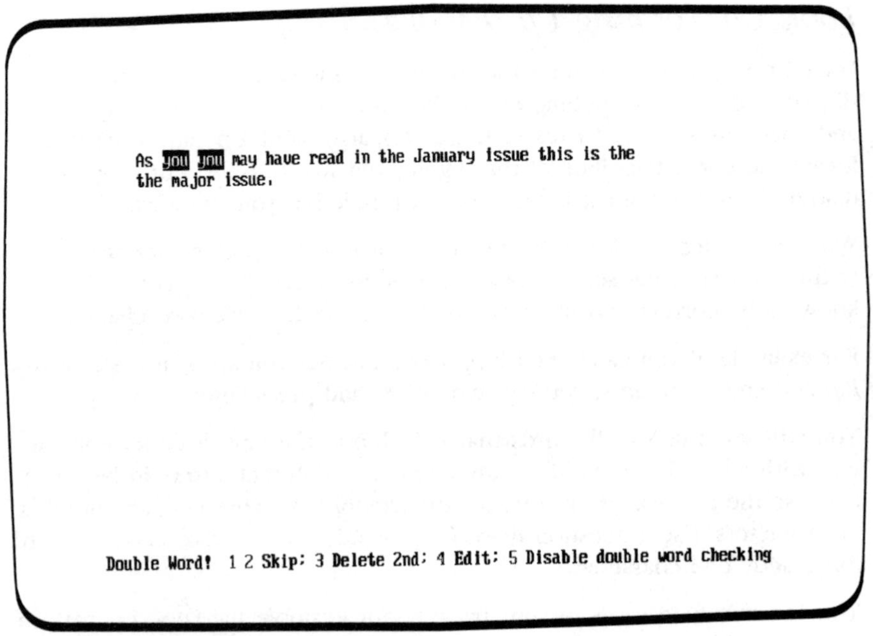

```
As ███ ███ may have read in the January issue this is the
the major issue.










Double Word?  1 2 Skip: 3 Delete 2nd: 4 Edit: 5 Disable double word checking
```

Fig. 7.4. WordPerfect's double-word Spell feature.

## Apparent Misspelled Words

WordPerfect cannot tell whether a word is used appropriately in the
context of a sentence. For example, WordPerfect will check words such as
*gnu* and *new* or *to* and *too* and decide that they are spelled correctly,
even though they are used inappropriately in the sentence.

## Changing Dictionaries

You can move to and from any special dictionaries you create. To change
to a specialized dictionary, choose 4 Change Dictionary from the initial
Spell menu. If you want to keep the main dictionary the same and change
only the supplementary dictionary, then enter the name of the
supplementary dictionary but press Enter when asked for the main
dictionary. Type the disk, path name, and file name of those supplemental
dictionaries you want to use in the spelling check.

The "Altering the Speller Dictionary" section in this chapter explains how
you can create a supplemental dictionary.

## Counting Words

Everytime you run the Speller on a page of text, a block of text, or an entire document, WordPerfect counts the words. If you want a word count at any other time, you can select option 6 on the Spell menu. Option 6 instructs WordPerfect to count the words in a file without checking the spelling.

## Spell-checking a Block

If the section of text you want to spell check is something other than a word, a page, or an entire document, block the text you want checked before pressing the Spell key. To check a block, move to the first character in the text you want checked, and press the Block key (Alt-F4). Move the cursor to the end of the block and press the Spell key (Ctrl-F2). The program checks the highlighted words only.

## Exiting the Speller

To exit the Speller, press Cancel (F1) until the typing screen appears. On a floppy disk system, remove the Speller disk from Drive B and insert your data disk (the disk on which you have stored your document).

## Altering the Speller Dictionary

With the WordPerfect Speller Utility, you can customize the Speller dictionary. You also can create your supplemental dictionaries for special purposes. You should also check with WordPerfect Corporation and your state and national legal or medical associations for special WordPerfect supplemental dictionaries.

The easiest way to add a number of words to a Speller dictionary is to create a WordPerfect document that lists each word on a separate line. Remember the name of your file so that you can use it when you run the *Speller Utility* (which is explained in a later paragraph). You can view the words in a LEX.WP or a .SUP supplemental dictionary by retrieving them just as you retrieve any other WordPerfect document.

"Word" is defined to mean any string of characters that neither begins with a number, nor contains any spaces. If a space is required, as is true with some foreign phrases, you must use a hard space (press the Home key then the space bar) between the characters.

To use the Speller Utility if you are using a dual floppy disk system:

**1.** Exit to DOS

**2.** Replace the WordPerfect Program disk in Drive A with the Speller disk

**3.** Insert your dictionary or word file data disk in Drive B

After the prompt B:>

**4.** Type **A:SPELL**

If you are using a hard disk, the SPELL.EXE file should be in the WordPerfect subdirectory. If SPELL.EXE is not in the directory you will receive an error message. In that case, after the prompt C:>

**1.** Type **SPELL**

The Speller Utility menu shown in figure 7.5 appears.

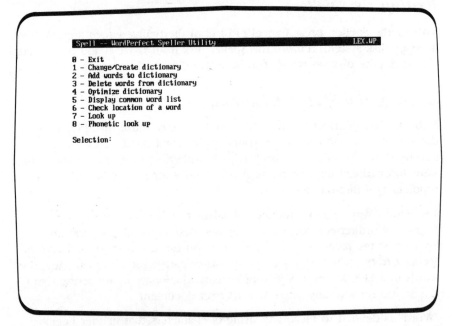

```
Spell -- WordPerfect Speller Utility                    LEX.WP

0 - Exit
1 - Change/Create dictionary
2 - Add words to dictionary
3 - Delete words from dictionary
4 - Optimize dictionary
5 - Display common word list
6 - Check location of a word
7 - Look up
8 - Phonetic look up

Selection:
```

*Fig. 7.5. The Speller Utility menu.*

If you use special terminology (legal or medical terms, for instance), or if you want to add the names of your clients and their businesses to your dictionary, create a supplemental dictionary housing only those terms. You can add single words to the dictionary or create a list of words as described earlier.

You must select 1 Change/Create dictionary to either change to a different dictionary, or to create a new dictionary, before you make any other choice from the Speller Utility menu shown in figure 7.5.

Add words to the dictionary you have chosen by selecting 2 Add words to dictionary. Typing 2 causes WordPerfect to display the Add Words menu shown in figure 7.6. From this menu you can enter the name of the file containing additional words, or you can add individual words by typing them directly from the keyboard.

*Fig. 7.6. The Add Words menu.*

Add individual words by choosing option 1 or 3 and typing in the words. If you are adding words that you have already typed as a list into a WordPerfect file, then select option 2 or 4. After you type the file name and press Enter, all the words in that file are added to the Speller dictionary. Any word you add to the common word list is automatically added to the main dictionary. Make sure you enter all the words, or the file name, before pressing Enter because one word can take as long as many words to be added to the dictionary.

Delete words from the dictionary using the same method. Select 3 Delete words from dictionary, from the Speller Utility menu. The Delete Words menu will display as shown in figure 7.7. This menu permits you to enter, from the keyboard, the word(s) to be deleted. You can delete an entire file of words by entering the name of the file containing the words to be deleted.

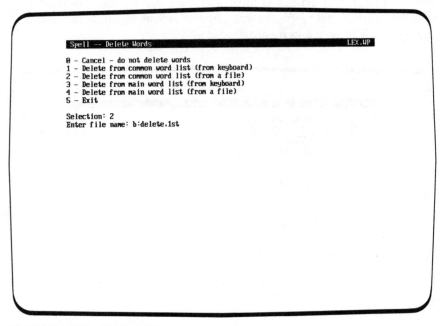

```
Spell -- Delete Words                                    LEX.WP
  0 - Cancel - do not delete words
  1 - Delete from common word list (from keyboard)
  2 - Delete from common word list (from a file)
  3 - Delete from main word list (from keyboard)
  4 - Delete from main word list (from a file)
  5 - Exit

Selection: 2
Enter file name: b:delete.lst
```

Fig. 7.7. The Delete Words menu.

After you have created a new dictionary you must *optimize* it by choosing 4 Optimize Dictionary from the Speller Utility menu (illustrated in fig. 7.5). Selecting 5 Display common word list displays the words on the common word list. The first screen of the common word list is shown in figure 7.8.

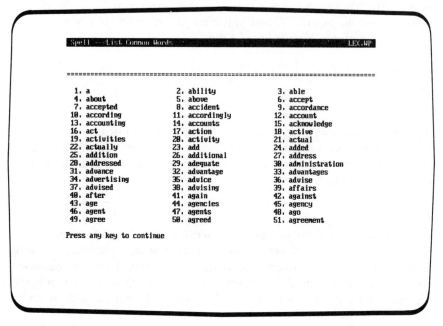

Fig. 7.8. The List Common Words menu.

Choosing option 6 Check location of a word, from the Speller Utility Menu, displays this prompt:

Word to check:

SPELL checks to see whether the word appears in the main or common word list.

Options 7 and 8, Look up and Phonetic look up, work much the same as spell check. *Look up* prompts for the word pattern, and *Phonetic look up* prompts for a phonetically similar spelling to the word you want to check.

# Using the Thesaurus
# To Find Alternate Words

The Thesaurus is similar to a dictionary but the Thesaurus contains synonyms, words with the same or similar meaning. The Thesaurus in WordPerfect 4.2 will provide antonyms, words with the opposite meaning, as well. The Thesaurus permits you to request synonyms for a specific word in your document, request synonyms of synonyms, and request synonyms for words outside of your file.

## ■ Warning

Be careful when using the Thesaurus. Please don't obfuscate the obvious! The Thesaurus is a valuable communication tool when you use it to find words that clearly state your intent or when you use it to find dramatic alternatives for overused words.

Don't use the Thesaurus to make your writing *sound* sophisticated. It never works. The *Wall Street Journal* is written at an eighth-grade reading level; not because subscribers read at the eighth-grade level, but because writing at the eighth-grade level demands that journalists select words that are clear and concise. Information can be absorbed more quickly if you select your words to communicate ideas clearly.

As noted previously, if you are using WordPerfect for the IBM PS/2, the Speller *and* the Thesaurus files are combined on one 3 1/2-inch master disk labeled *Speller/Thesaurus*. Keep this combination in mind when encountering subsequent references to the *Thesaurus* disk.

## *Starting the Thesaurus on a Dual Floppy Disk System*

To use the Thesaurus on a dual floppy disk system:

    **1.** Remove the data disk from Drive B and insert the Thesaurus disk

The WordPerfect program disk must remain in Drive A. Don't forget to put the disk that contains the document back in Drive B when you have finished with the Thesaurus.

## *Starting the Thesaurus on a Hard Disk System*

To use the Thesaurus on a hard disk system, you must copy the Thesaurus disk to the WordPerfect directory on the hard disk.

## Replacing a Word

The example text at the top of figure 7.9 contains a word that interrupts the natural flow of the sentence. To find an alternate (and clearer) word, move the cursor anywhere in the word *obfuscates*, and press the Thesaurus key (Alt-F1).

The text surrounding *obfuscates* moves to the top of the screen, as shown in figure 7.9. The majority of the screen surface is used to display alternative words from the Thesaurus.

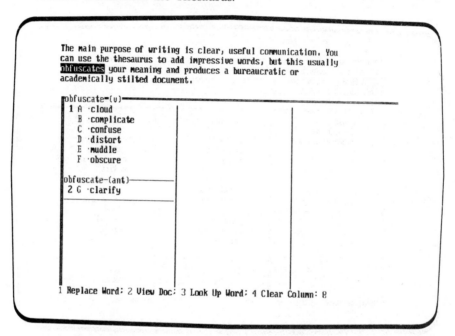

The main purpose of writing is clear, useful communication. You
can use the thesaurus to add impressive words, but this usually
obfuscates your meaning and produces a bureaucratic or
academically stilted document.

```
obfuscate-(v)
  1 A ·cloud
    B ·complicate
    C ·confuse
    D ·distort
    E ·muddle
    F ·obscure

obfuscate-(ant)
  2 G ·clarify
```

1 Replace Word: 2 View Doc: 3 Look Up Word: 4 Clear Column: 8

*Fig. 7.9. Finding alternate words.*

As illustrated in the left column on the lower part of the screen, the Thesaurus suggests six synonyms and one antonym for *obfuscate*. The words displayed are six verbs (v), and an antonym (ant). But, for other words there also might be nouns, verbs, adjectives, and antonyms. A letter—and in some cases, a dot—precedes each word. The dot indicates that the word is a *headword*. WordPerfect will provide additional synonym suggestions for headwords.

To replace *obfuscates* you must type 1 Replace Word, and type the letter that appears before the alternate word (typing *A* selects *Cloud*, for example).

## Finding More Alternatives

Suppose you decide that the word *obscure* is a good alternative to *obfuscate*. Before choosing *obscure*, you'll probably want to see what words are alternatives to *obscure*.

*Obscure* is preceded by a dot which means there are alternatives in the Thesaurus. To see the selection of alternate words, type the letter F. The selection of synonyms and antonyms for *obscure* appears as shown in figure 7.10.

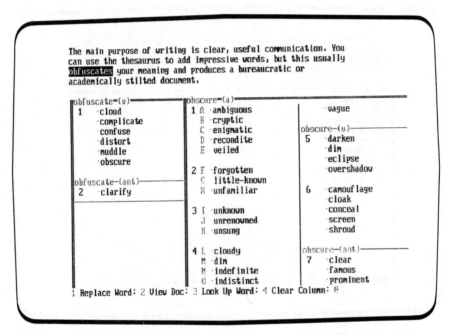

Fig. 7.10. Finding an alternate for "obscure."

Notice that the leading letters and dots before each alternative moved into the columns holding alternatives for the word obscure. You can now choose one of these words to replace the original obfuscate. Just press 1 for Replace Word, then type the letter preceding the word you want inserted. After you make your choice, you are returned to the normal typing screen.

## Clearing a Column

Choosing 4 Clear Column erases the columns of suggested alternatives. To clear the words from a column in the Thesaurus, use the left- and right-arrow keys to activate the column that you want to clear. Then select option 4 on the Thesaurus menu to clear that column.

## Moving the Cursor in Thesaurus Columns

Notice that when the synonyms for *obscure* appear (see fig. 7.10), the letters preceding the words in the list move into columns two and three. You can move the selection letters from column to column by pressing the left- and right-arrow keys. To select a word from the Thesaurus the word must be preceded by a letter.

To see those synonyms that extend beyond the portion of the screen that is currently displayed, use the cursor movement commands: the up- and down-arrow keys, PgUp, PgDn, and the plus (+) and minus (–) keys on the numeric keypad.

To move the cursor to a subgroup, a numbered group of words in the current column, use the Go To command (Ctrl-Home [number]). Home-Home-up arrow moves the cursor to the first subgroup, and Home-Home-down arrow moves the cursor to the last subgroup in the current column.

## Viewing a Word in Context

After viewing several synonyms, you may not be sure which one best fits in the context of your sentence. Checking each word in the context of individual sentences is difficult because the Thesaurus occupies most of the screen; you see only four (or fewer) lines of your document.

To check the context of the original word in the document, press 2 View Doc. Pressing 2 moves the cursor into the document at the top of the screen. Now, scroll the text and read the document. After checking the word within the context of the sentence, press Exit (F7) or press Enter to bring the cursor back to the Thesaurus menu.

## Looking Up Words

You also can locate synonyms for a word that is not a headword or a word that is not in your document. You'll need to do this if no alternate words are displayed when you enter the Thesaurus, or when there is no appropriate headword in the Thesaurus list.

Press the Thesaurus key (Alt-F1). The cursor location doesn't matter. If the cursor is on or following a word, you can ignore the Thesaurus's suggestions. Press 3 Look Up Word, and after the prompt, Word:, type a word similar to the word for which you'd like an alternative. Use your imagination to come up with a "seed" word that will produce more alternatives. If the cursor rests on a blank line, the Word: prompt immediately displays at the bottom of the screen.

The functions presented in this chapter will help you create and edit with a keener appreciation for the impact that clear and concise written communication has on all of us.

Using WordPerfect as a writing tool allows you the luxury of getting your ideas on the screen as quickly as they come to you—while they are fresh.

After you've recorded your thoughts, the next step in the writing process involves reorganizing the text (using the Move commands) so that your ideas are presented in the order that seems to make the most sense.

An often overlooked, but very important, next step requires that you review what you have written for spelling, grammar, and punctuation errors. WordPerfect's Spelling check and Search and Replace functions provide invaluable aid as you perform, what are usually, tedious manual tasks.

To add the coat of professional polish (that makes all the difference in how people respond to your words!), use WordPerfect's Thesaurus to help you select the clearest, most accurate, and most dramatic words with which you can carry your ideas to the reader.

It can't be overemphasized that you should use the Thesaurus to improve the clarity of your text as well as to add vitality to your writing. Don't hide your ideas in bureaucratic and pompous words or in academic stuffiness. Look for alternate ways of saying things!

Now that you have "done all that you can do" with the words in your document, go on to Chapter 8 where you will explore refining the *arrangement* of your text.

# Formatting Document Text

**W**e all have our own ideas about how the words that make up our letters, reports, and memos should be organized on the printed page. Some of us prefer business letters printed with ragged-right margins; others like the end of each line of text to fall perfectly even with the right margin. While you may prefer a memo that always includes an indented topic line, your boss may prefer a memo format that does not. In this chapter, you will learn how to format (and reformat) document text.

*Format* is the word used to describe the layout or design of your text on the printed page. Although WordPerfect permits you to make many format changes, you first should know how to change the margins and the tabs. A simple alteration in margin or tab setting can change the visual impact of your document dramatically.

With WordPerfect you can create as many as seven tab formats. The Tab formatting option alone permits you to create newspaper-style columns of text, columns of numbers for financial reports, personnel rosters, and so on. And, you can vary the type of column you use throughout your document—as many times as you want. Changes in margin settings permit you to create a very formal-looking document by specifying *full justification*, causing text to align on the right margin. For a less structured format, you might turn full justification off and use *ragged-right* margins.

But don't just read about these formatting options; place *Using WordPerfect,* 3rd Edition, beside your keyboard and experiment as you read!

This chapter also explores several line spacing options. With WordPerfect, you can triple-space your printed work to make your editing tasks easier; or you can double-space your personnel reports for easy reading; or you can half-space a lengthy list of telephone numbers.

This chapter is all about formatting your text—that is, planning how your words will appear on the printed page. Chapter 9 goes one step further and explores how you can format the pages that make up your document.

# Changing Margins

WordPerfect's default margins are 10 left and 74 right—approximate margins for 8 1/2-by-11-inch U.S. business letters. Full left-to-right margins for 10 *pitch* (the number of characters per inch) on paper 8 1/2 inches wide are 0 left and 85 right. For wider paper or smaller pitch, you can extend the right margin to 250. Pica type is 10 pitch and Elite type is 12 pitch.

Before changing a margin setting, position the cursor at the left margin of the line where you want the new margin setting to begin. The margin setting you enter will affect all of the text that follows until another margin setting is encountered. New margin settings override previous settings; you can change margins throughout a document.

To change the margins:

1. Move the cursor to the location in your document where you want the new left or right margin to begin

2. Press Line Format (Shift-F8) to display the Line Format menu shown at the bottom of the screen in figure 8.1

3. Type 3 Margins

This prompt appears:

```
[Margin Set] 10 74 to Left =
```

The numbers 10 and 74 represent the left- and right-default margin settings. Since the current margin settings are displayed in the prompt, your prompt may display different numbers if you have previously changed from the default margins in the document.

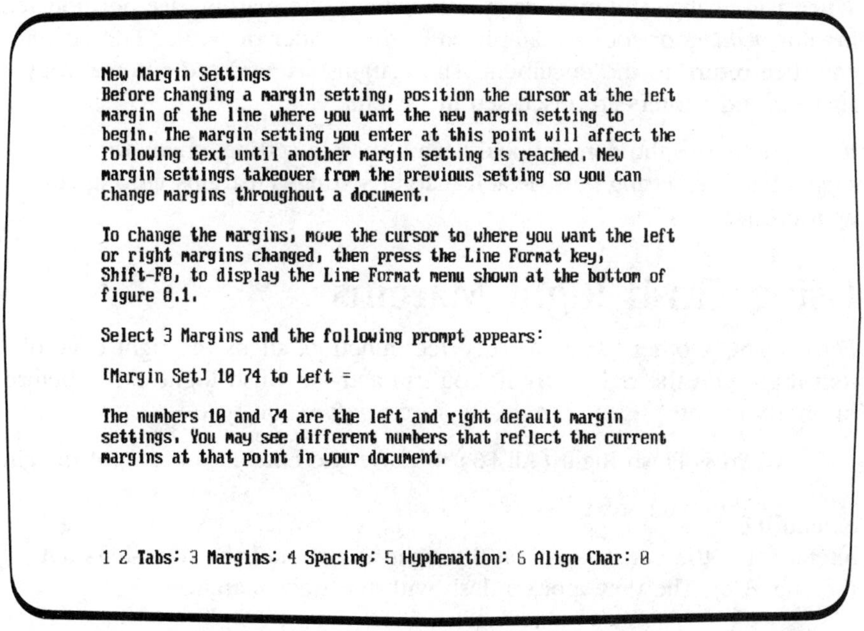

New Margin Settings
Before changing a margin setting, position the cursor at the left
margin of the line where you want the new margin setting to
begin. The margin setting you enter at this point will affect the
following text until another margin setting is reached. New
margin settings takeover from the previous setting so you can
change margins throughout a document.

To change the margins, move the cursor to where you want the left
or right margins changed, then press the Line Format key,
Shift-F8, to display the Line Format menu shown at the bottom of
figure 8.1.

Select 3 Margins and the following prompt appears:

[Margin Set] 10 74 to Left =

The numbers 10 and 74 are the left and right default margin
settings. You may see different numbers that reflect the current
margins at that point in your document.

1 2 Tabs; 3 Margins; 4 Spacing; 5 Hyphenation; 6 Align Char: 0

*Fig. 8.1. Line Format menu.*

After the equal sign (=):

4. Type the **new left margin**

5. Press Enter

When the prompt Right = appears

6. Type the **new right margin**

7. Press Enter

Pressing Cancel at this time won't cancel the margin command. You must use Reveal Codes (Alt-F3) to delete the [Margin Set:] code. The margin code that precedes the code you've deleted then takes control of the margin settings. Saving your document to disk will save new margin settings.

Documents lacking embedded margin codes assume the margin setting of the document or blank screen into which they are retrieved. If you exchange copies of your documents with colleagues, you should either agree on a standard default margin setting or insert a margin setting at the beginning of your documents. If you do not, margin settings may be inconsistent when they are retrieved.

When you change the margins in a document, the margins are not updated in your *headers* or *footers*. Simply enter the Header or Footer Edit screen and then return to the document. The margins are updated automatically. Headers and Footers are discussed in Chapter 9.

If you rarely use the conventional default margin setting, check the suggestions for setting new default margin settings (margins used at start-up) in Chapter 17.

## Using Flush Right Margins

*Flush Right*, another useful WordPerfect function, aligns the right edge of text flush with the right margin. You can activate Flush Right either before or after you enter text. To right-align text *before* you type:

1. Press Flush Right (Alt-F6) to move the cursor to the right margin

2. Type your text

As you type, the cursor stays on the right margin and the text shifts left (see fig. 8.2). The text appears flush with the right margin.

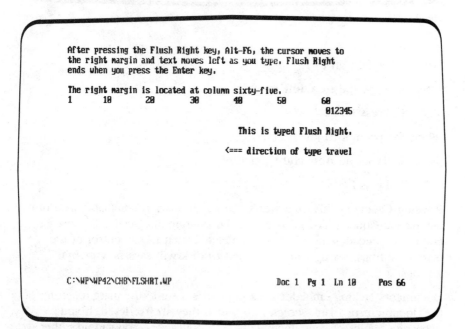

Fig. 8.2. Flush right margins.

To align *existing* text with the right margin:

1. Place the cursor at the beginning of the text

2. Press Flush Right (Alt-F6)

3. Press the down-arrow key

   Or

3. Press the right-arrow key

When you first use Flush Right to align the text, some of the text may disappear from the right edge of the screen (similar to what has happened in fig. 8.3) but pressing the down-arrow key adjusts the text.

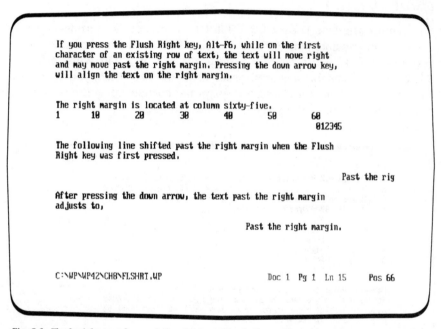

```
If you press the Flush Right key, Alt-F6, while on the first
character of an existing row of text, the text will move right
and may move past the right margin. Pressing the down arrow key,
will align the text on the right margin.

The right margin is located at column sixty-five.
1       10        20        30        40        50        60
                                                          012345

The following line shifted past the right margin when the Flush
Right key was first pressed.

                                                   Past the rig

After pressing the down arrow, the text past the right margin
adjusts to,

                                      Past the right margin.



C:\WP\WP42\CH8\FLSHRT.WP              Doc 1  Pg 1  Ln 15    Pos 66
```

*Fig. 8.3. Flush right text beyond the right margin, before adjustment.*

Flush Right turns off when you press Enter. If you want to make the next line flush right as well, you must give the command again.

You can use two methods to delete a Flush Right command. The easiest method is positioning the cursor at the beginning of the text, pressing the Backspace key, and then typing Y to answer the prompt Delete [Aln/ FlshR] (Y/N). The text is repositioned at the left margin.

To use the second method, enter Reveal Codes (Alt-F3) and delete either the [A] or [a] code surrounding the flush right text.

# Setting Tabs

Generally, tabs are set to mark paragraph beginnings and indents are used to set off quotations, and columns of text and numbers within the body text.

WordPerfect's preset (default) tab settings are spaced five characters apart but you can change the setting by simply pressing the Line Format key (Shift-F8) and following the directions.

## Using the Tab Ruler

You can use the Line Format key (Shift-F8) to change tab settings anywhere in your document. From the Line Format menu, shown at the bottom of the screen in figure 8.1, press either 1 or 2. (In WordPerfect 4.1, choose 1 Tabs for tabs from positions 1 to 159.) When you select 1,2 Tabs, the WordPerfect 4.2 screen displays the current tab settings on a ruler at the bottom of the screen, as shown in figure 8.4.

```
WordPerfect 4.2 has seven types of tab settings to make column
entries easier. These tabs will align text left, right, centered
or aligned on a decimal. They can also precede the entry with a
row of dots. The types of tabs are;

Letter      Alignment         Dot Leader
L           Left aligned          .
R           Right aligned         .
D           Decimal aligned       .
C           Centered

Manually enter these tabs by moving on the tab ruler to the
location where you want the tab and then typing the letter. Move
with the left or right arrow, or use Home-left and Home-right to
move a screen at a time.




....,L....,L....,L....,L....,L....,L....,L....,L....,L....,L....,L....,L....,L..
1234567890123456789012345678901234567890123456789012345678901234567890123456
     10        20        30        40        50        60        70
Delete EOL (clear tabs); Enter number (set tab); Del (clear tab);
Left; Center; Right; Decimal; .= Dot leader; Press EXIT when done.
```

*Fig. 8.4. WordPerfect 4.2 tab ruler.*

WordPerfect 4.2 displays a single ruler that shows the column positions 1 to 79. (WordPerfect 4.1 shows the tab ruler as two rulers, one above the other, and a combined length of 159 columns.)

When you select the Tab menu item, WordPerfect 4.2 moves the cursor from its current column position on the typing screen to the same position on the tab ruler. (In WordPerfect 4.1, the cursor moves to the beginning of the tab ruler line when you select Line Format, 1 Tabs.)

Use the left- and right-arrow keys to move the cursor along the tab ruler at the bottom of the screen. Move to tab locations beyond 79 by pressing the right arrow. (In WordPerfect 4.1, you must select 2 ETabs from the Line Format menu to access tabs beyond 159.)

## Selecting Tab Stops

WordPerfect 4.1 designates tab positions on the tab ruler by an uppercase *T*. The left edge of your typed material aligns on the *T* marker. To set a tab manually, move the cursor to the position where you want the tab and type either an uppercase or a lowercase *T*. The cursor automatically wraps to the lower line of the tab ruler when moved past location 79.

The seven types of tab settings offered by WordPerfect 4.2 make entering column text and characters easy. These tabs align text to the left of the tab marker, to the right of the tab marker, centered around the tab marker, or aligned on a decimal tab marker. They also can precede the entry by a row of dots (dot leader). The types of tabs are

| Letter | Alignment | Dot Leader |
| --- | --- | --- |
| L | Left aligned | . |
| R | Right aligned | . |
| D | Decimal aligned | . |
| C | Centered | |

## Entering Single Tabs

To enter tabs manually:

1. Move the cursor to the position on the tab ruler where you want to set the tab

Use the left- and right-arrow keys or Home, left and Home, right to move a screen at a time.

**2.** Type the **letter** that represents the type of tab

Type an *L* or left-aligned tab for a normal tab; *R* or right-aligned tabs align the right edge of your typing with the tab. These work well for columns of numbers that cannot be aligned on a decimal point. *D*, or decimal tabs, align numbers on the decimal.

**3.** Type a **period** (.) over the L, the R, or the D on the tab ruler

Notice how the letter on the tab stop displays in reverse to indicate that it now has a dot leader.

This dot leader prints a string of dots between the typing at the current tab and at the previous tab. The dot leader is an excellent feature for tables of contents and listings. The periods guide the reader's eye to the page number.

You can set as many as 40 specialized tabs in your document. After you have set 40 specialized tabs, WordPerfect permits you to set only L tabs.

You also can insert new tab positions by typing the number of the position where you want the tab set. For example, if you want a tab at position 32, type 32 and press Enter to set the tab.

If you want another tab at position 50, type 50 over the top of your last number, and press Enter. You can use this method repeatedly to enter new tab stops.

**4.** Press Exit (F7) to record the tab settings

Or, if you've changed your mind:

**4.** Press Cancel (F1) to return to the typing screen without recording the tab setting changes

A hidden tab set code has been embedded in the text at the cursor's location. The new tab stops take effect from the point where you entered the command to the end of the document, or until another tab stop command is encountered. You can change tab stops throughout your documents by invoking another Tab Stop command wherever you want to make a change.

Display and delete tab codes by pressing the Reveal Codes key (Alt-F3).

If you use multiple tab settings at even intervals, make sure you read this section about setting multiple tabs.

## Setting Multiple Tabs

WordPerfect permits you to quickly create evenly spaced columns of text by entering multiple tabs. First preview the section "Deleting Tab Settings" since you'll need to use the Ctrl-End procedure to clear a portion of the tab ruler before setting multiple tabs.

To set the left, L or T, tabs at even intervals:

1. Type the **number of the first new tab position**

2. Type a **comma** (,)

3. Type the **tab interval**

For example, if you want the first tab at 10 and a tab every 14 spaces thereafter: **10,14**

4. Press Enter

The new tabs start at 10 and are marked every 14 character positions.

5. Press Exit (F7) to save these tab settings and to return to the typing screen

To set multiple specialized tabs:

1. Move the cursor to the spot on the tab ruler where you want the first special tab

2. Type the **R, C, D,** or **dot leader** tab that you want to duplicate

3. Type the **location of the first tab**, for example 10

4. Type a **comma** (,)

5. Type the **interval**, for example 14

6. Press Enter

The special tab located at 10 will be duplicated at intervals of 14.

## Creating Extended Tabs

If you want to set tabs beyond position 160 in WordPerfect 4.1, you can select 2 Extended Tabs from the Line Format menu. Tabs must be entered by typing the numbers, such as 180, and then pressing Enter. To enter tabs at intervals, type the first tab, a comma, and the interval (for example, 180,10).

In WordPerfect 4.2, both choices 1 and 2 present the same tab ruler. To set extended tabs in WordPerfect 4.2, move the cursor to the right, to the desired tab position, or type the number of the tab location. To move rapidly through the extended ruler, press the Home key and then press the right- or left-arrow key, or press the End key.

## Deleting Tab Settings

The procedure for deleting specific tabs is the procedure you've used to delete text characters. Move the cursor to the tab you want to delete on the tab ruler and press the Del key. You can move the cursor across the tab line and eliminate or add tabs anywhere you want.

To delete multiple tab settings (all of them at one time), move the cursor on the tab ruler until the tab settings that you want to delete lie to the right of the cursor. Press the Delete to End of Line key (Ctrl-End) to delete all tabs to the right of the cursor. On the typing screen, Delete to End of Line also deletes material from the cursor to the end of the current line of text.

# Creating Indented Text

To use a temporary margin to set off a section of typing, such as a quote or a table, use either the Left Indent key or the Double Indent key.

## Using Left Indents To Create Lists

To indent a paragraph on the left side, press the Left Indent key (F4), which is marked on the template by a right-pointing arrow. The cursor moves to the next tab setting to the right, and you then can begin typing. See figure 8.5 that follows.

The left edge of your typed material aligns with the indent. As soon as you press Enter, the indent is turned off and the typed material returns to the usual margin settings. If you want to indent multiple paragraphs, then you must press the Left Indent key at the beginning of each paragraph.

You can indent an existing paragraph by moving the cursor to the first character in the text you wish to indent, and pressing the Left Indent key (F4). The line of text shifts right, to the next tab stop. Press the down-arrow key to redraw the screen so that the entire paragraph is indented.

```
ITEM              DESCRIPTION
Item 1            This is an item description that is longer
                  than one line. The use of the Left Indent key
                  gives this column of text a clean and even
                  appearance.

Item 2            This is another description that also extends
        beyond one line however; because only a Tab was used to start the
        sentence, each line of text wraps to the left margin.




C:\WP\WP42\CH8\LTINDENT.WP                      Doc 1  Pg 1  Ln 1      Pos 1
```

Fig. 8.5. Left indented lists.

## Creating Double Indents for Quotes

There will be times that you'll need to set off a portion of text from the body copy or to use a direct quotation longer than three lines in your documents. To call attention to a particularly important section of your text, indent both sides of that section of text. Figure 8.6 illustrates text that has been formatted using double indents.

Use the Double Indent key (Shift-F4), shown on your keyboard template as an arrow on each side of Indent. Each time you press this key, WordPerfect indents both the left and the right sides of the text to the next tab position.

To create a double indent, move the cursor to the left margin of the line where you want the indentation to begin. Press Double Indent (Shift-F4) once to indent one tab stop. Type the text. Press Enter to turn off the Double Indent. Text that has been typed already can be indented by this same procedure. Move the cursor to the beginning of the paragraph, and press Shift-F4.

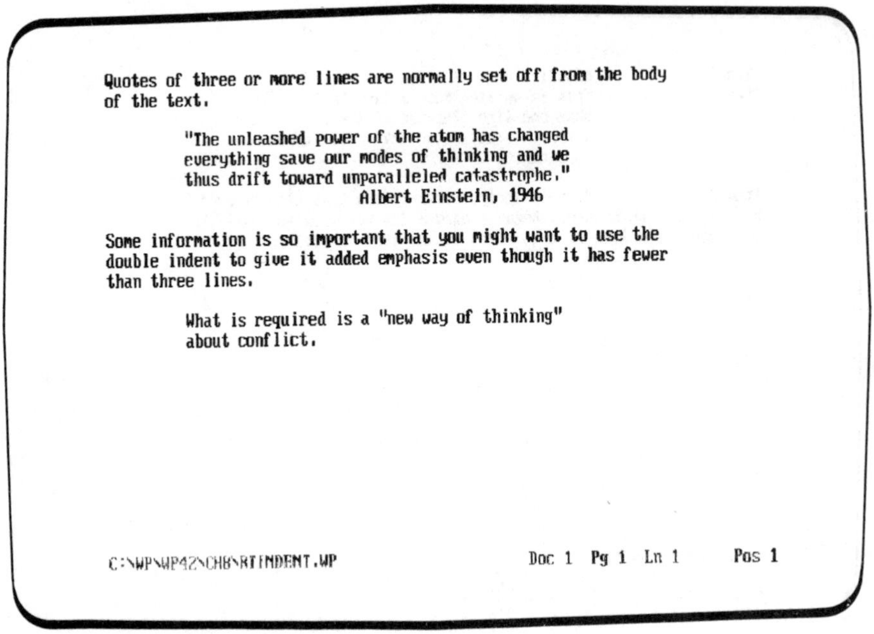

```
    Quotes of three or more lines are normally set off from the body
    of the text.

            "The unleashed power of the atom has changed
            everything save our modes of thinking and we
            thus drift toward unparalleled catastrophe."
                    Albert Einstein, 1946

    Some information is so important that you might want to use the
    double indent to give it added emphasis even though it has fewer
    than three lines.

            What is required is a "new way of thinking"
            about conflict.




    C:\WP\WP42\CHB\RTINDENT.WP              Doc 1  Pg 1  Ln 1       Pos 1
```

*Fig. 8.6. Double indented quotations.*

You can create left and right indents of varying widths by changing the tab setting before the area of the indent and then restoring the original tab setting after the indent.

## Changing Line Spacing

If your document requires more space between each line, use the Line Spacing function. Although you can insert extra lines by pressing Enter, you'll find that adding lines with the Enter key is time-consuming. WordPerfect is preset for single-spaced lines; you may select any spacing option in half-space increments.

To change the line-space setting:

1. Place the cursor at the left margin of the line where you want the new spacing to begin

2. Press Line Format (Shift-F8)

3. Select 4 Spacing

This prompt appears on your screen:

```
[Spacing Set]
```

The prompt is followed by the current spacing number.

**4.** Type the **line spacing interval**

Your entry must be a decimal number in half-space increments. For example, .5 indicates half-space; 1 indicates single-space; 2.5 indicates two and one-half spaces; and 4 indicates four spaces.

**5.** Press Enter

The screen shows how the text will be spaced when it is printed. If the text doesn't reformat completely, press either the down-arrow key or Rewrite (Ctrl-F3), and then press Enter.

Half-space lines appear on-screen as whole spaces; however, you can see from the Ln indicator on the Status Line that lines change in .5 increments.

The new spacing takes effect from the point where you entered the command to the end of the document, or until another line-spacing command is encountered. You can change line spacing throughout your documents by invoking another line spacing command wherever you want to make a change.

To check the current line spacing, press Reveal Codes where the line spacing starts, or give the spacing command. The current spacing appears in the prompt (for example, [Spacing Set] 2). Press the Cancel key (F1) to leave the current setting unchanged.

Because spacing commands don't affect headers and footers, or footnotes and endnotes (they all remain single-spaced), you must change them by editing them for new spacing.

You'll find that it's easier to enter certain numeric formulas if you set the line spacing to .5, a setting that makes the typing of divided and parenthetical terms easier to perform.

# Hyphenating Words

WordPerfect's Hyphenation function permits you to divide words that cross the right margin. By hyphenating long words instead of wrapping them to the next line, you create a more evenly spaced printed copy, and a right margin that aligns more evenly on the page. You decide whether

WordPerfect inserts hyphens automatically or whether you will place the hyphens manually.

## Beginning Hyphenation

To turn on the Hyphenation function, press Line Format (Shift-F8) and select 5 for Hyphenation. The Hyphenation menu displayed at the bottom of the screen in figure 8.7 is displayed. Type 1 and press Enter to turn on the feature. A [Hyph on] code is inserted in the text at the cursor location. The hyphenation feature remains on in the document until you turn it off.

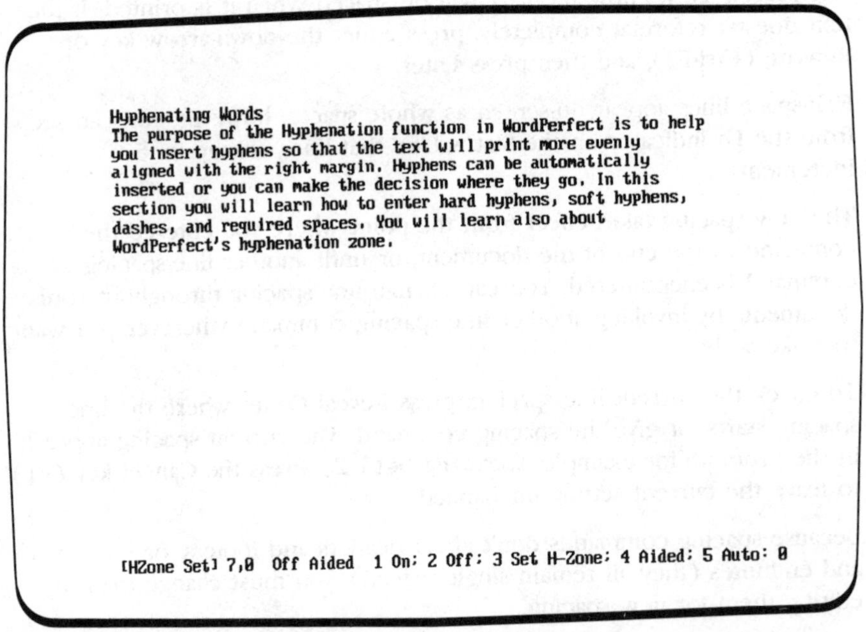

```
Hyphenating Words
The purpose of the Hyphenation function in WordPerfect is to help
you insert hyphens so that the text will print more evenly
aligned with the right margin. Hyphens can be automatically
inserted or you can make the decision where they go. In this
section you will learn how to enter hard hyphens, soft hyphens,
dashes, and required spaces. You will learn also about
WordPerfect's hyphenation zone.




[HZone Set] 7,0  Off Aided  1 On; 2 Off; 3 Set H-Zone; 4 Aided; 5 Auto: 0
```

Fig. 8.7. Hyphenation menu showing default H-Zone settings of 7 and 0 (before turning on hyphenation and scrolling document).

As you type or scroll through a reformatted document, WordPerfect will call your attention to those words that should be hyphenated by displaying this message and the word to be hyphenated:

Position hyphen; Press ESC

If you decide to hyphenate the word, use the arrow keys to move the hyphen between the appropriate syllables and then press the Esc key. Continue typing.

If you decide that the word should *not* be hyphenated, press Cancel and the word will wrap to the next line. A Cancel Hyphenation code is inserted in front of the word. The code can be deleted if you decide, later on, to hyphenate the word.

To end hyphenation, insert the [Hyph off] code by displaying the Hyphenation menu and selecting 2.

WordPerfect's default settings turn off the hyphenation. If you want hyphenation always set to on or off, use the Set-up menu (described in Chapter 17) to change the default setting.

## Selecting Auto/Aided Hyphenation

WordPerfect 4.2 tries to insert hyphens automatically if you choose 5 Auto from the Hyphenation menu. If the hyphens cannot be inserted automatically, the program temporarily enters Aided Hyphenation mode, and you must position the hyphens manually.

If you want to position hyphens manually, choose 4 Aided from the Hyphenation menu. (WordPerfect 4.1 always operates with manually positioned hyphens.)

## Controlling Which Words Hyphenate

WordPerfect decides which words to hyphenate by comparing those words to the Hyphenation Zone (H-Zone) on either side of the right margin. The following diagram may help you to see how WordPerfect decides which words to hyphenate.

| *Left H-Zone* | *Right Margin* | *Right H-Zone* | |
|---|---|---|---|
| A | ———— | | Stay |
| B | ——————————— | | Word Wrap |
| C | ———————— | | Word Wrap |
| D | ———————————————————— | | Hyphenate |

The diagram shows the Left and Right H-Zones with respect to the right margin. Each zone is measured by the number of characters separating it from the right margin. The horizontal lines represent words of different lengths at different locations in the document.

When hyphenation is turned on, three things can happen to words that fall near the right margin:

- Words that start on or after the Left H-Zone but do not reach the right margin (like the word in line A) will remain in position

- Words that begin on or after the Left H-Zone and pass the right margin, such as the words in lines B and C, wrap to the next line

- Words that start before the Left H-Zone and pass over the Right H-Zone, like the word in line D, require hyphenation

The distance between the Left and Right H-Zones determines the size of words selected for hyphenation. The shorter the distance between the two zones, the more hyphenation is needed. Although some people are bothered by too many hyphenated words, more hyphenation produces a smoother right edge when justification is off. With justification on, a shorter distance between zones results in more even spacing of text across the printed line. You must weigh the difference between the number of hyphens and the appearance of the page.

What difference does the right margin's position between the Left H-Zone and the Right H-Zone make? If you compare two H-Zones with the same distance between the Left and the Right H-Zone, the one with the larger Left H-Zone will wrap fewer words to the next line.

Notice the effect of the different H-Zone sizes in the following examples:

| Left H-Zone | Right H-Zone | Effect on Text |
|---|---|---|
| 7 | 0 | The Right H-Zone is on the right margin. No word extends over the right margin. Words shorter than seven characters wrap if they cross the right margin. Words with eight or more characters are hyphenated if they cross the right margin. (7,0 is the default H-Zone setting.) |
| 5 | 5 | Right margin centered in H-Zone. Words must be 10 characters or longer before hyphenation is required. Largest blank left before the right margin will be five characters or less. Largest |

extension past the margin will be
five characters.

7          3          Fewer words wrapped to the next
line than the 5,5 example. Words
must still be 10 characters or
longer before hyphenation is
required.

If your documents require hyphenation, you should experiment with
different H-Zone settings on a sample page of text to find the best setting.
The H-Zone in figure 8.7 is set at 7 and 0. If the settings were 4 and 0
rather than 7 and 0, the paragraph would look like the one shown in
figure 8.8.

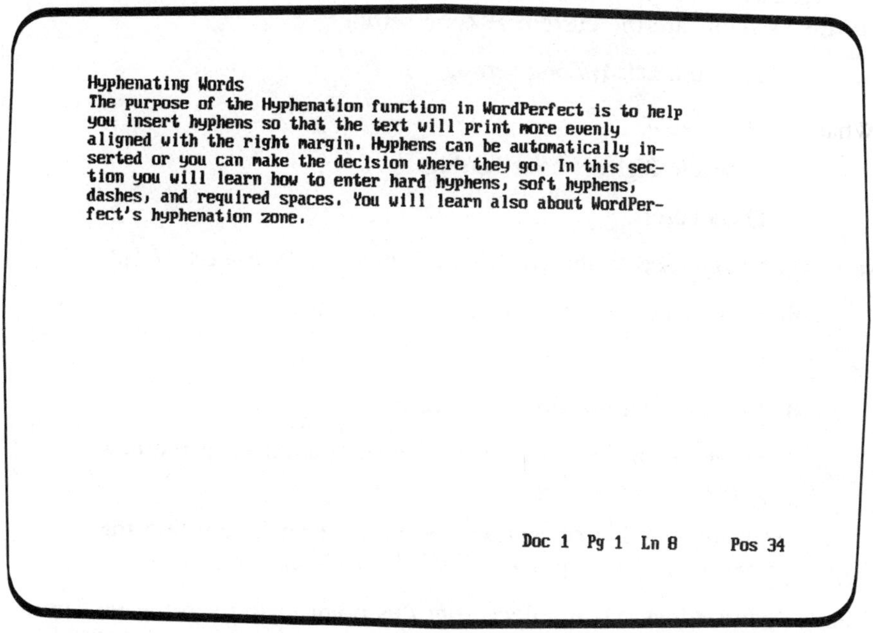

```
Hyphenating Words
The purpose of the Hyphenation function in WordPerfect is to help
you insert hyphens so that the text will print more evenly
aligned with the right margin. Hyphens can be automatically in-
serted or you can make the decision where they go. In this sec-
tion you will learn how to enter hard hyphens, soft hyphens,
dashes, and required spaces. You will learn also about WordPer-
fect's hyphenation zone.




                                   Doc 1  Pg 1  Ln 8     Pos 34
```

*Fig. 8.8. Effect of setting H-Zone at 4 and 0, turning on hyphenation, and scrolling the document.*

## Setting the H-Zone

Although changing the hyphenation-zone settings is quite simple, you may prefer to type your draft with hyphenation turned off and then turn on hyphenation after you have a finished copy.

To change the H-Zone:

1. Press the Line Format key (Shift-F8)

2. Select 5 Hyphenation

3. Select 3 Set H-Zone

A prompt similar to

        [HZone Set] 7,0  to Left =

will appear at the lower left corner of the screen. The two numbers, 7,0 in this example, are the current H-Zone settings.

4. Type the Left H-Zone setting

5. Press Enter

6. Type the Right H-Zone setting

7. Press Enter

You will be returned to the Hyphenation menu in WordPerfect 4.2.

8. Press Enter to return to the typing screen

    Or

8. Choose 1 On to turn hyphenation on

9. Scroll down the typing screen to see the effect of the new hyphenation

If you are using Aided Hyphenation, you must manually position the hyphen when each new hyphenated word scrolls on the screen.

The H-Zone settings stay in effect from this point forward in the text until they are reset or until hyphenation is turned off. You can set one H-Zone for part of the document and another for the rest of the document. If you want to change the H-Zone for the entire document, you must place the cursor at the beginning of the document before you specify the settings.

# Creating Justified or Ragged-Right Text

Justification causes the text to be printed so that full lines of text are aligned with both the left and right margins. WordPerfect inserts extra spaces between some of the words in each line so that the words will align at the right margin. You cannot see justification on the screen. It is visible only when your text prints.

Because justification is preset to be on, all of the text you print will appear justified unless you turn justification off. When you turn justification off, the text is printed as *ragged right*.

You can turn off the justification function, either before you begin typing your text or at any point within the text where you want the justification to stop. To turn off justification, press Print Format (Ctrl-F8), and then select 3 Turn Off. The feature remains off in the document until you turn it on again by pressing Print Format and 4 Turn On. You can use justification in some portions of the document and not in other portions of the document.

To change the default setting so that justification off is the default setting, read Chapter 17 for information about how to use the *WP/S* start-up to change default settings.

# Using Special Word Separators

In this section, you will learn how to enter *hard hyphens*, *hard spaces*, *soft hyphens*, and *dashes*. Each is used to link words or syllables in a special way.

## Keeping Two or More Words Together with Hard Spaces

Some characters, numbers, and words are not normally hyphenated, but should not be divided within the text. The formula, HCL, for instance cannot be divided; word units, such as San Francisco, should not be divided; WWII is another example of an abbreviation that loses meaning if it's divided.

You can keep these character strings together by pressing the Hard Space key (Home, space bar) where blanks are between words. For instance, if you wanted to keep the formula $a + b = c$ on one line, you would type $a$, press a Hard Space, type +, press another Hard Space, and so on. Entering a character string in this manner prevents WordPerfect from dividing it.

## Using Special Types of Hyphens

To change the location of a hyphen so that a word will break only where you want it to, insert a hard hyphen (Alt-hyphen) or a soft hyphen (Ctrl-hyphen) in the desired location. Use the Reveal Codes function to delete the unwanted hyphen.

A hard hyphen is part of the spelling of a word. *Father-in-law* and *jack-of-all-trades* are examples of words that use hard hyphens. A hard hyphen displays and prints at all times. A soft hyphen appears only when it is needed to hyphenate the word. To insert a hard hyphen in a previously unhyphenated word, press the Hard Hyphen key combination (Alt-hyphen). (Be sure to use the hyphen key that lies at the top of the keyboard, *not* the minus sign key on the numeric keypad.)

WordPerfect will use the hyphen, when appropriate, to divide the word at the end of a line.

If you do not want a hyphenated word, such as a hyphenated name or place, to be divided at the end of a line, use the minus sign to produce the hyphen. To enter the minus sign, press the Home key and then a hyphen. This minus-sign hyphen is not used as a syllable or a word break. (Again, do not use the regular minus sign on the numeric keypad.)

Insert soft, or conditional, hyphens in words to be certain that word breaks always are correct. For example, if you see that the word *automatically* is going to be printed near the end of a line and may be hyphenated, you can press the Soft Hyphen key (Ctrl-hyphen) between the letters where the word can be divided. The hyphen appears on the screen only when the word actually is divided. You can see soft hyphens, however, if you use Reveal Codes.

## Using Dashes

Dashes are used to set off or emphasize an idea within a sentence. To type a dash (a double hyphen), type the minus sign (Home, hyphen) and a hyphen. This keystroke sequence prevents WordPerfect from separating the two hyphens—should they fall at the right margin.

Now you've worked your way through all of the WordPerfect commands you'll need to complete the majority of your professional and personal word-processing tasks. You can create documents, proofread and edit text, format text, save your documents, retrieve files from disk, and print your documents—an impressive array of new skills!

The two most frequently used formatting commands discussed in this chapter are the margin and the tab commands.

Use this procedure to change the margins (as many times as you like) in your document:

☐ Move the cursor to the position where you want the new margin to begin

☐ Press the Line Format key (Shift-F8)

☐ Select 3 Margins

☐ Type the left margin setting

☐ Press Enter

☐ Type the right margin setting

☐ Press Enter

You must use a few more keystrokes when you change tabs because you have several alternatives. Remember that you can use several different types of tab settings: Left (L) tab, Right (R) tab, Centered (C) tab, and Decimal (D) tab. Left, right, and decimal tabs also can be preceded by a line of dots.

Use these steps to enter new tab settings:

☐ Move the cursor to the position where you want the new tabs to begin

☐ Press the Line Format key (Shift-F8)

☐ Select 1,2 Tabs

☐ Move the cursor to the position where you want the tab

☐ Type L for left, R for right, C for center, or D for decimal tab (Type T if you are using WordPerfect 4.1)

☐ Press the Exit key (F7) to return to the typing screen

Chapter 17 explains how you can set defaults that respond to the way *you* use WordPerfect. If you find that you are using many of your own tab, margin, and justification settings in most of the documents you create, refer to the Set-up menu section in Chapter 17.

More global formatting commands, such as page numbering, defining page breaks, and inserting headers and footers, are discussed in the next chapter—you'll move away from the idea of formatting text to the broader concepts of formatting the pages that make up your document.

# Formatting Your Document Pages

**B**efore your eye focuses on a single word on this page and before you understand the meaning of the words on the page, you unconsciously form an impression of the text in front of you. The format (or layout) of the text on the page creates that impression.

Think about the printed pages you've seen that looked as though they contained complicated or difficult material. Chances are the pages were covered with very dense text, little "white space," narrow top, bottom, and side margins, lengthy paragraphs, no indented sections, and no variation in type size, or line or page length. Documents that are created with little regard for page layout will almost always appear more difficult and forbidding.

On the other hand, consider those documents you've seen in which the text has been broken into manageable "chunks" of information, documents in which the margins are generous enough to frame lines of text for easy reading, written materials in which the text varies in size and placement, and documents in which important text is set apart from regular text by indents or tabs. Those documents almost always appear "friendly"—regardless of their level of complexity.

You can, in large measure, control how your readers react to your printed materials by using the features and functions presented in this chapter. You can control such page-layout elements as top and bottom margins, page size, page breaks (where one page ends and another begins), footnotes, and endnotes.

To begin, the functions discussed in this chapter offer you four approaches to defining where (and how) you may divide the pages of your document:

- You may create typed page breaks

- You may create breaks that assure that a specific number of lines appear on the page

- You may create page breaks that protect tables and charts from being divided between two pages

- You may create breaks that automatically protect against "widows" and "orphans"

As you move on in the chapter, you'll use page-layout commands to position your text (exactly where you want it) on a variety of paper sizes. You'll learn how to control:

- Page numbering and page number location

- How the text is centered (top to bottom) on a page

- The position of your text on letterhead paper

- Print line advance for line drawing and formulas

Finally, if you're responsible for preparing technical reports or research papers, which demand strict adherence to a footnote or endnote style, you'll explore how WordPerfect creates both footnotes and endnotes. You'll be pleased to discover how easy it is to create footnotes and endnotes, and how simple the formatting and numbering of those footnotes and endnotes is.

# Using Page Breaks

You have several options for controlling where, in your document, WordPerfect begins and ends each page. WordPerfect's methods are as straightforward as a single keystroke to: enter a page break, automatically calculate the number of lines that must remain together on a page, and automatically protect against single lines of paragraph text appearing either at the top of a page or at the bottom of a page. Read about these page-break techniques, and when you must make a page-break decision, refer to this section for the the most appropriate solution.

As you work through the following sections, remember that the WordPerfect default is 54 single-spaced lines of text on a 66-line page.

You can see (on your screen) where page breaks occur because WordPerfect inserts a dashed line, and both the Pg and the Ln indicators on the Status Line change as the cursor moves between pages.

## Soft Page Breaks

An advantage that WordPerfect enjoys over other word processors is that WordPerfect shows you on-screen where page breaks occur.

As you type, WordPerfect counts the number of text lines used per page and compares that number to the number of single spaced lines per printed page. When all the lines on a page have been used by text, headers/footers, and footnotes, WordPerfect does two things:

- The page number following Pg on the Status Line changes

- And, a dashed line appears on-screen to separate the previous and current pages—the *Soft Page break*

You can see exactly where the Soft Page break occurs from the Reveal Codes screen by looking for the [SPg] code.

As you edit, text flows across the Soft Page break. When your work requires a page break that maintains its location in text, use the manually inserted *Hard Page break* described in the next section. For more flexible automatic positioning of Soft Page breaks use the Conditional End of Page, Block Protect, and Widow/Orphan commands.

## Using the Hard Page Break Command

To determine where a page breaks, use the Hard Page key (Ctrl-Enter). If you place the cursor at the end of a line and press Hard Page, the program inserts a double-dashed line immediately below the cursor position. (A single-dashed line is used in WordPerfect 4.1.) This dashed line marks a Hard Page break. If you then press the Reveal Codes key (Alt-F3), you can see the code for a Hard Page break [HPg].

Use a Hard Page break when you have several tables or charts that each require a full page. Although you can save each page in a separate file, a more convenient solution involves putting all of the tables or charts at the end of the major document that uses them. To keep the tables or charts from running together, use the Hard Page break to separate them.

Do not assume that the Hard Page break solves all your page-break problems. If you insert or delete text above a Hard Page break, the Hard

Page break may move to a position that produces a page which has only a few lines. If you need a more discriminating page break, read about the Conditional End of Page, Block Protect, and Widow/Orphan commands.

## Canceling Hard Page Breaks

You have several choices for canceling Hard Page breaks. If you have only one page break to cancel, place the cursor at the end of the last line above the new page-break line and press Del; the page break disappears from the screen. You also can move the cursor to the first character of the new page and press Backspace.

To remove several Hard Page codes at one time, and force WordPerfect to distinguish between Hard Page and automatic page breaks, use the Replace function described in Chapter 7.

1. Move the cursor to the beginning of the document by pressing Home, Home, up arrow

2. Press Replace (Alt-F2)

3. Type **N** to answer the confirm question

This prompt appears on your screen:

> Srch:

4. Press the Hard Page key combination (Ctrl-Enter); then press the Search key (F2)

When WordPerfect asks you to enter the character that will replace the [HPg] code, press the Search key. All the Hard Page breaks are erased, and nothing replaces them.

## Using the Conditional End of Page Command

Whenever you have text, graphs, tables, or charts that must remain together on one page, use the Conditional End of Page command. This page-break method eliminates the problems that can occur with the Hard Page break during major revisions.

You can be certain that when you use this command with charts and tables, that the chart and table text will remain associated with the correct headings. The Conditional End of Page command assures that charts and tables aren't divided by page breaks.

To use the Conditional End of Page (EOP) command:

1. Count the lines that must remain together on the page

2. Place the cursor on the line immediately before the section you want to keep intact

3. Press Page Format (Alt-F8)

4. Select **9** Conditional End of Page

5. Type the **number of lines** counted in Step 1

6. Press Enter, twice

A page break is inserted at the point of the Conditional End of Page command if there are not enough lines left on the page to accommodate your section of text. The entire section then moves to the new page. No matter how much you rearrange material later, the text won't be broken between two pages—the lines that you've indicated must remain together will always stay together.

A Hard Page break command *always* begins a new page, the Conditional End of Page command begins a new page *only if the number of lines you've specified are not available on the page where the conditional text starts.*

## *Using the Block Protect Command*

The Block Protect command binds together lines so that a page break won't split them. To protect a block of text, such as a table or a chart:

1. Use the Block command (Alt-F4) to highlight the text that you want to protect

Figure 9.1 illustrates what a highlighted table looks like on your screen.

2. Press the Page Format key (Alt-F8)

This prompt is displayed on your screen:

    Protect Block?(Y/N)

3. Type **Y** to keep page breaks from separating lines of text

WordPerfect 4.2 has seven types of tab settings to make column
entries easier. These tabs will align text left, right, centered
or aligned on a decimal. They can also precede the entry with a
row of dots. The types of tabs are,

| Letter | Alignment | Dot Leader |
|--------|-----------|------------|
| L | Left aligned | . |
| R | Right aligned | . |
| D | Decimal aligned | . |
|   | Centered |   |

Manually enter these tabs by moving on the tab ruler to the
location where you want the tab and then typing the letter. Move
with the left or right arrow, or use Home-left and Home-right to
move a screen at a time. Use an L or left aligned tab for a
normal type of tab. R or right aligned tabs, align the right edge
of your typing with the tab. These work well for columns of
numbers that cannot be aligned on a decimal point. D, decimal
tabs, align numbers on the decimal. The Dot Leader shown in the
table is entered by typing a period over the top of the L, R, or
D on the tab ruler. A dot leader puts a string of dots between
the typing at the current tab and the previous tab. This is
excellent for use in tables of contents and listings.

Block on                                Doc 1  Pg 4  Ln 48      Pos 1

Fig. 9.1. First step in implementing Block protection.

## Protecting against Widows and Orphans

Try to eliminate the situation in which a single line from a paragraph falls
either at the bottom of the page or at the top of the page. "Disassociated"
lines of text are distracting to readers. (See fig. 9.2.)

These breaks in text are called *widows* and *orphans*. A widow occurs
when the first line in a paragraph falls at the bottom of one page, and the
rest of the paragraph appears on the next page. An orphan occurs when
the last line in a paragraph appears at the top of one page, but the rest of
the paragraph appears on the preceding page.

You can correct the widow and orphan problem using Conditional End of
Page. But, you'll have to use Conditional EOP every time a widow or an
orphan appears! WordPerfect's built-in feature that automatically eliminates
widows and orphans solves the problem more easily.

After you set the Widow/Orphan protection feature, it works throughout
the document. Position the cursor at the top of the document, press Page
Format (Alt-F8), and select A for the Widow/Orphan protection. Respond

Single lines of a paragraph that occur at the bottom or top of a
page appear poorly in printed documents and should be prevented.
Such breaks are called widows and orphans. WordPerfect's
documentation defines a widow as the first line of a paragraph at
the bottom of one page, with the rest of the paragraph found on
the next page. An orphan is the last line of a paragraph at the
top of one page, with the rest of the paragraph on the preceding
page.

To correct the widow and orphan problem, you could use
Conditional End of Page. However, you would have to use it every
time a widow or an orphan occurred. To make solving the problem
much easier, WordPerfect has a built-in feature that
automatically eliminates widows and orphans. After you set this
feature, it works throughout the document. Position the cursor at
the top of the document, press Page Format (Alt-F8), and then
select A for the Widow/Orphan protection. Answer the prompt
Widow/Orphan Protect (Y/N): with a Y for Yes to invoke the

New page ──────▶ protection feature. ◀───────────────────────── An orphan

Single lines of a paragraph that occur at the bottom or top of a
page appear poorly in printed documents and should be prevented.
Such breaks are called widows and orphans. WordPerfect's
documentation defines a widow as the first line of a paragraph at
the bottom of one page, with the rest of the paragraph found on
the next page. An orphan is the last line of a paragraph at the
top of one page, with the rest of the paragraph on the preceding
page.

To correct the widow and orphan problem, you could use ◀────────── A widow

New page ──────▶ Conditional End of Page. However, you would have to use it every
time a widow or an orphan occurred. To make solving the problem
much easier, WordPerfect has a built-in feature that
automatically eliminates widows and orphans. After you set this
feature, it works throughout the document. Position the cursor at
the top of the document, press Page Format (Alt-F8), and then
select A for the Widow/Orphan protection. Answer the prompt
Widow/Orphan Protect (Y/N): with a Y for Yes to invoke the
protection feature.

*Fig. 9.2. An example of a widow and an orphan.*

to the prompt Widow/Orphan Protect (Y/N): with Y (for yes) to invoke the protection feature.

Remember that there are two differences between Conditional EOP and Widow/Orphan Protect:

1. You must set Conditional EOP for each instance in the file; Widow/Orphan Protect operates with one setting for the whole file.

2. You can use Conditional EOP to tie together any number of lines; Widow/Orphan Protect applies to traditional paragraphs only.

# Formatting the Body of Printed Text

Most organizations use a format they consider unique for their typed reports and documents. The vertical positioning of text on the page and the positioning of page numbers are part of that format. In this section you'll learn how to control where page numbers are printed and how they are numbered. You'll also learn how to position text on the page by controlling the top margin or the number of lines of text per page. If you use odd-sized paper, such as labels or envelopes, you'll be interested in this section for its information on changing paper size.

## Numbering Pages

If you use WordPerfect's command to automatically number pages, you can select the position of the page number as well.

To set page-number positions:

> **1.** Press Page Format (Alt-F8)

When the menu shown in figure 9.3 appears:

> **2.** Select **1** Page Number Position

```
Page Format

        1 - Page Number Position

        2 - New Page Number

        3 - Center Page Top to Bottom

        4 - Page Length

        5 - Top Margin

        6 - Headers or Footers

        7 - Page Number Column Positions

        8 - Suppress for Current page only

        9 - Conditional End of Page

        A - Widow/Orphan


    Selection: 0
```

*Fig. 9.3. Page Format menu.*

The Position of Page Number menu that appears offers the positions for page-number placement shown in figure 9.4.

```
Position of Page Number on Page

    0 - No page numbers

    1 - Top left of every page

    2 - Top center of every page

    3 - Top right of every page

    4 - Top alternating left & right

    5 - Bottom left of every page

    6 - Bottom center of every page

    7 - Bottom right of every page

    8 - Bottom alternating left & right




Selection: 0
```

Fig. 9.4. Position of Page Number menu.

3. Select the location of the page number by typing the corresponding menu number

4. Press Enter twice to return to the typing screen

Page numbers don't appear in position on the screen, although the Status Line indicates the current page number. The pages are numbered in sequence automatically when your document is printed. If you are using WordPerfect 4.2, you can see the page numbers on-screen by choosing 6 Preview from the Print menu (Shift-F7).

When you change the margins of the document, you may need to change the column on which the number prints with 7 Page Number Column Positions on the Page Format menu to reset the left, right, and centered column numbers. Figure 9.5 shows the default settings on this menu.

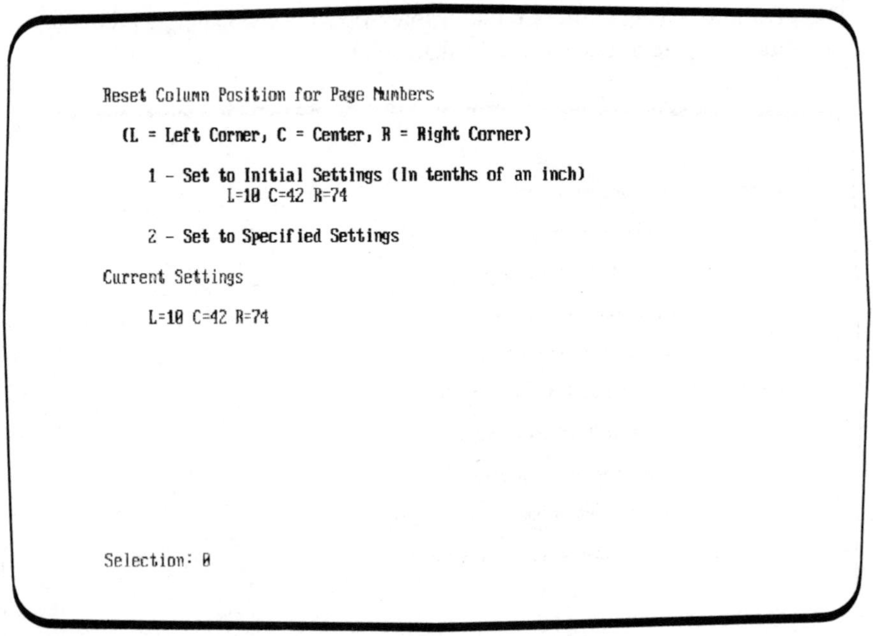

```
Reset Column Position for Page Numbers

   (L = Left Corner, C = Center, R = Right Corner)

      1 - Set to Initial Settings (In tenths of an inch)
             L=18 C=42 R=74

      2 - Set to Specified Settings

Current Settings

      L=18 C=42 R=74




Selection: 8
```

*Fig. 9.5. Page number column positions.*

## Turning Off Page Numbering

To turn page numbering off in the document, move to the location where you invoked the code. Remember, you can save time by using the Search command to find the code. Press Reveal Codes (Alt-F3) and delete the [Pos Pg#:] code. To terminate page numbering that appears later in the document, return to the Page Number Position menu and select 0.

There will be times that you won't want a particular page numbered—the foreword page or the trademark acknowledgment page in a book, for instance. You can suppress (eliminate) the page number on a single page by moving the cursor to the page on which you want numbering suppressed and return to the Page Format menu (Alt-F8). Choose 8 Suppress for Current Page Only and choose the features that you do not want printed on the current page.

## Creating New Page Numbers

Although WordPerfect automatically renumbers the pages in your document if you add or delete pages, you may want the numbers in a sequence to start with a number other than 1. For example, if your document is stored in two files, you may want to begin numbering the second file where the first file finished.

1. Move the cursor to the top of the page where you want a new page number to be used

2. Press Page Format (Alt-F8)

3. Select **2** New Page Number

This prompt appears on your screen:

New Page #:

4. Type the **starting page number** and press Enter

You then are asked to select Arabic or Roman styie numbers.

5. Type **1**

   Or

5. Type **2**

6. Press Enter

7. Press Enter again to return to the typing screen

The new number should appear in the Status Line. All subsequent pages are numbered in sequence automatically. You can check or delete the page numbering code, [Pg#:], with Reveal Codes.

You can use Arabic numerals (such as 1, 2, and 3) as well as lowercase Roman numerals (such as i, ii, and iii) to number pages. The Roman numerals are useful for numbering the front matter in documents (the table of contents, the preface, and the acknowledgments, for instance).

If you use New Page to number multiple files (using the same sequence), you must change the starting page number of each file manually if the length of preceding files changes. For example, if 3 pages are added in the first part of a document, the automatic numbering in the 32 pages of the first file changes the last page number from 32 to 35. However, you have to change the New Page number code on the first page in the second file from 33 to 36.

## Centering Text Top to Bottom

If you've ever had to retype a letter because it wasn't properly centered between the top and bottom margins, you know what an aggravation it can be—measuring and retyping and remeasuring and retyping until you get it right! With WordPerfect, you won't be faced with the problem again. WordPerfect automatically centers text from top to bottom on the pages you specify.

1. Place the cursor at the top left margin of the page

2. Press Page Format (Alt-F8)

3. Select 3 Center Page (Top to Bottom)

4. Press Enter to return to the typing screen

Although the text does not move to the center of the screen, it will center when you print your document. All the lines you enter, both text and blank lines, are positioned so an equal number of blank lines lie above and below them.

Use the Reveal Codes key to remove the hidden [Center Pg] command if you no longer need the feature.

This letter illustrates the concepts presented in the next few sections of this chapter.

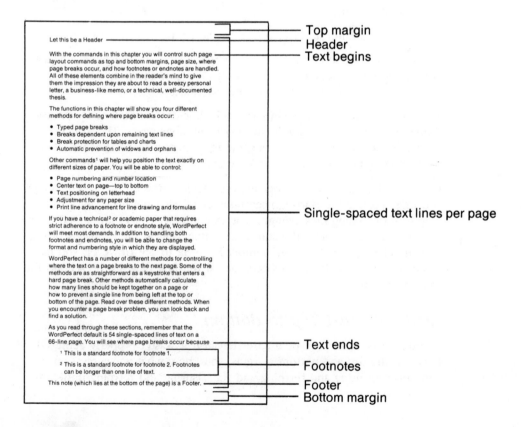

Let this be a Header — Top margin / Header / Text begins

With the commands in this chapter you will control such page layout commands as top and bottom margins, page size, where page breaks occur, and how footnotes or endnotes are handled. All of these elements combine in the reader's mind to give them the impression they are about to read a breezy personal letter, a business-like memo, or a technical, well-documented thesis.

The functions in this chapter will show you four different methods for defining where page breaks occur:

- Typed page breaks
- Breaks dependent upon remaining text lines
- Break protection for tables and charts
- Automatic prevention of widows and orphans

Other commands[1] will help you position the text exactly on different sizes of paper. You will be able to control:

- Page numbering and number location
- Center text on page—top to bottom
- Text positioning on letterhead
- Adjustment for any paper size
- Print line advancement for line drawing and formulas

If you have a technical[2] or academic paper that requires strict adherence to a footnote or endnote style, WordPerfect will meet most demands. In addition to handling both footnotes and endnotes, you will be able to change the format and numbering style in which they are displayed.

WordPerfect has a number of different methods for controlling where the text on a page breaks to the next page. Some of the methods are as straightforward as a keystroke that enters a hard page break. Other methods automatically calculate how many lines should be kept together on a page or how to prevent a single line from being left at the top or bottom of the page. Read over these different methods. When you encounter a page break problem, you can look back and find a solution.

As you read through these sections, remember that the WordPerfect default is 54 single-spaced lines of text on a 66-line page. You will see where page breaks occur because — Text ends

[1] This is a standard footnote for footnote 1.

[2] This is a standard footnote for footnote 2. Footnotes can be longer than one line of text.

Footnotes

This note (which lies at the bottom of the page) is a Footer. — Footer / Bottom margin

Single-spaced text lines per page

## Changing Paper and Printing Length

WordPerfect assumes that you use standard 8 1/2-by-11-inch U.S. business-size paper. With 6 lines per inch, WordPerfect uses a setting of 66 lines per page. Legal-size 8 1/2-by-14-inch paper demands a setting of 84 lines.

Other WordPerfect defaults are 6-line (1-inch) margins at both the top and bottom of the page. Therefore, 12 of the 66 or 84 lines available are used for default top and bottom margins. Fifty-four lines remain for text on an 11-inch sheet of paper, and 72 lines remain for a 14-inch sheet.

Page numbers, headers, footers, and footnotes also must fit in the allotted number of text lines. These print in text range between top and bottom margins of lines 7–60 (11-inch paper) and 7–78 (14-inch paper). The only exception is a 2-line footer; the second line is placed on line 61 (11-inch paper) or line 79 (14-inch paper).

## Changing Paper Size

If you use 8 1/2-by-11-inch paper and are satisfied with the six-line top and bottom margins, don't change any settings. If you want to use legal-size paper:

1. Press Page Format (Alt-F8)

2. Select **4** Page Length to go to the Page Length menu shown in figure 9.6

3. Select **2** Legal Size Paper to set the automatic paper size and text per page of legal-size paper

4. Press Enter to return to the typing screen

The legal-size paper setting remains in effect in your document until you delete the code or change the setting. When you save the file, the command also is saved.

## Changing the Top Margin

With WordPerfect, you can use a variety of paper sizes (including mailing labels), you can add more lines of text to a page, or use fewer lines of text on a page, you can use nonstandard top and bottom margin settings, you can even turn the standard paper sideways and roll the 11-inch edge into the printer! With WordPerfect, you can place text anywhere your printer can print on the paper.

```
    Page Length

            1 - Letter Size Paper: Form Length = 66 lines (11 inches)
                Single Spaced Text lines = 54 (This includes lines
                used for Headers, Footers and/or page numbers.)

            2 - Legal Size Paper: Form Length = 84 lines (14 inches)
                Single Spaced Text Lines = 72 (This includes lines
                used for Headers, Footers and/or page numbers.)

            3 - Other (Maximum page length = 100 lines.)

    Current Settings

            Form Length in Lines (6 per inch): 66

            Number of Single Spaced Text Lines: 54




    Selection: 0
```

*Fig. 9.6. 4 Page Length menu from Page Format menu.*

If you've decided to use a top margin of 10 lines, you can change the top margin setting:

**1.** Press Page Format (Alt-F8)

**2.** Select **5** Top Margin

WordPerfect prompts you to change the number of half-lines (12 half-lines equal 6 full lines; 6 lines always equal an inch in a top or bottom margin).

You can increase the top margin by as much as you want or you can decrease it to 0, a setting that instructs the printer not to space down any lines before printing.

You can change the top margin setting after you've created your document, as well. Remember, however, that such a change reformats the rest of the document from the point where you selected the Top Margin command.

WordPerfect assumes that hand-fed sheets of paper are rolled down one inch when the printer starts printing. That inch is subtracted from the top margin setting that you enter, so the paper does not roll up as far as it does on a printer using tractor-fed paper. The one-inch compensation allows the paper bail to catch the paper.

As you might guess, when you change the top margin on a page or when you change the lines of text per page, you affect the bottom margin as well. Read the following section about adjusting the bottom margin.

## Changing the Bottom Margin

When you increase the top margin on a page, WordPerfect pushes the text on the page down so that less room is available for the bottom margin. As the top margin increases, you must decrease the number of lines of text per page—if you want the bottom margin to remain the same.

For example, standard business-letter-size paper has both a top and bottom margin of 6, a text length of 54, and a total paper length of 66. If you increase the top margin to 10 and keep a text length of 54, only two lines remain for the bottom margin. In this example, you should decrease the text lines per page to 50 if you want a bottom margin of 6.

| | |
|---|---|
| total lines per page | 66 |
| –the top margin | 10 |
| –the desired bottom margin | 6 |
| text lines per page | 50 |

## Changing the Number of Text Lines Per Page

You can change the number of Text Lines per Page from the same menu that you used to change the page length. Return to the menu by pressing the Page Format key (Alt-F8) and then selecting 4 Page Length. From the Page Length menu, choose 3 Other, which is the same choice you use for custom-size paper. The menu is shown in figure 9.6.

When you type 3, the cursor moves to the Form Length in Lines (total lines per page), which is always measured in 6 lines per inch. Press Enter if you don't want to change it. When the cursor lies next to Single Spaced Text Lines (text lines per page), enter the number of lines of text you want. The example in the previous section used 50 lines. Consider single-spaced lines only; the program compensates for any line spacing you select.

## Changing the Number of Text Lines Per Inch

WordPerfect will change body copy lines from 6 to 8 lines per inch. The length of the page, lines in the top and bottom margins, and headers and footers are always calculated at 6 lines per inch.

Many printers can print 8 as well as 6 lines per inch. You can change the number of lines per inch from 6 to 8 by pressing Print Format (Ctrl-F8) and selecting 2 Lines Per Inch. Change the 6 to an 8, and press Enter twice. When you change the number of lines per inch, you also should change the number of lines per page. On 11-inch paper, you can print 72 lines of text at 8 lines per inch. On legal-size paper, 96 text lines fit on a page. Any adjustments you make should be added to or subtracted from these totals.

When you change the number of lines per inch, the number of text lines also changes, as stated earlier. The form length, however, continues to be defined as 6 lines per inch. For example, to print 8 lines per inch on a standard 11-inch paper, you leave the page length at 66 but set the number of text lines to the actual number—72, in this case. You must remember that the page length, as stated on the Page Length menu, always assumes 6 lines per inch.

## Advancing Lines on the Page

The Advance Line function moves the printer forward to any line and restarts printing. On some printers, you can "advance" to an earlier line so that you can print over the top of previous typing. You need Advance Line for at least two purposes: with some laser printers, Advance Line is necessary to position text over line drawing; and Advance Line provides a means for lowering text on a page to compensate for letterhead and logos. (Some printers are not capable of "advancing" backward to a line already printed.)

Advance Line moves the cursor to any specified line on the page. If the letterhead occupies the first 8 lines of the page, for example, and you want to begin printing text on line 12 rather than on line 7 (assuming a default top margin of 6 lines), then you will find that using Advance Line is easier than changing the Top Margin setting. Unlike the Top Margin command, the Advance command affects only the current page.

To activate Advance Line, place the cursor in the top left margin, press the Super/Subscript key (Shift-F1), select 6 to advance to a specific line, and type the line number where you want the text to begin. For instance, if you want your letter to begin on line 12, type 12 and press Enter.

If you use Line Drawing on a laser printer, you may not be able to type the text and the lines on the same screen line because a different font is used for lines than is used for text. To solve this problem, first draw your lines with the Line Drawing function. Record the Ln and Pos indicators displayed on the Status Line so that you'll know where text should be entered over the top of the line drawing. After the last line of line drawing, use the Advance Line feature to "advance" backward to a text line inside the drawing. This step lets you type text on the screen below the line drawing that will print over the top of the line drawing.

Figure 9.7 shows a drawing at the top of the screen and a line of text near the bottom of the screen. The Advance Line function has been used to give the text line the same line number (notice the Ln indicator) as the middle of the box. Some laser printers require that you use this technique to print text over the top of line drawings.

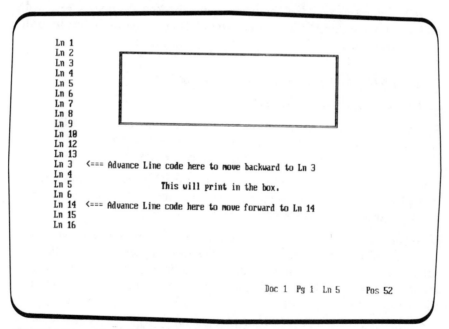

Fig. 9.7. Advance Line function.

In the Advance Line function, enter the line number of the first line in the line drawing where you want to type text. When you enter the command, the Ln indicator changes to reflect the fact that you are typing over the line drawing. (The text will still display below the line drawing on the screen. You won't see the text superimposed over the drawing until it is printed.)

Each time you press Enter, the Ln indicator moves one line down in the drawing. Refer to your notes to determine the line and column position for each text entry over the drawing. When you have typed all the text, use the Advance Line function again to advance forward to a line number past the end of the line drawing. Until you develop experience (or a good template), this process can involve much trial and error.

Advance can be tricky because the display on-screen does not match the text that prints. The screen displays sequential portions of text that print on top of, or after, one another. You can tell what is printing only by watching the Pg, Ln, and Pos indicators on the Status Line. Remember that some printers are not capable of rolling the paper backward, so they are unable to "advance" to previous lines.

To delete the Advance Line command, enter the Reveal Codes screen with Alt-F3 and delete the [AdvLn:] code. The text on-screen prints in the order you see on-screen.

## Advancing Half Lines for Extended Superscript and Subscript

The Advance Up and Advance Down command prints lines half a line above or below the standard line position. Advance Up and Down work like a subscript or superscript for multiple characters.

Place the cursor at the beginning of the text that you want to move up or down half a line space. Press Super/Subscript (Shift-F1), and then select either 4 Advance Up or 5 Advance Down.

WordPerfect records the command and moves the text up or down from that point to the end of the line. You won't see the text move on the screen (only the Status Line indicates that the line spacing is a half-line above or below the normal typing line), but when your document prints, the text is printed correctly.

If you use the Advance Up or Down command like an extended superscript or subscript—that is, to print several words raised or below the normal typing line—you return to the normal line of print by choosing the alternate option. For example, if you selected Advance Up at the beginning of the text, select Advance Down at the end of the text.

Some printers cannot print half-line spacing and, therefore, cannot print Advance Up, Advance Down, Superscripts, or Subscripts. Check your printer manual to determine what your printer can do for you.

# Creating Headers and Footers

A *header* is information automatically placed at the top (head) of the page above the regular text. A *footer* is information printed at the bottom (foot) of the page. Typical header and footer information includes running chapter heads, revision numbers and revision dates, section titles, and so forth.

You create headers and footers just one time; thereafter, WordPerfect prints them automatically. Press Page Format (Alt-F8) and select 6 Headers or Footers. Figure 9.8 shows the Header/Footer Specification menu that you will see.

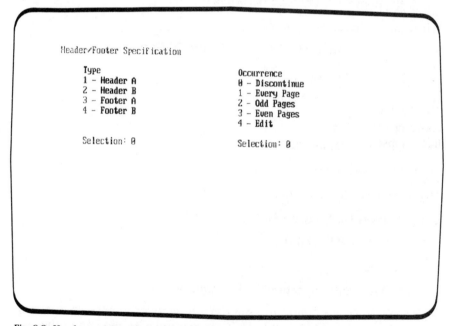

```
Header/Footer Specification

    Type                              Occurrence
    1 - Header A                      0 - Discontinue
    2 - Header B                      1 - Every Page
    3 - Footer A                      2 - Odd Pages
    4 - Footer B                      3 - Even Pages
                                      4 - Edit

    Selection: 0                      Selection: 0
```

*Fig. 9.8. Header and Footer Specification menu from Page Format menu.*

After you enter the header or footer choices, the screen clears and the program asks you to type the text. Type everything you want in the header or footer; press Exit (F7) then press Enter. The program records the header or footer, and the document returns to the screen. If you want to edit a header or footer later, go to the Header/Footer Specification menu and select 4 Edit from the right-hand menu labeled *Occurrence*.

As many as two headers and two footers can be used on the same page. If you want two headers or two footers, you must make sure that they appear in different locations at the top or bottom of the page. You can place one heading at the left margin and one at the right margin. For example, look at this text header:

**USING WORDPERFECT, 3rd Edition**                                    **CHAPTER 9**


To set up these two headings:

1. Move the cursor to the first character position on the page where you want the header to appear

2. Select Header A from the Header/Footer menu

3. Choose **1** Every Page occurrence

When the blank screen appears:

4. Type **USING WORDPERFECT, 3rd Edition** at the left margin

5. Press Exit (F7)

When the Page Format menu reappears:

6. Press **6** again

This time, select Header B

7. Choose **1** Every Page occurrence

When the blank screen appears:

8. Press Flush Right (Alt-F6)

9. Type **CHAPTER 9**

10. Select Exit (F7)

11. Press Enter to return to the typing screen

Both headers are set. You can begin using headers or footers anywhere in the document, but they'll print only from that point to the end of the document. That is, if you specify a header in the middle of the sixth page, the header starts printing at the top of the seventh page. If you want the header to begin on the sixth page, the cursor must be at the top left margin of the screen on the sixth page when you give the command. They don't appear on the typing screen, but you can check them by using Reveal Codes or the Preview function (available in WordPerfect 4.2).

Headers and footers are printed on the same line as are the page numbers. Therefore, you must make sure that the page-number position does not overlap the header or footer.

An automatic one-line skip occurs between the header and the beginning of the text. To insert more blank lines between the header or footer and the text, you must include blank lines when you define the header or footer. Lines are not drawn between the headers or footers and the text; if you want lines to appear, you must type them when you enter the header or footer.

## Page Numbering in Headers and Footers

You can include page numbers within header and footer text if you prefer. Using this page-numbering technique is useful when you write letters that are several pages long. Place the recipient's name and the page number at the top of every page, as shown in figure 9.9.

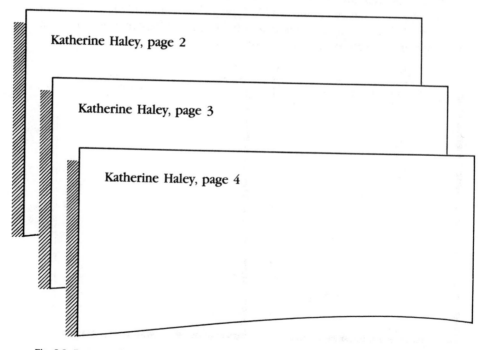

*Fig. 9.9. Page numbers included in Header text.*

To set up automatic page numbering within headers or footers:

    **1.** Follow the same steps that you used to create a header

After you invoke the Header/Footer Specification screen:

    **2.** Type **Katherine Haley, page**

    **3.** Move the cursor to the location where you want the number to appear in the header

    **4.** Press Ctrl-B

The screen will display ^B

This command instructs WordPerfect to print the current page number in that position on the page. You can use Ctrl-B to place the page number anywhere in a header or footer. Be sure, however, that you use the Ctrl key and the B key. Do not type the caret (^) and the B key.

## Printing Headers and Footers on Alternate Pages

You can place different headers or footers on odd- and even-numbered pages, or you can choose the same settings for both right-hand and left-hand pages (see figs. 9.10 and 9.11). Typing different headers on the right-hand and left-hand pages means that you can put a chapter heading on the left page and a section heading on the right page.

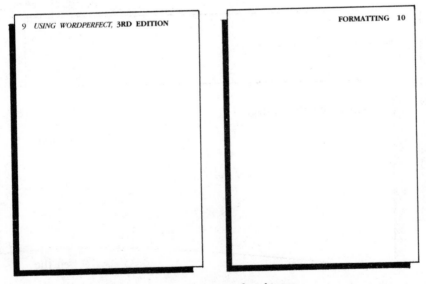

9  *USING WORDPERFECT,* 3RD EDITION

FORMATTING  10

*Fig. 9.10. Different Header on odd- and even-numbered pages.*

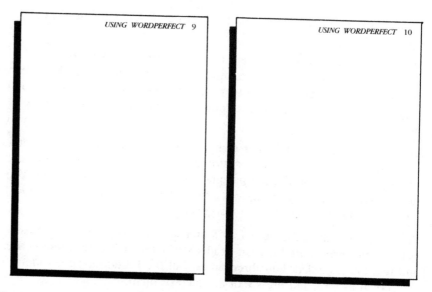

*Fig. 9.11. Same Header on right-hand and left-hand pages.*

One advantage to combining page numbers in headers and alternating pages is that you can place page numbers in different spots on left- and right-hand pages. Define one header (or footer) by typing ^B at the left margin on even pages, and define another header (or footer) by typing ^B at the right margin on odd pages. Now if the pages are copied or printed on both sides of the paper, the page number always appears on the outer edge of the page.

If you want to use headers or footers to print only alternating page numbers (that is page 1, page 3, page 5, and so forth), use this technique: press the Page Format key (Alt-F8), select Page Number Position, and choose the Alternating option.

## Editing and Setting Margins in Headers and Footers

After you've selected your header and footer specifications and begun entering the text for them, you can use most of the regular text-editing features, such as centering and tabs. To edit a header or footer, press the Page Format key (Alt-F8), and choose 6 Headers or Footers. When the Headers/Footers Specification menu appears, choose 4 Edit. To use the Edit option, you should place the cursor after the header or footer entry because the program searches backward when it looks for headers and footers.

When you change margin settings, the new margin settings are not automatically reflected in the headers and footers. When your document is printed you could end up with text that lies between left margin 20 and right margin 80, and headers and footers that lie between left margin 10 and right margin 74.

To change the header or footer margins, move to the headers and footers and select the Header/Footer function as though you are planning to edit them (as described in the last paragraph). That's all you have to do! You don't need to make any changes because the act of selecting the header/footer edit function updates the margins automatically.

Press Exit (F7) after the header or footer appears on-screen. You must perform this procedure for each header or footer. If you have one header and two footers, select Edit three times, call the header and each footer to the screen in turn, and press Exit for each of them.

## Suppressing Page Formats for Current Page

You can cancel or "suppress" instructions for headers, footers, or page numbers on any page. By setting header or footer instructions for all pages and then suppressing the instructions for pages where they should not appear, you can control the pages that receive headers, footers, or page numbers.

To keep headers, footers, or page numbers from being printed on a specified page, move the cursor to the top left corner of the page. Press Page Format (Alt-F8) and select 8 Suppress for Current Page Only. The Suppress Page Format menu, shown in figure 9.12, lists choices for turning off any or all of the possibilities for headers, footers, and page numbers.

You can turn off several page-format features simultaneously by using plus signs to connect the menu item numbers: 1+3+5+7. Press Enter after typing the numbers of the features that you want to suppress. WordPerfect stores the page suppression commands with the document. Remember that they affect only the page on which the code appears.

If you suppress headers, footers, or page numbers temporarily, you must remove the instructions if you want headers, footers, or page numbers printed again later. To remove the code, use Reveal Codes to find and remove the [Suppress:] code.

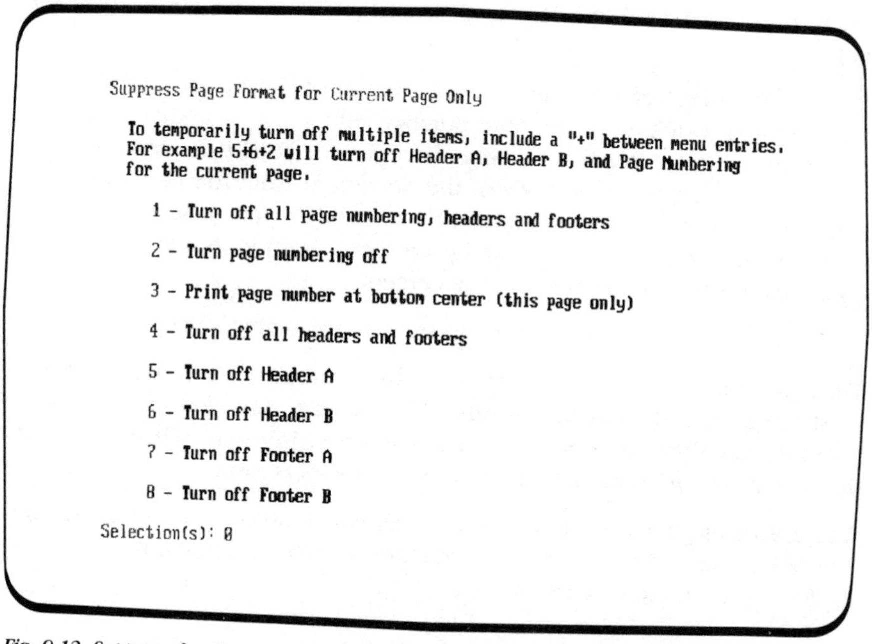

```
Suppress Page Format for Current Page Only

    To temporarily turn off multiple items, include a "+" between menu entries.
    For example 5+6+2 will turn off Header A, Header B, and Page Numbering
    for the current page.

        1 - Turn off all page numbering, headers and footers

        2 - Turn page numbering off

        3 - Print page number at bottom center (this page only)

        4 - Turn off all headers and footers

        5 - Turn off Header A

        6 - Turn off Header B

        7 - Turn off Footer A

        8 - Turn off Footer B

    Selection(s): 0
```

*Fig. 9.12. Suppress for Current Page only from Page Format menu.*

# Creating Footnotes and Endnotes

*Footnotes* are source citations or explanations that print at the bottom of the referenced page. *Endnotes* provide identical information but they are printed collectively at the end of the document. WordPerfect makes creating and formatting both footnotes and endnotes easy.

The steps involved in creating footnotes and endnotes are nearly identical:

1. Place the cursor where you want the reference number to appear (at the end of a quote, for example)

2. Press the Footnote key (Ctrl-F7)

The Footnote menu (see fig. 9.13) appears.

3. Type **1** to create a footnote

   Or

3. Press **5** to create an endnote

4. Type the note

After you press 1 or 5, the screen is cleared and ready for you to type the note.

Because WordPerfect automatically numbers and formats, you have only to type the text. Don't enter the note number, either in the body of the document or in the text of the note. Also, do not indent the note text or draw a line to separate the body of the document from the footnote. *All these steps are performed automatically by WordPerfect.* Just type the source or the sentences that make up the note. Both footnotes and endnotes can be used in the same document.

**5.** Press Exit (F7) to return to the normal typing screen

The Cancel key will not back out of the footnote or endnote screen. You must press Exit. The cursor remains where it was when you invoked the Footnote function, but a note number is inserted in place. When you print the document, the note number appears as a superscript.

Figure 9.13 displays the typing screen with two footnotes, 1 and 2, already inserted at the end of the second and third sentences. The Footnote menu displays at the bottom of the screen.

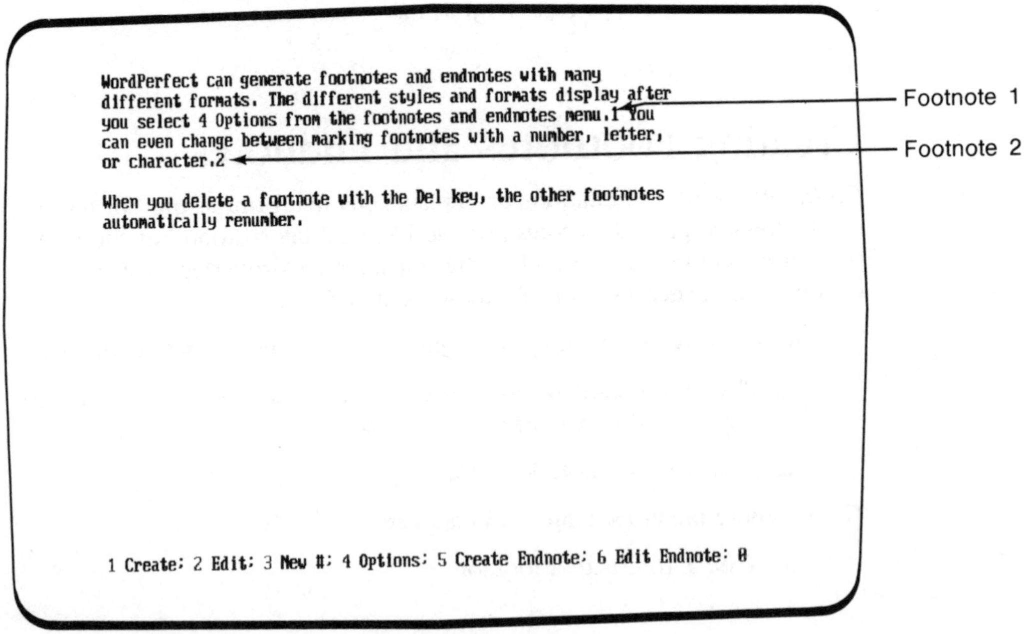

```
WordPerfect can generate footnotes and endnotes with many
different formats. The different styles and formats display after
you select 4 Options from the footnotes and endnotes menu.1 You      ──── Footnote 1
can even change between marking footnotes with a number, letter,
or character.2 ◄───                                                  ──── Footnote 2

When you delete a footnote with the Del key, the other footnotes
automatically renumber.




1 Create; 2 Edit; 3 New #; 4 Options; 5 Create Endnote; 6 Edit Endnote; 0
```

*Fig. 9.13. Footnote menu from the Footnote key (Ctrl-F7).*

Neither the footnotes nor the endnotes appear at the end of the typing page on-screen. In WordPerfect 4.2, you can select 6 Preview from the Print key (Shift-F7) to display how footnotes will appear. In both WordPerfect 4.1 and 4.2, you can read the first 50 characters of a note by using Reveal Codes. The program adjusts the page breaks to allow for the notes.

## Editing Footnotes and Endnotes

To edit an existing footnote, press Footnote (Ctrl-F7) and select either 2 Edit Footnote or 6 Edit Endnote. A prompt asks for the number of the note that you plan to edit. Enter the number and press Enter. The note text appears on the screen. Edit the note just as you would edit ordinary text.

You can move quickly through a document to each footnote or endnote by using the Search key (F2) to search for the Footnote or Endnote code hidden in the text. For example, to search forward for the next footnote, press the Search key (F2). When the prompt for the search characters appears, press the Footnote key (Ctrl-F7) and select 1 Create; then press F2 to start the search. To find the next footnote, just press F2 twice.

You can perform most of the standard WordPerfect typing and editing functions as you create your footnotes and endnotes. For example, you can use the Move function to copy a footnote that you will use again later, and you may use the Macro function to enter sources that are footnoted repeatedly. You'll read about Macros in Chapter 14.

Footnotes can be inserted at any time, either while you type text or after you enter it. WordPerfect automatically renumbers all footnotes when you add or delete them and reformats the pages after you edit footnotes.

Each footnote is printed at the bottom of the page with the reference number. If a footnote is too long to fit on the page, WordPerfect prints at least three lines on the page and carries the rest to the next page. In WordPerfect 4.2, you can choose an option to print a *Continued* . . . message when the footnote continues on a following page.

WordPerfect begins printing endnotes on the last page of the document. To make sure that your endnotes start printing on a new page, press Hard Page at the end of the document.

## Footnote and Endnote Options and Formats

To change footnote or endnote formats, move the cursor to the point in the text where you want the new format to start, press the Footnote key (Ctrl-F7), and select 4 Options. The Footnote Options menu displayed in figure 9.14 is displayed. Format changes entered from this menu affect the format of footnotes and endnotes following the cursor.

```
Footnote Options

    1 - Spacing within notes                      1
    2 - Spacing between notes                      1
    3 - Lines to keep together                     3
    4 - Start footnote numbers each page           N
    5 - Footnote numbering mode                    0
    6 - Endnote numbering mode                     0
    7 - Line separating text and footnotes         1
    8 - Footnotes at bottom of page                Y
    9 - Characters for notes                       *
    A - String for footnotes in text             [SuprScrpt][Note]
    B - String for endnotes in text              [SuprScrpt][Note]
    C - String for footnotes in note                  [SuprScrpt][Note]
    D - String for endnotes in note              [Note].

    For options 5 & 6:              For option 7:
        0 - Numbers                     0 - No line
        1 - Characters                  1 - 2 inch line
        2 - Letters                     2 - Line across entire page
                                        3 - 2 in. line w/continued string

    Selection: 0
```

*Fig. 9.14. Footnote 4 Options menu.*

Some of these options are self-explanatory; you may need help with others. Select 3, Lines to keep together, to change the number of lines the program will keep together at a page break that occurs in a footnote or endnote. The selection 4, Start footnote numbers each page, restarts footnote numbering at the top of each page if you type Y.

To identify your footnotes or endnotes with letters (A, B, C, . . . ) or characters (*, **, ***, . . . ), choose 5 Footnote numbering mode or 6 Endnote numbering mode. Enter the identifier type (0, 1, or 2) from the list at the lower left section of the menu shown in figure 9.14. If you choose characters to identify each footnote or endnote, you can select the type of character used from option 9 Characters for notes.

To create a *Continued* . . . message when footnotes wrap to the next page, select 7, Line Separating text and footnotes, and enter 3 from the menu at the bottom right of the menu.

When you want footnotes printed at the bottom of the page, check the setting in 8 Footnotes at bottom of page for Y. If you want footnotes directly below the text, even on short pages, then type N.

## Deleting Footnotes and Endnotes

To delete a footnote or an endnote, position the cursor on the reference number in the document, press Del, and type Y to the deletion prompt. The program then deletes the note and automatically renumbers any notes that follow.

## Renumbering Footnotes and Endnotes

Because WordPerfect automatically numbers footnotes and endnotes, you'll seldom need to change footnote numbers.

If you do need to make a change: Place the cursor anywhere in the text before the note that must be renumbered, press the Footnote key (Ctrl-F7), and select 3 New #. A prompt asks you for the new number. Type the number and press Enter. All of the footnotes or endnotes that follow are renumbered sequentially.

## Numbering Your Document's Lines

If you frequently prepare manuscripts (for books, plays, poetry, technical reference materials) you'll find WordPerfect's Line Numbering function helpful.

Line numbering includes all document text including footnote and endnote lines, but it does not include headers and footers. To begin (and you can begin and end line numbering anywhere and any number of times in your document), move the cursor to the location in your document where you want the numbering to begin and press Print Format (Ctrl-F8). Select Line Numbering option B and make the appropriate selections from the menu displayed on your screen.

Just as you and I are influenced by our initial impression of others, we form initial impressions about the printed materials we see every day. The way in which text "presents itself" makes a dramatic first impression on most of us. In the span of a few seconds, we decide how complete a document is, how technical a document is, how complicated a document is, how formal a document is, and even, how important a document is. Often, without reading a word, we decide whether the document is worthy of the time and effort it'll take to read it.

The page formatting features and techniques presented in this chapter will help you elicit the kind of positive response most of us seek in our writing efforts.

This chapter explored four methods for determining the location of page breaks. Of course, each page-break method works best in specific situations:

| Method | Key | Result |
|---|---|---|
| Widow/Orphan | Alt-F8, A | Prevents single lines at the end of a page or at the beginning of a page |
| Block protect | Block, Alt-F8 | Protects a chart or a table from being divided between pages |
| Conditional EOP | Alt-F8, 9 | Holds a specified number of lines together on the same page |
| Hard Page break | Ctrl-Enter | Breaks lines of text into separate pages at the end of a document |

Most businesses use many different forms, labels, and letterheads. To adjust for different paper sizes and lines of text per page, use the Page Format key (Alt-F8) to display the Page Length menu, choose 4 Page Length, set the page size for a specific form, and adjust the top margin from the same menu by choosing 5 Top Margin. (Remember that changing the top margin affects the space remaining for the bottom margin.)

A *Continued...* message feature is available from the Footnote Options menu. If the footnote is continued to the next page, WordPerfect separates the text from the footnote with a two-inch line and prints (Continued . . .) in the last line of the footnote. (Continued . . . ) is printed in the first line of the footnote on the next page, as well.

1. Press Footnote (Ctrl-F7)

2. Select 4

3. Select 7 Line Separating Text and Footnotes

4. Type 3

5. Press Enter to return to your document

Finally, you may work in a technical or academic environment where every person claims to know "the only acceptable way" to write footnotes or endnotes. If you are faced with a unique footnote or endnote requirement, don't fret. WordPerfect is extremely flexible. Create a small sample document and experiment with the different footnote and endnote options available with Ctrl-F7, 4 Options.

To continue the topic of formatting, you also might refer to the tab and margin setting information in Chapter 8. If you write scripts or newsletters, read Chapter 11. Any work with footnotes and endnotes may require repetitive typing, but the macros described in Chapter 14 can save you lots of keystrokes!

# CHAPTER 10

# More about Your Printer

This chapter is a collection of facts that can affect how you control printed *output*. You'll find information about setting up printers, changing between printers, using special print features, and troubleshooting printer problems.

When a solution to a printer question is best handled by a format code, you'll be directed to other, more appropriate, chapters of *Using WordPerfect*, 3rd Edition.

Perhaps more than any other potential difficulty, the printer's installation and daily operation can pose a challenge for even the most efficient word-processing operations. If the printer is set up correctly and its special features are understood by those using it, it demands few changes and little attention. Getting to that point, however, can be very exasperating.

WordPerfect provides a feature that will save you both time and frustration—the capability to print from a *queue* (a list of documents)—while you continue typing and editing other documents. This chapter will also introduce you to:

- Working with multiple printers

- Making multiple copies

- Using different types of paper-feed mechanisms

Some printers use sets of characters that differ from those you see displayed on-screen. Never fear, you'll learn how to match keys to printed characters. With WordPerfect, you'll be able to see exactly how your document will look after it's printed, including, of course, the page numbers, headers, footers, footnotes—all the special features you've selected.

# Previewing What Will Print

Before you print your document, you can take advantage of the WordPerfect 4.2 Preview feature. Preview shows you on-screen exactly how your document will look when it is printed—including headers, footnotes, page numbers—every format element you've specified. To request Preview:

1. Press the Print key (Shift-F7)

2. Select **6** Preview

You are asked if you want to preview 1 Document or 2 Page. Select 1 to view each page of the entire document. Select 2 to see how the current page will print. Scroll through the pages with the normal cursor movement keys. When you want to return to the typing screen, press Exit (F7).

# Printing the Display

There'll be times when you'll want to print the screen just as you see it, including Reveal Codes, Status Lines, and menus. If, for instance, you find an error or an unusual code and want a record of it, print the screen.

Print the screen by holding down the Shift key and pressing PrtSc. The printer prints all of the text on that screen. Be sure your printer is on and attached before you use this (and any other) function.

PrtSc works only if you use a parallel printer. Parallel printers are usually dot matrix and are connected to an LPT port when installed.

# Printing While Editing Another Document on the Screen

As mentioned before, one of WordPerfect's nicest timesaving features is the capability to create or edit a document on-screen while you print one or more documents from disk. You can create a queue, or list of documents, that will print while you continue working on the screen.

Because your computer must handle both typing and printing operations simultaneously, both the editing and printing tasks may be slowed. This slowdown is normal and doesn't pose any threat either to your on-screen work or to the output.

You can request that your documents print from the disk in two ways. One of the easiest methods is:

1. Enter the List Files menu (F5)

2. Move the cursor to the file you want printed

3. Press 4 Print

The highlighted document is added to the print queue and prints either immediately or when it assumes the first position in the queue. After pressing 4, you can return to your typing. Another procedure for adding documents to the print queue is to:

1. Press Print (Shift-F7)

2. Select 4 Printer Control

From the menu at the upper right corner of the screen:

3. Type **P**

You have prompted WordPerfect for the name and the pages of the document you want to print. Figure 10.1 illustrates the prompt and two files that are already in the queue to be printed.

More documents can be held in the print queue than will display in the space allowed in figure 10.1. To see the entire print queue, type D from the Printer Control screen. After adding documents to the queue, you can return to the typing screen and continue typing.

# Moving between Printers

Some systems are set up so that more than one printer is attached to each computer. A common configuration is to attach both a high-speed dot-matrix printer to print drafts, labels, and graphics, and a letter-quality or laser printer to print higher quality final documents. If your computer is set up like this, you must tell WordPerfect that it will be interacting with two different printers—only then will WordPerfect be able to communicate correctly with each printer model.

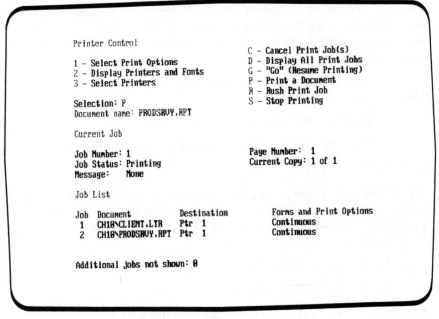

Fig. 10.1. Printer Control menu displaying queue and print prompt.

Before changing between printer definitions, you must see which printer definitions are available and which of six different printer numbers they are assigned to. You can see the six printers (and definitions) that are currently available by pressing the Print key (Shift-F7) and selecting 4 Printer Control. From the Printer Control menu, type 2 to select 2 Display Printers and fonts. A screen similar to figure 10.2 will display showing you the printer number, the printer model, the paper-feed type, and the available fonts. Jot down the number of the printer you'll be using.

If you don't find your printer, press the space bar for the next screen. Three printers are displayed on each screen. WordPerfect can accommodate six printers, each with either different or similar printer definitions attached to them. If your printer is not one of the six definitions currently available, then you must return to the chapter about installing printers and install the printer definition for your printer model.

Now that you have identified the printer number that you'll use, you can choose it temporarily (for the next printed document only), or you can use it for the rest of your work session. If you want to change printers

```
1:  Epson MX-Graftrax/MX-Type IIIContinuous

        1 Dot Matrix 1/60      2 Epson Graftrax
        3 Epson Graftrax       4 Epson Graftrax
        5 Epson FX&Type3       6 Epson FX&Type3
        7 Epson FX&Type3       8 Epson FX&Type3

2:  LaserWriter Times Portrait  Continuous

        1 Times 12pt           2 Times Ital 12pt
        3 Times Bold 12pt      4 Times BItl 12pt
        5 Times 9pt            6 Times Ital 9pt
        7 Times 5pt            8 Times Bold 18pt

3:  LaserWriter Times Landscape  Continuous

        1 Times 12pt           2 Times Ital 12pt
        3 Times Bold 12pt      4 Times BItl 12pt
        5 Times 9pt            6 Times Ital 9pt
        7 Times 5pt            8 Times Bold 18pt



    Press any key to continue
```

*Fig. 10.2. Display printers and fonts options.*

temporarily, give the Print command (Shift-F7) and select 3 Change Options. The menu shown in figure 10.3 displays. Compare the heading on this menu, Change Print Options Temporarily, with the permanent change menu.

To specify a different printer and its printer definition, press 1 to select Printer Number. Type the number of the printer that has both the printer definition and paper-feed type that you want. Press Enter to return to the typing screen.

If you're changing to another printer for the rest of your work, press the Print key (Shift-F7) and choose 4 Printer Control. From the menu at the upper left corner, choose 1 Select Print Options. The Select Print Options menu looks exactly like the Change Print Options Temporarily menu. Type 1 and enter the number of the printer. Press Enter twice to return to the typing screen. On this menu, you can change between printers whenever you want.

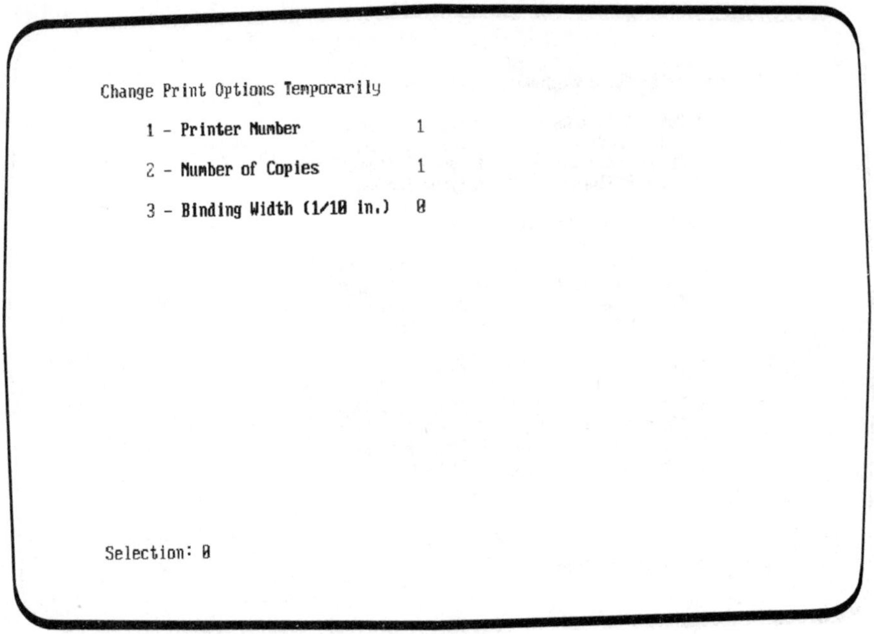

```
Change Print Options Temporarily

     1 - Printer Number        1

     2 - Number of Copies      1

     3 - Binding Width (1/10 in.)  0




Selection: 0
```

*Fig. 10.3. Change Print Options Temporarily menu.*

# Changing Number of Copies
# or Binding Width Options

You'll change Print Multiple Copies and Binding Width in exactly the same manner that you change the printer. You can change the number of copies or the binding width for the next print job only or for the rest of your work session, as you did for your printer.

To make a change for the next job only:

> **1.** Enter the Print menu (Shift-F7)
>
> **2.** Select **3** Options

To change for the rest of the work session:

> **1.** Enter the Print menu (Shift-F7)
>
> **2.** Select **4** Printer Control
>
> **3.** Select **1** Select Print Options

To print multiple copies, select 2 Number of Copies and type the number of copies you want. Option 3 Binding Width offsets the text on the printed page to allow two-sided copying and binding. You can offset the text in increments of 1/10 inch.

For example, to shift the text one half of an inch on the page, type 5. The text on odd-numbered pages moves to the right; text on even-numbered pages shifts to the left.

# Printing a Portion of Your Document

You can print just a portion of your document. If, for instance, you've called a sales meeting to discuss one idea presented in a lengthy report, use the Block function to highlight only the text to be discussed. Press the Print key. A prompt asks Print Block? (Y/N). When you type Y, the highlighted block of text prints. You have saved copying time and money—and those participating in the meeting won't have to shuffle through pages of text to be able to focus on the matter at hand.

Use any of the cursor movement keys and the Go To key to help highlight the block of text. Look at Chapter 6, "Using the Block Function To Rearrange Your Text," for more information about printing with the Block.

# Printing Letterhead and Multipage Documents

When you instruct WordPerfect to print multiple-page and odd-size documents, you may have to make format changes in the number of text lines on a page, the top-margin setting, the page numbers, the line spacing, and other elements that affect the amount of text that can appear on the page. Chapter 9 describes how to set these formatting features for different types of documents.

If you're using a bin feeder to feed single sheets of paper for a multipaged document, read the section called "Using Bin Feed Single Sheets."

# Printing with a Variety of Feed Mechanisms

Your printer may have the capability to print with any of the three sheet-delivery mechanisms:

- Continuous paper

- Single sheets that are hand-fed

- Single sheets fed from a bin-fed mechanism

Each type of sheet feeding mechanism requires a different printer. For example, the Display Printers and Fonts screen, figure 10.2, may show the QuietWriter® as continuous fed in printer 1, hand fed in printer 2, and bin fed in printer 3. You must change between printers to select the printer that will handle your paper-feed method.

## Using Continuous Feed Paper

If you use continuous feed paper, your printer is fed from a continuous stack of sheets linked by a perforated edge. WordPerfect automatically advances to the next sheet at the appropriate time. You'll find an illustration of the various kinds of printer sheet feed mechanisms in Chapter 1.

If the printer starts with the correct top margin but prints over the perforated edge between sheets, then you must reset either your top margin or the number of text lines per page. The sections "Changing the Top Margin" and "Changing the Number of Text Lines per Inch" in Chapter 9 describe these procedures.

## Using Hand Feed Single Sheets

WordPerfect assumes that hand-fed sheets of paper are rolled one inch past the print head. This measurement is considered automatically when the paper advances at the top margin. WordPerfect knows if the printer uses hand-fed single sheets because you designated that feed mechanism when you installed the printer definition. For more information about selecting paper-feed mechanisms refer to Chapters 1 and 9. If you are using a single-sheet paper feeder and select the 1 Full Text print option, the printer does not print immediately but waits for you to indicate that you have inserted a sheet of paper.

To give the printer the "go" command, press the Print key (Shift-F7) a second time, select 4 Printer Control, and type G for go. The printer stops after each page is printed and waits for you to insert the next sheet. Type G after you insert a sheet.

### Using Bin Feed Single Sheets

Bin feeders automatically feed single sheets of paper as they are needed by the printer. Some bin feeders have two bins, one for letterhead and the other for bond. Your printer must be specifically designed to work with a bin feeder.

The bin-feed option is selected when you select your printer definition. When you choose bin feed as the paper-feed method, you are shown a list of bin-feed types from which you must choose. If your bin feeder has a single bin from which to pull paper, it may work satisfactorily if the printer is selected for continuous feed.

To prepare your bin-feed mechanism, you normally place letterhead paper in bin 1 and plain-bond second sheet paper in bin 2.

After typing your document, specify the bin from which each page should be pulled. Because the letterhead is stored in bin 1 and the default is bin 1, no change needs to be made for single-page correspondence or for the first page of a document beginning with letterhead.

Move the cursor to the first character on the page where you'll call the first sheet from bin 2. Use the Reveal Codes screen to make sure the cursor is positioned both at the first location and before any hidden codes.

Press Print Format (Ctrl-F8) and select 9 Sheet Feeder Bin #. Type the number of the bin you want (2, in this case). Press Enter to return to the typing screen. You have inserted the hidden code [Bin#:2], which can be deleted by the Reveal Codes key. You can enter a bin number on another page to return to bin 1.

# Printing on Nonstandard-Size Paper

When you print on nonstandard-size sheets of paper, use the Page Length command under the Page Format key (Alt-F8) to change both the paper size and the number of text lines per page. Change the width of the paper by changing the margins. If you have a wide carriage printer but the printer does not print on wide paper (even though you have set wide margins), check the printer manual index for the DIP switch settings for the printer.

## Printing Mailing Labels

Because of their speed, dot-matrix printers are most often selected for printing mailing labels. *Don't use standard pressure-sensitive labels with laser printers!* The fixitive causes major problems if it melts in the high-temperature rollers. To print labels on a laser printer:

- Use Avery® labels designed specifically for laser printers

- Use dry-adhesive sheet labels

- Print on a paper form and then photocopy the form to sheets of labels

If you print labels on single-column continuous-feed sheets, then you may need to refer to the changing Left Margin, Page Length, and Top Margin procedures in Chapters 8 and 9.

For more information about generating labels, Chapter 15 explores the idea of building a label-field database, and Chapter 11 discusses the procedure for printing labels in a multicolumn format.

# Choosing Print Pitch and Font

Many printers offer several options for type styles and sizes; sometimes the printer's instructions for selecting these options are confusing. WordPerfect eliminates the need to rely on obscure printer instructions by offering standard settings for pitch (characters per inch), font (type style), and number of text lines per vertical inch. Selecting these options is simple, and using the program's options is generally easier than entering printer commands from the printer manual.

## Changing Pitch and Font

WordPerfect is compatible with the options for spacing and pitch available on most printers. If your printer offers fonts or print styles, enter the appropriate font-change codes at the point in your text where you want the printing change to occur. If you must physically change print elements such as wheels, thimbles, and balls, the printer will stop when it reaches the code in your document. The printer stops to allow you to change the

print element. To designate a change in fonts, press the Print Format key
(Ctrl-F8) and type 1. The cursor moves into this option:

```
1 - Pitch          10
    Font            1
```

The cursor flashes at the Pitch number (which indicates the number of
characters per inch). Type the new Pitch setting. Press Enter or use the
down-arrow key to move the cursor to the next line and change 1 to the
new font setting. Press Enter to return to the typing screen.

You can see the fonts available for each printer. From the typing screen,
switch to the Printer Control menu with the Print key (Shift-F7) and
select 4 Printer Control. From the Print menu, type 2 for 2 Display
Printers and Fonts. Eight fonts and the recommended pitch setting for
each printer definition are displayed.

Some fonts on the Display Printers and Fonts screen may look alike. You
may see a few listed by the same name, but they may be different in style
or orientation (vertical or sideways). To see the difference in fonts and
pitches, retrieve and print the PRINTER.TST or PRINTER2.TST documents.

When you change pitch, you change the number of characters per
horizontal inch. For example, if you've printed with 10 pitch (10
characters per inch) and change to 12 characters per inch, WordPerfect
will fit more characters in each inch of space across the line. Compare the
lines that appear in figure 10.4.

```
This text has been printed with a 10-pitch setting.
This text has been printed with a 12-pitch setting.
```

*Fig. 10.4. Pitch setting examples.*

You must adjust the right margin if you want to retain the same line
length when you change pitch. Changing the pitch on some laser printers
does not affect the output. The pitch is set permanently for each font.

Because larger fonts may occupy more vertical space than normal fonts,
you may need to change the line spacing and the number of text lines for

the page. Because the larger fonts also occupy more horizontal space, you may have to shorten the length of the line, and you also may have to change the hyphenation zone to include more or less hyphenation.

## Creating Proportionally Spaced Text

WordPerfect offers you another option—proportional spacing. Proportional spacing occurs when the printer makes spacing adjustments based on the width of each character. For example, *m* and *w* are wider than *i* and *l*. If you select proportional spacing, the number of characters that fit on a line varies from one line to the next.

```
This sentence is printed using the proportional spacing option.

This sentence is printed without the proportional spacing option.
```

Fig. 10.5. Proportional spacing example.

Your printed documents will take on a more "professional" look because proportional spacing produces more readable, typeset-like text. To set proportional spacing, go to the Print Format menu and select 1 Pitch. Enter the pitch number and type an asterisk (*). For example, if the pitch remains at 10 but is proportional, type 10* and press Enter.

The cursor should lie to the right of the Font prompt. Type the number of the font that represents the proportional font in your printer definition, and press Enter. You can look at the available fonts on your printer by pressing the Print key (Shift-F7), selecting 4 Printer Control, and choosing 2 Display Printers and Fonts.

Your text will be proportionally spaced—if your printer is capable of performing proportional spacing. To turn off proportional spacing, return to the Print Format menu, remove the asterisk (*) from the pitch number, and change back to a nonproportional font.

If you plan to use proportional spacing every time you print, make proportional spacing the default setting. Refer to the Set-up Menu section in Chapter 17 for more information.

# Using Printer Control Codes

Some printers have features that you may not be able to use with WordPerfect. You also may have a printer for which a printer definition is not available. In either case, you can use printer control codes to control the printer's features.

You might change commands (on a dot-matrix printer, for example) to switch the printer from draft to letter-quality printing, to change the font, to change the type size, or to change the type style to styles that are not available in WordPerfect. The codes for these and many other printer options are listed in your printer manual. Each printer uses different codes; however, many of these codes begin with the Esc (escape) key character. Because the code begins with the Esc character, the printer understands that the next set of characters will change printer settings and should not be printed like normal characters. To see examples of these codes, look in the manual index under *Escape code* or *printer control code*. You'll probably find the codes arranged like this:

Esc "E"     for emphasized print

You cannot press the Esc key in WordPerfect to type an Esc key. When you press Esc, you invoke the repeat function or an escape from a menu. Instead, you must refer to the Esc key by its numeric computer code—027, the ASCII code.

To enter these codes in WordPerfect so that the printer will understand them, move the cursor to the position where you want the command to take effect. Press Print Format (Ctrl-F8), and select A for Insert Printer Command. The prompt Cmnd: appears. Enter the control code, and make sure that you type angle brackets (<>) around the 027.

*Example:* Cmnd:<Ø27>E

Press Enter. In this example, <027> represents the Esc character, and the E cues the printer to print in emphasize mode. The Printer Control Code is stored in the text as a hidden code that you can see only with the Reveal Codes function.

You can combine the effects of some codes by typing them in sequence. Each must contain the Esc code, if indicated. Some codes cannot be combined with others; they take precedence over all other codes. Usually, one code, such as Esc "@" or <027>@, resets the printer so that it forgets all codes that have been sent.

When you print the document, WordPerfect sends the command to the printer as though it were text. The printer, however, recognizes the <027> code as a control code and will not print it.

Like other WordPerfect commands, the printer command takes effect from the point where you enter it in the document through the remainder of the document.

If you intend to begin the document with letter-quality print, place the cursor at the beginning of the document and enter the code. Later, if you want to change to condensed characters, move the cursor to the position where condensed characters should begin, and enter the code for condensed characters. To return to letter quality, move the cursor to the position where the letter-quality print should begin again, and enter the letter-quality print code. Each time WordPerfect encounters a printing code, the program orders the printer to change accordingly—without interrupting the printing process.

# Troubleshooting Your Printer

The most frequently encountered printer problem is—*the wrong printer is selected.* WordPerfect sends signals and commands for one type of printer when, in fact, a different printer is attached to the computer. This error in selecting the proper printer can cause the printer to behave in very strange ways. If you're experiencing this problem, read the section in this chapter about changing printer options. Be sure that the printer you have selected matches the printer model that is physically attached to your computer.

The second most frequently encountered printer trouble involves the signals received from WordPerfect. The printer and WordPerfect may not "talk" to one another, or the commands may be garbled. Often these communication problems are a result of a faulty cable, or a faulty printer controller card inside the computer, a faulty program disk, or a damaged data file.

Check to be certain that you specified the correct port and communication settings when you installed the printer definition. For example, you may be sending print signals to COM2 when your printer is attached to COM1; or WordPerfect may send information at a rate of 9600 baud when the printer can receive at a rate of only 1200 baud.

The communication settings, usually described in your printer manual, were set when the printer definition was installed. Be sure that all cables are connected securely. Some of these problems may require assistance from a hardware technician.

The third trouble category is a faulty printer. This problem has nothing to do with WordPerfect, but it does prevent the program from printing properly. Check your computer manual index for a self-test procedure. If the self-test does not work correctly, consult your dealer.

## What To Do When Characters Print Incorrectly

WordPerfect displays standard characters found within the IBM-graphics character set. If your printer uses different characters for some of the symbols and line shapes, symbols and lines may not print as they display on-screen.

You have two solutions to this problem. Your printer may be capable of printing with the IBM-graphics character set by changing switch settings within the printer, or by using font cartridges or down-loadable character sets. Your printer manual and dealer can help you.

As an alternative, some printers have graphics characters and symbols similar to the IBM-graphics character set, but the manufacturer has assigned them to different keys. You can see the characters that match the keyboard keys by retrieving the file FONT.TST to a blank screen.

Figure 10.6 shows how this file displays characters in a matrix. Print this file to see how the corresponding screen characters appear on paper. If you want to reassign characters to different keyboard keys permanently, refer to Chapter 13 for information about the Ctrl/Alt keys selection from the Screen key. The printed copy of FONT.TST is necessary for reassigning characters in Chapter 13.

## Checking Command Codes

If your printer prints, but the printout doesn't seem to match what you've typed, an incorrect command may be causing the problem. For example, the vertical positioning of the text may not appear as you expected it. If this happens, place the cursor at the top of the page that begins printing incorrectly and press Reveal Codes (Alt-F3). Some formatting command codes—such as Advance, Top Margin, Center Page Top to Bottom, or Conditional EOP—may be causing the printer to scroll down the page before printing.

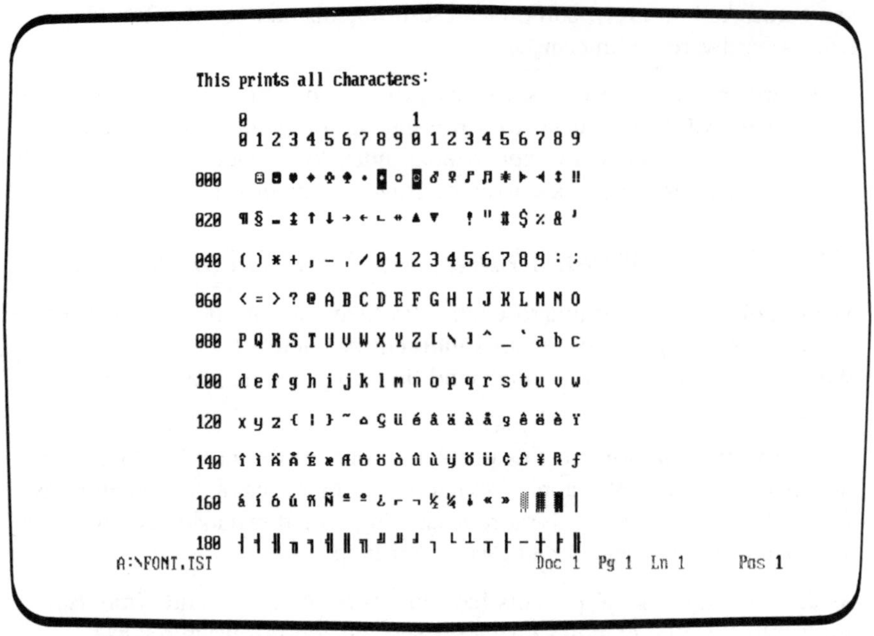

*Fig. 10.6. Font text matrix.*

Other codes, such as Center, Tab Align, Flush Right, Margin Release, or Indent, can cause the printer to move across the page before printing. And, some of these codes can conflict with each other because the program may not be capable of applying both of them to the same text.

If several like codes fall together in the text (such as several margin-set command codes recording different settings, for instance) WordPerfect uses the last in the sequence of commands. To avoid confusion, eliminate all but the desired code. Usually, the Reveal Codes command traces printing problems. Look for extra codes that you can remove from the document. Check also for omitted codes—cases in which you entered the commands but the codes don't appear in the document.

If you've identified the problem but cannot find the code, use the Search function (F2) to find it. When prompted for the Search string, press the function keys that evoke the command for which you are searching.

In this chapter you've explored how to make the most of WordPerfect's powerful printing features. One of the most dramatic timesaving features (a feature you'll use all of the time!) is the capability to queue documents to print while you continue to work on-screen with other documents. To create a print queue, the documents must be saved to disk, then:

☐ Select the documents in sequence with the 4 Print selection from the List Files screen, or

☐ Type the document name and the pages from the 4 Printer Control menu after pressing the Print key (Shift-F7)

If you work with different printer models or if you work with a single printer that has several sheet-feed methods, you must choose which printer will be used:

☐ Select a temporary printer for only the next print job with 3 Options from the Print key (Shift-F7), or

☐ Select a printer for the remainder of the work session from 1 Select Print Options from the 4 Printer Control menu after pressing the Print key (Shift-F7)

If you use hand-fed single sheets, remember that the printer does not print until you tell it to print. Although you give the printer a print command, it waits for you to insert a sheet. Give it the "go" signal by entering the 4 Printer Control menu and typing G.

Finally, you probably have noticed the frequency with which the Printer Control menu, (Shift-F7) 4 Printer Control, is used. The menus at the upper left and upper right corners of figure 10.1 give you control of many print functions. The messages that display at mid-screen indicate printing problems. Should you need to verify printer operation, look at these two menus and check the screen message.

# Creating
# Special Documents

To:     Communications Department Staff
From:  John Roberts
Re:     Quarterly Project Schedule

As promised, here is our production schedule for this quarter. By the way, this comes to you by way of WordPerfect's special formatting features.

| Item | Number | Price | Production Team |
|------|--------|--------|------------------|
| 73 | 278-5 | 239.95 | Allen, Smith |
| 267 | 305-7 | 111.95 | Jones, Walters |
| 98 | 295-8 | 319.95 | Roberts, Johnson |
| 276 | 134-0 | 129.95 | Thompson, Brown |

### Reporting Milestones

Monday, May 6th
Wednesday, May 22nd
Thursday, June 3rd
Friday, June 29th

Anticipated number of units moved:

| Item 73 | 239.95 * 600 = 143,970.00 |
| Item 267 | 111.95 * 100 = 11,195.00 |
| Item 98 | 319.95 * 50 = 15,997.50 |
| Item 276 | 129.95 * 25 = 3,248.75 |

J. Roberts

# Creating Newspaper and Parallel Columns of Text

**F**or those of you who create and produce newsletters, brochures, bulletins, sales presentations, scripts, training guides, and catalogs—documents that require a columnar text format—WordPerfect has a special feature you'll find invaluable. This chapter introduces you to the procedure you can use to create both newspaper-style columns of text and parallel columns of text.

Both of these types of columns are created in the same way:

- Move the cursor to the line immediately above the position in your document where you want the columnar text to begin

- Define the column type and appearance

- Turn on the column function

- Enter text (if it doesn't exist already)

- Turn off the column function at the end of the text

If you create text that others need to be able to read and understand quickly, try the newspaper-style format. Newspaper-style columns format text that flows from the bottom of one column to the top of the next column. Parallel columns format text in columns that usually are read as groups of horizontal text, such as scripts, catalogs, or price lists.

WordPerfect's text-column functions format both on-screen text and printed text which means that you'll be able to make layout and editing decisions before you print your document. The column functions presented in this chapter are intended for text, not for numeric columns. Numeric columns are better handled with Tab Align or the decimal tab (D) function.

# Creating Columns

Both newspaper-style columns and parallel columns are created with this WordPerfect procedure:

1. Move the cursor to the line immediately above the position where you want columns to begin

2. Press Math/Columns (Alt-F7,4) to display the Text Column Definition menu

3. Type **Y** or **N** to select evenly spaced columns or create your own column margins. Enter the number of spaces between columns if you typed Y

4. Type **1** to select Newspaper-style Columns

   Or

4. Type **2** to select Parallel Columns with Block Protect

5. Type the **number of columns** that will appear on your page

6. Press Exit (F7) to accept the column settings

7. Type **3** to turn on columns

8. Type your text

9. Press Alt-F7,3 to turn off columns

After you've defined the columns, you can turn them on and off throughout your document. The column definition that precedes a set of columns controls the column format and remains in control until you change column definitions.

# Creating Newspaper-Style Columns

To begin newspaper-style columns, press Math/Columns (Alt-F7) and select 4 Column Def. You must define your columns before you can turn the columns function on. After you select Column Def, the Text Column Definition menu appears, as shown in figure 11.1.

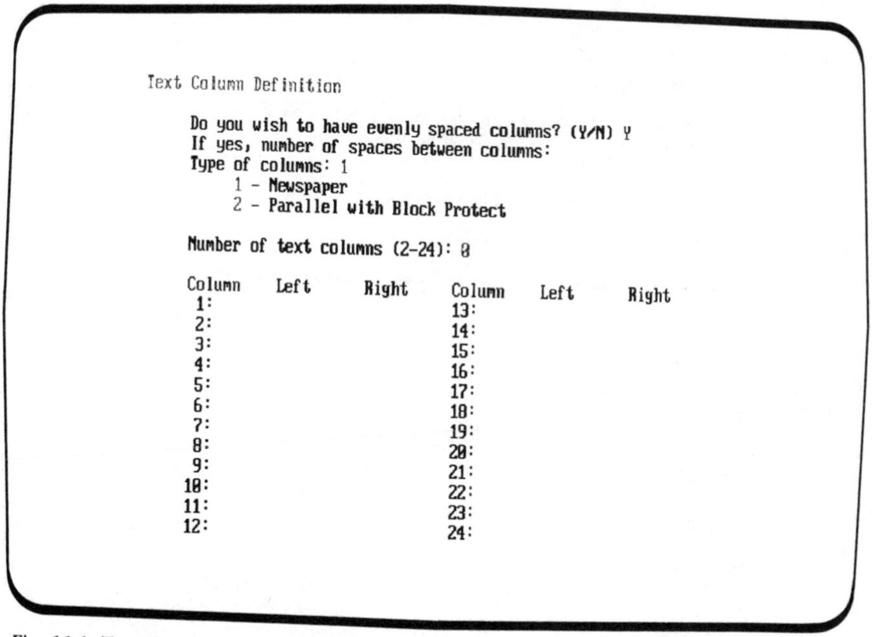

```
Text Column Definition

   Do you wish to have evenly spaced columns? (Y/N) Y
   If yes, number of spaces between columns:
   Type of columns: 1
       1 - Newspaper
       2 - Parallel with Block Protect

   Number of text columns (2-24): 8

   Column   Left    Right    Column   Left    Right
     1:                       13:
     2:                       14:
     3:                       15:
     4:                       16:
     5:                       17:
     6:                       18:
     7:                       19:
     8:                       20:
     9:                       21:
    10:                       22:
    11:                       23:
    12:                       24:
```

*Fig. 11.1. Text Column Definition menu.*

WordPerfect will prompt you to define your columns. Type Y if you've decided that all of your columns should be the same width. Then type the number of spaces that should separate the columns.

In WordPerfect 4.2, you then select newspaper-style columns by typing 1 after the Type of columns: prompt. (If you're using WordPerfect 4.1, type N to answer the prompt Do you want groups kept together on a page? (Y/N).)

Type the number of columns that should appear on the page (WordPerfect 4.2 permits from 2 to 24 columns), and press Enter.

The margins for each column are calculated automatically. Figure 11.2 illustrates margin settings for three columns of even width and five spaces between columns.

If you must make adjustments to column margins that have already been calculated, use the arrow keys to move the cursor to the margin you must change and enter the new setting. Press the Exit key (F7) to accept the settings and return to the Math/Column menu.

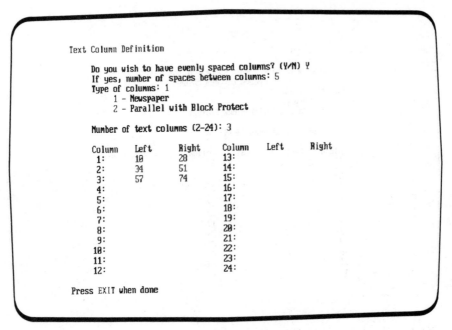

```
Text Column Definition

      Do you wish to have evenly spaced columns? (Y/N) Y
      If yes, number of spaces between columns: 5
      Type of columns: 1
            1 - Newspaper
            2 - Parallel with Block Protect

      Number of text columns (2-24): 3

      Column    Left    Right   Column   Left    Right
         1:      10       20      13:
         2:      34       51      14:
         3:      57       74      15:
         4:                       16:
         5:                       17:
         6:                       18:
         7:                       19:
         8:                       20:
         9:                       21:
        10:                       22:
        11:                       23:
        12:                       24:

   Press EXIT when done
```

*Fig. 11.2. Margin settings for three even columns set five spaces apart.*

If you want to calculate the column widths yourself, type N when the program asks Do you wish to have evenly spaced columns? (Y/N). Specify the type and number of columns and complete the margins for each column.

If you define a greater-than-usual number of columns or columns that are very wide, WordPerfect may require more space on the document page than the current margins provide. If this happens, an error message appears that cautions that the "columns are too wide, return to the typing screen." Move the cursor above the column definition position and set wider margin settings for the document.

Once you've defined the columns, the settings remain active in the document—until you either change them or delete the code. You can change column definitions throughout a WordPerfect 4.2 document. WordPerfect 4.1 permits only one column definition throughout the entire document. When you save your document on a disk, the column definitions also are saved.

## Beginning the Columns

After you define the columns, turn on the columns function by pressing Math/Columns (Alt-F7) and selecting 3 Column On/Off. You can turn on the column function at a location only after the columns have been defined. When the column function is on and the cursor rests within a column, the Col indicator appears on the Status Line to show you in which column the cursor rests.

## Typing Column Text

After Column has been turned on, you'll enter the text that will fill the first column until:

• You come to the end of a page

• You force a column break with the Hard Page command (Ctrl-Enter)

• You turn off the column function

The first two options move the cursor to the next column automatically. The text is printed on-screen only as wide as the column margins permit.

You can move the cursor to a column on the left by moving it to the first character at the top of the current column and pressing the left-arrow key. The cursor moves to the bottom of the preceding column. To move the cursor to a column that lies to the right, move it to the last character of your current column and press the right-arrow key. The cursor will move to the top of the column on the right.

The Advance Line, Margin Set, and Footnotes functions do not work when you are in column mode. To leave room for a logo or a newsletter heading, use the Advance Line function before turning on columns or after turning off columns. You can review how to use Advance Line in Chapter 9.

Hyphenation and Justification functions can affect the appearance of your columns. To achieve tighter word spacing, reset the H-Zone before you begin entering the text. Common H-Zone settings for text columns are 3 and 3, and 2 and 3.

## Creating Newspaper-Style Columns with Existing Text

Straight text, previously entered, can be formatted easily into columns. To reformat straight text, follow essentially the same steps that you'd use to create columns.

Move the cursor to the beginning of the text and define the columns. After defining the columns, place the cursor at the beginning of the text to be reformatted. Press the Math/Columns key (Alt-F7) and select 3 Column On/Off. The text will look as if nothing has changed. Press the down-arrow key and the text will reformat to column text. If the column format has been previously defined, you need only to turn Column on at the beginning of the existing text.

## Turning Off Newspaper-Style Columns

To turn Column off after entering the text, return to the Math/Columns menu (Alt-F7) and select 3 Column On/Off. Before you turn off the column function, remember that you should place the cursor at the end of the last text you want formatted in columns. You should turn Column on or off only while the cursor is at the beginning or the end of a line.

## Removing the Column Format

To cancel Column and return the columnar text to straight-text format, position the cursor at the beginning of the columnar material, enter Reveal Codes (Alt-F3), and delete the [Col On] code with the Del or Backspace key. The column definitions remain but the instructions to reformat that material in columns are removed.

## Ending Columns

To end a column before you reach the end of your page, press Hard Page (Ctrl-Enter) to insert a Hard Page code [HPg].

## Improving the Appearance of Columnar Text

Justified newspaper-style columns may not format as neatly as a full-page-width column because the spacing between words in the printed newspaper-style columns frequently is too wide for the text to look "right." Wider columns offer more room to adjust the words with spaces.

You can improve the appearance of text spacing in your columns by changing the H-Zone settings so the text aligns more evenly with the right margin. Change the H-Zone settings before you turn on Column. Another approach you might consider is resetting the column definitions for slightly different spacing between columns. Changing the space between columns changes the text-column widths and causes the Hyphenation function to divide the words differently.

# Printing Mailing Labels in Multiple Columns

Printing mailing labels in multiple columns (three-up, for example) can be a money-saver if you produce label after label each day. To create the labels from a secondary merge list (described in Chapter 15) carry out this procedure:

1. Create a secondary merge file that contains your mailing-list information (described in Chapter 15)

2. Create a primary document that prints the mailing list in a one-up (single column) label format

3. Use the Merge function to merge the secondary merge file with the primary document

This step creates a file that has a single column of mailing labels.

4. Measure the sheets on which you will print multiple columns of labels

5. Calculate the margin settings for each column and the page length for the sheet (most printers print at ten characters per inch and six lines per inch)

6. Set the text lines per page with the Page Length choice from the Page Format key (Alt-F8)

7. Define the newspaper-style columns at the top of the single column of labels

8. Turn on the columns function

9. Press the down-arrow key to see the single column of labels flow into three columns

# Creating Parallel Columns

Although parallel columns and newspaper-style columns are created in much the same way, the printed text is very different.

Parallel columns usually are read across the page rather than down the page. When you edit a parallel column, the related horizontal segments of text remain next to each other even when you insert or delete text in a preceding part of the column. (The items in the columns remain parallel to one another.) Here are some examples of, and uses for, parallel columns:

Schedules        Aligning names, routes, and times within
                 column formats.

Scripts          Aligning names and dialogue.

Catalogs         Aligning item numbers, descriptions, and
                 prices.

Figure 11.3 is an example of how you might use three parallel columns.

```
                          TASK TEAM LIST

      March 3, 1987


                    Complete    Team           Action
      Action Item   Date        Members        Description
      ============  ========    =======        ===========

      Appraisal of  3/13/87     Smalle, R,     Multi-office
      Janus site                Teddis, K,     site analysis
                                Black, R,      near Holcomb

      Acctg S/W     4/15/87     Ira, D,        Service
      selected                  Cache, S,      oriented
                                Gelt, G,       acctg




      C:\WP\WP42\CH11\FIG11WK3.WP        Col 2  Doc 1  Pg 1  Ln 15    Pos 28
```

*Fig. 11.3. Parallel columns.*

You can, of course, use the Left Indent key to create two columns but, if you need three or more columns, use the Parallel Columns function.

Parallel columns should be used for groups of text that fit on a single page. If a segment of columnar text requires more than one page, the extra text wraps to the next column and destroys the format of parallel columns. To prevent text from wrapping to the next page, separate long segments of text with the Hard Page key (Ctrl-Enter).

## Defining Parallel Columns

To define parallel columns, press the Math/Columns key (Alt-F7), then select 4 Columns Def as you did for newspaper-style columns. Type Y or N for evenly spaced columns. If you typed Y, enter the number of spaces desired between columns. Choose 2 Parallel with Block Protect to select Parallel Columns. In WordPerfect 4.1, type Y to the prompt Do you want groups kept together on a page? (Y/N) to choose Parallel Columns.

Enter the number of columns; the margins will be calculated and displayed in the lower section. The Text Column Definition screen in figure 11.4 is set for four parallel columns and manually entered margins.

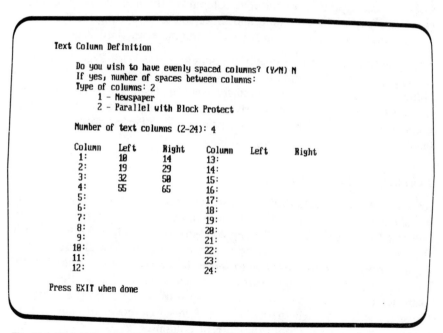

Fig. 11.4. Text Column Definition menu set for four parallel columns.

Be sure that you select margins that allow for your text; narrow columns demand excessive hyphenation. If you format existing text for parallel columns, turn off hyphenation until you can determine how the text will fit within the column parameters.

## Beginning Parallel Columns

After defining the columns, turn on Parallel Columns by pressing the Math/Columns key and choosing 3 Column On/Off to begin the columns. Make sure you start the parallel columns after the character position where you've defined the columns.

## Typing Parallel Column Text

Entering text in parallel columns differs from normal typing. Move the cursor beyond the character position where you turned on Parallel Columns, and type text for the first column on the line. Press Hard Page (Ctrl-Enter) to end the column and move to the next column. Type the text for the second column and end the column with Hard Page.

After you type the last of a group of columns, press Hard Page to return the cursor to the first column for typing the next group of parallel columns. When the program calculates page breaks, it keeps all the lines of a related group on the same page. The columns of text are aligned on the screen as they will appear when printed. WordPerfect inserts one blank line to separate the groups of text.

## Editing Parallel Columns

After the text is formatted in columns, you can edit the text column and not affect the text in the neighboring columns. Move the cursor between columns by pressing the Go To key combination (Ctrl-Home), followed by the left- or right-arrow keys. If the cursor rests on the first character of a column, press the left-arrow key to move the cursor to the column on the left. Similarly, press the right-arrow key when the cursor is on the last character of a column to move the cursor to the column on the right. Pressing the left- or right-arrow keys by themselves moves the cursor from character to character within the current column.

If two columns suddenly wrap together, you have accidentally deleted the Hard Page code, [HPg], which separates columns in a text group. To fix this, move the cursor to the location in the text where you want the column break and then press the Hard Page key (Ctrl-Enter).

After moving through the text and the columns, the text may not format correctly as you begin to type. The cursor may appear to be correctly positioned for additional column text, but it is outside the hidden codes that control parallel columns. To position the cursor so that you can type, go to Reveal Codes by pressing Alt-F3. Use the left- or right-arrow keys to position the cursor according to these guidelines:

• Groups of parallel text columns begin with [BlockPro:On][Col on]

• Columns in a group are separated with [HPg]

• Last column in a group at the right margin ends with [Col off]

### Ending Parallel Columns

If a text group does not fill the page but does extend beyond the page break, insert a Hard Page break. The Block Protection codes automatically move the text group to the top of the next page in your document.

## Using Column Display

Make creating and editing columns more efficient by speeding up both scrolling and rewriting the screen. Display each column on a separate page instead of side-by-side by selecting Column Display (Alt-F7,5). Type N to display columns on separate pages. Each column displays in the position it would normally occupy but the columns are divided by Hard Page breaks.

To display the columns side-by-side again, press Column Display (Alt-F7,5) and type Y.

You don't have to own (or even have access to) expensive typesetting equipment, graphic artists, pasteup people, or publishing software to produce a slick in-house publication. You can put out a high-quality publication with just a 24-pin dot-matrix printer (or a laser printer) and WordPerfect's newspaper-style and parallel column formatting options—plus a few other WordPerfect tricks.

If your printer supports line drawing, create borders for photos and charts. Leave space for photographs by pressing Enter to insert hard returns and use the Block Protect function to keep the photo area from being divided by a page break. Photos, logos, and line drawings can be added to your newsletter by the print shop.

Use the format that works best and most efficiently for the job you are doing. Try newspaper-style and parallel column formatting on a few simple jobs before you attempt them on more complex and time-sensitive work.

Both newspaper-style and parallel column formats use nearly identical keystrokes:

- ☐ Move the cursor to the location where new column definition should appear

- ☐ Press the Math/Columns key (Alt-F7)

- ☐ Select 4

- ☐ Enter the type of format and number of columns

- ☐ Type in new column margins, if necessary

- ☐ Press Exit (F7) to accept the definition

- ☐ Select 3 Column On/Off to turn on columns

- ☐ Enter the column text. Press Hard Page break (Ctrl-Enter) to end each entry in parallel columns

- ☐ Select 3 Column On/Off to turn off columns

It's wise to choose a simple column project as your first effort, and work toward more complex projects. As you become more familiar with WordPerfect's column functions, you'll realize significant time gains on catalog, scheduling, script, and newsletter projects.

# Working with Numbers in WordPerfect

**B**y now, you probably consider WordPerfect pretty close to magic because of all of the things it can do with words. WordPerfect does amazing things with numbers as well!

If, in the course of your work day, you're expected to create price lists, inventory sheets, budgets, or balance sheets, you'll be interested in WordPerfect's number-handling capabilities. Although WordPerfect is *not a spreadsheet* like Lotus 1-2-3, Microsoft® Excel, or SuperCalc®, WordPerfect *can* total columns of numbers and manipulate as many as four formulas.

It is important that you read this chapter from start to finish because skipping ahead may make the Math function seem confusing. Even if all you do is enter columns of numbers, reading the first section "Aligning Numeric Columns" will make editing numeric columns easier for you.

Math in WordPerfect is a six-step process:

- Set the tab stops for columns

- Define the type and format of column

- Turn on the Math/Columns function

- Enter the numbers and math operators in the column

- Calculate the column

- Turn off the Math/Columns function

# Aligning Numeric Columns

There are many reasons for typing columns of numbers in WordPerfect. You may need to type financial reports, price lists, inventory sheets—any of the hundreds of documents requiring numeric columns.

If you are unfamiliar with WordPerfect, you may be tempted to take what appears to be the easy way out—pressing the space bar to align columns of numbers. By inserting spaces, you can align numbers in columns exactly as you want to. The procedure works just fine. Until . . .

Until you find that you estimated incorrectly and you need to move the columns to accommodate new data. Or until the boss says "Add this one last column," or "Wouldn't it look better if this column appeared a few more spaces to the left?" Or, until you discover that your columns don't line up because you've printed with proportional spacing. Then, you must edit all of those spaces!

If you use tabs to align the columns, you can reposition a column simply by moving the tab stop. This method is much easier and much more flexible than working with individual spaces. In WordPerfect you use the Tab Align key to align math columns on any tab stop.

## Tab Align

With the Tab Align key, you can align a column of numbers or text on any character that appears within the numbers or text. The alignment character that everyone is most familiar with is the decimal point. Columns of numbers aligned so that all the decimals are in the same character position look like this:

```
  $  4,500.30
    15,678.90
       346.87
```

WordPerfect's Tab Align feature is more flexible than the usual decimal tab, however. With Tab Align, you can choose the character upon which the columns will align. For example, you might want to align on the equal sign (=):

```
        3 * 6 = 18
        4 * 5 = 20
    1 + 10 * 5 = 51
```

In normal typing, you can use Tab Align to align on a chosen character. In the Math function, Tab Align is always used to align columns of numbers.

## *Tabbing with Tab Align*

You can line up the align character on any tab stop:

1. Set your tab stops with the Line Format key (Shift-F8)

2. Select **1** Tabs

Tab settings are described in Chapter 8.

Pressing the Tab Align key (Ctrl-F6) moves the cursor to the right to the next tab stop. At the same time, the character that is used for alignment is displayed in the lower left corner of the screen, following the prompt:

    Align Char =

After you press the Tab Align key, you can begin typing. Your cursor remains stationary on the tab stop. Characters will move to the left until you type the alignment character, after which characters will move to the right.

To align the next set of characters:

1. Move down to the following row

2. Press Tab Align (Ctrl-F6) until the cursor rests under the first alignment character

3. Begin typing

You can use the Del or Backspace key to delete Tab Align codes ([A][a]) from the Reveal Codes screen. Pressing Del or Backspace while the cursor is on a Tab Align code will produce the message:

    Delete [Aln/FlshR]? (Y/N)

Type Y to delete the code. Deleting the code does not delete the tab setting.

## *Changing the Align Character*

For some projects, you will need to align on a different alignment character. For example, assume that you want to align on the equal sign (=).

To do so:

1. Press the Line Format key (Shift-F8)

2. Select **6** Align Char

The prompt:

```
Align Char =
```

followed by the current alignment character, appears in the lower left corner of the screen. When you type the new alignment character, WordPerfect immediately returns you to the typing screen.

    **3.** Type the new alignment character

To see the current alignment character, look for the [Align:] hidden code in the Reveal Codes screen.

## Aligning Columns of Whole Numbers

Occasionally, you'll want to right-align whole numbers that do not have a decimal or ending character. Although you cannot enter a blank as the align character, you can align on the right. In WordPerfect 4.2, you can use the R tab stop during normal typing. If you need to right-align numbers in a math column or at any time in WordPerfect 4.1, follow this procedure:

    **1.** Change the alignment character to a character that will not be typed in any column

    **2.** Press the Tab Align key until the cursor is at the tab stop for right alignment

    **3.** Type the number or text to be right-aligned (Notice that the number or text stays right-aligned as you type)

    **4.** When you are ready to move to the next column, press the Tab or Tab Align key

What you've typed will remained right-aligned. *Do not type the alignment character at any time.*

# Using Math Columns

WordPerfect math feature includes subtotaling, totaling, and grand totaling columns of numbers. The feature can be a quick aid when you must produce columns of figures for accounting reports. This section shows you how to carry out columnar math.

Math in WordPerfect is basically a six-step process:

1. Set the tab stops for columns

2. Define the type and format of column

3. Turn on the Math/Columns function

4. Enter the numbers and math operators in the column

5. Calculate the column

6. Turn off the Math/Columns function

## Setting Tabs for Columns of Numbers

The first step in calculating columns of numbers is to position the columns. Set tabs so that your numbers or text will align on the alignment character or right-align on the tab stop. Be sure to set tab stops in such a way that the columns will be wide enough to contain all the text, digits, and decimal points in the longest number. If your numeric columns overlap, your calculations will be incorrect.

It doesn't matter what types of tab stops you set. Within a Math area, all Tab and Tab Align keystrokes act as a tab align on any tab stop.

## Using Math Column Terminology

Columns are referenced in left-to-right order, as *A* through *X*. The left margin is not a column, and numbers in it cannot be added. The first tab stop is column A, the second tab stop is column B, and so on.

---

### ■ Warning

---

Because the left margin is not a column, numbers in it cannot be added.

---

Four types of columns are available in WordPerfect: *numeric, total, text,* and *calculation.*

The default column setting is *numeric* because most columns in a math area will be columns of numbers.

The *total* column is useful for accounting work. *Total* columns display a total derived from numbers in the column to its left. (The *numeric* column also can include totals.)

In *text* columns, all entries (including numbers) are considered text. There is no math capability in a text column.

*Calculation* columns are described in the formula section of this chapter.

Consider this example:

| A | B | C |
|---|---|---|
| Item Description | Stock Number | Dollars On Hand |
| Felt-tip pens | 4175 | 45.60 |
| Erasers | 3345 | 12.15 |
| Mech pencils | 4560 | 36.90 |

Because columns A and B are descriptions, and will not involve math, they should be defined as text columns. Column C is a numeric column that can be used in calculations. The text in column C will not affect the calculations. You can set up as many as 24 numeric columns.

When you define math columns, refer to a column as A, B, C, and so on. You can tell WordPerfect whether negative results should be displayed with a minus (-) or whether they should be enclosed in parentheses (###). You can specify also the number of decimal digits, from zero to four.

## Defining Math Columns

Now that you are familiar with the types of columns and their formats, you can set the math column types and format for each tab stop.

To do this, press Math/Columns (Alt-F7) and you'll see the menu displayed at the bottom of the screen in figure 12.1. From that menu, select option 2 Math Def. WordPerfect displays the Math Definition screen shown in figure 12.2.

In figure 12.2, the letters *A* through *X* identify the 24 possible math columns. Descriptions at the bottom of this figure indicate the Type of Column under each column letter. Notice that all the columns are preset to numeric, the default type. You can see also how negative numbers and the decimal places shown for results will display. (Remember that column A refers to the first tab stop, not to the left margin.)

```
                        Inventory List

        Item                 Qnty on    Cost on     Cumulative
        Description    Code   Hand       Hand        Cost












        1 Math On; 2 Math Def; 3 Column On/Off; 4 Column Def; 5 Column Display: 0
```

*Fig. 12.1. The Math/Columns menu.*

```
        Math Definition        Use arrow keys to position cursor

        Columns                A B C D E F G H I J K L M N O P Q R S T U V W X

        Type                   2 2 2 2 2 2 2 2 2 2 2 2 2 2 2 2 2 2 2 2 2 2 2 2

        Negative Numbers       ( ( ( ( ( ( ( ( ( ( ( ( ( ( ( ( ( ( ( ( ( ( ( (

        # of digits to         2 2 2 2 2 2 2 2 2 2 2 2 2 2 2 2 2 2 2 2 2 2 2 2
        the right (0-4)

        Calculation   1
        Formulas      2
                      3
                      4

        Type of Column:
            0 = Calculation   1 = Text    2 = Numeric    3 = Total

        Negative Numbers
            ( = Parenthesis (50.00)       - = Minus Sign  -50.00

        Press EXIT when done
```

*Fig. 12.2. The Math Definition menu.*

Now set the column types and formats:

**1.** Using the arrow keys, move the cursor under a column letter

**2.** Type the **number appropriate to the column type**

**3.** Type ( or – (to specify how negative math results will display)

**4.** Type the **number of decimal digits for the display**

Decimals are rounded to whatever accuracy you specify.

**5.** Press the Exit key (F7) after you finish setting the column types and formats

**6.** Press Cancel (F1) if you want to return to the typing screen without making changes

Figure 12.1 shows an on-screen form with a description at the left margin, and four columns. To accommodate this form, the Math Definition screen has been changed (see fig. 12.3). The columns in figure 12.3 are defined as:

- Code
- Text (column A, Code)
- Numeric (columns B and C, Qnty and Cost on Hand)
- Total (column D, the Cumulative Cost column)

Columns B and D are specified for zero decimals in math results.

## Turning Math On

Before you enter data and math operators (such as subtotal and total), turn Math on:

**1.** Make sure that the cursor is positioned after the location of the math definition code and before the math area

**2.** Press Math/Columns (Alt-F7)

**3.** Choose 1 Math On

Notice that the prompt:

```
Math
```

appears in the lower left corner of the screen.

**4.** Press Enter

**5.** Press the Tab key once

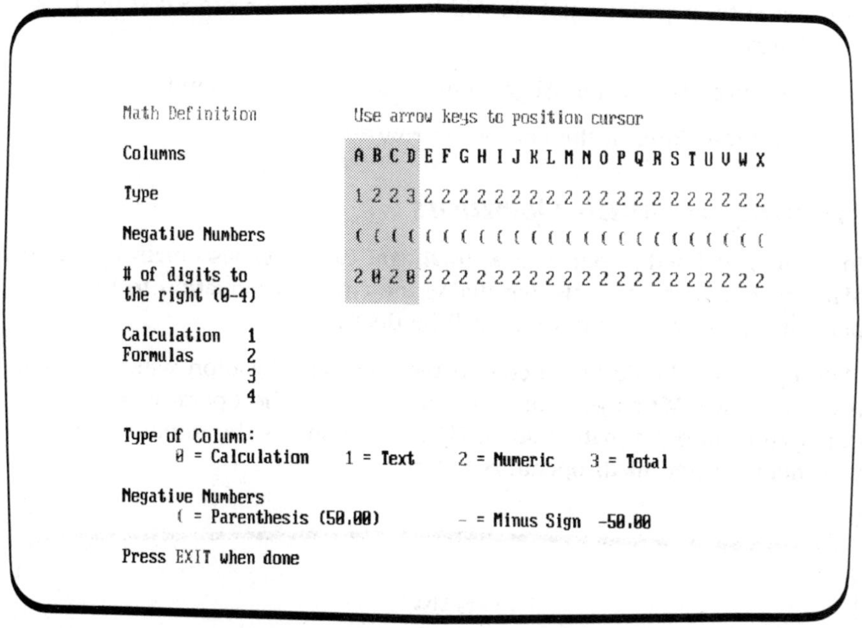

```
Math Definition          Use arrow keys to position cursor

Columns                  A B C D E F G H I J K L M N O P Q R S T U V W X

Type                     1 2 2 3 2 2 2 2 2 2 2 2 2 2 2 2 2 2 2 2 2 2 2 2

Negative Numbers         ( ( ( ( ( ( ( ( ( ( ( ( ( ( ( ( ( ( ( ( ( ( ( (

# of digits to           2 0 2 0 2 2 2 2 2 2 2 2 2 2 2 2 2 2 2 2 2 2 2 2
the right (0-4)

Calculation    1
Formulas       2
               3
               4

Type of Column:
     0 = Calculation    1 = Text    2 = Numeric    3 = Total

Negative Numbers
     ( = Parenthesis (50.00)        - = Minus Sign  -50.00

Press EXIT when done
```

*Fig. 12.3. Math definition for figure 12.1.*

You'll see the prompt:

    Align Char

which indicates that WordPerfect is aligning on this tab stop.

While you are in Math mode, pressing either the Tab or Tab Align key activates the Tab Align function and moves the cursor right to the next tab stop. The Align character works in Math mode as it does in word processing.

## Entering Numbers

In numeric columns, you can enter either positive or negative numbers for use in calculations. To enter numbers:

1. Press the Tab or Tab Align key until the cursor is on the tab stop under the appropriate column heading

2. Type the number

You can enter negative numbers within parentheses or preceded by a minus sign.

   **3.** Press Tab or Tab Align to move to the next column

   **4.** Press Enter at the end of the row

## Entering the Math Operators

In columns defined as numeric or total, you can enter also math operators. Math operators are symbols that define the type of calculation to be performed, and where the result will be displayed.

Math operators should be entered at the Tab Align location where a result is to be shown. When you enter an operator, only the operator will be displayed (without a math result). Figure 12.4 shows the sample form with numbers and math operators entered.

```
                          Inventory List

       Item                 Qnty on    Cost on      Cumulative
       Description   Code   Hand       Hand         Cost

       Pencils, wood  514    36         54.15
       Pencils, mech  525    12         48.90
          Subtotal                        +

       Eraser, pink   402    20         12.20
       Eraser, gum    314    13          9.00
          Subtotal                        +

       Paper, bond    112    12        t22.25
          Total                                        =

       Desk           678     1        t89.90

       Chair, swivel  615     3        150.00
       Chair, wood    616     2        154.50
          Subtotal                        +
          Total                                        =

       Grand Total                                  *
       Math                           Doc 1  Pg 1  Ln 24      Pos 56
```

*Fig. 12.4. Inventory with numbers and operators but no results.*

Math operators are:

| | | |
|---|---|---|
| + | Subtotal | Add all numbers above this cell until a blank cell is reached. |
| t | Extra subtotal | Insert a typed number with the same priority level as a subtotal. |
| = | Total | Add all subtotals (+) and extra totals (t) since the last total. |
| T | Extra total | Insert a typed number with the same priority level as a total. |
| * | Grand total | Add all totals (=) and extra totals (T). |
| N | Negate | Use the result at this location as a negative number in further calculations. |

Notice that Subtotal, Total, and Grand Total operators work on the numbers above them in the document, but they work on numbers or results that are at a lower priority level. When you look at the results in figure 12.5 from the operators in figure 12.4 it will be apparent.

When you want to type a number at the subtotal ($t$) or total ($T$) level:

1. Press the Tab key until the cursor rests in the correct column

2. Type the **t** or **T** math operator, followed immediately by the number you want in that location

Figure 12.4 illustrates such an entry.

3. Press the Tab key to move to the next column

   Or

3. Press Enter to move to the next row

The Negate function is available only in WordPerfect 4.2. This function enables you to retain the negative of a result so that future calculations use the negative of that result.

To enter a Negate:

1. Press the Tab key to move to the appropriate column

2. Type **N** followed immediately by the appropriate number

To Negate a result:

1. Tab to the appropriate location

2. Type an **N** followed by a math operator, such as **N+**

## Calculating a Subtotal

Notice that, even though you have entered all the numbers and operators as shown in figure 12.4, there are no results. You must tell WordPerfect to calculate the results.

No matter where the cursor lies on the screen:

1. Press Math/Columns (Alt-F7)

2. Select **2** Calculate

WordPerfect calculates the results, inserts them next to the math operators, and aligns them on the tab. The results will look like the example in figure 12.5.

```
                      Inventory List

        Item                  Qnty on    Cost on    Cumulative
        Description   Code    Hand       Hand       Cost

        Pencils, wood  514    36         54.15
        Pencils, mech  525    12         48.90
           Subtotal                      103.05+

        Eraser, pink   402    20         12.20
        Eraser, gum    314    13          9.80
           Subtotal                      22.00+

        Paper, bond    112    12         t22.25
           Total                                    147=

        Desk           678     1         t89.90

        Chair, swivel  615     3         150.00
        Chair, wood    616     2         154.50
           Subtotal                      304.50+
           Total                                    394=

        Grand Total                                 541*
        Math                             Doc 1  Pg 1  Ln 24      Pos 56
```

*Fig. 12.5. The calculated inventory list, with results.*

Don't worry about the math operators on the screen. Only the numeric results will print on paper.

### Turning Math Off

When you reach the bottom of the area in which you want column math performed, you need to turn Math off:

1. Press the Math/Columns key (Alt-F7)

2. Choose 1 Math Off

By turning Math on and off in different parts of the document, you control which portions will be included in the calculations when you give the Calculate command. As you move through a document that contains both text and math areas, watch the lower left corner of the screen. When the cursor lies in a Math area, you'll see the Math indicator.

### Editing the Math Definition

When you try to change the Math Definition from within the Math area, you will find that 2 Calculate has replaced 2 Math Def on the menu.

To edit the Math Definition:

1. Use the Reveal Codes function to move the cursor to a position immediately following the [Math Def] code

2. Press the space bar to return to the typing screen

3. Press the Math/Columns key (Alt-F7)

4. Select 2 Math Def

5. Change your definitions

6. Press Exit (F7) to return to the typing screen

Reenter the Reveal Codes screen, and you'll see two [Math Def] codes. The old code is the one on the left. Delete it.

# Calculating Formulas in WordPerfect

WordPerfect does more than total columns of numbers. Using the numbers in a row, WordPerfect can calculate formulas and record the results in the column you've specified. This feature is helpful if you work with price lists that include sales tax or margins. You might use this feature also to calculate the total cost of goods on hand, given the number of units and cost per unit.

The rest of this section assumes that you are familiar with column math. For a refresher, read through the previous sections in this chapter.

## Calculation Columns

You can create as many as four formulas. Then each formula can be assigned to a specific Calculation column.

Look back at the Math Definition screen in figure 12.2. Notice that one of the column types you can enter is represented by a zero (0). The zero indicates a Calculation column.

If you want a column to contain the result of a formula:

1. Use the arrow keys to move the cursor in the Type row until the cursor rests under the appropriate column letter

2. Type a **0**. The cursor jumps to the next available formula line (labeled Calculation Formulas)

3. Type the **formula**

4. Press Enter to leave the formula line and return to the upper portion of the screen

## Entering Formulas

Formulas use four operators:

+    Add
–    Subtract
*    Multiply
/    Divide

And, formulas are composed of numbers, column letters, and math operators. If you use a column letter, such as *A*, the formula uses the number in that column.

Some sample formulas are:

| Formula | Result |
|---------|--------|
| 3*3–2 | 7 |
| 3*A+B | 17 (if column A contains 4, and B contains 5) |

When you specify a column letter, the formula takes the number in the same row as the formula result.

Certain special math operators must be entered by themselves on the formula line:

+   Add the numbers in the numeric column
+/   Average the numbers in the numeric column
=   Add the numbers in the total column
=/   Average the numbers in the total column

Unlike algebra, the formula is calculated from left to right. If you want something to calculate before other items, enclose that math term in parentheses. You cannot, however, use nested parentheses, as in (3+(3*A))−B, for example.

## Calculating Formulas

To calculate your formulas:

1. Press the Math/Columns key (Alt-F7)

2. Select 2 Calculate

The columns containing formulas will calculate their results as well as calculating the numeric and total columns. Each line in a formula column contains the result of the formula using the numbers from that line.

## Editing Formulas

To change a formula:

1. Using the Reveal Codes function, move the cursor so that it immediately follows the [Math Def] code

2. Press Alt-F7

3. Select 2 Math Def to display the Math Definition screen

4. Move the cursor to the *0* in the Type row under the column that contains the formula you want to edit

5. Type a **0** to move the cursor into the formula line

6. Edit the formula

*Beware! Entering the formula line and pressing Enter without making a change will erase the entire formula.*

7. Press Enter

## *Entering Numbers in a Calculate Column*

When you tab the cursor into the calculate column, an exclamation mark
(!) will display. If you want to enter a number instead of using the
formula result, delete the exclamation mark with the Backspace key.

WordPerfect's math features are designed for straightforward and simple math projects—columns of sales figures that must be updated frequently, for instance.

Attempting to use WordPerfect for complex calculations and electronic spreadsheet work is frustrating . . . at best! It is much wiser to create a spreadsheet in a package like Lotus 1-2-3, or Supercalc, and save or "print" the spreadsheet results to a disk file in ASCII-text format. Then, retrieve the ASCII file to WordPerfect using the techniques described in Chapter 17.

When using Math, remember:

☐ The left margin cannot be a column. Column A is the first tab

☐ If the results appear with the wrong format or if no results appear, display the Math Definition screen as though you are going to edit it. Check to make sure that you have the correct definition for each column

☐ Make sure that the cursor directly follows the [Math Def] code before you try to change or edit the math definition

☐ Often the easiest way to enter new numbers and math operators is to delete the previous number and its tab-align code. Press the Tab Align key, then enter the new number

# Using Special Characters and Document References

**T**he WordPerfect features presented in this chapter were developed in response to word-processing needs in a specific work environment. Although you may not use these features in the majority of your work, *don't skip this chapter.*

At the very least, flip through the pages and scan the section headings. While most of the features are designed for special circumstances, a few, such as special characters and line drawing, can be used in a variety of word-processing projects.

Much of this chapter deals with the WordPerfect features used by those who create books, legal documents, scientific papers, foreign-language papers, and academic tomes.

- If your work involves entering special characters or characters in nonstandard locations within a document, you'll want to read the first section, "Shifting Character Line Position." The section explores how to use superscript and subscript, and how to create formulas

- When you need help using special characters or symbols that are not available on the keyboard, refer to this chapter. You'll learn how to create characters by overstriking, how to type normally unavailable characters, and how to change character sets in some printers

- Drawing lines with WordPerfect should be helpful for you if you develop forms, draw simple bar graphs, or build organizational charts. The forms you can produce with WordPerfect and a laser printer are so professional that you may never make another trip to the print shop

- If you are involved in legal or academic work, WordPerfect's capability to automatically generate tables of contents, indexes, and lists saves hours of typing and retyping. And, WordPerfect automatically generates outline numbering and paragraph numbering as you enter the text

Even if you don't plan to use these features immediately, look through the chapter. At least you'll know where to turn for the answer if you suddenly find yourself faced with an extraordinary word-processing challenge.

# Shifting Character Line Position

Scientific and technical writing generally requires the use of subscripts and superscripts. The most convenient method for typing *single* subscripts and superscripts is with WordPerfect's Super/Subscript key.

If you type *many* equations or lines of text that contain subscripted or superscripted characters, you'll probably want to use either the half-line technique for equations, or the Adv Up or Adv Down functions. These techniques are presented after a discussion of subscripts and superscripts.

## *Creating Subscripts*

The Subscript command instructs the printer to print subscripted characters one-third of a line below the other characters on the line. The *exact* spacing, however, depends on your printer's capabilities. (Some printers may not be able to subscript.) You'd use the Subscript function to type the following sentence:

Now insert the $CO_2$ cartridge in the machine.

With the cursor positioned where you want the subscripted number *2* to appear:

1. Press Super/Subscript (Shift-F1)

2. Select 2 Subscript

A lowercase *s* appears at the lower left corner of the screen to indicate that the next character typed will be a subscript.

**3.** Now type the subscript character, **2**

The subscripted *2* looks normal on the screen but will print subscripted.

After you've read Chapter 14 you'll want to consider creating a subscript macro to reduce the number of keystrokes you must enter each time you create a subscripted character.

## Creating Superscripts

Superscript works like Subscript but places a superscripted character one-third of a line above the other characters on the line. (Some printers may not be able to do this.) For example, to enter the superscripts in the following formula:

$$A^2 + B^2 = C^2$$

Position the cursor where the superscripted character should appear.

**1.** Press the Super/Subscript key (Shift-F1)

**2.** Select **1** Superscript

**3.** Type the superscript character, **2**

Notice that an uppercase *S* appears at the lower left corner of the screen to indicate that the next character typed will be a superscript.

## Erasing Subscripts and Superscripts

You can erase the Subscript or Superscript command (but leave the characters) by displaying the Reveal Codes screen and erasing the hidden code, [SubScrpt] or [SuprScrpt].

To erase subscript and superscript characters:

**1.** Place the cursor to the right of the sub- or superscripted character

**2.** Press Backspace to erase the character

**3.** Press Backspace again

WordPerfect prompts:

    Delete [SubScrpt] (Y/N)

or

```
Delete [SuprScrpt] (Y/N)
```

4. Type **Y** to erase the command

## *Continuous Subscript or Superscript*

An easy way to temporarily print half a line above or below the standard line is to use the program's Advance Up or Advance Down commands. (Notice that this is a half-line rather than the one-third line used by subscript or superscript.)

To raise or lower a string of letters by half a line:

1. Press the Super/Subscript key (Shift-F1)

2. Select **4** Adv Up

   Or

2. Select **5** Adv Dn

An arrow in the lower left corner of the screen will indicate the current line advance. The Ln indicator in the Status Line will also indicate a half-line adjustment.

You won't see a change in the appearance of your text on the screen. Changes occur when the document is printed.

To return to the normal typing line, select the Advance Up or Advance Down command that is the opposite of your first selection.

## *Entering Equations with Half-Line Spacing*

If you are entering a complicated equation such as the one shown in figure 13.1, changing the line spacing to half a line is easier than using subscripts and superscripts. (Subscripts and superscripts must be activated for each character—a long process in a complex equation.)

$$P(X) = \sum_{x = x_1}^{x = x_n} {}_nC_x p^x q^{n-x}$$

*Fig. 13.1. A complex equation to be entered using Half-Line Spacing option.*

Beware of mixing subscripts, superscripts, and half-line spacing in the same area—remember, subscripts and superscripts are raised or lowered by one-third (not one-half) line.

To prepare an area for equations, you must:

1. Change the line spacing to .5 (half-line)

2. Use the space bar to insert blank spaces in all areas where the equation will be typed

3. Type in Insert mode

To make these preparations:

1. Position the cursor at the left margin of the first line where the equation will appear on the page

2. Press Line Format (Shift-F8)

3. Select 4 Spacing

At the prompt:

[Spacing Set] 1

4. Type .5 for one-half spacing

5. Press Enter

6. Press Print Format (Ctrl-F8)

7. Select 3 Turn Off to turn off justification

8. Press Enter

This procedure prevents WordPerfect from inserting extra spaces for justified text.

9. Count the number of lines in the equation

Count subscripts, superscripts, and "normal" print lines as separate lines. For example, figure 13.1 has three lines.

10. Hold down the space bar until blank spaces have been inserted in as many lines as you need for the equation. Be sure to press Enter at the end of each line

These blank spaces will make it easy to move the cursor to any location in the "equation area."

11. Use the arrow key to move the cursor up to the line where you'll type the equation

12. Press the Ins key to activate Insert/Replace mode

The prompt:

    Typeover

appears in the lower left corner of the screen.

Now you are ready to type the equation. Begin by drawing the division line with the underscore key. Then, using the arrow keys to move the cursor, fill in the equation. If you make a mistake, you can type over the incorrect character because WordPerfect already is in Typeover mode. To delete a character, type over it by using the space bar instead of deleting the character with the Del or Backspace keys.

After you type the equation, move to the end of the equation area and turn off Insert/Replace mode by pressing the Ins key and, if necessary, turn on justification. Change the spacing from .5 to 1. After making these changes, you can resume normal typing.

Look at the equation on the screen and you'll see that the subscripts and superscripts appear on separate lines. Notice that as you move the cursor down through the equation area, the Ln indicator shows that lines are in half-line increments. When the equation prints, the lines will print in half-line increments.

For additional information about entering special symbols used in equations, see the section "Assigning Special Characters to Keys" in this chapter.

# Typing Specialized Characters

With WordPerfect, you can type specialized characters for documents using foreign languages or for scientific and technical writing. These special characters are produced in three ways.

To form a combined character, you can use WordPerfect's overstrike capability to print one character over another. This method is useful for creating diacritical marks in foreign languages.

Another method is to *remap* or reassign special characters to keyboard keys to type characters that are not normally available on the keyboard. You map or assign these special characters to special keystroke combinations, such as Alt-S or Ctrl-K.

The third method of printing with special characters depends on your printer. Printers with print wheels or thimbles can be changed to a foreign-language print element. Some dot-matrix and laser printers use foreign-language or technical character sets.

## Striking Over Text

The Overstrike option, which is part of the Super/Subscript feature, is activated by the Shift-F1 key combination.

To use Overstrike:

1. Type a character that requires an overstrike

2. Press Super/Subscript (Shift-F1)

3. Select 3 Overstrike

The cursor jumps back to the character you've typed, and now you can type another character in the same position.

4. Type the diacritical mark or overstrike character

The cursor moves to the right, ready for text entry, and the original character disappears from the screen. Only the second character remains visible.

You can use Reveal Codes to check the command. If you want $\tilde{n}$, for example, Reveal Codes would show n[Ovrstk]~. When you print the document the first and second characters will overlap.

You also can insert diacritical marks after you enter text:

1. Position the cursor to the right of the character

2. Press Overstrike

The cursor jumps back to the character specified as the one to receive the diacritical mark. When you enter the mark, the character disappears, leaving only the diacritical mark.

To erase a diacritical mark:

1. Place the cursor to the right of the mark

2. Press the Backspace key once

The mark disappears.

**3.** Press Backspace again

WordPerfect prompts:

> Delete [Ovrstk]? (Y/N)

**4.** Press **Y** to erase the Overstrike command

To return the "missing" character to the screen, press the down-arrow key.

If you want to overstrike with special characters that are not shown on your keycaps, go on to the following section.

## Assigning Special Characters to Keys

Many characters and symbols that are not marked on the keys *are* available to your computer and printer. Many of these characters are useful for foreign languages and scientific or technical writing. A few of them are just plain fun.

To see all of the characters in the computer, retrieve the file FONT.TST. The file probably is located on your *Learning* disk. Figure 13.2 shows the first screenful of this document.

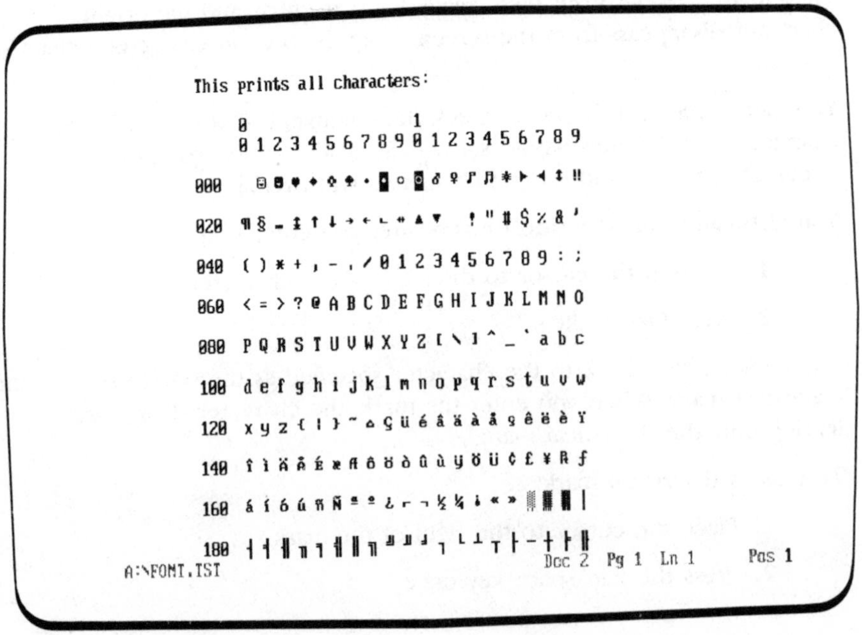

*Fig. 13.2. FONT.TST file screen display.*

Your computer and printer have an ASCII number assigned to each letter, number, and symbol. There can be as many as 255 numbers and assigned characters. Figure 13.2 displays only the first 199 of the characters. Many of the keyboard characters are represented by the numbers that fall between 32 and 126.

You can use the nonkeyboard characters that appear in FONT.TST by assigning them to key combinations, such as Alt-S or Ctrl-K.

In legal or accounting work, for example, you will need the subsection symbol, §. Look at figure 13.2 and you will see that the subsection symbol is ASCII decimal number 021 (in column 1 of symbol row 020). To make the subsection symbol easy to type and easy to remember, you might assign it to the key combination, Ctrl-S.

To assign the subsection symbol to Ctrl-S:

1. Press the Screen key (Ctrl-F3)

2. Select 3 Ctrl/Alt keys

The symbols and prompts shown in figure 13.3 appear on-screen. Notice that the matrix of characters and their numbers are the same as those shown in FONT.TST. (They are laid out differently.) You can see that the subsection symbol is still in position 021. The top of the screen shows two columns for assigning Alt key combinations and two for assigning Ctrl key combinations.

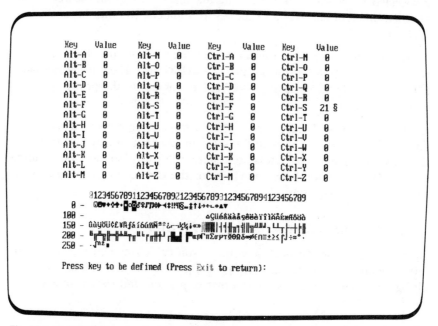

*Fig. 13.3. Ctrl/Alt key menu displaying ASCII set.*

3. Type **Ctrl-S** to move the cursor to the right of Ctrl-S at the top of the screen

4. Now type **021** (the number that corresponds to the subsection symbol)

5. Press Enter. The subsection symbol displays to the right of the 021

You can continue to assign more special characters to Ctrl and Alt key combinations.

6. Press Exit (F7) when you are finished

Or

6. Press Cancel (F1) to ignore the assignments you have made

When you return to the typing screen you can type the subsection symbol by pressing Ctrl-S. (Remember to hold down the Ctrl key while you press the *s*.)

## Printer Characters that Don't Match Screen Characters

Your computer display probably uses a character set known as the IBM graphics character set. As you have learned, each character within the set is assigned to an ASCII number. If the manufacturer of your printer assigned different characters to the ASCII numbers, you may have problems.

To see whether your screen characters match your printer characters, retrieve the file FONT.TST from the *LEARNING* disk. Then, using normal printing procedures, print the FONT.TST document to the printer you want to examine.

Compare the printed characters to the corresponding screen characters (in the same location and with the same number). You may find that a few of your printer's characters are different. If this is so, use your printed copy of FONT.TST to choose numbers for the characters you assign to Ctrl and Alt key combinations.

## Special Characters and Your Printer

By changing the print wheel or thimble, you can change character sets for letter-quality printers that use changeable print elements. You also can change character sets for some dot-matrix printers and laser printers.

There are four often-used methods for changing character sets in dot-matrix and laser printers. If one or more of these methods is available for your printer, it will be referenced in your printer manual:

- Miniature DIP switches inside or in the back of the printer can be set to enable or disable foreign character sets

- Front panel switches with control lights may enable or disable different character sets

- Software available from the manufacturer or dealer can *download* new character sets from the computer to the printer

- Font cartridges that are plugged into the printer can change the font, print style, and character set

Whenever you change fonts or character sets, print another copy of FONT.TST to ensure that the characters you want to use still have the same numeric designations.

## Using Line Draw

Certain forms, equations, organizational charts, and simple graphs require line drawing. Although WordPerfect is in no way intended to be a graphics package, you can draw forms and boxes with the Line Draw feature. You can use a variety of graphics characters to create lines and boxes on the screen, and the results will be impressive.

To invoke the Line Draw feature:

1. Press Screen (Ctrl-F3)

2. Type 2

The Line Draw menu, shown at the bottom of the screen in figure 13.4, appears.

3. Select option 1, 2, or 3

You can create a line using any of these graphic options. Use the arrow keys to move the cursor (which draws the line). The drawing character can be changed by selecting options 1 through 4.

In figure 13.4, the lines that surround *Client/Customer* and *Select Client Customer* were created with option 2. The remaining boxes were created with option 1. The ends of the arrows were created with option 3.

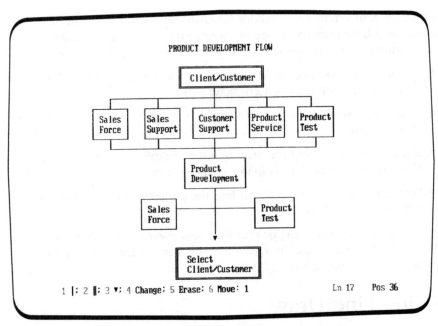

*Fig. 13.4. The Line Draw menu and figure created with Line Draw function.*

## Erasing Lines and Moving through Lines

Select 5 Erase to erase lines. Option 6 Move temporarily turns off the Line Draw feature so that you can move the cursor to another position on the screen. To resume drawing, press the number of the desired drawing character. You exit Line Draw by pressing Cancel (F1).

## Printing Your Line Drawing

The printed results of your on-screen line drawing largely depend on your printer's capabilities. To print the on-screen drawings, your printer must use the IBM graphics character set. Printers that do not contain this character set will print characters that do not provide the appropriate lines and corners.

If your printer will not print the lines and corner characters shown on screen, refer to the section, "Assigning Special Characters to Keys." You may be able to use one of the characters displayed in FONT.TST for drawing by identifying this special character as the drawing character selected with the custom drawing character. Or, you may be able to change your printer's character set to a character set containing the correct line-drawing symbols (check the "Special Characters and Your Printer" section). Look back at the section, "Line Drawing on Laser Printers," in Chapter 9.

# Marking Text To Add or Delete

To alert your readers to proposed changes, use the Redline and Strikeout features. When you redline text, WordPerfect inserts a vertical line in the left margin of the text you propose to add. If, for instance, there is a change in your personnel manual that must be approved before publication, use the Redline feature to call out the text to be added—let your boss see the change, and approve of it before finalizing the document. The Strikeout function marks text for deletion by printing hyphens over the indicated section of text.

## *Redlining Text To Be Added*

To insert redlining codes as you type:

1. Press Mark Text (Alt-F5)

2. Select 3 Redline

The hidden code [RedLn] is inserted at that location, and a plus sign (+) appears to the right of the position number (Pos) in the lower right corner of the screen.

To end redlining:

1. Press Alt-F5

2. Type 3 Redline

Whenever the cursor enters an area marked for redline, the + sign displays to the right of the character position number in the lower right corner of the screen.

To redline text that you've already typed:

1. Mark the text as a Block with Alt-F4

2. Press the Mark Text key (Alt-F5)

3. Select 3 Redline

Redlined text can be identified (in your printed document) by a double vertical bar printed in the left margin. If you don't want the vertical bars to print, see this chapter's section on removing Redline and Strikeout or use Reveal Codes to delete the [RedLn] hidden code.

## Strikeout Text To Be Deleted

You'll find the Strikeout feature very useful as you edit. With Strikeout, you can print a document so that proposed deletions are printed with an overstruck hyphen. Later, you can go back and use the Remove feature to delete the strikeout text in a single operation.

The Strikeout feature works on existing text. To identify text for strikeout:

1. Use the Block function (Alt-F4) to highlight the text

2. Press the Mark Text key (Alt-F5)

3. Select 4 Strikeout

A minus sign appears to the right of the position number (Pos) whenever the cursor is inside a Strikeout zone. When you print, the text marked for strikeout is printed with overstruck hyphens.

## Removing Redline and Strikeout Text

Of course you won't want the final printed version of your document to contain redline and strikeout markings. You can quickly remove both redline markings and overstruck text:

1. Press Mark Text

2. Choose 6 Other Options

From the Mark Text Options menu:

3. Select 6 Remove all Redline Markings and all Strikeout text from document

Or, if you use WordPerfect 4.1:

1. Press Mark Text

2. Choose 4 Remove

WordPerfect will prompt you with:

```
Delete Redline Markings and Strikeout text? (Y/N)
```

3. Type a Y to proceed

Understand that you are deleting the actual text marked for strikeout, not just the strikeout symbols.

If you want to selectively remove a Redline mark or a Strikeout mark:

1. Move the cursor to the character position before the area you want to examine

2. Press the Replace function (Alt-F2)

3. Type **Y** at the `with Confirm? (Y/N)` prompt

4. Press Mark Text (Alt-F5) at the `Srch:` prompt

5. Select **Redline** or **Strikeout** from the menu

6. Press →Search (F2)

When WordPerfect prompts you for the replacement character, you'll press →Search because you don't want to replace the code with anything.

When a Redline or Strikeout code is found:

7. Type a **Y** to remove the Redline or Strikeout code

Or

7. Type **N** to keep the code

# Referencing Text: Outlines, Indexes, and Tables of Contents

Paragraph and outline numbering are essential if you work in the legal profession, create or type contracts and proposals, or need to document your work with indexes, outlines, or tables of contents. WordPerfect is capable of creating these references for you—automatically.

## *Automatic Outlining and Paragraph Numbering*

Remember how awful it was when you had to do outlines by hand? You had to organize and reorganize, number and renumber, write and rewrite, cut and paste.

With WordPerfect, you enter the text and WordPerfect generates the outline numbering. When you move a section, WordPerfect automatically renumbers the outline. You also can mark text that you want to include in lists, tables of contents, and indexes, and WordPerfect will organize and print them in the style you designate.

WordPerfect's Automatic Outlining feature numbers outline headers according to the level of the tab stop on which the outline header begins. Before you start an outline, make sure that the tabs are set in the correct locations. (You can always return and change the tab stop locations.) Automatic outlining will execute as many as seven tab-stop levels.

The outline in figure 13.5 shows four tab-stop levels, and level numbering.

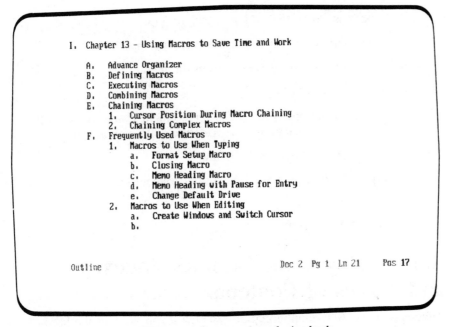

```
    I.  Chapter 13 - Using Macros to Save Time and Work

        A.  Advance Organizer
        B.  Defining Macros
        C.  Executing Macros
        D.  Combining Macros
        E.  Chaining Macros
            1.  Cursor Position During Macro Chaining
            2.  Chaining Complex Macros
        F.  Frequently Used Macros
            1.  Macros to Use When Typing
                a.  Format Setup Macro
                b.  Closing Macro
                c.  Memo Heading Macro
                d.  Memo Heading with Pause for Entry
                e.  Change Default Drive
            2.  Macros to Use When Editing
                a.  Create Windows and Switch Cursor
                b.



    Outline                                    Doc 2  Pg 1  Ln 21      Pos 17
```

*Fig. 13.5. A sample outline illustrating tab stop and numbering levels.*

To create an outline:

1. Move to the position at which you want to begin outlining

2. Press Mark Text (Alt-F5)

3. Select **1** Outline

No hidden code is inserted, but Outline appears at the bottom left corner of the screen.

4. Press Enter to see the first number of the outline

5. Press Tab to go to the next deeper outline level

Or

5. Press the Left Indent key (F4) to freeze an outline level number or letter in its current place and value

Or

5. Type spaces after the outline number to freeze the outline level

6. Type the **heading or text** for that level

When you press Enter at the end of a heading, the next outline number automatically appears. If an outline number has not yet been "frozen" by the Indent key, you can:

1. Press Enter to insert a blank line between the current and previous number

Or

1. Press the Left Indent key (F4) to freeze the outline number

Or

1. Press Tab to move to a lower level of the outline to create a subheading

Each new tab stop causes the next lower outline number or letter to display. When you reach the level you want:

1. Stop pressing Tab

2. Press the Indent key to freeze the level number without an entry

Or

2. Type the heading or entry

To back up to a previous level of heading:

1. Move the cursor to that level number

2. Press the Left Tab key (Shift-Tab)

If you press the Backspace or left-arrow key, you will lose the automatic number for that line.

When the outline is complete, turn off the outline feature:

1. Press Mark Text (Alt-F5)

2. Choose **1** Outline

The easiest way to type text into an outline is to create the outline, turn off the outline function, and then enter the text at the appropriate level of the outline. Use the Indent key to left-align text under subheadings.

## Editing Your Outline

To change the levels of subheadings:

1. Move the cursor to the left margin of the subheading's line

2. Press the Tab key to move the heading right to a deeper level

   Or

2. Press Del to move the heading left to a higher level

3. Press the down-arrow key to see the heading numbers or letters adjust to their new locations

To delete a level number:

1. Position the cursor under the number

2. Press Del

   Or

1. Move the cursor to the right of the number

2. Press Backspace

When you move the cursor through the outline or press Rewrite, WordPerfect renumbers the headings for you.

To add an outline heading within an existing outline:

1. Move the cursor to the left margin on the line on which you want to add the outline heading

2. Press Alt-F5 (Ctrl-F4, 1)

3. Choose 1 Outline (Ctrl-F5, 5)

Now, outline as before. WordPerfect will renumber those entries that follow the new entry.

To move blocks of your outline:

1. Use the Block function to highlight from the left margin to the end of the section you want to move

2. Cut the block (Ctrl-F4, 1)

3. Move the block to the new location (Ctrl-F5, 5)

WordPerfect automatically renumbers your outline.

## Automatic Paragraph Numbering

Paragraph numbering is similar to outline numbering except that a number is *not* inserted automatically whenever you press Enter. Paragraph numbering permits you to choose the level number that displays—regardless of cursor position.

To number a paragraph:

1. Tab the cursor to the position at which you want to insert the number

2. Press Mark Text (Alt-F5)

3. Select **2** Para #

This prompt asks you for the level of the number:

```
Paragraph level (Enter for automatic):
```

4. Press Enter

WordPerfect automatically inserts the number that matches the tab stop upon which the cursor rests. When you add and delete paragraph numbers, the program automatically renumbers these numbers as it does for outline numbering.

If you want the appropriate paragraph number regardless of cursor position:

1. Press Mark Text (Alt-F5)

2. Select **2** Para #

At the prompt:

```
Paragraph level (Enter for automatic):
```

3. Type a number (from 1 to 7) to indicate the level of the paragraph number

Use the editing procedure described for outlining to edit paragraph numbering.

## Selecting Numbering Styles

WordPerfect presets a numbering style for its Outline and Paragraph Numbering features. You can use WordPerfect's preset style, or choose from several other available styles, or design your own.

To select the predefined numbering style:

1. Press Mark Text (Alt-F5)

2. Select **6** Other Options

3. Select **1** Define Paragraph Outline Numbering

   Or, if you are using WordPerfect 4.1:

2. Select **6** Define

3. Select **7** Paragraph/Outline Numbering

The Paragraph Numbering Definition screen shown in figure 13.6 will appear.

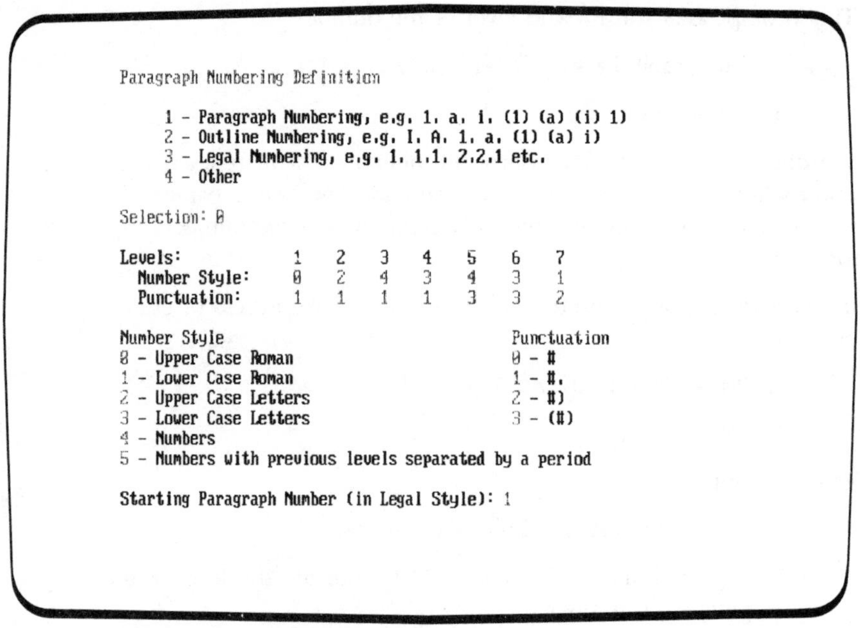

```
Paragraph Numbering Definition

        1 - Paragraph Numbering, e.g. 1, a, i, (1) (a) (i) 1)
        2 - Outline Numbering, e.g. I, A, 1, a, (1) (a) i)
        3 - Legal Numbering, e.g. 1, 1.1, 2.2.1 etc.
        4 - Other

Selection: 0

Levels:          1   2   3   4   5   6   7
  Number Style:  0   2   4   3   4   3   1
  Punctuation:   1   1   1   1   3   3   2

Number Style                          Punctuation
0 - Upper Case Roman                  0 - #
1 - Lower Case Roman                  1 - #.
2 - Upper Case Letters                2 - #)
3 - Lower Case Letters                3 - (#)
4 - Numbers
5 - Numbers with previous levels separated by a period

Starting Paragraph Number (in Legal Style): 1
```

*Fig. 13.6. Paragraph Numbering Definition screen.*

From the top of the Paragraph Numbering Definition screen, you can choose 1, 2, or 3 for predefined numbering styles. Choose 4 to move the cursor into the area at midscreen to design your own numbering scheme. Plan ahead before making style changes because you can't back up in the Paragraph Numbering Definition screen.

Move the cursor through the Number Style: and Punctuation: lines, entering numbers that correspond to the Number Style and Punctuation choices shown at the bottom of the screen.

To remove old paragraph numbering styles, delete the [Para#Def] code that precedes the paragraphs or outline.

## Creating Multiple Outlines or Groups of Numbered Paragraphs

When you must create more than one outline or have created several dissimilar groups of numbered paragraphs in the same document, generate a new Paragraph/Outline Numbering definition for each of them. Use the procedure described in the final paragraph of the preceding section.

## Generating Tables of Contents, Lists, and Indexes

You can mark words or headings (in your document) so that they will be included in such listings as the table of contents, the list of figures or tables, or the index. As you mark text, you must identify which list that text will be a part of. At the end of your document, you'll issue a command that generates the listings automatically from the text you have marked.

Creating tables of contents, figure and table lists, and indexes is a three-step process:

1. Mark the text to be included

2. Define the style

3. Generate the listing at the end of the document

When you create a list or a table of contents, WordPerfect uses the text from the document. If you are creating an index, you can use document text or enter your own text for the index listings.

## Marking Text for Tables of Contents and Lists

To highlight the text you want to include in the table of contents or list:

1. Invoke Block (Alt-F4)

2. Press the Mark Text key (Alt-F5) while the block is highlighted and the menu shown in figure 13.7 appears

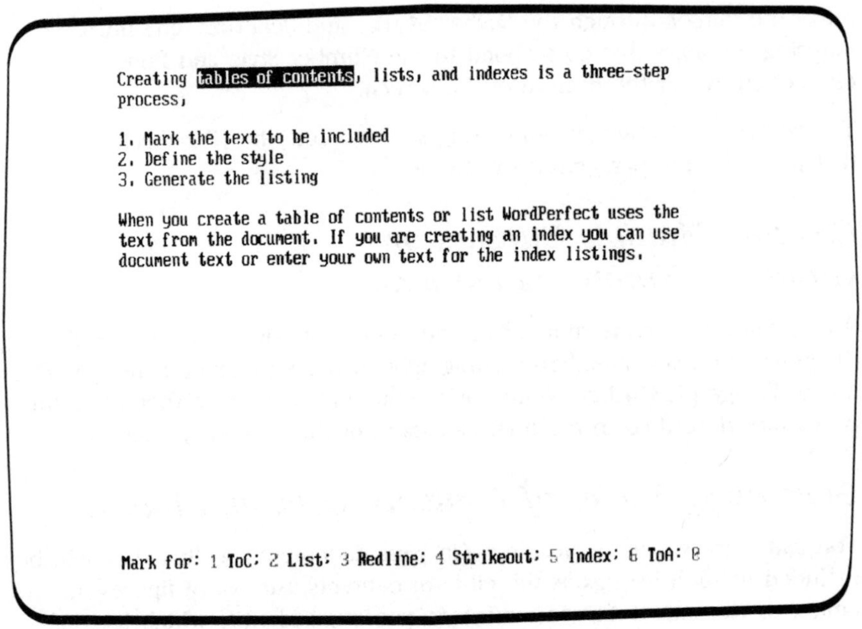

```
Creating tables of contents, lists, and indexes is a three-step
process,

1, Mark the text to be included
2, Define the style
3, Generate the listing

When you create a table of contents or list WordPerfect uses the
text from the document, If you are creating an index you can use
document text or enter your own text for the index listings,




Mark for: 1 ToC: 2 List: 3 Redline: 4 Strikeout: 5 Index: 6 ToA: 0
```

Fig. 13.7. Mark Text (Alt-F5) menu with TOC highlighted.

3. Type **1** for Table of Contents

   Or

3. Type **2** for List

4. Type a number between 1 and 5 to indicate the level in the
   table of contents

You can mark as many as five levels in the table of contents.

   Or

4. Type a number between 1 and 5 to indicate the number of the
   list

You can mark text for as many as five different lists.

## Marking Text for Indexes

To include text in the index:

1. Move the cursor to the word you want marked

   Or

1. Use the Block function (Alt-F4) to highlight multiple words

2. Press the Mark Text key (Alt-F5)

3. Select **5** Index

The message:

    Index Heading:

appears in the lower left corner of the screen, followed by the word or words you highlighted. You can type a new indexing word over the top of the existing word if you want a different index heading.

4. Press Enter

The message Subheading: appears. If you typed in your own heading, the word you marked in the text will appear here as the subheading.

5. Type a new subheading

   Or

5. Press the Del key to remove the subheading

6. Press Enter

To see the heading and subheading:

1. Move to the indexed text

2. Press Alt-F3 to display the Reveal Codes screen

The code will appear as [Index:heading,subheading]

## Defining Table of Contents Style

After you've marked text, you'll need to define the style to be used for printing the table of contents. The table of contents will be placed wherever the hidden code, [DefMark], specifying the table of contents style is located. You can use the Hard Page break, Ctrl-Enter, to define page breaks around the table of contents.

To define the style and location for the table of contents:

1. Move the cursor to the location in your document where the table of contents is to appear

2. Enter a heading for the table

3. You may want to center the heading by pressing the Center key (Shift-F6)

4. Press Mark Text (Alt-F5)

5. Select 6 Other Options

   Or

5. Select 6 Define for WordPerfect 4.1

6. Select 2 Define Table of Contents

   Or

6. Select 6 for WordPerfect 4.1

Figure 13.8 displays the Table of Contents Definition menu.

```
Table of Contents Definition

    Number of levels in table of contents (1-5): 8


                        Page Number Position
        Level 1
        Level 2
        Level 3
        Level 4
        Level 5


        Page Number Position
        1 - No Page Numbers
        2 - Page Number Follow Entries
        3 - (Page Numbers) follow Entries
        4 - Flush Right Page Numbers
        5 - Flush Right Page Numbers with Leaders
```

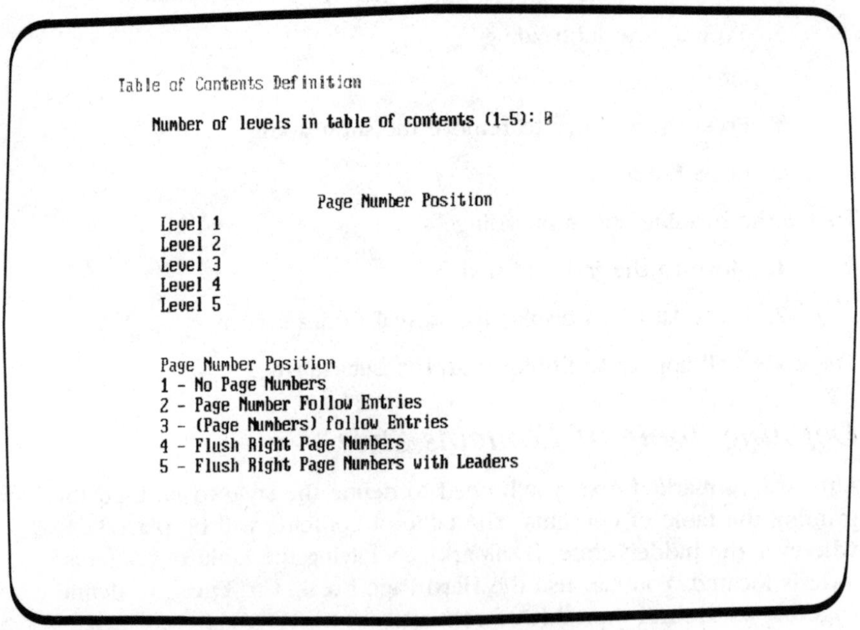

*Fig. 13.8. Table of Contents Definition menu.*

**7.** Enter the number of levels you want in your table of contents

You will see a prompt that asks whether you want the last level of contents wrapped around into a single paragraph. Each item in the paragraph will be separated by a semicolon.

**8.** Type **Y** if you do want the last item wrapped

If you select Y, WordPerfect will not permit Flush Right style for the last level of the table of contents.

The cursor then moves into the Page Number Position lines. If you prefer a page-number position other than 5:

**9.** Type the appropriate number from the menu at the bottom of the screen

**10.** Press Enter

To remove the current table of contents definition, delete the [DefMark:] code using Reveal.

## Defining List and Index Style

Because figure and table lists and indexes generally appear at the end of a document, and because only the marked index items that precede the Index Definition code will be used to create the index, move to the end of your document:

**1.** Press Home twice

**2.** Press the down arrow

**3.** Enter a heading for the list or index

**4.** Reposition the cursor for the beginning of the list or index

**5.** Press the Mark Text key (Alt-F5)

**6.** Select **6** Other Options

Or

**6.** Select **6** Text Marking Definition for WordPerfect 4.1

**7.** Type **3** to define a List

Or

**7.** Type **5** to define an Index

If you choose Index:

**8.** Press Enter if you are asked for the Concordance file name

The "if asked for" in Step 8 accounts for differences between 4.1 and 4.2. The menu of Index styles shown in figure 13.9 appears.

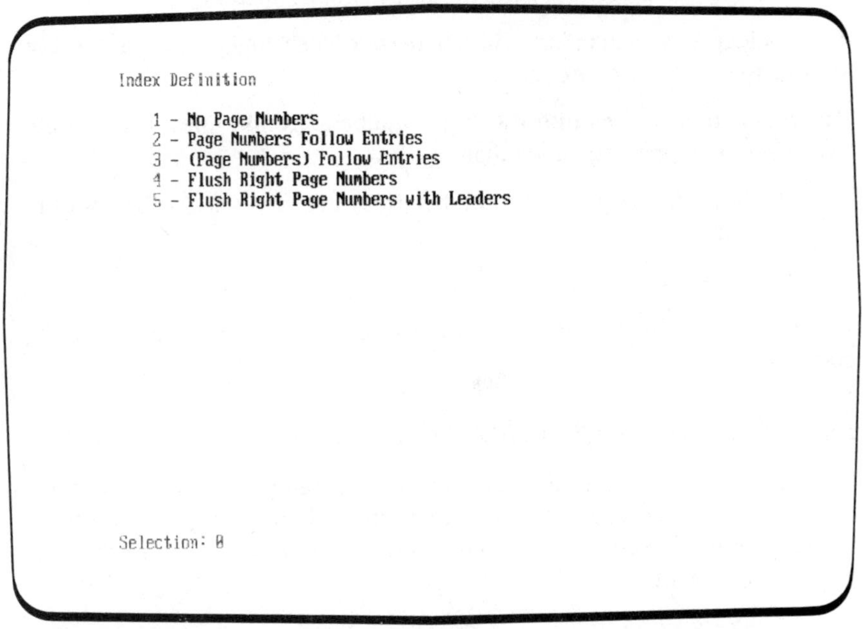

```
Index Definition

    1 - No Page Numbers
    2 - Page Numbers Follow Entries
    3 - (Page Numbers) Follow Entries
    4 - Flush Right Page Numbers
    5 - Flush Right Page Numbers with Leaders

















Selection: 0
```

*Fig. 13.9. Index Definition menu.*

**9.** Type the number of the index style you want

If you choose 3 to do a list:

**10.** Type the number of the list (1 to 5)

**11.** Type the style of the list from the menu that is displayed

In WordPerfect 4.1, you type the number of the list immediately after you choose 6 Text Marking Definition.

## *Generating Lists*

The final step, after you have marked the text and selected the printing styles, is to generate the table of contents, figures and tables list, or index:

1. Press Mark Text (Alt-F5)

2. Select **6** Other Options

    Or, if you are using WordPerfect 4.1:

2. Select **7** Generate

3. Select **8** Generate Tables and Index from the Other Options menu

Before WordPerfect will generate the tables and index, two criteria must be met:

1. The text must be marked correctly

2. There must be enough room in memory

If there is not enough room in memory, you will be asked to clear the second document (Doc 2). If you have not erased previous tables, lists, and indexes, you will be asked whether they can be erased. Other kinds of problems will cause WordPerfect to display a message asking you for corrections.

To change the format of the tables of contents, lists, or indexes you've generated, use the Reveal Codes screen to remove the [DefMark] codes from the document. Then, create a new style and generate new tables, lists, or indexes.

What you take from this chapter is a mix of techniques that separate "everyday" word processing from professional (and powerful) word processing. Although you may use these techniques only infrequently, you will be able to respond when these capabilities are required by industry standards or by higher management's expectations. You'll know how to put WordPerfect to work for you!

☐ Now, you'll think of Super/Subscript (Shift-F1) when you're asked to create scientific and technical documents

☐ You'll probably become involved with special characters in one of two ways—either because you need a special symbol for an equation or foreign language, or because the printer doesn't print the characters displayed on your screen

   To view what each keystroke will produce on the printer, retrieve the FONT.TST document from the *Learning* disk. Print the document and compare the printed characters to those you see on-screen.

☐ WordPerfect's line-drawing feature is easy to use with some printers—it makes drawing uncomplicated forms and graphs a pleasure

☐ If you type large projects that require tables of contents, figures and tables lists, or indexes, don't forget this three-step process:

   1. Mark the text to be included

   2. Define the style

   3. Generate the listing

Although *concordance* is covered thoroughly in Que Corporation's new book *WordPerfect Tips, Tricks, and Traps* and in WordPerfect's documentation, it is important that you know that this WordPerfect index feature is available for your use.

A concordance file is a normal WordPerfect document that contains text you wish to include in your index. The value of the concordance file feature is that by entering each word or phrase just once in the concordance file, you eliminate the need to mark each occurrence of the word or phrase in your document. If you create indexes as a part of your normal responsibilities, you'll be glad you took the time to learn how to put this feature to work for you.

The term *table of authorities* may be unfamiliar if you do not work with legal briefs or "scholarly" manuscripts daily, and there is the distinct possibility that the term is unfamiliar to you even if you do this kind of work!

WordPerfect permits you to create a table of authorities (which is similar to a table of contents) that contains as many as sixteen sections—one section for each type of authority you wish to reference. "Types" of legal authorities may include court cases, rules of court, statutes, and agency opinions. WordPerfect lists each citation alphabetically within each section and provides page references.

There are three basic steps in creating a table of authorities:

- Marking the authorities
- Defining the sections
- Generating the table

You may, of course, edit the authorities as well. A "typical" table of authorities looks like this:

I.

TABLE OF AUTHORITIES

Page

Cases

Anderson Drive-In Theater v. Kirkpatrick, (1953) 123
    Ind. App. 388, 392, 110 N.E. 2nd 506 . . . . . . . . . . . . . . . . . . . . 17, 19

Augustine v. First Federal Savings and Loan
    Association of Gary, (1979) _____ Ind._____,
    384 N.E. 2nd 1018 . . . . . . . . . . . . . . . . . . . . . . . . . . . . . . . . . . . . 12

Because this book is written for the WordPerfect "generalist" and the table of authorities feature is used in a very specific work environment, this feature is explored thoroughly in *WordPerfect Tips, Tricks, and Traps* as well. Your WordPerfect documentation also provides an explanation of the process.

Chapter 14 is devoted to one of WordPerfect's easiest-to-use, timesaving features—*macros*. Macros are another way to make WordPerfect work for you; this time, by remembering a series of keystrokes that you use frequently. WordPerfect will remember, and play back, those keystrokes each time you press a specially designated "macro" key.

# Streamlining
# with WordPerfect

To: Communications Department Staff
From: John Roberts
Re: Middle-of-the-night idea

Now that we've mastered the basics and some of the more advanced features of WordPerfect, let's put the technology to work for us!

First, use WordPerfect's Sort and Select feature and create a list of clients who:

- Do business in the Washington metropolitan area (check ZIP codes)
- Sell computer hardware
- Have a D&B AA rating

Then:

Using WordPerfect's Merge feature, develop a standard "sales" letter that you personalize to each client. Your letter should emphasize client benefit—tie those benefits to dollars, and increased sales, efficiency, and customer goodwill. Use macros to automate your efforts!

It'll be your responsibility to keep mailing lists up-to-date.

J. Roberts

# CHAPTER 14

# Using Macros To Streamline Editing and Printing

**A** *macro* is a special file which you create to hold a series of function keystrokes, or phrases, or paragraphs, or formats. The macro file can be "played back" (retrieved) with one or two keystrokes.

If you find the macro concept difficult to imagine, consider this: whenever you find yourself using the same keystrokes to complete a task (setting tabs and margins, periodically filling in a form with identical information, using a standard memo format) create a macro to record your standard memo format, and assign the macro to a keystroke combination (such as Alt-M perhaps). Then, the next time you have a memo to prepare, instead of typing in the *TO:* and the *FROM:*, just press Alt-M to play back the keystrokes that re-create the memo format.

Here's another example of the flexibility you'll enjoy with macros: you can format a new document, change paper feed bins, and type a heading just by pressing Alt-H.

If you build more macros than can be assigned to Alt-"letter" combinations, you can assign descriptive names, like *BILLFORM*. Using macros is quicker and more accurate than entering a series of complex instructions each time you must carry out a task. Macros can streamline your editing, saving, and printing tasks in any number of ways; the macros discussed in this chapter demonstrate only a fraction of the number of macro possibilities.

There are a couple of points you'll need to remember as you create your macros:

■ Retrieve a macro only with the Macro key (Alt-F10) or with Alt plus a letter between A and Z (Alt-C, for example)

   If you retrieve a macro any other way, the macro may not perform properly

■ You can erase macros from your disk by using the standard erase procedure from the List Files menu or from DOS

## Creating Macros

You'll follow these four basic steps as you create macros:

• Turn the macro-definition recorder on

• Name the macro

• Type the keystrokes and menu choices to be remembered

• Turn the macro-definition recorder off

And now for the procedure:

1. Press Macro Def (Ctrl-F10) to turn the macro-definition recorder on

The prompt

    Define Macro:

which appears in the lower left corner of the screen, asks you to name your macro.

Select a name that is relevant and easy to remember. Consider also whether you want to continue to use the macro with other documents or whether you'll be using it temporarily.

There are four ways to name macros:

- *Alt-"letter" macro:* To assign an Alt-"letter" combination to a macro, press and hold the Alt key while you type a letter between A and Z. You are limited to twenty-six Alt-"letter" macros, of course, because there are only twenty-six letters in the alphabet. *An Alt-"letter" name is best used for macros that you want to use frequently and in many documents.*

  The Alt-"letter" macro is saved to disk in a file named ALT"letter".MAC (ALTC.MAC, for example). The .MAC *file extension* identifies the file as a macro. This macro file will be saved to the default drive and directory.

- *Enter macro:* To create a temporary macro that you'll use until you exit WordPerfect, do not type a name. Just press Enter. WordPerfect names the macro.

- *One-letter macro:* Type one letter but do not hold down the Alt key. Naming a macro in this way is convenient if you have used up all of your Alt key macro names. One-letter macros are temporary and are not available after you exit WordPerfect.

- *Named macro:* To name a macro, type a two- to eight-character name and press Enter. With this technique, you can name many more macros than the twenty-six allowable Alt-"letter" combinations. Named macros are also saved to disk in a macro file. The file name is assigned the macro name plus the extension .MAC. This macro file will be saved to the default drive or directory.

Alt- and named-macros are saved to disk in the current directory and can be used in other documents and at a later time.

**2.** Type the **macro name** and press Enter

After you've named the macro, the Macro Def prompt flashes in the lower left of the screen while your keystrokes and almost all menu choices are recorded in the macro.

**3.** Type the keystrokes (keystroke combinations or text) you want recorded in the macro file

**4.** Press Macro Def (Ctrl-F10) to end macro definition

If you named the macro with an Alt key combination or a name, a file containing your keystrokes is saved in the default drive or directory.

*If you want to use a macro while you are working in another directory or on a drive other than the default drive, copy the file to that directory or drive by selecting 8 Copy from the List Files menu.*

If you attempt to view or retrieve a .MAC file, WordPerfect will prompt you with an error message which states that you have requested an invalid file name. Viewing a macro from the List Files screen will display only a screen full of machine symbols. A good rule of thumb is, never attempt to retrieve a macro file because doing so can cause errors in the file and may cause temporary problems in WordPerfect.

If you try to create a macro with a name that duplicates the name of an existing macro, WordPerfect asks whether you want to replace the existing macro. Type Y to replace the existing macro or select another name for the macro you're creating.

WordPerfect does not permit you to edit the macros you create. If your macro doesn't work, you must re-create the macro.

## Starting Macros

You can start your macro anywhere in a document. You must remember though, a macro created to start at a specific location within the document may not work correctly if you start it somewhere else.

To start an Alt key macro:

1. Hold down the Alt key while you type the letter assigned to the macro

If the disk light comes on but nothing happens, check to make sure that the current directory contains an ALT"letter".MAC file for that "letter."

To start a macro with a two- to eight-character name:

1. Press the Macro key (Alt-F10)

2. Type the **macro name**

3. Press Enter

If the macro does not work, check to make sure that the default directory contains a .MAC file with the appropriate macro name.

To start a temporary macro:

1. Press the Macro key (Alt-F10)

2. Press Enter and WordPerfect will find the temporary macro

   Or

1. Press the Macro key (Alt-F10)

   2. Press a single letter

   3. Press Enter

Because temporary macros are not stored on disk in a .MAC file they must be redefined if they don't work.

It is possible to create a macro or macros that start as soon as WordPerfect starts; use the */m* switch described in Chapter 17.

As you know, named macros and Alt macros are stored in a file. If that file does not reside in the current (default) disk or directory, the macro will not operate. There are two ways to handle the situation:

   1. Copy the macro files to directories in which you will need them

      Or

   1. Press Macro (Alt-F10) to start the macro

   2. Type the disk, directory, and macro name

# Stopping Macros

You can stop a macro while it is running simply by pressing the Cancel key (F1).

# A Sample Keystroke Macro

The simplest kind of macro inserts frequently used text: the closing of a letter, a memos heading, or a standard form, for instance. The following example demonstrates how easily you can record and store in one Alt key combination all the keystrokes necessary for typing a heading.

Follow these steps:

   1. Press the Exit key (F7) to clear the screen

   2. Make sure that the cursor is in the first character position at the top of the screen

   3. Press Macro Def (Ctrl-F10) to turn on the macro recorder

This message appears on your screen:

      Define Macro:

   4. Type the macro name **HEADING** and press Enter

   5. While the Macro Def prompt flashes in the lower right corner of the screen, type the heading shown in figure 14.1

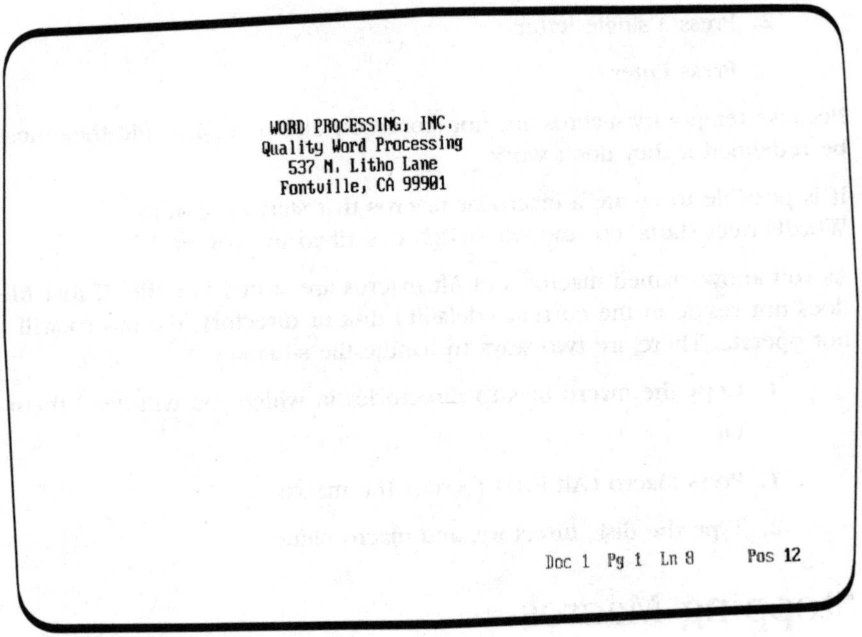

```
                    WORD PROCESSING, INC.
                    Quality Word Processing
                       537 N. Litho Lane
                      Fontville, CA 99901
```

Doc 1  Pg 1  Ln 8          Pos 12

*Fig. 14.1. Heading for sample macro file.*

6. Move the cursor to the location at which you want to start typing after the heading

7. Press Macro Def (Ctrl-F10) to turn off the macro recorder

The macro you've created is saved (under the file name HEADING.MAC) in the default directory or drive.

To test the macro:

1. Press the Exit key (F7) to clear the screen

2. Press the Macro key (Alt-F10)

At the prompt Macro:

3. Type **HEADING**

4. Press Enter

You'll see the heading retyped almost instantly on the screen. This process is not the same as retrieving a file. WordPerfect actually duplicated each of your keystrokes.

Try the seven-step exercise again. This time, however, press Alt and type H in Step 4, naming the macro with an Alt key combination. After you complete Step 7, you'll be able to call up the macro by pressing Alt-H.

Although naming a macro with an Alt key combination limits you to one of twenty-six key combinations, the Alt key combination does permit you to call up the macro very quickly.

As you will see in the next section, it's a simple matter to include formatting commands in the heading macro.

# A Sample Macro

If you consistently use one format for your documents, you can use the Set-up menu, described in Chapter 17, to set that format so that WordPerfect will execute it on start-up. More often though, you must frequently change margin and tab settings for the different types of documents you create—the shipping labels that must be created while you're busy writing letters, or the invoices that have to be completed while you're working on the board report.

Wouldn't you like to simply press Alt-L and have the format immediately set up for labels, or to press Alt-I and switch to invoice format?

Macros remember the function keys that you press, the menu choices you make, and the characters you type. Follow these steps to set up a simple formatting macro that changes margin and tab settings:

1.  Note your current margin and tab settings for reference

2.  Move to the left margin

3.  Press the Macro Def key (Ctrl-F10) to turn on the macro recorder. The Macro Def prompt will flash in the lower left corner of the screen

4.  Press Alt-F to name the macro

The F for *format* makes it easy to remember.

5.  Press the Line Format key (Shift-F8)

6.  Select 3 Margins

7.  Enter new margin settings of 12 left and 69 right

8.  Press the Line Format key (Shift-F8)

9. Select **1** Tabs

10. Clear the old tab settings by moving the cursor to location 1 and pressing Ctrl-End

11. Type new tab settings of **17, 22, 59,** and **64**

12. Press Exit (F7) to return to the typing screen

13. Press the Macro Def key (Ctrl-F10) to turn off the macro recorder

You can insert this format by moving to the left margin of any line in a document and pressing Alt-F.

To test the macro:

1. Type an **asterisk** (*) at each of the first four tab stops in your document

2. Move to the left margin of the line before the asterisks

3. Press Alt-F

All the asterisks should reposition with the new margin and tab settings.

Although you can stop a macro by pressing the Cancel key (F1), this macro works so fast that you won't be able to stop it before it is finished.

To check to be certain that this macro appears on the List Files directory:

1. Press the List Files key (F5)

2. Look for a file named ALTF.MAC

You can copy this file to other disks or directories where you need the macro.

# Making a Macro Pause for Keyboard Entries

There will be times that you'll want to create a macro that pauses, so that you can add text (typed from the keyboard) before the macro continues. Macros that include pauses are useful for filling in forms, typing *To* and *From* information in headings, and so on.

To insert pauses in your macro:

1. Create the macro to the point at which you want it to pause

2. Press Ctrl-PgUp while the Macro Def prompt flashes in the lower left corner of the screen

You will hear a beep.

**3.** Press Enter twice

This three-step procedure marks the spot at which the macro will pause. The "automatic reorganizer" macro in this chapter offers an example of another macro that utilizes pauses.

**4.** Continue creating the macro

The macro will run until it reaches the pause. You'll hear a beep, after which you can type text. As soon as you press Enter, the macro will continue.

# Entering Delays To Slow Macro Operation

You can use the pause capability in a macro also to slow down the macro so that you can see what's happening. Normally, when you run a macro nothing appears on the screen until the macro is complete. By slowing down macro execution, you can see each step of the macro on the screen as the instructions are carried out.

By entering delays of different lengths at different locations throughout a macro, you cause different sections of the macro to execute at different speeds. The delay number that you type is the delay (in tenths of a second) between each keystroke replayed by the macro.

To slow down a macro, enter a pause command (Ctrl-PgUp) followed by a number to indicate the length of the delay. This is the procedure:

**1.** Press Macro Def (Ctrl-F10) and name the macro

**2.** Insert a delay by pressing Ctrl-PgUp

A beep sounds.

**3.** Type the number of tenths of a second, between 0 and 254, that you want between each keystroke during replay

**4.** Press Enter

**5.** Continue creating the macro

When you run the macro, it will slow down or speed up at the appropriate location.

# Chaining Macros

You can "chain" macros so that one macro will call up another. There are two rules to remember:

- A macro can call up only one other macro which, in turn, calls up another macro—eventually creating a "chain" of linked macros

- When WordPerfect leaves one macro to work on another, the program can't return to the location it left in the original macro. The "link" to the next macro is always at the end of the current macro

To create a format macro that links to a heading macro, follow these steps:

1. Press the Macro Def key (Ctrl-F10) to turn on the macro-definition recorder

2. Type the macro name **FORMAT** and press Enter

3. Using the Line Format commands, create the format macro

4. Press the Macro key (Alt-F10) to indicate that another macro will start

5. Type the name of that macro **HEADING**

6. Press the Macro Def key (Ctrl-F10) to turn off the macro-definition recorder

Now you must create a HEADING macro, and of course, you could create the HEADING macro to call another macro.

When you call up the FORMAT macro, it will run until it reaches the instruction to start the HEADING macro. At that point, the FORMAT macro has completed its job and the HEADING macro will start.

Building large chained macros with conditional statements is comparable to programming in a computer language. To do the job effectively, you need a macro-editor program that lets you edit macros without having to re-create them. Call WordPerfect Corporation for information about purchasing their low-cost macro editor.

# Designing Macros

Remember that macros are like tape recorders—they play back your keystrokes and commands on demand. An incorrectly designed macro will not work as planned and may be difficult to record correctly.

Before you create a macro, decide what you want it to do and determine the necessary keystrokes. Entering simple keystroke macros that reproduce your typing is a fairly simple process. You can correct your entries, and the macro recorder will remember the corrections. However, you may have to do some advanced planning to create more complex macros.

If you want to develop large macros that work with chaining and merging of documents, you will need to describe in writing what you want to accomplish. The easiest way to write a complicated macro is by writing a series of statements. Each statement should be on a separate line and should describe one specific task to be performed in the macro. Such a *metacode* macro might look like this:

Move cursor to first character in document
Enter new margin settings
Enter new tab settings
Retrieve C:\WP\FORMS\INSURANC.STL document
Move to Addenda location
Enter new margin settings
Retrieve C:\WP\FORMS\ADDENDA document
Move to end of Addenda
Enter original margin settings
Move to first entry location
Pause for first name
Move to second entry location
Pause for last name
Invoke LASRPRNT macro to print form

# Eleven Frequently Used Macros

The following macros are divided into three broad categories: typing, editing, and printing. For each of these macros, you will find a general statement about the macro's task, a specific description of the macro, steps for creating the macro, and at least one possible variation.

You may want to change the macro names to make them more meaningful to you. In most cases, two methods for naming each macro are provided: one using the Alt key and one using a descriptive two- to eight-character file name. If you decide to use the Alt key to name macros, you may want to keep a handwritten list of the macro names and notes about what the macros do. Naming a macro Alt-A may seem logical to you today, but later in the week you may have problems trying to remember the contents of Alt-A.

# Macros for Typing

You can use macros in numerous ways to make entering text and formats faster and more accurate. Use a macro to type the closing of a letter, or use a macro to type the heading for a memo, or use a macro to set up the format for any kind of document.

## Format Setup Macro

**Task:** This macro sets up the format of a document. The format can include tabs, margins, line spacing, page numbering, pitch and font, page length, and even printer selection.

**Description:** Suppose that you need a format for short, one-page letters. This macro changes the margins to 15 and 70, turns off justification, sets tabs every 8 spaces across the line, inserts 12 blank lines at the top of the page to accommodate the letterhead, and automatically inserts the current date.

**Steps:**

1. Press Macro Definition (Ctrl-F10)

2. Name the macro Alt-F (for format) or LTR-FMT (for letter format)

3. Press Enter

4. Press Line Format (Shift-F8)

5. Select 3 Margins

6. Type 15 (left margin)

7. Press Enter

8. Type 70 (right margin)

9. Press Enter

10. Press Print Format (Ctrl-F8)

11. Select 3 Turn Off (Justification)

12. Press Enter

13. Press Line Format (Shift-F8), 1 Tabs

14. Move the cursor to the first position

15. Press Ctrl-End (delete all tabs)

16. Type **15,8** to enter tabs starting at 15 and continuing every 8 spaces

17. Press Enter

18. Press Exit (F7)

19. Press Enter 12 times to move the cursor to line 12

20. Press Date (Shift-F5)

21. Select **1** Insert Text to insert the text date

22. Press Enter four times to position the cursor for the inside address

23. Press Macro Definition (Ctrl-F10) to turn off the macro recorder

**To operate:**

1. Press Exit (F7) to clear the screen

2. Make sure that the cursor is at the first character location

3. Press Alt-F to invoke the macro

   Or

3. Press Alt-F10 and type **LTR-FMT**

4. Press Enter

**Variations:**

- Develop a similar macro for other documents such as memos, legal pleadings, or minutes

- If you plan to store the document and edit or reprint it in the future: in Step 21, select **3** Insert Function instead of **1** Insert Text. The Insert Function automatically inserts the current date whenever you retrieve or print the document

- If more than one printer is attached to your computer, you can include the printer-selection commands in the setup macro

## Letter Close Macro

**Task:** This macro automatically types a letter closing.

**Description:** After you place the cursor on the line where you want to print the closing of a letter, you can call up the Closing macro. This macro positions the closing in one of three places: at the left margin, centered, or tabbed to a specific position. The Closing macro can include the complimentary closing and signature block as well as notations for initial, enclosure, and copy.

**Steps:**

1. Press Macro Definition (Ctrl-F10)

2. Name the macro Alt-C (for closing)

   Or

2. Use the name or initials of the person whose name appears in the closing

3. Type all the text you want to include in the standard closing (If the closing will be aligned at a tab rather than at the left margin, you may want to set the tabs in the macro. This arrangement guarantees that the closing will be aligned properly even though the tabs in the letter are different from those in the closing)

4. Press Enter to generate the blank lines for the signature

5. Press Macro Definition (Ctrl-F10) to conclude the definition process

**To operate:**

1. Move to the left margin of the line at which you want the closing to begin

2. Press Alt-C (or, press Alt-F10 and type the initials you've selected) to call up the macro

3. Continue typing

   Or

3. Print the finished letter

**Variations:**

- Create a collection of closing macros, one for each closing that you use frequently

- Define a macro for any text you type frequently: company or department name, product names or descriptions, inside addresses for regular clients and customers, bibliographic citations, and so forth

## *Memo Heading Macro*

**Task:** This macro types the standard heading used for a memo.

**Description:** You can set up the macro to generate your usual memo heading: the word *MEMORANDUM* or *MEMO* across the top, with the *TO*, *FROM*, and *SUBJECT* headings automatically in place.

**Steps:**

1. Press Macro Definition (Ctrl-F10)
2. Name the macro Alt-M or MEMO
3. Press Center (Shift-F6)
4. Type **MEMO** or **MEMORANDUM**
5. Press Enter four times to move the cursor down four lines
6. Type **To:**
7. Press the Tab key
8. Press Enter twice
9. Type **From:**
10. Press the Tab key
11. Press Enter twice
12. Type **Subject:**
13. Press Tab
14. Press Enter twice
15. Type **Date:**
16. Press Tab
17. Press Date (Shift-F5)
18. Select 1 Insert Text
19. Press Enter twice
20. Move the cursor to the *To:* line and position the cursor for the first entry
21. Press Macro Definition (Ctrl-F10) to end the definition procedure

**To operate:**

1. Press Exit (F7) to clear the screen

2. Make sure that the cursor is at the first character location

3. Press Alt-M (or, press Alt-F10 and type MEMO) to call up the macro

**Variations:**

• Include pitch and font-change commands after pressing Center and before typing the text in Step 4. This will allow you to type the heading MEMO or MEMORANDUM in larger or more emphasized style. Change the pitch and font back to the default, following the centered text

• Use Indent (F4) instead of Tab in the preceding steps

## Memo Heading with Pause Codes

**Task:** This macro, which is similar to the Memo Heading macro, pauses during execution so that you can enter the TO, FROM, SUBJECT, and DATE information.

**Description:** Define this macro as you did the preceding macro, but add pause codes that instruct the macro to pause for keyboard input. To insert a pause code, press Ctrl-PgUp while defining the macro.

**Steps:**

1. Follow the steps provided for the preceding macro but, after pressing the Tab key following the TO, FROM, and SUBJECT entries, press Ctrl-PgUp to insert the pause (The computer beeps)

2. Press Enter twice to end the pause-insertion process. Continue defining the macro as in the preceding macro

**To operate:**

1. Press Exit (F7) to clear the screen

2. Make sure that the cursor is at the first character location

3. Press Alt-M to call up the macro

4. Whenever the macro beeps, the cursor will pause by the *TO*, *FROM*, or *SUBJECT* entries. Type the appropriate entry

5. Press Enter to continue the macro

**Variation:**

- Use the macro-pause feature to create other fill-in-the-blank documents, including standard letters and contracts

## Change Default Drive Macro

**Task:** This macro changes the default drive from within WordPerfect.

**Description:** This macro sets up Drive B as the default drive.

**Steps:**

1. Press Macro Definition (Ctrl-F10)
2. Name the macro Alt-B (for Drive B)
3. Press List Files (F5)
4. Type an equal sign (=)
5. Type **B:**
6. Press Enter twice
7. Press the space bar once
8. Press Macro Definition (Ctrl-F10) to end the definition process

**To operate:**

1. Press Alt-B

Make sure that the macro you want is in your current directory.

**Variations:**

- Set up macros to change to another directory on the hard disk. In Step 5, you simply type the disk and directory's full path name (C:\WP\LETTERS, for example)

- Use two- to eight-character macro names instead of Alt key combinations. Each name can designate the directory to which you want to change. For example, pressing the Macro key, Alt-F10, and entering LETTER could change the current directory to C:\WP\LETTER. If you want to move to any directory from any other directory, copy a full set of all directory-change macros into each directory

# Macros for Editing

Before you begin a complex, repetitious editing task, you should consider creating a macro that does the task automatically. Macros can save many keystrokes during editing. For example, you can use macros to save a document, and to open or close windows. The samples provided here are but a few suggestions.

## Windows and Switch Cursor Macro

**Task:** While you are editing a document, this macro lets you refer to another part of the same document or retrieve another document.

**Description:** This macro opens a second window and moves the cursor to the new, blank window. Then you can manually retrieve or create a document.

**Steps:**

1. Press Macro Definition (Ctrl-F10)

2. Name the macro Alt-W (for window) or WINDOW

3. Press Screen (Ctrl-F3)

4. Select **1** Window

5. Type the number of lines you want in the top window (Type **11** to create two windows of equal size)

6. Press Enter

7. Press Switch (Shift-F3) to move the cursor to the lower window

8. Press Macro Definition (Ctrl-F10) to turn off the macro recorder

**To operate:**

While you are working in the current typing screen:

1. Press Alt-W

   Or

1. Call up the WINDOW macro by name

After the cursor moves into the new, blank window:

2. Use List Files to retrieve a document

   Or

2. Begin typing a new document

**Variation:**

• If you frequently use windows to recall the same document, you may want to include in the second window the Retrieve function and the name of the document you retrieve. The second window is an excellent place to view outlines, project notes, or grammar notes as you write

## Close Window Macro

**Task:** This macro "undoes" the Window command—that is, it expands the window the cursor rests in so that the window fills the screen.

**Description:** This macro assumes that two windows are currently on the screen. The window that contains the cursor will become a full-screen document.

**Steps:**

1. Check to be certain that there are two windows displayed on the screen

2. Press Macro Def (Ctrl-F10)

3. Press Alt-C to name the macro

4. Press Screen (Ctrl-F3)

5. Select 1 Window

6. Type **25**

7. Press Enter

8. Press Macro Def (Ctrl-F10)

**To operate:**

This macro affects the screen only when two windows are displayed.

1. Press the Switch key (Shift-F3) to move to the window that will fill the screen

2. Press Alt-C

**Variations:**

• Try creating an Alt-W macro to quickly switch between full-screen documents

• Display the document with a tab ruler by specifying 23 instead of 25 as the number of lines (in Step 6)

## *Automatic Reorganizer Macro*

**Task:** After you type an original draft, you probably will need to do some reorganizing. Cutting, moving, and pasting more than a few segments of text can become tedious, but this macro almost automates the job.

**Description:** Use this macro to move highlighted sections of text to an appropriate area in an outline. Create an outline of key words at the beginning of your document. Then move the cursor to the text you want reorganized into the outline. When you press the macro key (Alt-M), you'll be asked to highlight the text and type the location identifier where the text should be moved. All the cutting, pasting, and moving are done automatically. The cursor returns to its original location.

This is the longest macro in the book. However, if you type your drafts directly into WordPerfect (an excellent way to work), this macro will be a real time-saver.

**Steps:**

If you have entered the section identifiers from Step 1 in each document, you can use the macro described in the following steps with any document:

1. Retrieve a test document to the screen. Having a document in the screen will make entering the macro easier visually

2. Type in unique identifiers at the beginning of the draft

The identifiers should serve as a miniature outline into which text will be moved. Identifiers should be preceded by double asterisks so the macro can find them easily. For example, **SECTION1, **SECTION2. Use two asterisks only—no spaces.

3. Move to the beginning of a paragraph that you will **pretend** to move

4. Press the Macro Def key (Ctrl-F10)

5. Name the macro Alt-M (for move)

6. Type a space and three pound signs, followed by another space ( ### ). (The spaces are important)

The macro will use these # signs to mark the original location of the cursor. At the end of the macro, the cursor will return to this same location.

7. Press the Block key (Alt-F4) to turn on the block. This gets the macro ready for a Block move

In the following steps you'll pretend to move a block; however, you won't actually highlight text.

8. Press the Ctrl-PgUp key to mark a pause in the macro for keyboard entry. You will hear a beep

9. Press Enter twice to mark the end of the pause

When the macro operates, you will use this pause to highlight the text to be moved. During the macro-building process, you won't actually highlight any text.

10. Press the Move key (Ctrl-F4) to display the Block Move menu

11. Select **1 Cut Block** to cut out the text that will be highlighted while the macro operates

12. Press Home, Home, PgUp to move to the top of the document

13. Press the Search key (F2). The forward Search will be used to find the location to receive the cut text

14. Press the Ctrl-PgUp key to mark a pause in the macro for keyboard entry. You will hear a beep

15. Press Enter twice to mark the end of the pause

When the macro operates, you will use this pause to enter the location identifier such as **SECTION2, where the block of text will be moved.

16. Press the Search key (F2) to activate the search

Because you haven't entered anything to search for, the cursor remains at the top of the screen. During actual macro operation, the cursor moves to the location identifier.

17. Press the down arrow

Because the macro moved the cursor to the identifier, the down arrow moves the cursor to the next lower line where the moved text will be inserted.

18. Press Home and left arrow to move the cursor to the left margin

19. Press the Move key (Ctrl-F4) to display the Move menu

20. Select **5 Retrieve** to retrieve the text that is being moved

21. Press Home, Home, up arrow to move to the top of the document

22. Press the Search key (F2). You are about to search for the ### marking the cursor's original location

23. Type a space and three pound signs, followed by a space ( ### ). This is the marker at the original cursor location

24. Press Search (F2) to activate the search for the original cursor location

25. Press Backspace five times to delete the original location marker ( ### )

26. Press the Macro Def key (Ctrl-F10) to turn off macro definition

**To operate:**

You must place location identifiers—for each area to which text will be moved—in the document to be reorganized. If you are doing a great deal of reorganizing, you may want to put all the identifiers in a semioutline at the beginning of the document.

When you find text that you want moved:

1. Move the cursor to the first character of the text

2. Press Alt-M to call up the macro. The Block on message will flash in the lower left corner of the screen and a beep will sound

3. Use the cursor movement keys to highlight the text you want moved. If the cursor is incorrectly positioned, turn off the macro by pressing the Cancel key (F1)

4. Press Enter when the text you want moved is highlighted

The text disappears from the screen.

5. The →Srch: prompt will appear in the lower left corner of the screen

6. Type the location identifier of the location you want to receive the text

For example, you'd type **SECTION1 if you wanted the text moved to the **SECTION1 location identifier.

7. Press Enter

8. The text will be moved and the cursor returned to its original location

**Variations:**

- Enter, in random order, notes for a project or report into a document. Or you can merge many note documents into one. Use this macro to reorganize the notes

- If all of your reorganizing is done by paragraph, you can create a macro that will search for paragraphs containing key words or phrases and then automatically move only those paragraphs to one location

  The macro should use the Search function to prompt you for a key word or phrase, and then move the cursor to that word or phrase. Then, instead of using the Block Move function used in this macro, the macro should use choice 2 Paragraph from the Move menu. Use a second Search function to move the cursor to the location you want the paragraph moved to. Don't forget to return the cursor to the top of the document before each search

# Macros for Printing

Macros can make printing easier. For instance, you can write macros that select printers, give the Print command, and interrupt or cancel printing.

## Resume Printing Macro

**Task:** If your printer is set up as a hand-fed printer, you need to tell it to resume printing after each page is inserted. Because this takes at least four keystrokes, it is a real interruption of your work when you are printing from the print queue while simultaneously typing on another document.

Although you must still take the time to insert the next sheet of paper, you can save time at the keyboard by letting the macro instruct the printer to resume printing.

**Description:** You must give the initial Print command to print from the screen or print from the print queue. After printing the first page, the printer stops. You insert a sheet of paper and then invoke the macro to send the "go" command to the printer.

**Steps:**

1. Press Macro Definition (Ctrl-F10)

2. Name the macro Alt-G

3. Press the Print key (Shift-F7)

4. Press 4 Printer Control

5. Press **G** ("Go") to restart the printer

6. Press Enter to return to the typing screen

7. Press Macro Definition (Ctrl-F10)

**To operate:**

Insert a sheet of paper and start the printer. Return to the typing screen and continue to work. When the printer finishes, insert another sheet of paper and press Alt-G. The printer will start and you will be returned immediately to the typing screen.

**Variations:**

- Define a macro that stops the printer. Use Print, 4 Printer Control, and S (Stop Printing)

- To cancel a print job, set the macro to go to the Printer Control menu and select C to cancel the job. Let the macro stop operation at that point. You can then select which job you want to cancel

## *Envelope Macro*

**Task:** This macro prepares the format for typing an address on a standard #10 business envelope.

**Description:** You can set up envelope macros in several ways. This macro's primary function is to set up the format for the envelope. You type the address manually after the macro executes.

**Steps:**

1. Press Macro Definition (Ctrl-F10)

2. Name the macro Alt-E (for envelope) or ENV or ENVELOPE

3. To change the top margin to 20 half-lines, press Page Format (Alt-F8)

4. Select **5** Top Margin

5. Type **20**

6. Press Enter twice

7. To change the side margins, press Line Format (Shift-F8)

8. Select **3** Margins

9. Type **40** (left margin)

10. Press Enter

11. Type **80** (right margin)

12. Press Enter

13. Press Macro Definition (Ctrl-F10) to end the macro

**To operate:**

Invoke the macro at the top of the document if you are going to type a single envelope.

If you are going to enter an envelope at the end of a letter, enter a Hard Page break (Ctrl-Enter) before you call up the macro.

**Variations:**

You can vary this macro to make it more useful. Several of the methods suggested are best suited to a hand-fed printer. Because you insert new paper into the printer for each page, you determine whether you will use regular paper or an envelope.

- If you are using a hand-fed printer or a printer with paper bins, you can select an envelope as the last "page" of a letter. End the letter portion of the document with a Hard Page break (Ctrl-Enter) to separate the letter from the envelope

- To alternate letters and envelopes in the same document, restore the initial document formats—left, right, and top margins—at the end of each envelope. You might do so by defining another macro (called, for instance, Alt-L for letter) that you invoke after each envelope address

- If you plan to follow letters with envelopes, you may want WordPerfect to automatically pick up the letter's inside address. To do this, the last step in the Alt-E (envelope) macro should move to the top of the letter (with Home, Home, up arrow) and then cursor down to the first line of the address. Use the Block copy technique to pick up as many lines as the longest address block for a letter. Move to the end of the document (with Home, Home, down arrow), reposition the cursor to the address area, and retrieve the address with the Move key

*Note:* When you print envelopes with a laser printer, you usually feed the envelopes one at a time. Include a font change in the macro to switch into landscape mode. Be sure to switch back to a portrait font to print on regular paper.

*Note:* If you use a continuous-feed printer, you can purchase envelopes that are "tacked" to continuous-feed paper so that you can print envelopes in a batch. To print many envelopes contained in one document, you may need to change the paper length to match the distance between the tops of succeeding envelopes.

## Change Printer Macro

**Task:** This macro lets you change easily between printers. You may decide to change to a (physically) different printer or to use the same printer with a different printer definition. Different printer definitions let you use different fonts and paper-feed methods on the same printer.

**Description:** This macro permits you to select a printer through the Printer Control menu. If you are using a laser printer, the macro assumes that you have inserted the necessary font cartridge or that you have the appropriate software fonts downloaded to the printer.

**Steps:**

1. Press the Print key (Shift-F7)

2. Select 4 Printer Control

3. Select 2 Display Printers and Fonts

4. Look for the number of the printer with the printer, font, and feed mechanism you want to use. Press the space bar to see the second screen. Remember the number of the printer

5. Exit to the typing screen

6. Press Macro Definition (Ctrl-F10)

7. Name the macro Alt-P (for printer) or a letter specific to the printer's name. If you name the macro, you can use a name (such as HPHELVET, HPTIMES, IBMBIN) that describes the printer, font, and feed

8. Press Print (Shift-F7)

9. Select 4 Printer Control

10. Select 1 Select Print Options

11. Select 1 Printer Number

12. Enter the printer number you found in Step 4

13. Press Enter twice to return to the typing screen

14. Press Macro Definition (Ctrl-F10)

**To operate:**

When your document is ready to print, invoke the macro for the printer definition you want to use. (The printer the macro changes to must already be selected with the appropriate font, printer connections, and paper feed. It must be one of the six printer alternatives.) After invoking the macro, you can print from the screen or from the print queue with the new printer.

**Variations:**

- If you assume that the document to be printed will be on the screen, you can include the Print command following Step 13

- You may want a macro that prints only once to the assigned printer and then returns to the WordPerfect default printer (used on start-up). For the macro to do this, choose 3 Options in Step 9 and then skip to Step 11. This changes printers for only the next print job

- Change also the font that is used when you switch between printers. Change fonts between Steps 13 and 14 by pressing the Print Format key (Ctrl-F8), selecting 1 Pitch/Font, and entering the font number you want. You can see the font numbers available in Step 3 of the preceding procedure

Once you have completed the *Quick Starts*, and become familiar with basic format commands, you can create macros to streamline editing, printing, and saving tasks. You can create macros to do such simple tasks as repeating a signature block, or you can create macros to handle more complex tasks, such as a completely automated legal document system.

Only four steps are needed to create a macro:

☐ Press the Macro Def key (Ctrl-F10) to turn on the macro recorder

☐ Name the macro

☐ Type the keystrokes and commands you want recorded

☐ Press the Macro Def key again to turn off the macro recording

Remember these tips when you create macros:

☐ Unless the macro reproduces simple keystrokes, make a list of the macro's functions and keystrokes before you enter the keystrokes

☐ Some macros rely upon the cursor location to start. Try to create your macros so that the macro positions the cursor in the correct location even if the user does not. Use the cursor movement keys for correct positioning

☐ Document your macros. Keep a log of the names of important macros; what they do, and how they should be used

☐ Use 8 Copy from the List Files menu to move a macro to another disk or directory. Macros are easiest to use if they are stored in the current disk or directory

Starting your macro depends on how you named it:

☐ Start Alt key macros by holding down the Alt key and pressing the letter

☐ Start the macros that you've named with the Enter key by pressing the Macro key (Alt-F10) and then pressing Enter

☐ Start macros you've named with one letter by pressing the Macro key (Alt-F10), typing the single letter, and then pressing Enter

☐ Start macros named with two to eight letters by pressing the Macro key (Alt-F10), typing the name, and pressing Enter

☐ If you want a macro to start as soon as WordPerfect starts, use the /m switch described in Chapter 17

To make sure that your macros don't give you problems:

☐ Never retrieve a macro file with the Retrieve or List Files keys. Macros end with the file extension .MAC

☐ Make sure that the cursor is in the correct location when executing a macro. Starting a macro in the wrong location could cause you to lose text

☐ Work your way up from simple text macros to longer and more complex macros

Before you consider creating a macro to help you fill in forms, look at the merge capabilities discussed in Chapter 15. WordPerfect's merge function can create forms in which the cursor automatically moves to each blank and prompts you for the text to be typed. The merge function handles mailing lists and form letters as well.

# Combining Documents with Merge

One of WordPerfect's most often overlooked features is the capability to merge text from one document with text in another document. Unfortunately, the feature is overlooked because it is perceived to be an "advanced" feature—requiring skill beyond new users' abilities.

The truth is, if you have completed the *Quick Start* sections, and you have learned to use WordPerfect's basic commands, you can put the Merge feature to work for you today!

Merge retrieves data from a *secondary merge file*, a text file, or from the keyboard and inserts it into a file called the *primary file*. The primary file actually orchestrates the merge process by calling for a client's name, or an address, a product name, a store location, or even a block of text, at specified points in the primary document.

With WordPerfect's merge features, you can create personalized form letters from an address list, or piece together complicated reports, or fill in forms. Merge operations make it easy to produce thousands of individualized letters or bills, which WordPerfect prints while you use the computer for other purposes.

This chapter explores the straightforward aspects of merge so you can begin "automating" the tedious and repetitive tasks that demand so much of your time and energy. WordPerfect's Sort capability (which helps add the finishing touches to the merge procedure) is described in Chapter 16.

# Merging Documents

WordPerfect can merge documents in more than one way. *Quick Start* 3 in Chapter 4 steps you through the *manual* technique for merging documents residing on disk to documents on the screen. This chapter describes how you can accomplish document merge *automatically*.

## Primary and Secondary Files

The merge function is frequently used for merging a mailing list to a form letter or to mailing labels. WordPerfect uses two documents to do this. One document contains the form letter or the mailing label format; the other document contains all of the pieces of data, such as names and addresses, that will be merged into the first document.

The *primary file* holds a skeleton document to which pieces of data are merged. Most of the primary file remains constant.

The *secondary file*, or data file, contains the data or variable information that will be merged into the primary file. Information in the secondary file is organized like information on filing cards. The information on one filing card is know as a *record*. Each record contains data about one entity.

Records are divided into *fields*, which represent the individual bits of information about the entity. For example, the types of data stored in mailing list fields usually are first name, last name, firm name, street address, city, state, ZIP, phone number, and so on.

The primary file and secondary file are used together in this way. Suppose that you are sending the same basic letter to several people. The letter is the primary file and the address list is the secondary file. In another example, if you are filling out a dentist's invoice, the invoice itself is (in) the primary file and the information about the patient and treatment is (in) the secondary file.

## Creating a Secondary File

Creating the secondary file—the data file—is frequently the first step in the merge procedure. You begin by dividing into records the information you want in the secondary file. For example, you divide a client mailing list so that each record holds information about a single client.

Next, you divide each record into fields, the categories of information the record holds. Fields in a mailing list might contain first name, last name, street address, city, and so on. Data such as the first name and last name or the address and city are in separate fields.

Separating fields into the smallest convenient blocks of data will give you greater flexibility later on. For example, if the first name and last name are stored in separate fields, you will be able to create a letter that refers to Ms. April Smith in the address, Ms. Smith in the salutation, and April in the text. Similarly, if you enter the ZIP code in its own field (separate from the address, city, and state), you will be able to sort labels by ZIP code. Sorted labels can save you money at the post office.

When you design a record, keep in mind two important things:

- First, every record must have the same number of fields. Even when a field is blank, you must acknowledge the blank field's presence. You do this by inserting a Merge R code (described later in this chapter). Blank fields are common in mailing lists because records include a field for the company name, but some clients have no company name.

- Second, the fields in all records must be in the same order. If the order of the fields is scrambled in various records, the merged results also will be scrambled. This happens because WordPerfect looks for the data being merged by the number of the field in the record. For example, if the first name is in field 1 in most records, but one record has the last name in field 1, WordPerfect will not be able to tell the difference. The resulting form letter will show a last name where the first name should have been.

## A Sample Record and Its Fields

Imagine that you are creating a mailing list of clients for a financial planner. The first field will contain the client's entire name and address.

Begin by clearing the screen and positioning the cursor at the top left margin. Then type the following client's name and address, stopping at the end of the ZIP code:

**Ms. Katherine Haley**
**5 Waverly Place**
**New York, NY 10021**

With the cursor immediately after the ZIP code, press the Merge R key (F9). A ^R appears at the end of the address.

```
Ms. Katherine Haley
5 Waverly Place
New York, NY 10021^R
```

WordPerfect interprets this code as the end of a field. You have declared that all the data from *Ms.* to *10021* belongs in field 1. The Merge R code that appears on-screen is not the same as typing the ^ symbol followed by an R.

The second field will contain the name to be used in the salutation of a letter. Later, this name can be used after the *Dear* in a form letter. Type Ms. Haley and press the Merge R key (F9) to generate the ^R. Now your record should look like this:

```
Ms. Katherine Haley
5 Waverly Place
New York, NY 10021^R
Ms. Haley^R
```

The third field you add is for the investment subject Ms. Haley is most concerned with. The phrase you insert here is designed to match the context of the letter you will type. Don't forget to press the Merge R key (F9) at the end of the field.

```
Ms. Katherine Haley
5 Waverly Place
New York, NY 10021^R
Ms. Haley^R
investing for Kim's college fund^R
```

Now you have completed the file of information on Ms. Haley. Your cursor should be on the blank line following the phrase "investing for Kim's college fund". If your cursor is somewhere else, move it to the correct position.

To indicate that Katherine Haley's record is complete:

Press the Merge E key (Shift-F9)

A ^E marks the end of the record.

The complete record for Katherine Haley follows:

```
Ms. Katherine Haley
5 Waverly Place
New York, NY 10021^R
Ms. Haley^R
investing for Kim's college fund^R
^E
```

To add another record to the data file, make sure that the cursor rests on the line after the ^E. (It should have moved there after you pressed the Merge E key.)

Enter your own name and address and other information as you did the data for Katherine Haley. Save this file under the name NAMES and then clear the screen by pressing the Exit key (F7).

Remember:

- Each record must contain the same number of fields (Merge R codes ^R)

- Even blank fields must be indicated by a Merge R code on that line

- The types of data in each record must be arranged in the same order

- Each record must end with a Merge E code (^E) on the last line

## Creating the Primary File

Now you will create the primary file, the form letter you will send to each client in the secondary (data) file. (If you typed the preceding example, there are only two clients, you and Katherine.) Type the primary file document and specify where information from the secondary file will merge. For example, suppose that an investment consultant wants to send out notices to remind clients of a seminar. The letter will read:

---

November 12, 1987

Ms. Katherine Haley
5 Waverly Place
New York, NY 10021

Dear Ms. Haley:

We spoke a short while back about investment opportunities. I wanted to let you know that we will be having another series of educational seminars next month. The meetings are from 7:30 to 9:30 on Tuesdays and Thursdays.

Ms. Haley, you mentioned to me that you were concerned with investing for Kim's college fund. This is an excellent way to learn more without feeling committed to a specific course of action.

If you are interested in attending, please call Carol, my assistant. I look forward to meeting you again.

---

Several variables in the letter change for each client. The variables are the client's name and address, the greeting, and the most important investment subject for the specific client. Notice also that the client's name is used again in the second paragraph. This variable information is taken from the data file.

## Entering Merge Codes

The letter in the preceding section shows what the completed letter looks like after the primary and secondary files have been merged. After a merge there would be a similar letter for the record you created about yourself. Before you can merge files, however, you must tell WordPerfect where to insert the variable information from the data file.

To create the letter that composes the primary file, follow these steps:

1. Clear the screen with the Exit key (F7)

2. Move the cursor to line 10 and press the Flush Right key (Alt-F6)

3. Press the Date key (Shift-F5) and select 3 Insert Function

This will automatically insert the computer start-up date in the letter when the letter is merged. (Remember that this default date format can be modified to be used in other types of correspondence. More on that in Chapter 17!)

4. Press Enter three times to move down to the address line

5. Press the Merge Codes key (Alt-F9) to display the menu shown at the bottom of the screen in figure 15.1

From this menu you can select different codes that will control how information merges into the letter.

6. Type f to select the ^F code, then type 1 and press Enter

This inserts the code ^F1^ into the letter. The code ^F1^ tells WordPerfect to put the information belonging to field 1 at this location.

Although the inside address in the data file is several lines long, do not allow extra lines in the primary file. WordPerfect will insert as many lines as are needed, moving the subsequent text down as necessary.

7. Press Enter twice after the ^F1^ address (for spacing)

8. Type **Dear** and a space

The cursor is positioned for printing the second field, the salutation.

9. Press Merge Codes (Alt-F9), type **F**, then **2**, and press Enter

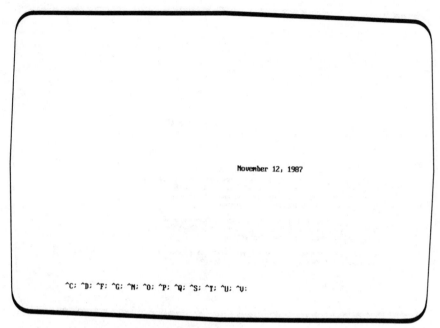

November 12, 1987

^C: ^D: ^F: ^G: ^N: ^O: ^P: ^Q: ^S: ^T: ^U: ^U:

*Fig. 15.1. Merge codes menu below Dated letter.*

WordPerfect inserts ^F2^. The second merge field, *Ms. Katherine Haley* or your name, will merge here.

**10.** Type the **colon** (:) after the merge code

The spacing you use after the merge code will be used also after the inserted text.

**11.** Press Enter twice

**12.** Continue typing the letter

Later in the letter, insert field 3, the investment subject. Use field 2, the salutation, to insert the client's name in the last paragraph. Your finished letter should look like the letter shown in figure 15.2. Save this document with the file name REMINDER.

## Merging the Primary File with the Secondary File

Now that you have created the primary file (REMINDER) and the secondary file (NAMES), you are ready for the most common merge operation: combining the primary and secondary files. The codes ^F1^, ^F2^, and ^F3^ will instruct WordPerfect to reach into the secondary file,

```
                              November 12, 1987


     ^F1^

     Dear ^F2^:

        We spoke a short while back about investment opportunities.
     I wanted to let you know that we will be having another
     series of educational seminars next month. The meetings are
     from 7:30 to 9:30 on Tuesdays and Thursdays.

        ^F2^, you mentioned to me that you were concerned with
     ^F3^. This is an excellent way to learn more without feeling
     committed to a specific course of action.

        If you are interested in attending, please call Carol my
     assistant. I look forward to meeting you again.


     A:\INVFORM.LTR                    Doc 1  Pg 1  Ln 29      Pos 10
```

*Fig. 15.2. Reminder letter with merge codes inserted.*

copy the appropriate field, and insert it into the letter where the ^F#^ appears.

If you have created the two files, combine them with these keystrokes:

1. Clear the screen with the Exit key (F7)

2. Press the Merge/Sort key (Ctrl-F9) and select option **1** Merge

At this prompt:

> Primary file:

3. Type the primary file name: **REMINDER**

4. Press Enter

WordPerfect will tell you if you have not created the file or if you have typed an incorrect file name.

At this prompt:

> Secondary file:

5. Type the secondary file name: **NAMES**

6. Press Enter

WordPerfect will tell you if you have not created the file or if you have typed an incorrect file name.

In a moment, you see the two merged letters on the screen. You can edit them, if necessary.

Notice that every ^F#^ code has been replaced with data and that a page break has been placed between the two letters. The name and address field, greeting field, and investment subject have been pulled from the secondary file and inserted into the primary file.

If the merge did not work properly, it is probably because the ^F#^ and ^R codes don't match. To remedy this situation, clear the screen and review the two files. Check the secondary merge file to see that it does not violate the rules set forth earlier. Make sure that the ^F#^ codes are correctly numbered and entered in the primary file. Once the merged document appears correctly on the screen, you are ready to start printing.

## Printing Merged Documents

When you see the merged letters on the screen, you can print them in one of two ways:

1. Press Print (Shift-F7) and select **1** Full Text

   Or

1. Save the merged letters to disk as a new document
2. Press the Print key (Shift-F7) and select **4** Printer Control
3. From the Printer Control menu, type **P** and the file's name

This will print the file from disk so that you can work on another document on-screen.

## Merging Directly to the Printer

When you are dealing with many form letters, the finished document may not fit in memory. This can occur if, for instance, you have a large number of names on a mailing list that you are merging into a long letter. To solve the problem, you can send the results of the merge operation directly to the printer.

When you create the primary file, you must enter a print command that will cause WordPerfect to print each letter when the merge for that letter

is complete. To do so in our example, enter the following code at the end
of the letter:

**^T^N^P^P**

The new merge codes ^T, ^N, and ^P are available from the Merge Codes
key (Alt-F9). This is what these codes do:

| Code | Function |
|------|----------|
| ^T | Send to the printer all the text that has been merged so far |
| ^N | Move to the next record of information in the secondary file |
| ^P*filename*^P | Start the merge again, using the file name indicated. If no file name is entered between the ^P codes, the same primary file is used again. |

To merge the sample primary and secondary files directly to the printer,
follow these instructions:

1. Press the Exit key (F7) to clear the screen

2. Press the List Files key (F5) and retrieve the primary file,
   REMINDER

3. Press Home, Home, down arrow, and Enter to move to the last
   new line in the file

4. Press the Merge Codes key (Alt-F9)

5. Type **T** to insert the ^T code

6. Press the Merge Codes key (Alt-F9)

7. Type **N** to insert the ^N code

8. Press the Merge Codes key (Alt-F9)

9. Type **P** to insert the ^P code

10. Press the Merge Codes key (Alt-F9)

11. Type **P** to insert the ^P code

12. Press the Save key (F10)

13. Type a new name for the primary file **PMERGE**

14. Save this file to disk (You will use the original REMINDER file later)

You have created a primary file that contains merge codes which direct the finished output directly to the printer.

Turn on the printer and start the merge operation:

1. Press Merge (Ctrl-F9) and select **1** Merge

2. Type the primary file name **PMERGE**

3. Type the secondary file name **NAMES**

Now sit back and watch while WordPerfect prints your letters.

You cannot merge to the printer if you are using hand-fed paper. If your printer accepts only hand-fed paper, separate the secondary file into a number of smaller files so that you can merge to the screen.

## Removing Blank Lines from Merged Fields

Occasionally, you will run into a problem with mailing lists because all the address lines are not filled in. For example, there may be space in each record for a company name but some of the records may not have company names. Two correctly completed records with this difference will look like:

```
John^R
Smith^R
Air Conditioning Masters^R
512 Plenum Way^R
Santa Rosa, CA^R
95406^R
^E
Suzan^R
Kramer^R
^R
616 Elm Lane^R
Santa Rosa, CA^R
95401^R
^E
```

When you merge to a primary file, the blank field where Suzan's company name should appear becomes a blank line. In WordPerfect 4.2 you can "collapse" such a blank field in the primary file so that it doesn't leave a blank.

To eliminate blank lines, follow this process when you insert a field code into a primary file:

1. Press the Merge Codes key (Alt-F9)

2. Type **F**

3. Type the number of the field, followed by a **?**

4. Press Enter

The field code ^F3?^ will appear on-screen.

In the following example, which shows blank lines, the merge codes on the left (in a primary file) create the merge results on the right when Suzan's record is merged:

| Primary File | Merged Result |
|---|---|
| ^F1^ ^F2^ | Suzan Kramer |
| ^F3^ | |
| ^F4^ | 616 Elm Lane |
| ^F5^ | Santa Rosa, CA |
| ^F6^ | 95401 |
| | |
| ^F1^ ^F2^ | Suzan Kramer |
| ^F3?^ | 616 Elm Lane |
| ^F4^ | Santa Rosa, CA |
| ^F5^ | 95401 |
| ^F6^ | |

## Customizing Form Letters from the Keyboard

At times during a merge, you may want to include information that is not in the data file. In other words, you may want to "fill in the blanks" during the merge. By putting another type of merge code into the primary file, you can make the merge pause so that you can type this information.

Suppose, for example, that you want to suggest an appointment date to a client. You might want to include the following sentence in the letter to Katherine Haley:

**We are reserving Tuesday, December 8, for you.**

To make this work in the REMINDER primary file, retrieve the file to a clear screen. Then position the cursor after the last sentence in the first paragraph and type:

**We are reserving ^C, for you.**

You generate the ^C by pressing Merge Codes (Alt-F9) and then typing C. Figure 15.3 illustrates how the ^C code appears on your screen. Save this file with the name REMINDER.TYP.

```
                                        November 12, 1987

        ^F1^

        Dear ^F2^:

            We spoke a short while back about investment opportunities.
        I wanted to let you know that we will be having another
        series of educational seminars next month. The meetings are
        from 7:30 to 9:30 on Tuesdays and Thursdays.

            ^F2^, you mentioned to me that you were concerned with
        ^F3^. This is an excellent way to learn more without feeling
        committed to a specific course of action.

            If you are interested in attending, please call Carol my
        assistant. We are reserving ^C, for you.

            I look forward to meeting you again.

        A:\INUFORM.LTR                      Doc 1  Pg 1  Ln 31     Pos 18
```

*Fig. 15.3. ^C code permits current typing to be merged to a form letter.*

To activate this automated letter clear the screen and:

1. Press the Merge/Sort key (Ctrl-F9) and select **1** Merge

2. Type the primary file name **REMINDER.TYP**

3. Press Enter

4. Type the secondary file name **NAMES**

5. Press Enter

The merge operation will begin. Merging runs automatically until it comes to the ^C code. The cursor moves to where the ^C was, and ^C disappears.

6. Type the client's reserved date

7. Press Merge R (F9) to resume merging of this record and continue to the next

Notice that you didn't press Enter after you finished typing. You can use the Enter key for normal typing when the cursor stops at ^C. You could have typed several paragraphs, pressing Enter to separate them.

The cursor will stop for each letter that belongs to each new record. When the merge is complete, you can edit, store, or print the completed letters.

## Creating Screen Prompts with ^O

Use the ^O command with ^C. The ^O command lets you write a message on the screen when the merge is stopped by the ^C command.

Suppose, for example, that you need to enter several items from the keyboard but don't know which item WordPerfect is waiting for you to enter. You can use the ^O command to display, at the lower left corner of the screen, a message in bold that reminds you of the entry. An example of such a message is

**Enter Social Security number**

The ^O code is available also from the Merge Codes key (Alt-F9). In the previous section's example of how to use the ^C code, you could precede the ^C with a prompt such as

`Enter Seminar Date`

The prompt must be preceded and followed by the ^O code.

The completed ^Omessage^O prompt and ^C pause code look like this:

`^OEnter Seminar Date^O^C`

When WordPerfect encounters ^C, the merge stops and the ^O codes cause your message to appear as a bold prompt at the bottom left corner of the screen. Type your response to the prompt and press Merge R (F9). The message disappears when you press Merge R (F9) and the merge operation continues. As with any ^C code, you can enter text or commands when the merge pauses.

## *Updating the Screen with ^U*

Because merges happen quickly, you may not see the results on the screen until the entire merge process is finished. You can view the screen whenever you want to, however, by inserting ^U, for *Update*, in the primary file. WordPerfect then displays one full screen of text.

## *Stopping a Merge with ^Q*

If you want to stop a merge operation, you can do so manually by pressing the Merge E key (Shift-F9). Another way to stop a merge is to place a Quit command (^Q) anywhere in a primary or secondary file.

Suppose, for example, that you want to merge only part of your NAMES list. Place a ^Q at the point in your NAMES file where you want the merge to stop. Inserting ^Q anywhere in either file causes the merge operation to stop at that point.

To invoke the ^Q command:

1. Place the cursor in the appropriate position within the file

2. Press the Merge Codes key (Alt-F9)

3. Type **Q**

# Automating Entry Forms

You can fill out medical forms, transcripts, insurance forms, and so on with WordPerfect. Usually, filling out forms is easier to do with a typewriter than with a word processor. However, you can really automate your form-completion process by using the ^O and ^C merge codes.

The on-screen typing that you do for a form may be nothing more than a few items scattered over the screen—a shotgun blast of words. Usually entries are typed on-screen without surrounding text so that knowing what to type next or where to type it is difficult. You can solve that problem with WordPerfect.

Create a line and character-space template that shows the line numbers and character positions, so that you will be able to see the location of each entry. To see which line and character positions correspond to entry blanks, you can lay a printed version of the template over your form.

Create a template with the same margin settings that you will use for the form. Down the screen's left margin, type the line numbers that follow the Ln on the Status Line. In a row across the page, type the character positions. You may have to use two lines for character positions, one for digits and another for tens. Figure 15.4 illustrates a printed template.

```
0123456789012345678901234567890123456789012345678901234567890123456789012345
2          2         3         4         5         6
3                                                              3
4                    position 33                              4
5                                                              5
6                                                              6
7                                                              7
8  <-line 8              x  (8,33)                            8
9                                                              9
10                                                            10
11                                                            11
12                   Positioning Template                    12
13                   Margins of 10,65                        13
14                                                            14
15                                                            15
16                                                            16
17                                                            17
18                                                            18
19                                                            19
20                                                            20
21                                                            21
22                                                            22
23                                                            23
24                                                            24
```

*Fig. 15.4. Blank template for form entries positioning.*

As you place the paper in the printer to print the template, note *exactly* how the paper is positioned. You will need to position the forms in the same way. Print the template, lay it over your form, and note the line and character position of each entry blank.

## Creating the Automated Entry Form

After you have written down the line and character positions for each entry blank, you can create an automated form.

Follow this procedure:

1. Clear the screen with the Exit key (F7)

2. Move the cursor to the line and character position for the first entry

3. Press the Merge Codes key (Alt-F9)

4. Type O to insert the ^O code

5. Type your first prompt message

6. Press the Merge Codes key (Alt-F9)

7. Type **O** to insert the closing ^O code immediately after the prompt message

8. Press the Merge Codes key (Alt-F9)

9. Type **C** to insert the ^C pause code

The result should look like:

```
^OFirst Name^O^C
```

The line and character position of the caret (^) in the first ^O code is the position at which the first character you type will print.

10. Return to Step 2 and move to the next location at which you want the automated entry form to pause and prompt

11. When you finish entering all the ^O and ^C codes, save the document. You may want to use a .PRM file extension to indicate that this is a primary file

## Using the Automated Entry Form

When you need to generate a form from the file you created:

1. Insert the blank form in the printer in the same way that you inserted the paper on which you printed the template

(To ensure that the lines and character positions will print at the same locations.)

2. Clear the screen with the Exit key (F7)

3. Press the Merge/Sort key (Ctrl-F9)

4. Choose **1** Merge

5. Type the name of the primary file (your automated form file)

6. Press Enter when WordPerfect prompts you for the secondary file name

There is no secondary file because the data being merged is generated from your keyboard.

7. Watch the lower left corner of the screen for a bold prompt

8. Type your response to each prompt

If you press Enter while you type, an extra line will be inserted in the document. This may throw off the form alignment of following entries.

9. Press the Merge R key (F9) to move to the next entry

10. When there are no more merge fields, you can move the cursor as you normally would to edit, save, or print the completed form

Figure 15.5 shows the screen of an automated form. Some form entries have already been made. Notice the prompt in the lower left corner for the current keyboard entry.

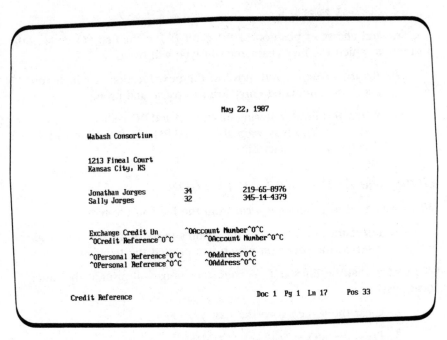

```
                          May 22, 1987


        Wabash Consortium

        1213 Fineal Court
        Kansas City, KS


        Jonathan Jorges        34        219-65-8976
        Sally Jorges           32        345-14-4379


        Exchange Credit Un      ^OAccount Number^O^C
        ^OCredit Reference^O^C      ^OAccount Number^O^C

        ^OPersonal Reference^O^C    ^OAddress^O^C
        ^OPersonal Reference^O^C    ^OAddress^O^C


        Credit Reference                 Doc 1  Pg 1  Ln 17    Pos 33
```

*Fig. 15.5. Screen displaying an automated form containing entries from the keyboard.*

## Editing the Automated Entry Form

You can retrieve the primary file you created for automatic form entries just as you retrieve any other document—use the Retrieve or List Files key. The file also can be edited as a normal document. However, remember that if you change the line spacing or character spacing, entries may no longer match the form's blanks.

The automated entry-form file's automatic functions work only when you retrieve the file with the Merge/Sort key.

# Creating a More Complex Secondary File

You can include as much information in your data file as you like, but you don't have to use all of the data during a merge. In the previously described data file, you included only as much data as you needed in the merge letter. However, you could include also such client information as business address, telephone numbers, and client history.

> Although WordPerfect's merge capabilities are excellent, WordPerfect is not a true database program, and does not have the power or ease of a database for sorting, searching, and reorganizing mailing lists. (WordPerfect's Sort function is described in Chapter 16.)
>
> If you want to create complex files such as sales histories, client transaction profiles, or accounts receivable files, you should use a list manager or database program. The list manager in the WordPerfect Library program is designed specifically to handle WordPerfect secondary files.
>
> Other databases also can be used to manage your data. These databases can transport their data to WordPerfect via ASCII file format. The WordPerfect CONVERT utility (stored on one of your master disks—which disk depends on the version you are using) will then convert the ASCII file into a secondary merge file. This process is described in Chapter 17.

When you design your secondary data file, be certain that each record has the same number of fields and that the types of fields are in the same order. If the name and address are the first field in Katherine Haley's record, the name and address must be first for every other client in the data file. Whether one client's address is longer than another's doesn't matter, as long as the addresses hold the same position. Before setting up a data file, consider all the data you may want to include in that file.

A set of dental patient records might be recorded as:

| | |
|---|---|
| ^F1^ | Name and address |
| ^F2^ | Greeting |
| ^F3^ | Preferred appointment time |
| ^F4^ | Business address |
| ^F5^ | Phone numbers (home, business, and spouse) |
| ^F6^ | Name(s) of spouse or children |
| ^F7^ | Dates of appointments and services performed |
| ^F8^ | Most recent appointment date and services performed |
| ^F9^ | Outstanding balance |
| ^F10^ | Patient's medical file number |

^F11^          Insurance company

^F12^          Insurance company's regulations for billing

Be sure to keep a master copy that shows how data is arranged in each record.

If you decide that this data file covers every aspect of all the patients' records, use this field order for each patient, even if all the data does not apply to every patient. Not everyone has a business address, a spouse, or an insurance company. Even if you don't have data in some fields, you still must enter the Merge R code (^R) for each item in every patient's record. Otherwise, the fields that WordPerfect retrieves during the merge will be out of order and inappropriate.

The following record of information for Alice Schwarzen corresponds to the field numbers and data in the preceding list of field numbers and types of data:

```
Mrs. Alice Schwarzen
15 Wongahelah Place
New York, NY 10025^R
Ms. Schwarzen^R
during your lunch hour^R
Merrill Lynch Realty
94 Wall Street
New York, NY 10022^R
234-7069(h), 237-3618(o),
                417-5500(s)^R
Robert Schwarzen (husband)^R
3-12-85 X ray, filling, cleaning
12-5-85 checkup
6-4-86 checkup, cleaning^R
^R
^R
1078^R
Predential^R
three copies of bill^R
^E
```

Although Mrs. Schwarzen does not have an outstanding balance and has not been in recently for an appointment, you still must place a ^R on each of those lines. Without an ^R for those two fields, WordPerfect reads the medical file number, which is really ^F10^, whenever the program encounters ^F8^ in a primary file.

After you set up a data file and are sure that the data is consistent from one record to the next, you can manipulate the file in many ways.

For example, after each patient makes an office visit, you can use the Search function to find the patient's name, then fill in new data for ^F8^ and ^F9^. Then, at the end of the month, you can ask WordPerfect to select and send an invoice to all those patients who should be billed that month.

You can also create a field for the next checkup due, asking WordPerfect each month to prepare a reminder notice for everyone whose annual checkup is near. You can perform all these tasks with WordPerfect's sort features, which are described in Chapter 16.

Every record in this data file must have 12 fields, each ending with the ^R code. And each record must have a ^E after the last line. Any deviation causes WordPerfect to read the wrong information. If your own data file is as extensive as this one, you might want to use a macro (see Chapter 14) to create a template of ^R codes that you can fill in for each record.

# Creating Mailing Labels

Another common use for WordPerfect's Merge function is creating mailing labels from the data file. To extract the names and addresses, create a primary file with the field number codes in those locations where you want information to print on the labels. Then execute a merge.

The page length for label backing may differ from standard paper. To make the page breaks correct, measure the distance in inches from the top of one label to the top of the next one. Multiply this number by 6 to determine the page length. For example, the page length for a 1-inch label is 6 lines; for a 3-inch label, 18 lines.

You need to enter the Page Length command at the top of the primary file. Also, enter a number equal to or less than the page length for the number of text lines to print on the page.

When printing on small labels, you also may need to turn off the top margin. Retaining the one-inch top margin can cause every other label to be left blank if the page measures only two inches.

Try printing a few labels. If necessary, change the left margin in the primary file to position the text correctly on the label.

If you need to print labels in Chesire or three-up format, merge standard primary and secondary files to create a single column of labels. Move to the top of the merged document and use the Newspaper Columns commands to "wrap" the single column of labels into multiple columns on each page. If some of the labels have "collapsed" blank lines (so that they do not show), you'll have to scroll manually through the labels and insert blank lines between addresses to align the labels horizontally.

# Compiling Reports with Merge

You can use the merge feature to compile the same text in a different order for reports, contracts, or proposals. After the text data is organized, treat it as you would any other document.

## Using Merge To Organize Report Sections

Suppose that a vice president of marketing wants to disseminate the recent quarterly report to the heads of three departments (A, B, and C) and to the salespeople in each department. Furthermore, the vice president wants to arrange the text in each report so that the recipient's sales performance is placed first in the report. The vice president's quarterly report would be organized in the following way:

| | |
|---|---|
| Section 1 | Summary of quarterly activities |
| Section 2 | Quarterly sales from Department A |
| Section 3 | Quarterly sales from Department B |
| Section 4 | Quarterly sales from Department C |
| Section 5 | Outstanding salespeople in Department A |
| Section 6 | Outstanding salespeople in Department B |
| Section 7 | Outstanding salespeople in Department C |

To turn the report into a secondary file that can be reorganized, you must enter a field code at the end of each section. (Each section of the report will be just like the name, address, or ZIP in a mailing label.) To designate the fields, place a ^R at the end of text for each section. The resulting report will look like:

| | | |
|---|---|---|
| | Section 1 | Summary of quarterly activities (text of summary) |
| ^R | | |
| | Section 2 | Quarterly sales from Department A (text of Dept. A sales) |
| ^R | | |
| | Section 3 | Quarterly sales from Department B (text of Dept. B sales) |
| ^R | | |
| | Section 4 | Quarterly sales from Department C (text of Dept. C sales) |

^R

    Section 5    Outstanding salespeople in Department A
                    (text of Dept. A people)

^R

    Section 6    Outstanding salespeople in Department B
                    (text of Dept. B people)

^R

    Section 7    Outstanding salespeople in Department C
                    (text of Dept. C people)

^R
^E

Save the file you have just created under a new name. In this large secondary file, each section is a field (even though a section may contain paragraphs or pages). You can merge these fields into a primary file in any order you want.

The sections in this file now have these field numbers:

| ^F1^ | Section 1 | Summary of quarterly activities |
| ^F2^ | Section 2 | Quarterly sales from Department A |
| ^F3^ | Section 3 | Quarterly sales from Department B |
| ^F4^ | Section 4 | Quarterly sales from Department C |
| ^F5^ | Section 5 | Outstanding salespeople in Department A |
| ^F6^ | Section 6 | Outstanding salespeople in Department B |
| ^F7^ | Section 7 | Outstanding salespeople in Department C |

## Building Patterns for Reorganized Reports

Starting with a blank screen, create a primary file. The order in which you insert ^F#^ codes will determine the order in which sections from the vice president's report will appear after merging.

For Department B, organize the fields in the primary file so that the group's sales numbers and salespeople appear first:

^F1^
^F3^
^F6^
^F2^
^F5^
^F4^
^F7^

To attract the attention of the salespeople in Department C, use a primary
file with fields in the following order:

```
^F1^
^F7^
^F5^
^F6^
^F4^
^F2^
^F3^
```

When you rearrange the full report, you can eliminate any sections that
are inappropriate for certain recipients. Perhaps the salespeople should
receive information that pertains to their departments only.

When you are ready to produce a reorganized report:

1. Press the Merge/Sort key (Ctrl-F9)

2. Specify one of the primary files that contains only field codes in
   the order needed for a department

3. For the secondary file, specify the vice president's file that has
   had ^R and ^E codes inserted

# Linking Secondary Files

In some merge operations, one secondary file must be linked to another.
With mailing lists, for example, you might want to draw from several
different files. To demonstrate how this procedure works, create a second
name list:

1. Clear the screen

2. Type this information:

   **Mr. Jeffrey Halston**
   **16 Fifth Avenue**
   **New York, NY 10019^R**
   **Jeff^R**
   **investing in local real estate^R**
   **^E**

Remember, press F9 (^R) at the end of each field, and Shift-F9 (^E) at the
end of each record.

3. Save the file under the name *NAMES2*

4. Clear the screen with the Exit key (F7)

5. Retrieve the file *NAMES* that you created earlier in this chapter

6. Move the cursor to the bottom of the NAMES list, after the final ^E

7. Type **^SNAMES2^S**

The code ^S*filename*^S alerts WordPerfect to switch to another secondary file. The file name between the codes tells WordPerfect the name of the secondary file to use next.

8. Save the file as *NAMES*

9. Clear the screen

Now execute a merge, using *REMINDER* as the primary file and *NAMES* as the secondary file. After WordPerfect finishes merging the first file, the program reads the command ^S*NAMES2*^S and switches to the secondary file you have named NAMES2. You can continue to link secondary files as long as each has the ^S*filename*^S after the last ^E in the file.

# Changing Primary Files

Just as you can switch secondary files during a merge, you also can switch primary files. Doing so can be useful when you have to assemble documents such as contracts and reports.

Suppose, for example, that your business maintains WordPerfect files about:

    research and development
    financial planning
    marketing strategy
    community relations
    international trade
    personnel relations

And, as the Manager of Corporate Communications, you must create more than one report from these files. The sections in each report must appear in a different order. To assemble these sections, you might assign a file name such as *R&D*, *Finan*, *Market*, *CommRel*, *InterTrd*, and *PerRel* to each division. To assemble the files, you need to tell WordPerfect which files to retrieve and print in the report.

The code for switching primary files is ^P*filename*^P. For a modified report on the corporation's financial future, you might create the following primary file:

```
^PFinan^P
^PMarket^P
^PInterTrd^P
```

and save this primary file under the name *REPORT1*.

To build the merged report:

1. Clear the screen

2. Press the Merge/Sort key (Ctrl-F9)

3. Type the primary file name **REPORT1**

REPORT1 contains the names and order in which the additional primary files will merge.

WordPerfect asks you for the secondary file name.

4. Press Enter

WordPerfect assembles the document, using the files you requested in the order you requested.

The length of the primary file specified between ^P codes does not matter. WordPerfect places the next file beneath the previous one. If you had wanted a space between the first, second, and third files, you could have created the primary-file order form with double spaces.

Hopefully, this chapter's step-by-step explanation of some of the more frequently used merge applications has convinced you to use merge features to further streamline your word-processing tasks.

As you have learned, WordPerfect's merge functions can automate the process of creating and producing labels, form letters, fill-in forms, and reports or contracts.

When you create a secondary (data) file, remember that:

☐ Each record must contain the same number of fields, and even a blank field must contain a line with the Merge R code ^R

☐ The data present in each field must appear in the same order in all records

☐ Each record must end with a Merge E code ^E

To merge existing documents:

☐ Press the Merge/Sort key (Ctrl-F9)

☐ Select 1 Merge

☐ Enter the name of the primary file

☐ Press Enter

☐ Enter the name of the secondary file

☐ Press Enter

Some merges do not require a secondary file name. In that case, press Enter.

You can merge to the screen, then save or print the document. However, if a large document results from a merge, that document may not fit in memory. If you anticipate that a merge will create a large document, it's best to use merge codes that send the merge results directly to the printer.

To take the Merge function one step further, explore the Sort and Select function described in Chapter 16. With the Sort function you can sort records in the order you prefer and select only those records you need.

Chapter 17 describes the procedure you must follow to convert ASCII text files (created by a database) into a merge file for use with the Merge function.

# Using Sort and Select

**I**f you've ever been given the task of sorting through hundreds of files to identify only those clients who do business in the state of New York, and to further identify those businesses by city, you'll appreciate WordPerfect's Sort and Select features. Or, if you've ever been given the task of sorting through a mailing list to identify only those contributors who gave over one hundred dollars in the last fiscal year, you'll be delighted you've found Chapter 16, "Using Sort and Select."

If you generate lists, labels, or secondary merge files, you must investigate the power of WordPerfect's Sort and Select. Although the Sort and Select functions are not intended to provide the flexibility of a database program, they do offer features capable of manipulating the kinds of lists and secondary merge files used in inventory lists, form letters, and mailing lists.

With Sort, you can quickly and easily sort lines of text, paragraphs, or secondary merge file records. A simple application of the Sort feature is sorting lines to create alphabetical and numerical lists and rosters.

Sorting paragraphs permits you to create a reference report. For example, imagine that you've prepared a document describing a sampling of stocks and how those stocks fit into various investment strategies. The first word of each paragraph names the stock; the text follows. You can sort these paragraphs into alphabetical order for quick reference by your clients.

Sorting records in secondary merge files lets you sort by ZIP code or name. For example, you may want to sort a secondary merge file into ZIP code order for printing letters, envelopes, or labels. Then, you can sort the names within each ZIP code in alphabetical order.

The Sort feature contains a Select function that you can use to select from a data file the records that match certain criteria, such as *all the customers in Connecticut* or *all the patients who have not been contacted since May*. The result of such a select is a subset of the original file.

Before you jump to the sections on the Select function, read the following section on terms used in the Sort and Select process.

# Using Sort and Select Terms

Before you tell WordPerfect how you want to sort or select information, you need to understand the terms used by the functions.

*Keys.* WordPerfect sorts and selects according to the characters or numbers in a specific location in the file. These locations are known as *keys*. The words in the specific locations are *key words*. For example, phone books list information by line:

  Saunders, Robert    768 Skyview Dr.    452-0976

Listings in the phone book are sorted first by last name and then by first name. In WordPerfect, the last name is referred to as *Key1*, the first name as *Key2*. Files are sorted by the priority number of the key. For example, phone listings sort first by surname, Key1, and then by first name, Key2.

There can be as many as nine keys. Keys identify information by its location within the file. For example, Key3 may be the location in a mailing list of all the state abbreviations. You will need to tell WordPerfect which field, line, and word to examine when it compares different addresses.

*Alphanumeric.* Alphanumeric groups of characters are made up of letters and numbers. The numbers must be of equal length to be sorted correctly. You will be asked if a key is alphanumeric (*a*) or numeric (*n*).

*Numeric.* Numeric groups contain only numbers, and may contain numbers of different lengths. Numeric keys may contain also numeric punctuation and currency symbols. You will be asked if a key is alphanumeric (a) or numeric (n).

*Location Identifiers.* You will need to tell WordPerfect how to locate the position of key words in a file. To describe the location of a key word, you will use the words *record, field, line,* or *word.*

A record is the largest group of information in a file. Within a record, information can be segmented by field, line, or word. For example, you might need to tell WordPerfect to sort a secondary merge file of mailing labels by using the second word in the third field as Key1. Here are the terms used to describe locations:

*Records.* A record is a collection of related information in a file. In the phone book example, one line of data is a record. In written notes, one paragraph might be a record, and in secondary merge files each name and address collection ending with ^E is a record. Records are separated by:

| Unit | Separated by |
|------|--------------|
| Lines | Hard or Soft Returns |
| Paragraphs | Two or more Hard Returns |
| Merge file | Merge E code, ^E |

*Fields.* Fields make up a record. Fields may contain multiple words. As in secondary merge files, each field should contain the same type of information, such as state or ZIP. Fields are numbered sequentially, with the first field identified as 1, the second 2, and so on. Fields are separated by:

| Unit | Separated by |
|------|--------------|
| Lines | Tabs or →Indents |
| Paragraphs | Tabs or →Indents |
| Merge file | Merge R code, ^R |

*Lines.* Lines exist in paragraphs and secondary merge files. You will be asked for the line number of each key word. When specifying a line, count from top to the bottom. For secondary merge files, you can indicate (by entering a negative line number) that WordPerfect should count from bottom to top. Lines end with Soft or Hard Returns.

*Words.* Words, the smallest unit, are characters separated by blank spaces. Fields, lines, and paragraphs all contain words. When you enter the number of the word for WordPerfect to compare, count from left to right on the line. Enter a negative number if you want WordPerfect to count from right to left.

## *Reviewing the Sort and Select Screen*

When you enter the Sort or Select functions, the screen splits in half (see fig. 16.1). If the file you are sorting is on-screen, you will see it in the upper half of the screen; the lower half displays the Sort and Select screen.

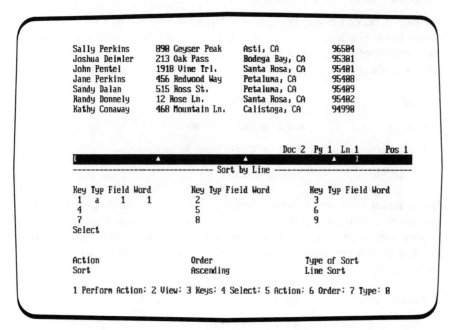

```
     Sally Perkins      898 Geyser Peak     Asti, CA           96584
     Joshua Deimler     213 Oak Pass        Bodega Bay, CA     95381
     John Pentel        1918 Vine Trl.      Santa Rosa, CA     95481
     Jane Perkins       456 Redwood Way     Petaluma, CA       95488
     Sandy Dalan        515 Ross St.        Petaluma, CA       95489
     Randy Donnely      12 Rose Ln.         Santa Rosa, CA     95482
     Kathy Conaway      468 Mountain Ln.    Calistoga, CA      94998


                                        Doc 2  Pg 1  Ln 1        Pos 1
     [                  ▲               ▲               ▲   ]
     -------------------------------- Sort by Line ------------------------------

     Key Typ Field Word         Key Typ Field Word       Key Typ Field Word
      1   a    1     1            2                        3
      4                          5                        6
      7                          8                        9
     Select


     Action                     Order                    Type of Sort
     Sort                       Ascending                Line Sort

     1 Perform Action; 2 View; 3 Keys; 4 Select; 5 Action; 6 Order; 7 Type: 8
```

*Fig. 16.1. The split Sort screen.*

Notice that the tab bar cuts through at midscreen. Its triangles point to the current tab settings. These tab locations are important because they control the numbering of fields. The title below the tab bar displays the type of sort currently selected. Below the "type of sort" heading, three columns allow room for you to enter the locations of Keys, from Key1 to Key9.

As an example, Key1 in figure 16.1 is defined as alphanumeric (a), and is located in the first word of field 1. This represents the individual's first name. Notice in the figure that there is one tab set for each field. There are no unused tabs. The entry for Key1 appears as:

| Key | Typ | Field | Word |
|-----|-----|-------|------|
| 1   | a   | 1     | 1    |

The numbers you enter underneath headings such as Field and Word determine where the Sort function will look for a specific key word.

## Sort Menu Alternatives

At the bottom of figure 16.1 is a menu of sort and select alternatives. Some of these alternatives are little more than toggles that let you select one choice or another. The menu options, which are described here for your convenience, are referenced in the examples as they are used.

| *Choose* | *To* |
|---|---|
| 1 Perform Action | Perform the current sort or select |
| 2 View | Move the cursor from the Sort screen into the document so that you can scroll and view a new text area |
| 3 Keys | Move the cursor into the key-definition area so that you can specify whether keys are numeric or alphanumeric and the location of each key |
| 4 Select | Move the cursor into the Select area so that you can enter a description of the information you want selected |
| 5 Action | Choose between Sort and Select or Select only |
| 6 Order | Choose between Ascending and Descending sort |
| 7 Sort Type | Change the title line so that WordPerfect knows whether to sort by line, paragraph, or secondary merge file |

All of these menu items display a prompt showing which key to press to return to the Sort and Select menu.

# Sorting Information

Whether you have lists composed of inventory line items, duty rosters, or client mailing labels, you will, at some point, want to sort the information. Because you're using WordPerfect, you can sort the information in almost any way you want.

As was mentioned earlier, to use WordPerfect's sorting function, you must understand a few simple terms. Terms such as *key*, *word*, and *record* tell WordPerfect how to locate the words in a file that WordPerfect will sort by. If you have not reviewed these terms, this is a good time to return to the first section of this chapter for a review.

## *Steps to Sorting and Selecting*

You can sort files on the screen or files on disk, and you can return the results to the screen or to a new file on disk. No matter which method you use, *save a copy of your file before sorting*. Then, if you have not specified the sort correctly, you will be able to return to the original file.

The following procedure lists the steps for sorting any type of file. Examples that follow this section demonstrate how to enter locations, and how the steps vary with different types of files:

1. Save your original file so that you can return to it, if necessary

2. Retrieve a file with the List Files key (F5) if you want to sort the screen display

3. Press the Merge/Sort key (Ctrl-F9)

4. Select **2** Sort

The prompt:

        Input file to sort: (Screen)

will appear in the lower left corner of the screen.

5. Press Enter if you are sorting the file on the screen

    Or

5. Type a file name if you are sorting a file on the disk

This prompt appears in the lower left corner of your screen:

        Output file to sort: (Screen)

6. Press Enter if you want the sorted results to replace the screen display

Or

6. Type a file name if you want the sorted results saved to disk in a new file

The Sort menu shown in figure 16.1 displays. If the tabs in the tab bar do not reflect your one-tab-per-field setting, press 2 View and move the cursor into the middle of the data you are sorting. When the tab bar displays your correct tab settings, press Exit, F7.

7. Choose 7 Type from the Sort menu

8. Select the type of records you are sorting: secondary merge files, lines, or paragraphs. The type of sort currently selected appears as the top line in the Sort screen; Sort by Line in figure 16.1, for example

9. Select 6 Order and select 1 Ascending for A-to-Z order or 2 Descending for Z-to-A order

10. Choose 3 Keys from the main Sort menu

The cursor will move into the Key area so that you can enter the location of each key.

11. Type a for alphanumeric sort for Key1

Or

11. Type n for numeric sort for Key1

12. Enter the location of Key1 by typing the numeric position for the field, line, and word being used for sorting

13. Press the right-arrow key to move to the entry area for Key2

14. Enter the key location for Key2

15. Move to and enter information for other keys. Press the Del key to delete the location information for a key

16. Press the Exit key (F7) to return to the Sort menu

17. Enter a selection statement if you want to select records meeting your criteria. *Do not use this step if you are sorting only*

18. If you entered a selection statement, select **5** Action from the main menu and choose either **1** Select and Sort or **2** Select Only. *Do not use this step if you are sorting only*

19. Select **1** Perform Action to execute the sort and/or selection

## Sorting Lines

When you need to sort rosters and lists, you probably will sort lines. If you are sorting lines, be sure to select 7 Type and choose 2 Line. The title on the Sort menu will change to "Sort by Line."

When you select the line sort, the key-location headings change to Field and Word. Identify the location of key words by their Field and Word number within each line. Remember that fields are separated by tabs and words are separated by spaces.

Figure 16.2 displays a seven-line file in the upper half of the screen and the Sort screen in the lower half. The triangles point to each tab stop (each tab stop indicates a field). In this figure, 3 Keys has been selected from the main Sort menu and the locations of Key1, Key2, and Key3 have been entered.

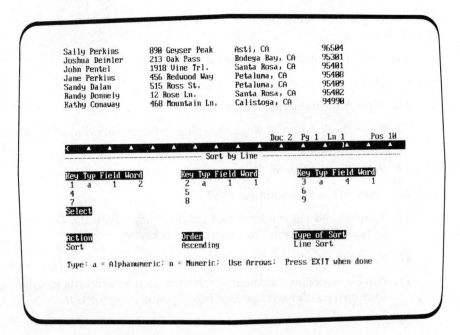

*Fig. 16.2. Split screen displaying seven-line file and Sort screen.*

Key1 is identified as the surname, the second word in the first field. Key2 is the first name, the first word in the first field, and Key3 is the ZIP code, the first word in field four. Notice that the ZIP code can be sorted alphanumerically (*a*) because each ZIP code is the same length.

After entering the key locations, return to the main Sort menu by pressing the Exit key (F7). Select 1 Perform Action from the main Sort menu. Figure 16.3 illustrates the results of this sort. (Because there were no conflicts between people with the same surname and first name, there was no need for a sort by ZIP.)

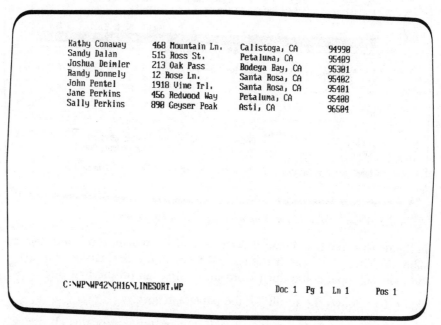

| Kathy Conaway | 468 Mountain Ln. | Calistoga, CA | 94990 |
| Sandy Dalan | 515 Ross St. | Petaluma, CA | 95409 |
| Joshua Deimler | 213 Oak Pass | Bodega Bay, CA | 95301 |
| Randy Donnely | 12 Rose Ln. | Santa Rosa, CA | 95402 |
| John Pentel | 1918 Vine Trl. | Santa Rosa, CA | 95401 |
| Jane Perkins | 456 Redwood Way | Petaluma, CA | 95408 |
| Sally Perkins | 890 Geyser Peak | Asti, CA | 96504 |

C:\WP\WP42\CH16\LINESORT.WP        Doc 1  Pg 1  Ln 1        Pos 1

*Fig. 16.3. Line Sort results.*

## Sorting Paragraphs

Sorting paragraphs is handy when you want to sort notes by index words, or to sort references and lists of citations. Paragraphs are defined as collections of information separated by two or more Hard Returns. Key words in paragraphs are located by their line, field, and word location.

Before you enter the key locations, select 7 Type and choose 3 Paragraph. The heading of the main Sort menu will change to Sort by Paragraph.

The paragraphs in figure 16.4 are all contained in field one, because only the left margin is used. However, the first three words in each paragraph are an index for each quote; speaker, main topic, subtopic.

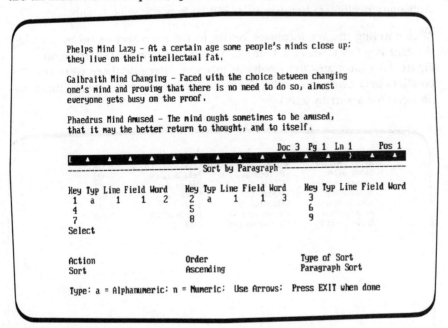

Fig. 16.4. Sort menu set to sort first by main topic, then by subtopic.

In figure 16.4, the Sort menu is set to sort first by main topic and then by subtopic. The main topic is the second word in the first tab on the first line. The subtopic is the third word in the first tab on the first line.

Figure 16.5 shows the results of the paragraph sort.

Another powerful feature that is described near the end of this chapter is the global select function. Global select extracts paragraphs from a file no matter where a word is located in the paragraph. It's an excellent way to organize paragraphs by words located anywhere within the body of text.

## Sorting Secondary Merge Files

The Sort function is helpful for people who use secondary merge files for form letters and mailing lists. Figure 16.6 shows a short secondary merge file containing three records. Remember, each record in a secondary merge file ends with the Merge E code, ^E, and each field ends with the Merge R code, ^R. (For additional information about secondary merge files, go back to Chapter 15.)

```
        Phaedrus Mind Amused - The mind ought sometimes to be amused,
        that it may the better return to thought, and to itself.

        Galbraith Mind Changing - Faced with the choice between changing
        one's mind and proving that there is no need to do so, almost
        everyone gets busy on the proof.

        Phelps Mind Lazy - At a certain age some people's minds close up;
        they live on their intellectual fat.












        A:\PARASORT.WP                          Doc 1  Pg 1  Ln 1      Pos 1
```

Fig. 16.5. Paragraph Sort results.

```
        Sandy Jenkins^R
        890 Pineridge Ct.^R
        Bodega Bay, CA^R
        95301^R
        ^E
        Joshua Jenkins^R
        213 Cedar Pass^R
        Bodega Bay, CA^R
        95301^R
        ^E
        John McGee^R
        1850 Gold Trail^R
        Anchorage, AK^R
        99508^R
        ^E






        A:\MERGSORT.WP                          Doc 1  Pg 1  Ln 16     Pos 1
```

Fig. 16.6. Secondary file merge before sort.

After you activate the Sort function, select 7 Type and then choose the sort type 1 Merge. The Sort screen heading changes to Sort Secondary Merge File.

The location headings for each key become Field, Line, and Word for merge file sorting. You know that fields end with the Merge R code, lines end with a Hard or Soft Return, and words are separated by a blank space.

To enter the key locations:

1. Select **3** Keys from the main Sort menu

2. Press the right- or left-arrow key to move between keys

In figure 16.7 WordPerfect is set to sort first by state abbreviation, second by surname, and third by first name.

The figure shows locations and types entered for Key1, Key2, and Key3. Key1 is the state abbreviation, the first word from the right in the third field. Key2 is the surname, the first word from the right in the first field. Key3 is the first name.

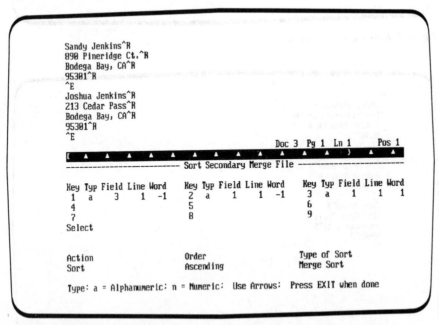

*Fig. 16.7. Sort first by state abbreviation, second by surname, and third by first name.*

The minus one (-1) in the word location for Key1 and Key2 indicates that words should be counted from right to left rather than from left to right. This technique is important if fields contain a number of words. By counting from the right, WordPerfect always finds the state abbreviation and the last name no matter how many words are in the city or the person's first name.

After you activate the sort by selecting 1 Perform Action, the result appears (see fig. 16.8) on your screen. Compare these results with the key specifications shown in figure 16.7.

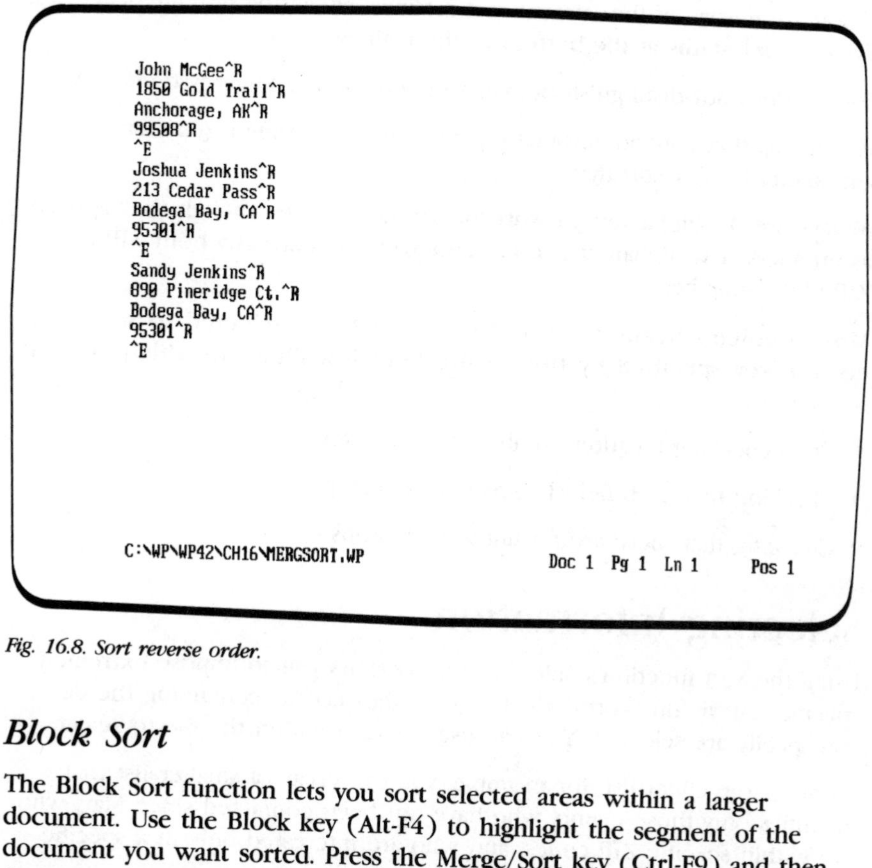

```
        John McGee^R
        1850 Gold Trail^R
        Anchorage, AK^R
        99500^R
        ^E
        Joshua Jenkins^R
        213 Cedar Pass^R
        Bodega Bay, CA^R
        95301^R
        ^E
        Sandy Jenkins^R
        890 Pineridge Ct.^R
        Bodega Bay, CA^R
        95301^R
        ^E




    C:\WP\WP42\CH16\MERGSORT.WP              Doc 1  Pg 1  Ln 1     Pos 1
```

Fig. 16.8. Sort reverse order.

## Block Sort

The Block Sort function lets you sort selected areas within a larger document. Use the Block key (Alt-F4) to highlight the segment of the document you want sorted. Press the Merge/Sort key (Ctrl-F9) and then (starting from Step 7) continue with the sorting procedure.

Block Sorts are done from the screen display and the results are returned to the block area. It's a good idea to save before doing a Block Sort.

## Special Sorting Considerations

If you are unfamiliar with the sorting process, practice sorting a few records (lines, records, or paragraphs) from one of your files. If you use just a few records, you can check visually to be sure that the file is sorting as you want it to.

After you select 3 Keys, use the left- or right-arrow key to move between key locations. Press the Del key to delete the entries beneath a location.

Because Sort keys are remembered during a session, you can save the file to disk and retrieve the file with the current sort settings retained.

If you are unsure of the current sort settings, check the Action, Order, and Type of Sort status at the bottom of the main Sort menu.

Sorting does not distinguish between uppercase and lowercase characters.

Paragraphs that contain automatic paragraph numbering renumber automatically after sorting.

Always use the alphanumeric sort for ZIP codes, even though they appear as numbers. The alphanumeric (a) sort will sort correctly both ZIP and ZIP plus 4 numbers.

Most problems occur because the key that was selected to sort on is not the key specified by the location entries. Eliminate this potential problem by:

- Cross-checking location numbers for each key

- Checking that each field begins on a tab stop

- Checking that there are no unused tab stops

# Selecting Information

Using the Sort function's Select feature permits you to impose extremely specific criteria on WordPerfect so only the records containing the data you specify are selected. You can use any data within the file to select.

From a large client list, for example, you can create a smaller list that identifies only those clients who have not been contacted since May, who live within specific ZIP codes, and who are interested only in a specific subject.

## Preparing a Selection

The steps in the selection process are the same as those in the sorting process, but include a selection statement which describes the records you want. When you select records from a file, include Steps 17 and 18 from the "Steps to Sorting" list earlier in this chapter.

Before you type a select statement, you must define the Sort keys as described earlier in this chapter. The keys are necessary so that WordPerfect will know which words to examine for the information in your selection criteria.

For example, if Key3 contains the state abbreviation in a mailing list, your criteria might be to select all records where Key3 contains the abbreviation NY. If Key3 has not been defined, WordPerfect will not know where to look for the state abbreviation.

## Entering a Selection Statement

After you define the keys, enter the selection statement by choosing 4 Select from the main Sort menu (refer to fig. 16.1). Figure 16.9 shows a simple selection statement entered below the word Select at the lower left side of the screen. The selection statement:

```
Key1=perkins
```

will select only those records from the lines where the last name is *perkins* or *Perkins*. Press the Exit key (F7) to return to the Sort menu.

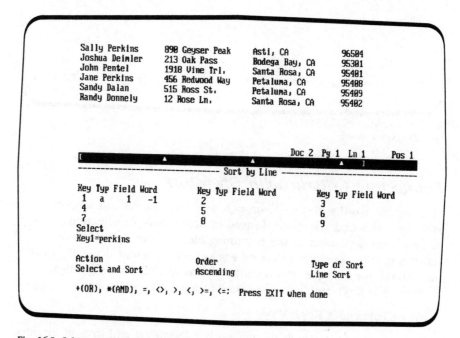

Fig. 16.9. Select statement entered below the word Select.

Then, from the Sort menu, select 5 Action and choose 1 to select and then sort records matching the criteria. Choose 2 to select records but not sort them. WordPerfect returns you to the Sort menu.

Now activate the selection by choosing 1 Perform Action. Figure 16.10 shows the result of the simple selection statement to find "perkins." Two people on the list share that last name.

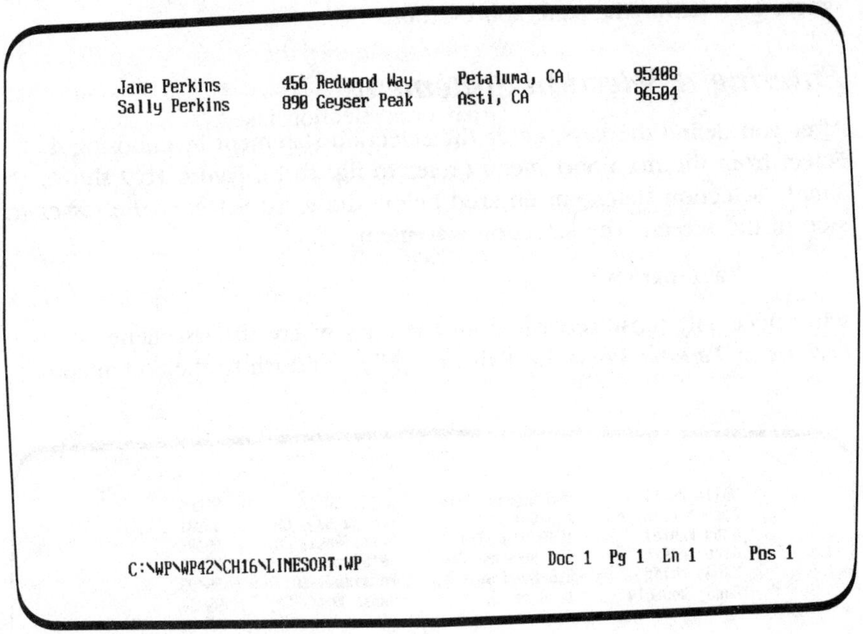

```
     Jane Perkins      456 Redwood Way    Petaluma, CA    95488
     Sally Perkins     898 Geyser Peak    Asti, CA        96584




















   C:\WP\WP42\CH16\LINESORT.WP                    Doc 1 Pg 1 Ln 1      Pos 1
```

Fig. 16.10. Select results.

## Connecting Criteria with Operators

You can use WordPerfect's *operators* to connect criteria and simplify entering compound selections. Instead of doing multiple selections, each one for a smaller subset of the remaining file, you can link selection statements with operators to create a selection statement that satisfies all the criteria. For example, if a record contains an individual's political preference in Key1 and his or her state in Key2, this statement:

Key1=Democrat * Key2=VA

will select records in which the person is a Democrat and lives in Virginia.

The statement specifies that Key1 must contain *Democrat* and Key2 must contain *VA*. The AND operator, an asterisk (∗), specifies that **BOTH** condition one **AND** condition two must be met.

For cases in which **EITHER** one condition **OR** another is met, use the plus sign (+) to indicate an OR operation. For example, to select everyone in Virginia or Kentucky, you would type:

**Key2=VA + Key2=KY**

Unless told otherwise, WordPerfect examines the selection statement from left to right, working on keys and operators as it comes across them. But some selections may require that one selection take place before another. In such cases, enclose in parentheses the criteria that should work first. If you do not use parentheses, WordPerfect may misinterpret what you want. For example, the statement:

Key1=Democrat ∗ Key2=VA + Key2=KY

will be interpreted as:

Select the records of people who are Democrats *and* Virginians, *or* who are Kentuckians of any political party

Use parentheses to make the *Democrat* condition apply to both states:

Key1=Democrat ∗ (Key2=VA + Key2=KY)

This select statement means:

Select the records of people who are Democrats *and* are from *either* Virginia *or* Kentucky

If you are not sure how a select statement will work, try using the statement with different sample records. See how different groupings of parentheses select different sets of records.

The selection statement shown in figure 16.11 is interpreted as:

Select the records of people with the first name Sally *and* the last name Perkins, *or* anyone from Petaluma

Figure 16.12 shows the result of this selection. Jane Perkins was selected, not because of her last name Perkins, but because she lives in Petaluma.

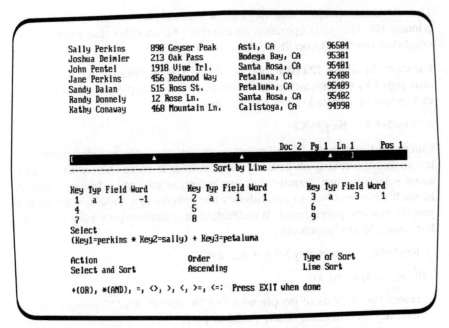

```
        Sally Perkins      890 Geyser Peak    Asti, CA          96504
        Joshua Deimler     213 Oak Pass       Bodega Bay, CA    95301
        John Pentel        1918 Vine Trl.     Santa Rosa, CA    95401
        Jane Perkins       456 Redwood Way    Petaluma, CA      95408
        Sandy Dalan        515 Ross St.       Petaluma, CA      95409
        Randy Donnely      12 Rose Ln.        Santa Rosa, CA    95402
        Kathy Conaway      468 Mountain Ln.   Calistoga, CA     94990




                                        Doc 2  Pg 1  Ln 1      Pos 1
[             ▲                ▲                   ▲   ]
───────────────────────── Sort by Line ─────────────────────────

Key Typ Field Word       Key Typ Field Word       Key Typ Field Word
 1   a    1    -1         2   a    1    1          3   a    3    1
 4                        5                        6
 7                        8                        9
Select
(Key1=perkins * Key2=sally) + Key3=petaluma

Action                   Order                    Type of Sort
Select and Sort          Ascending                Line Sort

+(OR), *(AND), =, <>, >, <, >=, <=;  Press EXIT when done
```

*Fig. 16.11. Select first name Sally, and last name Perkins, or anyone from Petaluma.*

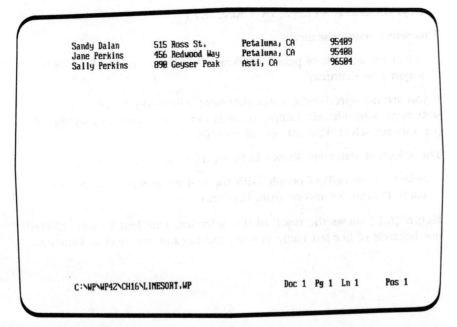

```
        Sandy Dalan        515 Ross St.       Petaluma, CA      95409
        Jane Perkins       456 Redwood Way    Petaluma, CA      95408
        Sally Perkins      890 Geyser Peak    Asti, CA          96504
```

```
C:\WP\WP42\CH16\LINESORT.WP             Doc 1  Pg 1  Ln 1      Pos 1
```

*Fig. 16.12. Sort result.*

When you specify criteria, use the operators in the following list:

| Operator | Meaning |
|----------|---------|
| =        | Equal to |
| <        | Less than |
| <=       | Less than or equal to |
| >        | Greater than |
| >=       | Greater than or equal to |
| < >      | Not equal to |
| +        | OR |
| *        | AND |

*You must include a space on either side of operators in a Select statement. Do not use spaces elsewhere.*

## Selecting Data Ranges

In previous examples, the equal sign (=) represented the connection between a key and its acceptable values. When Key1 was used to select a state, an equal sign was used to indicate the only state that would satisfy the condition:

Key1=VA

WordPerfect's Select function enables you also to select a range of numeric values. Suppose that you want to send a "let us refinance your home" letter to everyone whose mortgages have 10 to 15 years remaining. If Key1 contained the field of remaining mortgage years, you could use the following selection statement:

Key1>=10 * Key1<=15

which means:

Select the records in which the remaining years of the mortgage are 10 years or greater and 15 years or less

Notice that the AND symbol (*), not the OR symbol, references the range between end points.

*When you select items between the two end points of a range, make sure that the greater than (>) and less than (<) symbols both point toward an AND symbol (*).*

If you want a list of everyone whose mortgage has more than 15 years remaining (16 years or greater), enter either of the following Select statements:

Key1>15

Or

Key1>=16

Remember the following rules about entering compound selection statements:

- The keys must be defined before they can be used in a selection statement

- Criteria enclosed in parentheses are calculated first

- The operator symbols must have a space on either side of them

- No other spaces are used in the selection statement

## Finding and Selecting from Anywhere in Text

To select records that contain a specific word that may be located anywhere in the record, use a global select. So far, you have used WordPerfect to select only records in which a specific word matched a key in a specific location.

With a global select, the word by which you select can be located anywhere in the record. From 50 pages of notes, for example, you could select the paragraphs containing the word *automobile*. Paragraphs that didn't contain the word *automobile* would be filtered out.

When you want to examine all words in a record with a global select, use *Keyg* instead of using *Key1*, *Key2*, and so on. The *g* indicates that the search is global. WordPerfect will look in every position in every record for whatever word or number you are selecting by.

Use *Keyg* in the select statement in the same way you use other keys. To find if any word in a mailing list is Democrat, use the following select statement:

Keyg=Democrat

Global selections are an extremely powerful method of selecting:

- Lines or paragraphs that reference a topic anywhere in context

- Records in which data is entered in an inconsistent format

- Records from secondary merge files in which Merge R codes are missing

The global select works like the Search key—it can help you find something that has been misplaced. For example, you may fail to enter ^R at the end of a field when you create a secondary merge file to be used as a mailing list.

Some of the field numbers in that record, therefore, are incorrect. If you try sorting by field number, you may never find the incorrect record. You can find it, however, by using *Keyg* as the select key in the Select statement. Doing so causes the global key to search every word in every field rather than only a specific key.

With a global select, you can select from records in which data is entered with an inconsistent format. For example, a selection statement that uses a single numbered key, such as Key1, would *not* select *both Alice and John* in the following file:

```
Alice B. Miller^R
515 Ross St.^R
Kansas City, Kansas^R
^E
Miller, John T.^R
645 19th St.^R
Pocatello, Idaho^R
^E
Jonathan Samuels^R
413 Miller Rd.^R
Springston, Illinois^R
^E
```

The global select statement:

Keyg=Miller

will select both Alice and John. The problem is that it will select also records (such as Jonathan Samuels' record) with Miller in the address. While it is true that global select is a powerful technique for selecting records—you may get more records than you bargained for!

In a final example of global select, imagine that you have pages of notes, citations, or references in paragraph format. From all of these notes, you need to create a new file containing only records about a specific topic. The topic may be one of the three index words at the beginning of each paragraph or it may be located anywhere in the paragraph.

Figure 16.13 shows an example of such a paragraph selection. The example contains quotations about how people use their minds.

Each paragraph begins with three index words: *speaker, main topic*, and *subtopic*. But you want to select only quotations containing the words *mind* and *proof*. You use the following selection statement:

Keyg=mind ∗ (Keyg=proof + Keyg=proof.)

which means:

Select those records containing the word "mind" and either the word "proof" or the word "proof."

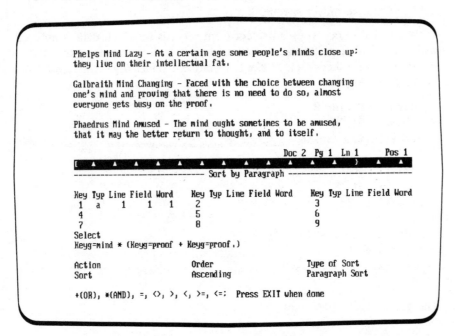

```
          Phelps Mind Lazy - At a certain age some people's minds close up;
          they live on their intellectual fat.

          Galbraith Mind Changing - Faced with the choice between changing
          one's mind and proving that there is no need to do so, almost
          everyone gets busy on the proof.

          Phaedrus Mind Amused - The mind ought sometimes to be amused,
          that it may the better return to thought, and to itself.

                                        Doc 2  Pg 1  Ln 1      Pos 1
          [  ▲   ▲   ▲   ▲   ▲   ▲   ▲   ▲   ▲   ▲   }   ▲   ▲
          ------------------------- Sort by Paragraph -------------------------

          Key Typ Line Field Word   Key Typ Line Field Word   Key Typ Line Field Word
          1    a   1    1    1       2                         3
          4                         5                         6
          7                         8                         9
          Select
          Keyg=mind ∗ (Keyg=proof + Keyg=proof.)

          Action                    Order                     Type of Sort
          Sort                      Ascending                 Paragraph Sort

          +(OR), ∗(AND), =, <>, >, <, >=, <=;  Press EXIT when done
```

*Fig. 16.13. Using global criteria to select paragraphs.*

Because WordPerfect selects exact matches, the selection statement must check for the word *proof* in a sentence or at the end of a sentence. If *Keyg=proof.* had not been included in the select statement, the word *proof* falling at the end of the sentence would not be selected. If you don't know where in a sentence a word is located, include any punctuation that might follow the word.

The result of the global select for *mind* and *proof* is displayed in figure 16.14.

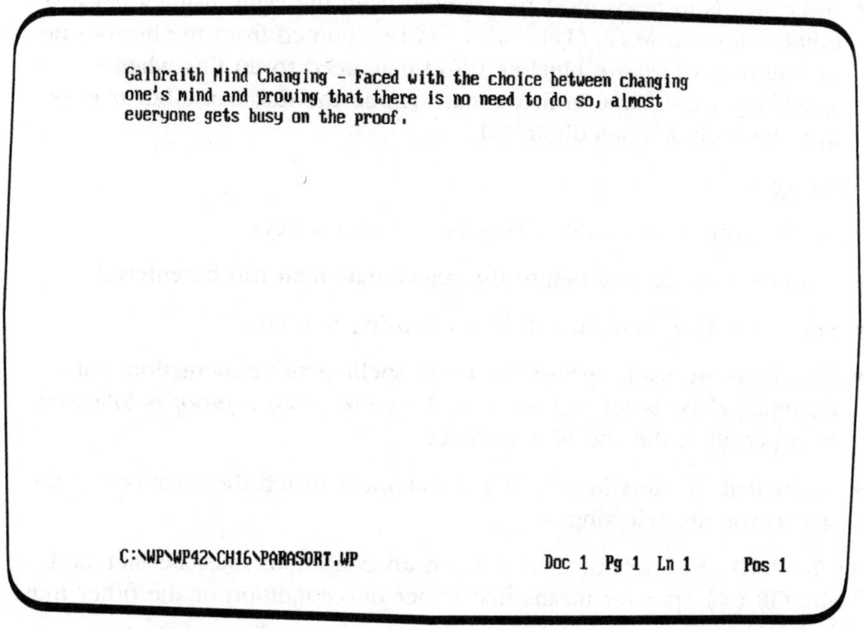

```
        Galbraith Mind Changing - Faced with the choice between changing
        one's mind and proving that there is no need to do so, almost
        everyone gets busy on the proof.




    C:\WP\WP42\CH16\PARASORT.WP                    Doc 1  Pg 1  Ln 1        Pos 1
```

*Fig. 16.14. Global select results.*

# Correcting Sort and Select Problems

At first, complex sorting and selecting can cause problems, so practice on simple, small files until you are familiar with the process. Then, if your sort or select does not work as you expected, check the following trouble-shooting list:

*Sorting*

- Set the type of sort with 7 Type before you set keys

- Use the tab ruler in the middle of the Sort screen to verify keys. The ruler's tab stops separate the fields

- Tabs must be set for fields. Set one tab per field with no unused tabs lying between fields

- Cross-check to be sure that words from one field are not mistaken for words from an adjacent field

- Be certain that fields in merge files end with ^R

- Check to be sure that the number of the key matches the key word's priority in the sort

- Some words in fields must be counted from the right, using a negative number for the word. (Lines also can be counted from the bottom up by entering a negative number.) You may need to do this when specifying a last name in fields that include the first name but may or may not include a middle initial

*Selecting*

- Set the type of sort with 7 Type before setting keys

- Keys must be defined before the select statement can be entered

- Enter the select statement before choosing 5 Action

- Selections are made against the exact spelling and punctuation. For example, *Keyg=proof* will not find the word *proof* if *proof* is followed by a period at the end of a sentence

- Verify that the keys in your select statement match the locations of the words you are selecting

- The AND (*) operator means that both conditions must be met, and the OR (+) operator means that either one condition or the other must be met

- Operators act from left to right in the select statement

- Parenthetical terms operate before any other operators

- Nested parenthetical terms (terms inside of terms) cannot be used

If you frequently work with lists or merge files, you'll save hours of manual sifting and sorting by learning how to operate WordPerfect's automated Sort and Select function. Once learned, the sort and select will become a constant support resource for you.

You can sort or select either from the document on the screen or from a document on disk—the results can be displayed on your screen or saved to disk.

The key steps for sorting or selecting are

☐ Always save the file to disk before sorting or selecting

☐ Choose 7 Type to set the type of sort or selection

☐ Choose 3 Keys to specify the location of keys

☐ Enter keys in the same order as sort priority. You must enter keys before you enter a select statement

☐ Choose 4 Select to enter a select statement

☐ Select 1 Perform Action to execute the sort or selection

If the sort or select function does not work as you expect it to, check to be sure that the key definitions refer to the lines, fields, and words which contain the words you are searching for.

Use a few records to check the operation of your sort or select. Cross-check to be sure that words from one field are not mistaken for words from an adjacent field. And, check to be certain that fields in merge files end with ^R.

# CHAPTER 17

# Managing Your System

After you've become familiar with WordPerfect's features and functions, you'll probably want to customize some of those features so that each time you boot WordPerfect, you'll be starting with the format settings you use most frequently—not necessarily the default settings you're using now. When you've identified which formats you use most often, use the Set-up menu to customize the start-up format. Changing WordPerfect default settings is not a difficult task.

You'll learn also how to customize the screen to display underlining or to change colors (if you use a color monitor), and you'll learn how to erase files, and how to copy files to new locations.

Because WordPerfect can convert and read files from other word processors, the last sections in this chapter will guide you through the procedure used to convert text from other software programs and word processors. WordPerfect's capabilities permit you to read "print outs" on disk from programs such as Lotus 1-2-3 and dBASE III.

# Using the Set-up Menu To Change WordPerfect Defaults

When WordPerfect starts, it uses preset (default) settings to specify characteristics such as margins, tab settings, spelling disk directory, date and time formats, and so on. These default settings are those that the WordPerfect Corporation believes will fit the needs of most users.

But, every user and every work environment must respond to special word-processing needs. WordPerfect offers optional settings that will permit you to make changes in the default settings to more closely match your needs. The following procedure will permit you to make default changes.

If you are using a hard disk, manually switch to your WordPerfect directory to access the Set-up menu shown in figure 17.1. This procedure will work only from within the WordPerfect directory.

1. Type: **CD\WP**

2. Press Enter

If you use a two floppy disk system, you will not need to change directories.

To see the Set-up menu before WordPerfect starts (on a hard disk drive system):

1. Type **WP/S** at the C> prompt

2. Press Enter

If you are using a dual floppy disk system, at the B> prompt:

1. Type **A:WP/S**

Ths screen in figure 17.1 will appear.

The changes you make from the Set-up menu are saved to disk so that they are used the next time you start. You can make Set-up changes as often as you want. These changes go into effect each time you load WordPerfect and remain in effect until you change them again.

## Setting Directories

Option 1 on the Set-up menu specifies where the Speller and Thesaurus files are located. If you are using a computer without a hard disk drive, you will insert the Speller and Thesaurus disks into Drive B when you use

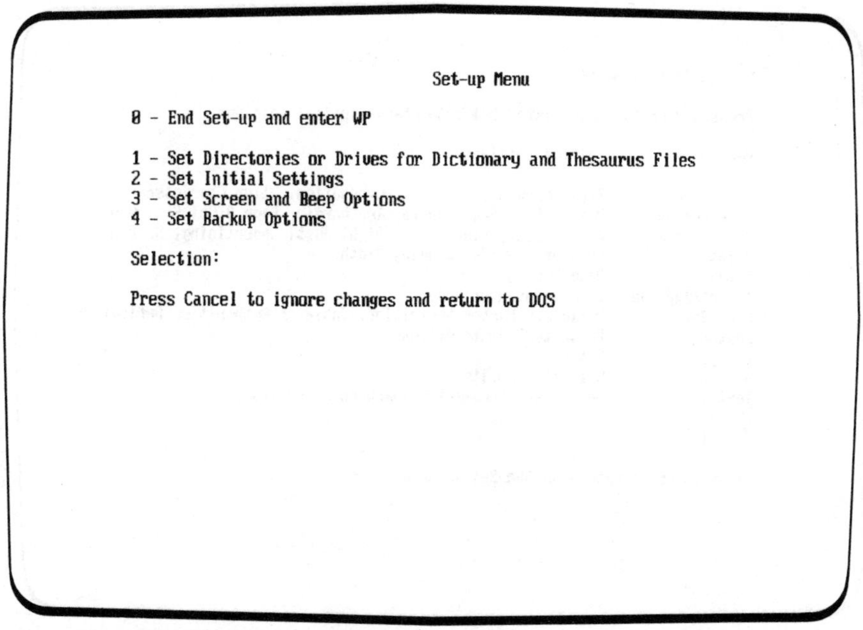

```
                              Set-up Menu

        0 - End Set-up and enter WP

        1 - Set Directories or Drives for Dictionary and Thesaurus Files
        2 - Set Initial Settings
        3 - Set Screen and Beep Options
        4 - Set Backup Options

        Selection:

        Press Cancel to ignore changes and return to DOS
```

*Fig. 17.1. The Set-up menu.*

them. On a hard disk system, the Speller and Thesaurus files are normally saved to C:\WP with the WP.EXE file. If you want to put the Speller and Thesaurus files in another location, you must identify (enter) the new location so that WordPerfect can locate them.

## Setting Initial Format Defaults

Format settings are the most frequently customized settings. To change the default format settings, select 2 Set Initial Settings from the Set-up menu. You will see the menu shown in figure 17.2. You can use this menu to change almost all format settings, such as those for margins, tabs, widow/orphan checking, page numbering, and date/time. Customize the format settings to those you use most often.

If you exchange documents with other users, remember that their default settings may not be the same as yours. A document may look different on your screen because a document that does not contain hidden format

```
Change Initial Settings

Press any of the keys listed below to change initial settings

Key              Initial Settings

Line Format      Tabs, Margins, Spacing, Hyphenation, Align Character
Page Format      Page # Pos, Page Length, Top Margin, Page # Col Pos, W/O
Print Format     Pitch, Font, Lines/Inch, Right Just, Underlining, SF Bin #
Print            Printer, Copies, Binding Width
Date             Date Format
Insert/Typeover  Insert/Typeover Mode
Mark Text        Paragraph Number Definition, Table of Authorities Definition
Footnote         Footnote/Endnote Options
Escape           Set N
Screen           Set Auto-rewrite
Text In/Out      Set Insert Document Summary on Save/Exit

Selection:

Press Enter to return to the Set-up Menu
```

*Fig. 17.2. Initial Settings Menu for format changes.*

codes takes on the format settings of the WordPerfect program that retrieves it. You can use either of two solutions to this potential problem:

- Everyone sharing files uses the same default format settings

  Or

- Everyone begins each document by entering important format codes, such as [Margin Set:] and [Tabs:]. The format codes that are entered from function keys or menus override the default format settings in different systems. Each user also could create macros to enter frequently used formats

As an example of customizing a setting, suppose that you want to change WordPerfect's defaults so that the margin is set to 12 left and 69 right. To do this:

1. Start WordPerfect with the **WP/S** command

2. Select **2** Initial Settings from the Set-up menu

When the screen shown in figure 17.2 displays:

3. Press the Line Format key (Shift-F8)

The Line Format menu will display.

    **4.** Select **3** Margins

    **5.** Enter the new margin settings

The Initial Settings menu will reappear so that you can enter additional default settings if you need to. A default that many WordPerfect users change is the Date/Time (Shift-F5) format. You can create hundreds of date and time display combinations from the standard December 25, 1989 to the more unusual 12/25/89—09:05am.

    **6.** Press Enter to return to the Set-up menu

    **7.** Type **0** to exit the Set-up menu, save the changes, and enter WordPerfect

    Or

    **7.** Press the Cancel key (F1) to exit the Set-up menu without saving the changes, and return to DOS

## Setting Screen Size and Beep Option

Menu item 3 on the Set-up menu lets you adjust WordPerfect to the number of lines and spaces that are displayed on your monitor. This option is useful if your monitor can show more than 25 lines or 80 columns.

For WordPerfect 4.2 users 3 Set Screen/Beep Options provides the opportunity to specify that the hard return default replace each hidden hard return code with an ASCII character (of your choice). After you've changed the default, each time you enter a hard return, the ASCII character will display on your screen. This is a useful default change if you'd prefer not to use Reveal Codes to "keep track" of hard returns. (See fig. 17.3.)

Option 3 also permits you to set the Beep Options. You can set WordPerfect to beep when an error message occurs, or when search commands fail. Normally, the beep feature is turned off. If you do not want the name of the current document to appear on the Status Line, type N to discontinue the file name display.

## Setting Backup Options

Select 4 Set Backup Options from the Set-up menu to instruct WordPerfect to save the document you're working on (at regular intervals) to the disk

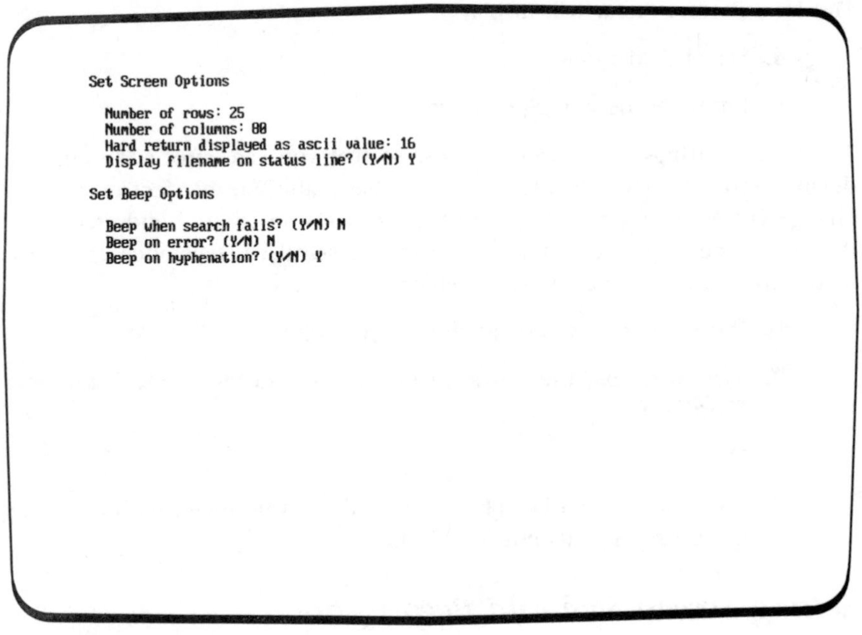

```
Set Screen Options

    Number of rows: 25
    Number of columns: 80
    Hard return displayed as ascii value: 16
    Display filename on status line? (Y/N) Y

Set Beep Options

    Beep when search fails? (Y/N) N
    Beep on error? (Y/N) N
    Beep on hyphenation? (Y/N) Y
```

Fig. 17.3. Set Screen Size and Beep Options screen.

drive or directory you've designated. You can specify the number of minutes that will elapse between these automatic saves.

If you like, WordPerfect will automatically retain a backup copy of each of your documents so that you will have the two most recent versions of the file. If you select this option (the default is No), WordPerfect will automatically create a backup carrying a .BK! extension.

# Using Macros on Start-up

If you'd like to add start-up features that cannot be customized in the Set-up menu, you may be able to set those features with a macro which executes automatically on start-up. Starting WordPerfect with the command:

   WP/M-macroname

will start WordPerfect and immediately call up the specified macro. The Alt-"letter" macros, such as Alt-R, are entered as:

   WP/M-ALTR

Use this macro streamlining technique to automatically switch to a specific directory, insert a heading, or retrieve a specific file on start-up.

# Adjusting for Graphics, COMPAQ, and Color Monitors

WordPerfect assumes that you are using a monochrome monitor without graphics capabilities. If you have a COMPAQ computer, or if your computer has a graphics card, you need to make an adjustment from within WordPerfect.

On monochrome screens (COMPAQ), the adjustment will cause underlined text to display in reverse text on your screen. On color screens, you can select from an assortment of colors to indicate bold, underline, and different areas of the screen.

If you are not sure whether you have a graphics card, go ahead and try the following procedure. It won't hurt anything because WordPerfect won't allow you to enter the menu if you do not have graphics.

To change display characteristics for a color screen, from the normal typing screen use this procedure for a monochrome monitor with graphics capability:

1. Press Screen (Ctrl-F3)

2. Select 4 Colors

3. Select 1 Color Monitor

4. Type N in response to the message fast text display

5. Type a letter next to that screen item you wish to change

Each letter corresponds to a color from the color menu at the top of the screen. Use the up- or down-arrow keys to move through the list of items on the screen. You can change colors as many times as you want. Note the effects of the different colors on the sample text in the lower right corner of the screen.

6. Press the Switch key (Shift-F3) to switch to the other document

7. Change the colors in the other document

8. Press Exit (F7) to return to the typing screen

When you exit WordPerfect, the color selections you have made will be saved and used the next time you start WordPerfect.

If you have a COMPAQ internal (green) monitor or other monochrome graphics monitor:

    **1.** Press Screen (Ctrl-F3)

    **2.** Select **4** Colors

    **3.** Select **2** Single Color Monitor (e.g., Black & White or COMPAQ)

Single-color monitors also may be green on black or amber on black.

    **4.** Type **N** for fast text display

    **5.** Select **1** Underline Display as Reverse Video

Notice the change in the sample text in the lower right corner of the screen.

    **6.** Press the Switch key (Shift-F3) to switch to the other document

    **7.** Type **1** again to choose reverse video for underlined display on this document

    **8.** Press the Exit key (F7) to return to the typing screen

When you exit WordPerfect, the underline selections you made will be saved and used the next time you start WordPerfect.

# Deleting WordPerfect Program Files

For the program to run correctly, certain files must always be stored on your copy of the WordPerfect system disk or in the WordPerfect directory on your hard disk—others can be deleted. The WordPerfect commands themselves are contained in file WP.EXE. Printer information is stored in the three files, WPFEED.FIL, WPFONT.FIL, and WPRINTER.FIL.

If the printers you use don't have sheet feeders, you can remove the WPFEED.FIL from your *backup* copy of the program system disk. *Never delete any files from your master disk*. Eliminate them only from your backup disk—your everyday working copy.

Remember also, *never retrieve or edit any of the WordPerfect program files*. WordPerfect may function improperly if you retrieve WordPerfect files with Retrieve or List Files because they are program files, not text files. And, what you see as these files are displayed on your screen is machine language and, for the most part, unintelligible.

In addition to the program files, WordPerfect creates several files while it runs. These files generally are identifiable by the name within braces—for example, {WP}.SPC. *Do not remove any of these files.*

*Macro files, which end with the extension .MAC should not be retrieved.*

## Managing Files and Disks

You can do many DOS file-management functions from the WordPerfect List Files menu. This convenient feature of the program saves time. Here are a few examples:

When you press the List Files key (F5), WordPerfect displays all the files in the drive or directory you specify. You can also retrieve, delete, rename, print, or copy a file; retrieve a DOS (ASCII) text file; view the contents of a document or of another directory; change the default directory; and search for files that contain a specified word. Figure 17.4 shows the List Files screen.

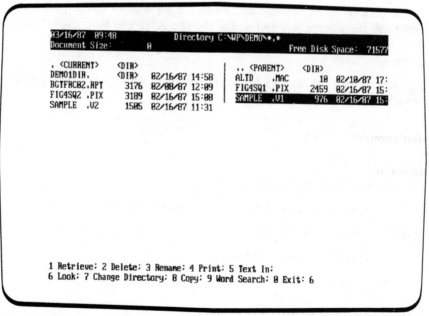

*Fig. 17.4. List Files screen.*

After you press the List Files key (F5), you can also list files that meet specific file-name requirements.

For example, if you type *.LTR when the Dir is displayed in the lower left corner of the screen, WordPerfect will display (from the current directory only) files that carry the extension .LTR

The asterisk indicates that any group of characters is acceptable. You can use a question mark (?) to indicate that any single letter in a file name is acceptable. For example, typing ANNUALV?.RPT will display both the file names ANNUALV1.RPT and ANNUALV2.RPT.

## Deleting Files

From the List Files screen, you can delete a file:

1. Press the arrow keys to highlight the desired file name

2. Choose 2 Delete

3. Type Y when prompted

If you want to delete several files, move the highlighter to each file name and press the asterisk key (*) to tag the file. After you have tagged all the files, give the Delete command, option 2. All the tagged files will be deleted.

You can remove the tag (*) from a file by highlighting the tagged file and again pressing the asterisk key.

## Renaming Files

To rename a file:

1. Highlight the file name

2. Select 3 Rename from the List Files menu

When prompted by WordPerfect:

3. Type the file's new name

4. Press Enter

## Checking Available Disk Space

The amount of available (free) disk space is displayed at the upper right of the List Files screen (see fig. 17.4). The size of the current document is displayed at the screen's upper left. If the space on your disk is almost full, you may want to delete files or change disks before you save the next document.

## Retrieving ASCII Files

ASCII text files are used to pass information between programs that do not normally communicate data. For example, in Lotus 1-2-3 you can use the command:

/Print File {filename} Range Go

to print a Lotus 1-2-3 worksheet to disk instead of printing it to paper. You can then retrieve this file into WordPerfect.

To retrieve an ASCII or DOS text file, select 5 Text In on the List Files menu. If, instead, you choose 1 Retrieve to retrieve ASCII text files, you probably will have problems when you edit. ASCII text files may contain special characters that hinder WordPerfect's operation.

ASCII text files frequently have *.TXT*, *.ASC*, *.PRN*, and in a few cases, *.DOC* file extensions. If you retrieve a file and see characters that are neither letters nor numbers, the file probably is not ASCII text. Files that end with *.DOC* may also be from MultiMate® Version 3.2 or Microsoft® Word.

ASCII text files contain a hard return [HRt] at the end of each line, which prevents sentences from wrapping as you edit. To remove these hard returns, use the Replace function (Alt-F2) to replace the [HRt] (Enter key) codes in the document with nothing. To enter "nothing" as the replacement character, press the Search key (F2) at the prompt: Replace with:

ASCII files created by programs such as Lotus 1-2-3 and dBASE III may have lines wider than your preset margin. Because of this, lines may wrap incorrectly and the document may appear out of alignment. So, before you retrieve the ASCII text file, reset margins on the screen so that they are wider than necessary.

Keep in mind that after you have displayed the document or edited it with WordPerfect, it is no longer an ASCII or DOS text file. The file now contains WordPerfect codes.

To save the file as a WordPerfect document:

1. Press the Save key (F10)

To save the document as an ASCII text file:

1. Press the Text In/Out key (Ctrl-F5)

2. Choose 1 Save from the menu

For information about retrieving and creating ASCII text files, refer to the index in *Using WordPerfect*, 3rd Edition, and the documentation provided with the other software you use.

## Looking at Files

The Look feature is useful for verifying the contents of a file before you retrieve it. Look (option 6 on the List Files menu) displays an unformatted view of the document but it will not retrieve the document. When you use Look, you cannot edit the document.

In WordPerfect 4.2, you can view a document also by highlighting the document name and pressing the Enter key.

## Changing Directories

From the List Files screen, you also can change the active directory or drive. For example, List Files may display the files in directory C:\WP\MEMO; you, on the other hand, want to use the directory C:\WP\REPORT

To move to a higher level (parent) directory:

1. Press the List Files key (F5)

2. Press Enter to accept the current directory

3. Highlight the directory named ⟨Parent⟩

4. Select 7 Change Directory

5. Press Enter twice

To move to a directory that is displayed in the list of files:

1. Press the List Files key (F5)

2. Press Enter to accept the current directory

3. Highlight the directory you want to change to

4. Select 7 Change Directory

5. Press Enter twice

In WordPerfect 4.2, you can change temporarily to another directory by highlighting the directory name on the List Files screen and pressing Enter, twice.

On a dual floppy disk system, you won't have much use for the Change Directory command because all of your work is saved on Drive B, and there is little room for directories.

## Copying Files

You can use 8 Copy to copy files, instead of exiting to DOS. To copy a file to the same disk or to another disk:

1. Press the List Files key (F5)

2. Press Enter

   Or

2. Change the directory name and press Enter

3. Highlight the file to be copied

4. Select **8** Copy

5. Type the **letter** of the destination disk drive, a **colon**, and **directory**. Enter a new file name if you want the duplicate to have a new name

6. Press Enter

For example, to copy a file from the hard drive to a floppy disk in Drive A, you would type:

   A:

A file copied from one location to another and renamed on the hard disk would have an entry like:

   C:\WP\LETTER\RECEIPT2.LTR

7. Press Enter

You can rename the copied file by typing a different name for the copied file.

## Using Word Search from the List Files Menu

Word Search (option 9 on the List Files menu) causes WordPerfect to search all the files on the list to locate one or more words of up to 20 characters. The screen then displays the names of the files containing the searched-for string of letters.

Here are some guidelines for specifying the search word (or words):

- If the phrase you want to locate contains any punctuation—spaces, commas, semicolons, or single or double quotation marks—you must enclose the entire phrase in quotation marks

- Capitalization is not significant

- You can use the question mark (?) to accept any single character for the ?s character location. For example, if you search for *bea?*, WordPerfect will locate words such as *bear*, *beam*, *beat*, and *bean*

- You can use the asterisk (*) to represent any group of characters. For example, if you search for *bea**, WordPerfect will locate the previous examples as well as *beatitudes*, *beautiful*, *beaus*, and *bears*

You can combine words using operators. For example, you can search for files containing both the words *vegetable* and *legume* by typing a semicolon or a space between the words:

    vegetable;legume

Or, by using a comma, you can specify that the files must contain one word or the other, but not necessarily both:

    vegetable,legume

You also can combine these two operators. For example, you can search for files that have both the words *vegetable* and *legume*, or the word *potato*:

    vegetable;legume,potato

## Exiting to DOS with Shell

WordPerfect permits you to remain "on hold" in memory while you return to DOS and run another program. You can then exit that program and return to WordPerfect exactly where you left off.

By issuing the Shell command (Ctrl-F1) and selecting 1 Go to Dos, you can exit WordPerfect temporarily and go to DOS (the operating system).

From DOS, you can execute DOS commands or run another program such as Lotus 1-2-3. You can access directories of disks or subdirectories, and you can copy, erase, or rename files. You also can create new subdirectories or format a disk in another drive.

Typing EXIT (the word, not WordPerfect's F7 Exit key) at the DOS prompt returns you to WordPerfect. The cursor returns to the character position it occupied before you gave the Shell command.

*DOS commands that affect the disk structure, such as CHKDSK/F, should not be run from the DOS shell.*

Because WordPerfect remains in memory while you temporarily exit to DOS, you may not be able to run large programs. The programs you can run will depend on the amount of RAM memory in your computer, the size of your current WordPerfect document, the size of the second program, and the amount of data in the second program.

## Setting File Protection

File protection, one of WordPerfect's special features, prevents an unauthorized user from reading those files you've protected with a password.

To lock and save the current document:

1. Press Text In/Out (Ctrl-F5)

2. Select 4 Save

   Or

2. Select option 3 if you are using WordPerfect 4.1

WordPerfect prompts you to enter a password, twice. The password can contain as many as 75 characters. You won't see the password on your screen as you type it.

WordPerfect then asks you for the name of the document you want to protect. After you respond, the program saves the document to disk and returns to your document.

After locking the document, you can use the Save or Exit key to save it again. When you do, you will be asked to enter the password. Entering the password will lock and save the file. If you simply press Enter, the file will be saved in its unprotected form.

If someone tries to retrieve a protected document and doesn't enter the correct password, the screen displays the error message:

        File is locked

The only way to retrieve a locked file is to:

1. Press the Text In/Out key (Ctr-F5)

2. Select **5** Retrieve

   Or

2. Select **4** Unlock and retrieve the locked document if you are using WordPerfect 4.1

3. Type both the file name and password when prompted

Use the protected save function to resave the document.

*Remember your password!* If you forget the password you won't be able to retrieve the file. Do not use passwords that are easy for someone to figure out, such as your name spelled backwards or your birth date.

Use your mother-in-law's middle name or the breed of your favorite dog. If you are protecting many files, you may want to set up a separate, protected file just for the passwords, so that all you have to remember is the one master password to the password file.

# Converting File Formats

The CONVERT.EXE file stored on your *Learning* master disk converts files created by other word processors such as WordStar® and MultiMate into WordPerfect format. And WordPerfect files can be converted into other formats such as WordStar or MultiMate Advantage. You also can convert data files created by other programs into WordPerfect secondary merge files for use with the program's merge features.

## Converting WordPerfect to Another Format

To convert a WordPerfect file to another format if you are using a dual floppy disk system:

1. Insert the disk with the CONVERT.EXE file in Drive A

2. From Drive B, type **A:CONVERT**

   Or

If you are using a hard disk drive system:

1. Change to the directory containing CONVERT.EXE

2. Type **CONVERT**

Then, for either type of system:

3. Type the **drive**, a **colon** (:), the **path name**, and the **name of the file** to be converted. For example, C:\WP\FILENAME

4. Press Enter

5. Type the **drive**, a **colon** (:), the **path name**, and the **name of the converted file** that will be created. For example, C:\WP\NEWNAME

6. Press Enter

Remember, the names cannot be the same.

7. Select **1** WordPerfect from the menu to indicate that the input file is in WordPerfect format

8. From the list of alternatives that appear, select the format you want the file converted to

IBM's DCA format is also known as Revisable Form Text.

You will be returned to DOS when the conversion is complete.

## Converting to WordPerfect Format

To convert a file to WordPerfect format if you are using a dual floppy disk drive system:

1. Insert the disk with the CONVERT.EXE file in Drive A

2. From the B drive, type **A:CONVERT**

If you are using a hard disk system:

1. Change to the directory containing the CONVERT.EXE file

2. Type **CONVERT**

Then, for either type of system:

3. Type the **drive**, a **colon** (:), the **path name**, and the **name of the file** to be converted

4. Type the **drive**, a **colon** (:), the **path name**, and the **name of the converted file** that will be created

The names cannot be the same.

5. Select from the menu the file format of the original file

IBM's DCA format may be referred to as Revisable Form Text.

Select Mail Merge if you want to convert an ASCII file, WordStar, dBASE, or other mail-merge file into a secondary merge file for WordPerfect.

After choosing Mail Merge, you will be asked what characters are used to separate fields and records in the original file.

You will be returned to DOS when the conversion is complete.

## Converting ASCII Files to WordPerfect Format

WordPerfect's CONVERT.EXE program cannot handle the format in some word processors and most spreadsheets and databases. If you are faced with this situation, use the original word processor to create an ASCII text file.

Look under the terms *ASCII* or *Text File* in the index of the program's manual. Use WordPerfect's Text In/Out key (Ctrl-F5) to retrieve the ASCII file. If you want to turn the ASCII file into a secondary merge file, refer to the previous section.

ASCII files contain all of the original letters, numbers, and symbols but will not contain formatting information. When the original program saves the file as ASCII text, it may change tabbed or indented areas into blank characters.

For this reason, it is best to prepare the original document as follows before saving it in ASCII format:

- Remove all tabs and indents used in text. This makes them easier to reenter in WordPerfect

- Remove all commands, such as centering and flush-right

- Do not remove tabs that separate columns of text or numbers

- Set the left margin to 0. Doing so prevents a leading blank space at the beginning of each line in the ASCII file

So, now that you're familiar with which WordPerfect formats you use most frequently, it's appropriate to set your own defaults (the WordPerfect start-up settings).

To change the start-up settings:

- [ ] If you are using a hard disk system, type **CD \WP** at the DOS prompt to change to the WordPerfect directory

- [ ] Type WP/S if you are using a hard disk

  Or

- [ ] Type A:WP/S if you are using a dual floppy disk system

- [ ] Select the custom feature you want to change. Choose 2 Set Initial Settings to customize the format

- [ ] Type 0 from the Set-up menu to start WordPerfect and accept the changes

  Or

- [ ] Press Cancel (F1) to return to DOS without accepting the changes

If you have a color monitor or a single-color monitor with graphics, you'll probably want to customize the colors and appearance of features on-screen. From the Screen key (Ctrl-F3), Colors menu, you can select colors to reflect features such as bold or underline. On single-color monitors, such as those used with a COMPAQ system, you can specify how you want underlining displayed.

When you use WordPerfect, remember that it isn't isolated from your other programs. One of the nicest aspects of using WordPerfect is that it can convert, retrieve, and edit formatted documents from many other word processors.

When you're faced with a format that the CONVERT.EXE program can't handle, use a format such as DCA (Revisable Text Format), ASCII text, or WordStar as an intermediary—three formats which are common language to many file converters.

It is fitting that the last chapter integrates all that has come before, and encourages you to modify WordPerfect for your special personal and professional word-processing needs.

You've come to the end of *Using WordPerfect*, 3rd Edition, except of course for the Appendix, which presents, in easy-to-read format, WordPerfect codes that may be viewed from the Reveal Codes screen.

# Appendix:

# Reveal Codes Screen Display

These are WordPerfect codes that display on the Reveal Codes screen ("n" = number).

|  |  |
|------|-------------|
| [^] (blinking) | Cursor Position |
| [ ] | Hard Space |
| [-] | Hyphen |
| -(blinking) | Soft Hyphen |
| /(blinking) | Cancel Hyphenation |
| [A][a] | Tab Align or Flush Right (begin and end) |
| [Adv ↑] | Advance Up 1/2 Line |
| [Adv ↓] | Advance Down 1/2 Line |
| [AdvLn:n] | Advance to Specific Line Number |
| [Align Char] | Alignment Character |
| [B][b] | Bold (begin and end) |
| [Bin#:n] | Sheet Feeder Bin Number |
| [Block] | Beginning of Block |
| [BlockPro:Off] | Block Protection Off |
| [BlockPro:On] | Block Protection On |
| [C][c] | Centering (begin and end) |
| [Center Pg] | Center Current Page Top to Bottom |
| [Cmnd:] | Embedded Printer Command |
| [CndlEOP:n] | Conditional End of Page (n=number of lines) |
| [Col Def:] | Column Definition |
| [Col Off] | End of Text Columns |
| [Col On] | Beginning of Text Columns |
| [Date:n] | Date/Time function (n=format) |
| [DefMark:Index,n] | Index Definition (n=format) |
| [DefMark:List,n] | List Definition (n=List Number) |

415

| | |
|---|---|
| **[DefMark:ToA,n]** | Table of Authorities |
| | (n=To A Level) |
| **[DefMark:ToC,n]** | Table of Contents Definition |
| | (n=ToC Level) |
| **[EInd]** | End of → Indent or → Indent ← |
| **[EndDef]** | End of Index, List, or Table of |
| | Contents |
| **[EndMark:List,n]** | End Marked Text |
| | (n=List Number) |
| **[EndMark:ToC,n]** | End Marked Text (n=To C Level) |
| **[E-Tabs:n,n]** | Extended Tabs (begin with n, |
| | every n spaces) |
| **[Font Change:n,n]** | Specify New Font or Print Wheel |
| | (n=pitch, font) |
| **[FtnOpt]** | Footnote/Endnote Options |
| **[Hdr/Ftr:n,n;text]** | Header or Footer Definition |
| | (n=type, occurrence) |
| **[HPg]** | Hard Page |
| **[HRt]** | Hard Return |
| **[Hyph on]** | Hyphenation on |
| **[Hyph off]** | Hyphenation off |
| **[HZone Set:n,n]** | Reset Size of Hyphenation Zone |
| | (n=left, right) |
| **[→ Indent]** | Beginning of Indent |
| **[→ Indent ←]** | Beginning of Left/Right Indent |
| **[Index:heading; subheading]** | Index Mark |
| **[LPI]** | Lines per Inch |
| **[← Mar Rel:n]** | Left Margin Release |
| | (n=positions moved) |
| **[Margin Set:n,n]** | Left and Right Margin Reset |
| **[Mark:List,n]** | Begin Marked Text for List |
| | (n=List Number) |
| **[Mark:ToC,n]** | Begin Marked Text for To C |
| | (n=ToC Level) |
| **[Math Def]** | Definition of Math Columns |
| **[Math Off]** | End of Math |
| **[Math On]** | Beginning of Math |
| !(blinking) | Formula Calculation |
| **t**(blinking) | Subtotal Entry |
| +(blinking) | Do Subtotal |
| **T**(blinking) | Total Entry |
| =(blinking) | Do Total |
| *(blinking) | Do Grand Total |

| | |
|---|---|
| **N** | Negate number (negative) |
| **[Note:End,n;[note#]text]** | Endnote (n=Endnote Number) |
| **[Note:Foot,n;[note#]text]** | Footnote (n=Footnote number) |
| **[Ovrstk]** | Overstrike Preceding Character |
| **[Par#;Auto]** | Automatic Paragraph/Outline Number |
| **[Par#:n]** | Fixed Paragraph Number (n=level number) |
| **[Par#Def]** | Paragraph Numbering Definition |
| **[Pg#:n]** | New Page Number |
| **[Pg#Col:n,n,n]** | Column Position for Page Numbers (n=left, center, right) |
| **[PgLnth:n,n]** | Set Page Length (n=form lines, text lines) |
| **[Pos Pg#:n]** | Set Position for Page Numbers |
| **[RedLn][r]** | Redline (begin and end) |
| **[Rt Just Off]** | Right Justification Off |
| **[Rt Just On]** | Right Justification On |
| **[Set Ftn #:n]** | New Footnote Number |
| **[Spacing Set:n]** | Spacing Set |
| **[SPg]** | Soft New Page |
| **[SRt]** | Soft Return |
| **[StrkOut][s]** | Strikeout (begin and end) |
| **[SubScrpt]** | Subscript |
| **[SuprScrpt]** | Superscript |
| **[Suppress:n]** | Suppress Page Format Options (n=format(s)) |
| **[TAB]** | Move to Next Tab Stop |
| **[Tab Set:]** | Tab Reset |
| **[Top Mar:n]** | Set Top Margin in Half-Lines |
| **[U][u]** | Underlining (begin and end) |
| **[Undrl Style:n]** | Underline Style |
| **[W/O Off]** | Widow/Orphan Off |
| **[W/O On]** | Widow/Orphan On |
| **[Smry/Cmnt:]** | Document Summary/Comment |
| **[Ln Num:On]** | Line Numbering On |
| **[Ln Num:Off]** | Line Numbering Off |

# Template for the IBM PC, XT, and AT Enhanced Keyboard*

| | Spell | Screen | Move | Ctrl | Text In/Out | Tab Align | Footnote | Print Format | Ctrl | Merge/Sort | Macro Def |
|---|---|---|---|---|---|---|---|---|---|---|---|
| Shell | | | | | | | | | | | |
| Thesaurus | Replace | Reveal Codes | Block | Alt | Mark Text | Flush Right | Math/Columns | Page Format | Alt | Merge Codes | Macro |
| Super/Subscript | ◆Search | Switch | ◆Indent | Shift | Date | Center | Print | Line Format | Shift | Merge E | Retrieve |
| Cancel | ◆Search | Help | ◆Indent | | List Files | Bold | Exit | Underline | | Merge R | Save |

\* can be used also on the IBM PS/2 Keyboard

**WordPerfect**
for the IBM PC, XT, AT

| | |
|---|---|
| Go To | Home |
| Hard Page | Enter |
| ◆Margin Release | Tab |
| Soft Hyphen | -/+ (num) |
| Screen Up/Down | -/+ |
| Word Left/Right | Backspace |
| Delete Word | |
| Delete to End/Lft/Pg | End/PgDn |

© WordPerfect Corp 1987. TMSWP01/4.2
ISBN 1-55692-200-0

# Index

---

## F

**T**

# More Computer Knowledge from Que

## LOTUS SOFTWARE TITLES

1-2-3 QueCards ............................. 21.95
1-2-3 QuickStart ............................ 21.95
1-2-3 Quick Reference....................... 6.95
1-2-3 for Business, 2nd Edition.............. 22.95
1-2-3 Business Formula Handbook............ 19.95
1-2-3 Command Language.................... 21.95
1-2-3 Macro Library, 2nd Edition............. 21.95
1-2-3 Tips, Tricks, and Traps, 2nd Edition ..... 21.95
Using 1-2-3, Special Edition................. 24.95
Using 1-2-3 Workbook and Disk,
   2nd Edition.............................. 29.95
Using Lotus HAL............................ 19.95
Using Symphony, 2nd Edition ................ 26.95

## DATABASE TITLES

dBASE III Plus Applications Library ........... 21.95
dBASE III Plus Handbook, 2nd Edition ........ 22.95
dBASE III Plus Advanced Programming,
   2nd Edition.............................. 22.95
dBASE III Plus Tips, Tricks, and Traps........ 21.95
dBASE IV Quick Reference .................. 6.95
dBXL and Quicksilver Programming:
   Beyond dBASE........................... 24.95
R:BASE Solutions: Applications and Resources  19.95
R:BASE System V Techniques
   and Applications ......................... 21.95
R:BASE System V User's Guide, 2nd Edition ... 19.95
R:BASE User's Guide, 3rd Edition ............ 19.95
Using Clipper............................... 24.95
Using Reflex ............................... 19.95
Using Paradox, 2nd Edition .................. 22.95
Using Q & A, 2nd Edition .................... 21.95

## MACINTOSH AND APPLE II TITLES

HyperCard QuickStart: A Graphics Approach.... 21.95
Using AppleWorks, 2nd Edition................ 21.95
Using dBASE Mac ........................... 19.95
Using Dollars and Sense .................... 19.95
Using Excel ................................ 21.95
Using HyperCard: From Home to HyperTalk .... 24.95
Using Microsoft Word: Macintosh Version....... 21.95
Using Microsoft Works....................... 19.95
Using WordPerfect: Macintosh Version ........ 19.95

## APPLICATIONS SOFTWARE TITLES

Smart Tips, Tricks, and Traps ................ 23.95
Using Dollars and Sense: IBM Version,
   2nd Edition.............................. 19.95
Using Enable, 2nd Edition ................... 22.95
Using Excel: IBM Version.................... 24.95
Using Managing Your Money.................. 19.95
Using Quattro .............................. 21.95
Using Smart ............................... 22.95
Using SuperCalc4........................... 21.95

## WORD-PROCESSING AND DESKTOP PUBLISHING TITLES

Microsoft Word Techniques and Applications.... 19.95
Microsoft Word Tips, Tricks, and Traps......... 19.95
Using DisplayWrite 4 ........................ 19.95
Using Microsoft Word, 2nd Edition ............ 21.95
Using MultiMate Advantage, 2nd Edition........ 19.95
Using PageMaker on the IBM ................ 24.95
Using Sprint................................ 21.95
Using Ventura Publisher ..................... 24.95
Using WordPerfect, 3rd Edition ............... 21.95
Using WordPerfect 5 ........................ 24.95
Using WordPerfect Workbook and Disk........ 29.95
Using WordStar............................. 18.95
WordPerfect QueCards ...................... 21.95
WordPerfect Quick Reference ................ 6.95
WordPerfect QuickStart...................... 21.95
WordPerfect Tips, Tricks, and Traps,
   2nd Edition.............................. 21.95
WordPerfect Advanced Techniques ............ 19.95

## HARDWARE AND SYSTEMS TITLES

DOS Programmer's Reference ................ 24.95
DOS QueCards............................. 21.95
DOS Workbook and Disk .................... 29.95
IBM PS/2 Handbook ........................ 21.95
Managing Your Hard Disk, 2nd Edition ........ 22.95
MS-DOS Quick Reference ................... 6.95
MS-DOS QuickStart......................... 21.95
MS-DOS User's Guide, 3rd Edition ........... 22.95
Networking IBM PCs, 2nd Edition............. 19.95
Programming with Windows................... 22.95
Understanding UNIX: A Conceptual Guide,
   2nd Edition.............................. 21.95
Upgrading and Repairing PCs................. 24.95
Using Microsoft Windows .................... 19.95
Using PC DOS, 2nd Edition.................. 22.95

## PROGRAMMING AND TECHNICAL TITLES

Advanced C: Techniques and Applications...... 21.95
C Programmer's Library ...................... 21.95
C Programming Guide, 2nd Edition ............ 19.95
C Quick Reference.......................... 6.95
C Self-Study Guide ......................... 16.95
C Standard Library.......................... 21.95
Debugging C ............................... 19.95
QuickBASIC Quick Reference ................ 6.95
Turbo Pascal for BASIC Programmers ......... 18.95
Turbo Pascal Program Library................. 19.95
Turbo Pascal Tips, Tricks, and Traps .......... 19.95
Using Assembly Language.................... 24.95
Using QuickBASIC 4 ........................ 19.95
Using Turbo Prolog ......................... 19.95

# MORE COMPUTER KNOWLEDGE FROM QUE

## WordPerfect Tips, Tricks, and Traps, 2nd Edition

*by Charles O. Stewart III and Daniel J. Rosenbaum*

Become a WordPerfect 5 power user with Que's *WordPerfect Tips, Tricks, and Traps*, 2nd Edition. This superb text presents a series of tips and advanced techniques that help you get the most efficient use possible from WordPerfect 5. Included is information on style sheets, keyboard mapping, the WordPerfect Library, Macro Commands, integrated text and graphics, and laser printers. *WordPerfect Tips, Tricks, and Traps*, 2nd Edition, is the perfect WordPerfect book for all intermediate and advanced WordPerfect users!

## Using PC DOS, 2nd Edition

*by Chris DeVoney*

DOS master Chris DeVoney has updated his classic *Using PC DOS* to include information on PC DOS 3.3. Critically acclaimed, this book is a combination of step-by-step tutorial and lasting reference. This new edition adds up-to-date information on IBM's PS/2 computers and shows how to work with 3 1/2-inch disks. Also featured is a comprehensive beginning tutorial and the popular Command Reference—an easy-to-use consolidation of essential DOS commands. No IBM microcomputer user should be without a copy of *Using PC DOS*, 2nd Edition!

## Using 1-2-3, Special Edition

*Developed by Que Corporation*

Acclaimed for its wealth of information and respected for its clear and concise style, *Using 1-2-3* is required reading for more than one million 1-2-3 users worldwide. This Special Edition of the classic text has more than 900 pages of up-to-date information and features, including comprehensive Command Reference and Troubleshooting sections, hands-on practice sessions, and information on Lotus HAL and other add-in/add-on programs. Discover for yourself why *Using 1-2-3*, Special Edition, is the ultimate tutorial and reference to 1-2-3, Release 2!

## Managing Your Hard Disk, 2nd Edition

*by Don Berliner*

Proper hard disk management is the key to efficient personal computer use, and Que's *Managing Your Hard Disk* provides you with effective methods to best manage your computer's hard disk. This valuable text shows you how to organize programs and data on your hard disk according to their special applications, and helps you extend your understanding of DOS. This new edition features detailed information on DOS 3.3, IBM's PS/2 hardware, and new application and utility software. If you own a personal computer with a hard disk, you need Que's *Managing Your Hard Disk*, 2nd Edition!

# REGISTRATION CARD

Register your copy of *Using WordPerfect*, 3rd Edition and receive information about Que's newest products. Complete this registration card and return it to Que Corporation, P.O. Box 90, Carmel, IN 46032.

Name _____ Phone _____

Company _____ Title _____

Address _____

City _____ ST _____ ZIP _____

*Please check the appropriate answers:*

Where did you buy *Using WordPerfect*, 3rd Edition?
- ☐ Bookstore (name: _____ )
- ☐ Computer store (name: _____ )
- ☐ Catalog (name: _____ )
- ☐ Direct from Que
- ☐ Other: _____

How many computer books do you buy a year?
- ☐ 1 or less      ☐ 6-10
- ☐ 2-5            ☐ More than 10

How many Que books do you own?
- ☐ 1              ☐ 6-10
- ☐ 2-5            ☐ More than 10

How long have you been using WordPerfect?
- ☐ Less than 6 months
- ☐ 6 months to 1 year
- ☐ 1-3 years
- ☐ More than 3 years

What influenced your purchase of *Using Word-Perfect*, 3rd Edition?
(More than one answer is OK.)
- ☐ Personal recommendation
- ☐ Advertisement
- ☐ In-store display
- ☐ Price
- ☐ Que catalog
- ☐ Que postcard
- ☐ Que's reputation
- ☐ Other: _____

How would you rate the overall content of *Using WordPerfect*, 3rd Edition?
- ☐ Very good      ☐ Not useful
- ☐ Good           ☐ Poor

How would you rate the *QUICK START SECTIONS*?
- ☐ Very good      ☐ Not useful
- ☐ Good           ☐ Poor

How would you rate the *KEYBOARD COMMAND MAP*?
- ☐ Very good      ☐ Not useful
- ☐ Good           ☐ Poor

How would you rate the *CHAPTER ON MACROS*?
- ☐ Very good      ☐ Not useful
- ☐ Good           ☐ Poor

What do you like *best* about *Using WordPerfect*, 3rd Edition?

What do you like *least* about *Using WordPerfect*, 3rd Edition?

How do you use *Using WordPerfect*, 3rd Edition?

What other Que products do you own?

What other software do you own?

Please feel free to list any other comments you may have about *Using WordPerfect*, 3rd Edition.

_____

_____

_____

_____

_____

_____